# THE TERRORISM TRAP

D1601590

COLUMBIA STUDIES IN TERRORISM AND IRREGULAR WARFARE

COLUMBIA STUDIES IN TERRORISM AND IRREGULAR WARFARE

*Bruce Hoffman, Series Editor*

This series seeks to fill a conspicuous gap in the burgeoning literature on terrorism, guerrilla warfare, and insurgency. The series adheres to the highest standards of scholarship and discourse and publishes books that elucidate the strategy, operations, means, motivations, and effects posed by terrorist, guerrilla, and insurgent organizations and movements. It thereby provides a solid and increasingly expanding foundation of knowledge on these subjects for students, established scholars, and informed reading audiences alike.

For the complete list of titles, see page 347.

# THE TERRORISM TRAP

## HOW THE WAR ON TERROR ESCALATES VIOLENCE IN AMERICA'S PARTNER STATES

HARRISON AKINS

Columbia University Press
*New York*

Columbia University Press
*Publishers Since 1893*
New York    Chichester, West Sussex
cup.columbia.edu

Library of Congress Cataloging-in-Publication Data
Names: Akins, Harrison, author.
Title: The terrorism trap : how the war on terror escalates violence in
America's partner states / Harrison Akins.
Description: New York : Columbia University Press, [2023] |
Series: Columbia studies in terrorism and irregular warfare |
Includes bibliographical references and index.
Identifiers: LCCN 2022034769 (print) | LCCN 2022034770 (ebook) |
ISBN 9780231209861 (hardback) | ISBN 9780231209878 (trade paperback) |
ISBN 9780231558150 (ebook)
Subjects: LCSH: War on Terrorism, 2001-2009. | Terrorism—United States—
Prevention. | Terrorism—Developing countries—Prevention. | Terrorism—
Developing countries. | United States—Foreign relations—Developing countries—
21st century. | Developing countries—Foreign relations—United States—21st century.
Classification: LCC HV6432 .A4323 2023 (print) | LCC HV6432 (ebook) |
DDC 363.3250973—dc23/eng/20221123
LC record available at https://lccn.loc.gov/2022034769
LC ebook record available at https://lccn.loc.gov/2022034770

Cover image: © Shutterstock
Cover design: Chang Jae Lee

FOR MARINA, MY LOVE

# CONTENTS

# NOTE ON SOURCES

In conducting extensive primary source research for *The Terrorism Trap*, the author has, to the best of his knowledge, relied only on open-source information and has not utilized classified government documents that were leaked to the public or otherwise improperly released. Instead, when referencing or discussing various government documents that contained classified or controlled information (such as intelligence reports, diplomatic cables, briefing documents, or internal memoranda), this book uses only those documents that have been formally declassified and publicly released according to official U.S. government policy.

# THE TERRORISM TRAP

# 1

## THE TERRORISM TRAP

As morning broke on September 12, 2001, countless people awoke to a world that would soon be reshaped by an all-consuming fear of al-Qaeda and the global mission to defeat it. Yet, in those early hours after the previous day's catastrophic events, they knew little of the repercussions that would follow the momentous decisions soon to be made by a handful of individuals within the U.S. government—hundreds of thousands of lives lost, tens of millions displaced, entire societies thrown into upheaval, and the world seemingly no safer from the lingering threat of terrorism over two decades later. But some U.S. officials were quickly cognizant of the global impact the U.S. response would have. One week after the 9/11 attacks, Secretary of Defense Donald Rumsfeld sent a memo to senior Pentagon officials outlining broad objectives to be included in plans for the coming campaign against al-Qaeda, which he warned would be "a marathon, not a sprint." He concluded with a rather banal and understated turn of phrase, though one that would be profoundly prophetic: "As we continue to go after terrorism, our activities will have effects in a number of countries. We have to accept that, given the importance of the cause."[1]

Within policy circles, academia, and the media, there has been an exhaustive analysis of and debate over the military invasions of Afghanistan and Iraq and the resulting political turmoil and persistent violence within both countries. In recent years, this has been matched by the focus on the less public side of U.S. counterterrorism efforts—covert operations, extraordinary rendition, and drone strikes. However, from the very outset of America's war on terror the cooperation of foreign governments has been of the utmost importance since U.S. officials understood al-Qaeda to be a global threat transcending national borders. The 9/11 Commission found that "practically every aspect" of U.S. counterterrorism efforts relied on international cooperation in some way.[2] Douglas Feith, the undersecretary of defense for policy from 2001 to 2005, similarly observed that "there was a general appreciation after 9/11 that for some purposes it would be necessary and for all purposes it would be desirable to have foreign partners."[3]

Over the past two decades, the U.S. government has worked with, and through, its partner states[4] to share the burden of counterterrorism out of a concern for such issues as legitimacy, expediency, legality, and effectiveness, especially when operating within partner states' borders. In the name of fighting al-Qaeda, partner states have reorganized their security forces, arrested high-value targets, conducted military operations, shared intelligence, cracked down on terrorist financing, passed stricter antiterrorism laws, increased border security, and implemented a wide variety of other counterterrorism policies in line with U.S. officials' demands and with U.S. support. While political leaders often described U.S. troops in Afghanistan and Iraq as confronting terrorism on the front lines, it is equally true that America's partner states have borne the overwhelming brunt of the war on terror's violence. A key challenge for U.S. officials was how to gain the cooperation of strategically vital states, such as Pakistan and Yemen, so that such states might do the "bidding" of the United States even when their threat perceptions and political interests were not aligned and their strategic importance provided them outsized leverage in the bilateral relationship.[5] Scholars have taken up the question of why some states are more cooperative than others with U.S. counterterrorism efforts.[6] But what has been the impact of this cooperation?

## THE PUZZLE

After two decades and costs totaling nearly $6 trillion, the results of the war on terror are decidedly mixed.[7] According to data from the Global

Terrorism Database, which is maintained by the University of Maryland's National Consortium for the Study of Terrorism and Responses to Terrorism, global terrorist attacks increased from 873 in 2000 to 6,352 in 2012.[8] By disaggregating these attacks into international and domestic events, international terrorist attacks—attacks in which the terrorist and victims are different nationalities—have increased from 144 in 2000, following a period of decline in the post–Cold War 1990s, to 351 in 2012. On the other hand, the figures for domestic terrorist attacks reveal a much more dramatic increase. In 2000, global domestic terrorist attacks added up to 729. By 2012, the number had climbed to 6,001. Figure 1.1 shows these two trends in global terrorism over the 1996–2012 period. Figure 1.2 further demonstrates that this increase in domestic terrorism was largely confined to regions of the world with significant Muslim populations— the focus of U.S. counterterrorism efforts—while other regions experienced a decline in domestic terrorism after 2001. It is logical that the number of domestic terrorist attacks would be higher given the proximity and greater availability of targets. Yet, it is not apparent why domestic terrorism increased so dramatically after 2001 while international terrorism did not, especially since scholars have demonstrated that states are more susceptible to international terrorism as a result of an

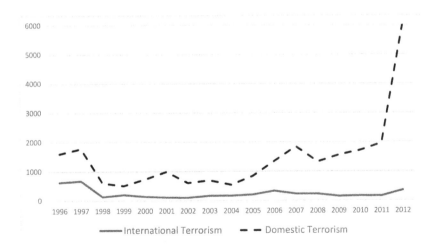

FIGURE 1.1 Annual count of global terrorist attacks, 1996–2012.

*Source:* Enders, Sandler, and Gaibulloev, "Domestic Versus Transnational Terrorism"; Gaibulloev, Piazza, and Sandler, "Regime Types and Terrorism."

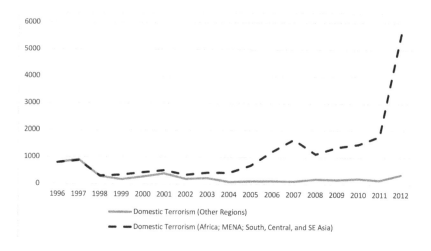

**FIGURE 1.2** Annual count of domestic terrorist attacks by region, 1996–2012.

*Source:* Enders, Sandler, and Gaibulloev, "Domestic Versus Transnational Terrorism"; Gaibulloev, Piazza, and Sandler, "Regime Types and Terrorism."

interventionist and militaristic foreign policy, as has been the case with the United States during the war on terror.[9]

While many studies of terrorism have examined only international attacks, or even aggregated international and domestic terrorism into a single measure of terrorist activity, scholars in recent years have increasingly examined domestic terrorism as a distinct phenomenon so as to explain its unique causes.[10] They have largely relied on more static domestic explanations using cross-national comparisons, such as the characteristics of states' political systems,[11] economic conditions,[12] governments' relationship with religious institutions,[13] social polarization,[14] gender imbalances,[15] or the presence of marginalized social groups.[16] Remaining relatively unchanged from the pre- to post-2001 periods, these causal factors do not account for the changing trend in domestic terrorism.

The answer, I argue, can be found by examining how U.S. counterterrorism policy shifted the domestic counterterrorism actions of key partner states and the resulting impact within their borders. After the high costs and attendant political turmoil of the military invasions of Afghanistan and Iraq, senior U.S. officials soon recognized the need for a new approach. At the outset of President George W. Bush's second term, U.S.

counterterrorism efforts shifted toward a "disaggregation" strategy focusing on breaking up the global al-Qaeda network and working with and through local security forces to target al-Qaeda-affiliated groups in various countries. The purpose of this strategy was to undercut al-Qaeda's efforts to aggregate its network of affiliates in pursuit of a transnational jihad against the United States. A senior official in the Obama administration similarly affirmed that its preference, "first and foremost," was "working with partners and strengthening their capacity to take action against terrorist networks," pointing specifically to U.S. efforts in Pakistan, Yemen, and Somalia in strengthening local security forces to target al-Qaeda and its affiliates.[17]

In particular, partner states' counterterrorism operations concentrated on the "ungoverned spaces" of their respective peripheries as these were the places where al-Qaeda's affiliates frequently operated.[18] The populations of these difficult-to-reach border regions often possessed languages, ethnicities, cultures, and political identities that set them apart from the dominant population in the centers of power. These differences laid the foundation for a history of conflict with the central governments, in some cases dating back centuries, which contributed to limited government presence and influence among local communities. Given these conditions, U.S. officials feared al-Qaeda could exploit these peripheral areas as safe havens from which to plan attacks against the United States and its interests abroad.

Following this shift in U.S. counterterrorism and under pressure from U.S. officials, partner states increasingly targeted al-Qaeda and its affiliates in the periphery with offensive military force, disrupting the status quo and often exacerbating long-standing points of contention between center and periphery. Given existing tensions, the local populations on the periphery saw the deployment of the military as an unwelcome intrusion by central governments into their territories, especially because of high civilian casualties amassed during the operations. The characteristics of these peripheries and the "foreignness" of the security forces made it difficult to distinguish legitimate targets from local civilians, forcing governments to rely upon indiscriminate violence and shifting the costs of such violence onto the civilian population. The deployment of the military for these counterterrorism operations helped to undermine the legitimacy of the state in the eyes of peripheral communities, drove recruitment for domestically oriented terrorist groups often nominally aligned with al-Qaeda, and provoked a violent backlash as these groups sought to expel the military from their territories and take revenge for government actions. Despite al-Qaeda's continued operational focus on targeting the United States, the overwhelming bulk of global terrorist activity after 2001 has been against local targets within terrorist groups' regions of operation.

From the perspective of key U.S. officials, the offensive actions taken to target al-Qaeda were necessary for protecting U.S. national security. As is evident from numerous public statements and policy documents, they frequently interpreted the resulting increase in terrorism abroad through the frame of a unified al-Qaeda network and as a threat to the United States, especially if terrorist groups internationalized their rhetoric or committed attacks against international targets. Officials across the U.S. government remained focused on stopping another potentially cataclysmic terrorist attack against the United States, often without fully grasping the local political and social dynamics driving patterns of violence. This led to heightened U.S. pressure on partner states to expand their counterterrorism operations at the periphery, feeding the very conditions that served as the original catalyst for a spike in domestic terrorism. As a result, partner states and terrorist groups became locked in a deadly, tit-for-tat cycle of violence—what I call the terrorism trap. In its global mission to defeat al-Qaeda and international terrorism, the United States unwittingly exacerbated the underlying drivers of intrastate violence and contributed to the increase in domestic terrorist attacks within its partner states.

By identifying this causal relationship, I am not arguing that it is the sole reason for or influence on global terrorist activities after 2001. The issue of terrorism, like so many other concepts studied in the social sciences, is an extremely complex social and psychological phenomenon with many varying and overlapping influences. Scholars have identified a variety of factors that interact with one another to drive the outbreak, frequency, and severity of terrorist attacks. I am not seeking a comprehensive, all-encompassing explanation for terrorism, nor am I conducting an overarching analysis of all aspects of the war on terror. Rather, in this study, I seek to understand the influence of U.S. counterterrorism policy and its impact on the levels of domestic terrorism in partner states in order to address the puzzle outlined above.

Moreover, I am not making any moral claims about the United States' or other governments' behavior as part of the war on terror or attempting to minimize the very real threat from al-Qaeda and other internationally focused terrorist groups. Rather, I am trying to empirically understand the impact of counterterrorism cooperation with the United States on partner states' domestic security environments and the implications for terrorist groups' behavior. As the historian Marc Bloch once observed, "It is so easy to denounce. We are never sufficiently understanding."[19] Looking back on the war on terror more than two decades after the 9/11 attacks and taking stock of U.S. counterterrorism efforts in the years since, this constructive and necessary exercise can help provide a better understanding of the ramifications of U.S. foreign policy. As political instability and violence abroad can negatively impact U.S. national security interests, it further demonstrates the need to reevaluate U.S. counterterrorism and reconceptualize the ongoing global fight against terrorism as governments continue to work to counter evolving security threats around the world.[20]

## THE TERRORISM TRAP: A THEORETICAL OVERVIEW

Rejecting the traditional division between international and domestic politics, scholars are increasingly cognizant of the role that domestic political constraints play in determining a state's foreign policy behavior, stemming from varying institutional structures or domestic political costs for unpopular foreign policy decisions.[21] With his "second image reversed," a phrase first coined in 1978 in a reexamination of the three images theory of realist scholar Kenneth Waltz, international relations scholar Peter Gourevitch argued that international politics also can influence states' domestic political processes and outcomes.[22] Factors such as the international economy, the structure of the international state system, hegemonic behavior, and interstate war impact a state's domestic political development by both limiting and directing opportunities for market growth, trade, political development, and security. With conflict increasingly occurring at the intrastate level, international politics plays a significant role in shaping governments' domestic security policies and conflict behavior.[23] Reflecting Gourevitch's "second-image reversed," the war on terror, a defining feature of U.S. foreign policy after September 11, 2001, has influenced the strategic calculus of many political leaders around the world and helped to shape and direct partner states' domestic security actions. As the war on terror progressed beyond U.S. military operations in Afghanistan and Iraq, U.S. counterterrorism efforts increasingly focused on the "ungoverned spaces" of the periphery as potential safe havens for al-Qaeda and its affiliates, with the United States pushing its partner states to shift their focus to terrorist activities in these regions.

These areas—including Pakistan's Federally Administered Tribal Areas (FATA), southern Yemen, northern Mali, the northeastern states of Nigeria, Egypt's Sinai Peninsula, and the southern Philippines—are on the peripheries of their respective national territories, places where a combination of weak government institutions, difficult terrain, historical marginalization of the local population, and conflicts with the central government have allowed terrorist groups to emerge and operate outside of state control. Akbar Ahmed, an anthropologist and former senior member of the Civil Service of Pakistan who served as a political agent in FATA, recognized in his 2013 book *The Thistle and the Drone* that many of the terrorist groups dominating international headlines emerged from lineage-based tribal societies in exactly these conditions,[24] including the Pakistani Taliban in Pakistan's northwestern frontier, Boko Haram in northeastern Nigeria, al-Qaeda in the Islamic Maghreb, Abu Sayyaf in the southern Philippines, and Ansar Dine in northern Mali.[25] Their actions, Ahmed argues, strongly resonated in the context of these tribal societies, with their "emphasis on honor and revenge."[26] He further observed that "a clear principle of cause and effect shapes the relationship between the attacking central authority and the resisting tribes. The draconian and often indiscriminate measures enacted by the center's security agencies and the military provoke the unrestrained retaliation of the desperate periphery. Indeed, the greater the brutalization of peripheral communities, the harsher their retaliatory violence."[27]

## CENTER VERSUS PERIPHERY

Governments throughout history—from ancient empires to modern states—have faced the challenge of extending their writ over tribal populations[28] residing in the distant and inaccessible mountains, deserts, jungles, and forests of the periphery. These regions remained untouched by the broader political developments of the faraway capitals that nominally ruled them thanks to the difficult nature of the terrain limiting access to outsiders and the fierce independence of the inhabitants themselves, who refused to accept outside interference in their internal affairs or to recognize the authority of a distant centralized government. The former governor of British India's North-West Frontier Province, Sir Olaf Caroe, saw Waziristan, the mountainous heart of FATA and future home of the Pakistani Taliban, as "a fortress built by nature for herself, guarded by mountains which serve it in the office of a wall."[29] In a more foreboding warning, a harsh desert region of southern Yemen was given the name Hadhramaut, meaning "death has come." Similarly, describing the Tuareg of the West African Sahel region, a British traveler wrote in the 1920s that they "are so little known even to-day that their very existence is almost legendary."[30]

While the line between center and periphery was fluid and often blurred, this was in essence a political division separating populations under government control from those that operated outside of such control.[31] The periphery began, according to political ethnographer James Scott, "where taxes and grain end."[32] Central governments made periodic attempts to conquer these areas, but these efforts were met with stiff resistance and were largely unsuccessful. Rulers came to understand that there was little economic return on the massive costs needed to assert control on the periphery and were therefore content to merely keep the regions' tribes at bay. Punctuated by periodic raiding and trade, successive governments often left the periphery to its own steady rhythm of life and largely allowed local populations to govern themselves according to their own political and social customs—a "delicate balance" and "uneasy truce" between center and periphery, as described by anthropologist Clifford Geertz.[33]

European colonialism hit these societies like a juggernaut. From the perspective of colonial authorities in distant European capitals, these

frontier regions were viewed as spaces of violence and contested authority beyond the reach of colonial authorities, a looming threat against
political control over their colonial possessions. In the late nineteenth
century, British historian Sir Alfred Lyall wrote that the frontier was
"the outmost political boundary projected, as one might say, beyond the
administrative border."[34] Backed by modern armaments, European powers keen to assert imperial dominance sought at best to "civilize," or at a
minimum to contain, the tribes in these frontier regions. In this way,
they hoped to establish a buffer zone against encroachments by imperial
rivals, as had been the ambition of the British and Russian Empires as
they jockeyed for position among the tribes of Central Asia during the
nineteenth century. As Lord Curzon, the British viceroy in India at the
turn of the twentieth century, once remarked, "Frontiers are indeed
the razor's edge on which hang suspended the modern issues of war or
peace, of life or death to nations."[35]

As imperial powers attempted to assert some level of political control
or influence in these regions, colonial officials often met any resistance
from the perceived "savages" and "barbarians" of the periphery with
overwhelming military force. Lord Curzon observed of the Tribal Areas
along the newly delineated border with Afghanistan that "No patchwork
scheme—and all our present recent schemes, blockade, allowances etc.,
are mere patchwork—will settle the Waziristan problem. Not until the
military steam-roller has passed over the country from end to end, will
there be peace." Aware of the potentially disastrous results of such an
approach, he continued, "But I do not want to be the person to start that
machine."[36] His successors were not so hesitant to rely on the military,
with British authorities launching several large-scale military operations
into the Tribal Areas through the first half of the twentieth century.
Other imperial powers likewise relied on military deployments and a
show of force to resolve challenges to their rule. The governor general of
French Algeria in the mid-nineteenth century, General Thomas-Robert
Bugeaud, argued that the massacres of Berber tribesmen in the Kabylie
region were "necessary to strike terror among these turbulent and fanati-
cal montagnards [mountain people]," and French parliamentarians went
so far as to call for a "war of extermination."[37] During the nineteenth and
early twentieth centuries, these tactics were mirrored by Russian imperial forces in the Caucasus, the Spanish military against the Riffian

Berbers in Spanish Morocco, the Italians in Libya and Somalia, and Dutch forces in the Aceh region of the Dutch East Indies.

The beleaguered status of the periphery continued as Europe's imperial holdings in Asia and Africa fell, one by one, in the years after World War II. Due to the borders haphazardly drawn by European officials, who often lacked local knowledge, newly independent states faced a daunting challenge in governing the dizzying mosaic of ethnicities, cultures, religions, and tribes under their rule. Walker Connor, a scholar of nationalism, points to the "illusion of homogeneity" that obtained for many postcolonial states, as different ethnic or social groups landed within the political boundaries of the same central government but with few historical interactions with one another. Such accidents of history undermined the political unity of the various populations who found themselves joined together within newly delineated borders. Facing these circumstances, their national consciousness and political identities were frequently bound with their group or region rather than the newly created state. As Connor writes, "The Asian pattern is also characterized by a number of major cultural pockets, each oriented to the periphery rather than to the interior. Contacts between the steppe- and highland-dwelling peoples on the one hand, and the riverine- and coastal dwelling peoples on the other have been insignificant."[38]

Faced with such divided societies, many of these relatively weak governments lacked the capacity to provide widespread government services, withstand internal challenges to their authority, or consolidate broadly recognized internal political legitimacy.[39] Robert Jackson, a political scientist specializing in issues of sovereignty within the developing world, classified such postcolonial states as "quasi-states" given the lack of widespread internal legitimacy.[40] He argued that many states that gained independence in the wave of decolonization following World War II earned formal international recognition largely by lobbying departing colonial powers and other international actors rather than as a result of domestic political processes. The governments of "quasi-states" often possessed only the legal trappings of domestic political sovereignty. They pursued the interests of a small group of elites dominating political and economic structures and lacked the capacity or political will to provide socioeconomic benefits or protect civil and human rights for the entire population. This undermined the domestic legitimacy of state

institutions, often Western imports, from the perspective of the populations they governed, especially the peripheral groups who received few
benefits from their new governments. Faced with mounting domestic
challenges to government authority, "quasi-states" were bolstered not only
by international recognition but often through external support, especially those shaped by the international rivalries of the Cold War. This
propped up and perpetuated weak governments despite large segments
of their own populations perceiving them as corrupt and illegitimate.
Within "quasi-states," empirical statehood, as opposed to juridical statehood, was still undergoing a process of construction.

For peripheral regions, little changed politically during the transition
from colonial rule to independence as they remained far outside the cor-
ridors of power. Many postcolonial states inherited peripheral regions
where central political control existed primarily on maps. "On the ground,"
historian Berenice Guyot-Rechard writes in her study of the border
regions of northeastern India and Tibet in the twentieth century, "the
presence of colonial authorities was scarce, to say the least. Most of the
region remained un-administered, if not unexplored."[41] In the early postcolonial period, efforts to extend and consolidate administrative and
political control into the periphery were frequently slow to achieve any
significant results, hampered as they were by the lack of political will or
interest on the part of government officials, limited government capacity
and resources, the periphery's difficult climate and terrain, local resistance, or conflicting interests within the central government. In the case
of India's northeastern frontier area within Assam, it was partly the
looming threat of Communist China and its claims on Indian territory
that spurred New Delhi's greater interest in establishing control over the
region through a variety of development, security, economic, and cultural initiatives.[42]

The populations of the periphery often possessed ethnic or tribal
identities, languages, informal governance structures, various social
customs, and, in some cases, religions that are distinct from the majority
population, which monopolized political and economic power at the
center.[43] Political theorist Will Kymlicka defined such peripheral groups
as "national minorities" in that they hold certain common characteristics of a nation-state—"a historical community, more or less institu-
tionally complete, occupying a given territory or homeland, sharing a

distinct language and culture"—but lack recognized political sovereignty within their respective national territories.[44] As a result, political leaders in the periphery have often sought to protect their communities' interests and distinct political identities (which often overlapped with these leaders' personal political interests) by pushing for various forms of political or cultural autonomy, if not outright independence from the postcolonial state. In support of the centralization of power and to dampen the strength of any political opposition, central governments often sought either the removal or co-optation of customary leadership at the periphery. This was matched by repressive policies aimed at assimilating the periphery into a common national identity so as to establish government control over these regions as part of the larger state-building process.[45]

Thus, the periphery represented a space of contested sovereignty, with those holding the reins of power in postcolonial governments quickly growing concerned at the potential for these regions to act as sources of early opposition to their efforts to assert political power and construct a national consciousness and unified national identity—or "imagined community," in the words of Benedict Anderson—often based in the characteristics and language of the dominant political group.[46] In his study of the "Celtic fringe" within British national development during the nineteenth and twentieth centuries, Michael Hechter described this process as a form of "internal colonialism" by which the state fosters the periphery's economic and political dependence on the center as it advances economically and technologically. He writes, "Policies determining the administration of these territories were subsequently to be decided in a larger political arena, one in which the Celts were destined to play only a minor role. The peripheral population, therefore, lost the privilege of determining its own fate."[47] This stratification of the center and periphery helped to strengthen the political salience of these different identities.

Peripheral communities often perceived this process as an illegitimate intrusion into their political or cultural autonomy, generating intense opposition and even violence against the state. As Donald Horowitz shows in his book *Ethnic Groups in Conflict*, political power in the ethnically diverse societies of former European colonies was frequently distributed unevenly after independence. This unequal access to political power gave different ethnic groups an awareness of their relative standing within the new political environment, undermining the state-building project and contributing to the outbreak of ethnic conflict. "Control of the state, control of *a* state, and exemption from control by others," Horowitz writes, "are among the main goals of ethnic conflict."[48] Many postcolonial states have been plagued by persistent rebellions and anti-state violence from the politically excluded periphery since independence, as many peripheral communities were effectively reduced to the status of second-class citizens.[49]

As postcolonial governments attempted to establish control over the periphery, their efforts often clashed with the strong identities, customs, and historical autonomy of local communities. The communities that often offered the strongest resistance were those organized along tribal lines. These were segmented societies defined by lineage, possessing informal governance structures exclusive of outsiders, and in which interactions were shaped by codes of honor emphasizing hospitality and revenge. The demand for revenge against slights of honor and other crimes was a key aspect of regulating behavior within tribal societies lacking state institutions and in which personal characteristics and reputation serve as the currency of social standing. With the compulsion to take revenge under the prevailing code acting as a deterrent, individuals were aware that any action violating the honor of another would be answered by violent acts of revenge against the transgressor or the transgressor's clan by the victim or the victim's clan.

Several tribal sayings capture this ideal of tribal behavior. A Pashtun proverb states that "He is not a [Pashtun] who does not give a blow in return for a pinch."[50] A Somali proverb similarly describes the ever-present role of blood feuds and tribal rivalries in society: "Me and my nation against the world. Me and my clan against my nation. Me and my family against the clan. Me and my brother against the family. Me against my brother."[51] Another saying among the Pashtun posits that "The [Pashtun] who took revenge after a hundred years said, I took it quickly," reflecting the fact that more serious crimes within society, such as murder, rape, or other attacks against women, could stir brutal cycles of revenge and counter-revenge that stretch across generations.[52] In the early 1970s, Akbar Khan Bugti, a Baloch tribal leader in Pakistan's Balochistan Province, remarked on the destructive nature of tribal feuding, clearly with a touch of hyperbole, that "No killing can ever go unavenged. . . . A lizard took refuge in a Baloch House. A Baloch of another tribe unwittingly killed it. The death of this refugee had to be avenged and the two tribes nearly became extinct in the resultant fighting."[53] The potential for acts of revenge to develop into deadly and disruptive cycles of violence highlight the important mediating role that tribal elders played in the settlement of blood feuds through negotiations between the aggrieved parties, often relying on blood payments or arranged marriages to resolve disputes. The goal of this mediation process was restorative justice rather than the punitive justice sought by modern legal systems. Religious leaders have also traditionally operated outside of tribal structures as neutral arbiters between competing clans or tribes, thereby helping to strengthen their reputation and influence among local communities.

However, the code of honor is not deterministic or a fixed institution. Among highly egalitarian communities on the periphery, the informal guiding principles of tribal codes have been subject to constant interpretation and reinterpretation amid the changing dynamics and pragmatic needs of day-to-day life.[54] While varying interactions with the modern state have altered or weakened tribal identities and customs in several ways, they ultimately have proven remarkably resilient and continue to resonant with many individuals at the periphery, where the limited reach of the state has allowed tribal customs to persist, including the impulse for blood revenge.[55] In 2012, a former Afghan government official explained that "the culture in the U.S. is about policy, it is about mutually rational interests. Revenge is at times more important in this part of the world, more important than any political or economic interest."[56] This reality has influenced the patterns of violence within many tribal societies and the conflicts between center and periphery. Revenge under prevailing codes was traditionally accomplished through discriminate action narrowly focused on the perpetrator or the perpetrator's clan, a means of regulating social relations within the tribe. Outside intrusions and military interventions relying on indiscriminate force, however, resulted in widespread social disruptions at the periphery and increasingly led to more generalized retaliatory acts against external enemies, helping to unite traditional tribal rivals against a common enemy. Following Russian military operations in Chechnya and the resulting societal-wide trauma, for example, psychological studies of Chechens have shown impacted individuals' desire for revenge shifting more toward generalized acts of vengeance against government targets or the majority population, the latter seen as collectively responsible for the violence.[57]

Such tribalism and the historical conflict between center and periphery provide the necessary context for understanding many of the regions classified as "ungoverned spaces" in the parlance of the war on terror and the terrorist groups that emerged from them.[58] In a 2005 speech, the head of al-Qaeda in Iraq, Abu Musab al-Zarqawi, stressed the importance of understanding the group's tribal context, rife as it was with shifting alliances and rivalries as tribes acted in their own interests in a fluid conflict environment. He referred to the tribes as "the most important mainstays of the Jihad," and, in the same breath, threatened local tribesmen with violence if they sided with "the Crusaders and their apostate lackeys" amid U.S. military operations in Iraq.[59] In May 2010, the al-Qaeda in the Arabian Peninsula (AQAP) ideologue Anwar al-Awlaqi likewise observed the importance of this tribal context. "The cradle for Jihad today are the tribes," he stated. "In Afghanistan there are tribes. In Iraq there are tribes. In Somalia there are tribes. Even in Pakistan there are tribal areas and non tribal areas and we find that the cradle for Jihad are the tribal areas, and so is the case in Yemen."[60]

Indeed, these terrorist groups' patterns of attacks and messaging frequently point more toward their tribal context than some putative concern for religious orthodoxy. Of course, many terrorists that emerged from tribal societies have relied on Islamic rhetoric and ideology to frame their grievances against the state and their motivations for fighting. And anthropologists have long pointed to the importance of religion and religious figures, with their broad appeal, to serve as mobilizing forces to unite competing clan groups and tribes to resist outside influences seen to be contrary to local practices and beliefs or to fight against an oppressive government. The history of European colonialism in Asia and Africa is replete with examples of indigenous groups uniting behind religious figures to oppose invading imperial forces, such as Mullah Muhammad Abdullah Hassan (known among the British as the "Mad Mullah") of Somaliland or the various mullahs within British India's Tribal Areas who led popular movements to resist British expansionism at the turn of the twentieth century.[61]

However, the harsh terrain of the periphery and tribal life traditionally made it difficult to maintain orthodox religious practices; scholars have recognized that religion is interpreted and practiced differently depending on local variations in social, political, economic, and even ecological conditions. Tribally organized Muslim societies, which take Islam to be a core aspect of their identity, have often viewed religion through the lens of prevailing social customs and practices that predate the historical conversion to Islam, synthesizing the two into a "tribal Islam."[62] Within these societies, tribal identities and many pre-Islamic customs, such as adherence to a code of honor, proved remarkably durable as they were maintained and given a religious sheen, even if such customs contradicted Islamic teachings. An early twentieth-century traveler among the Tuareg in western Africa remarked, "The Tuareg have nominally adopted the Mussulman religion, but they are not observant of the strict laws of the Koran. They have no mosques in their country, no Imam, or High Priest, and no Mufti. They still cling to a great many of their superstitions."[63] To demonstrate the inherent tension between religious ideals and social norms, a tribal elder in northern Pakistan described the Pashtun's adoption of Islam as follows: "When some Arab preachers came to introduce Islam to the area centuries ago, the Pashtun leadership responded by presenting the central features of the *Pashtunwali* (the way of the Pashtun) code and asked them if Islam was compatible with these values. It was only after the preachers agreed not to interfere with *Pashtunwali* that Pashtuns joined the fold of Islam."[64] Indeed, a Baloch scholar in Pakistan argued that even today "you don't understand these regions" without understanding the interaction between Islam and "tribal norms."[65]

In a study of the insurgency in the Dagestan region of the North Caucasus, for instance, Jean-Francois Ratelle and Emil Souleimanov argue that militants' embrace of an extreme Islamic ideology was a by-product of mobilization driven by a desire for blood revenge against repressive government forces.[66] These forces engaged in widespread abuses against the Dagestani population, including kidnappings, torture, blackmail, rape, beatings, and extralegal killings, often on unfounded suspicions of terrorist activity by young men, sometimes even for simply having a

"Wahhabi beard."[67] The mufti in Dagestan's capital city Makhachkala blamed this indiscriminate use of force for pushing Dagestanis to commit acts of violence. He explained, "The Russians knock on the apartment doors. They tell them to give up the people inside. So what happens? They shoot. That's why we have suicide bombers."[68] One former Chechen militant similarly explained, "In the beginning, no one was really willing to go to war. . . . After all, we all had families, households, elderly parents to care for. But when your younger brother is killed in an air strike, what are you supposed to do? Stay home and watch TV? For us Chechens, there was no other choice but to take up arms and seek revenge."[69] Another Chechen militant stated that "even those Chechens who hated [rebel Chechen leader] Dudayev ultimately drove into the war" due to the impulse for revenge against the Russian military and the civilian casualties it committed.[70] According to Ratelle and Souleimanov's analysis, the embrace of a religious-based extremist ideology became a vehicle for Dagestanis to express dissatisfaction with and challenge the Russian-backed Dagestani government, with militants' rhetoric and behavior more reflective of the Dagestani code of honor than any interpretations of Islam and its tenets. A 2009 survey of young men in the North Caucasus, in fact, found little support for fundamentalist views of Islam. According to this survey, the most salient motivations for joining militant activities were poor economic conditions and the repressive actions of the corrupt government.[71]

Within neighboring Chechnya, scholars similarly find that blood revenge served as the organizing principle of militant mobilization born out of the brutality of Russian military operations, in which as many as 250,000 Chechen civilians were killed between 1994 and 2004, along with reports of widespread rape.[72] Among Chechen suicide bombers analyzed by Anne Speckhard and Khapta Ahkmedova, every single one had undergone the trauma of a close relatives' death or near death by torture; the authors also point out that two would-be suicide bombers who did not follow through in their attacks were the only individuals in their study who did not experience this direct trauma.[73] Chechen militants embraced religious extremism as an ideology of opposition against the repressive government and an instrumental means to unify Chechen fighters across clan divisions. These militants, however, frequently framed their Islamic faith as compatible with the underlying impulse for

revenge within the Chechen code of honor, with terrorists often conflat-
ing religion and tribal customs without distinction. In June 2000, two
teenage girls, the first Chechen female suicide bombers, explained their
decision to drive a truck full of explosives into a Russian army base with
reference to a syncretic narrative of religion and tribalism, much like
other Chechen suicide bombers. "Sisters, the time has come," they
announced. "When the enemy has killed almost all our men, our brothers and husbands, we are the only ones left to take revenge for them. The
time has come for us to take up arms and defend our home, our land
from those who bring death to our home. And if we have to become
*shakhids* [martyrs] for Allah we will not stop. *Allah Akbar!*"[74]

### IGNITING KILCULLEN'S "ACCIDENTAL GUERILLAS"

An anthropologist, former Australian military officer, and expert in
counterterrorism, David Kilcullen has played a leading role in shaping
U.S. counterterrorism policy during the war on terror. He served as a
senior advisor to General David Petraeus, helping to plan the strategy for
the 2007 troop surge in Iraq, and as a senior counterterrorism advisor to
the secretary of state, leading field assessment teams in Afghanistan and
Pakistan. He has been on the front lines of the United States' fight against
terrorism, directly observing the behavior and tactics of terrorist groups
and helping to formulate U.S. strategy. During his time as an advisor for
the U.S. government, he witnessed U.S. forces in Iraq and Afghanistan
become increasingly bogged down fighting local militant groups. He
defined this phenomenon as the "accidental guerilla" syndrome.

In his 2009 book *The Accidental Guerilla: Fighting Small Wars in the
Midst of a Big One*, Kilcullen summed up this cyclical process. "[Al-
Qaeda] moves into remote areas," he writes, "creates alliances with local
traditional communities, exports violence that prompts a western intervention, and then exploits the backlash against that intervention in order
to generate support for its *takfiri* agenda [accusing other Muslims of
apostasy]." This process possesses four distinct phases. The first is the
*infection* phase, in which al-Qaeda "establishes a presence in a remote,
ungoverned or conflict-affected area." The second phase is *contagion*, in
which al-Qaeda "uses the safe haven to spread violence and *takfiri*

ideology to other regions." The third is *intervention*, where outside military forces challenge the al-Qaeda threat and "disrupt the safe haven." The fourth is *rejection*, as the "local population reacts negatively, rejecting outside intervention," often allying with al-Qaeda in the process.[75] The fourth stage leads back to the first as the violent resistance to the intervention brings further attention to and intervention into the region as a terrorist safe haven, starting the cycle all over again. Kilcullen continues, "Al Qa'ida's ideology tends to lack intrinsic appeal for traditional societies, and so it draws the majority of its strength from this backlash rather than from genuine popular support."[76] This process, as Kilcullen has argued, has driven much of the anti-American violence within Iraq and Afghanistan.

This same logic can be applied to the domestic conflict between center and periphery; Kilcullen himself acknowledged the applicability of the "accidental guerilla" syndrome to the center-versus-periphery dynamic in his discussion of the "internal colonialism" within the Patani region of southern Thailand and Pakistan's FATA.[77] With the advent of the war on terror, U.S. officials increasingly feared al-Qaeda could exploit the "ungoverned spaces" at the periphery of various partner states as bases of operation to spread their message and plan operations against the United States. An al-Qaeda presence or perceived al-Qaeda links to local groups in these regions, therefore, served as catalysts for U.S. pressure on partner states to militarily intervene to "disrupt the safe haven," particularly following the shift in U.S. counterterrorism to a "disaggregation" approach at the outset of Bush's second term.

Local communities in the periphery, however, viewed the resulting intervention by partner state security forces as an outside and unwelcome intrusion that disrupted the precarious status quo between center and periphery and destabilized the political environment. Rather than cowing the targeted groups into submission, these interventions led to an increase in retaliatory terrorist attacks as local groups targeted the state in revenge for counterterrorism operations. Making matters worse, the military escalation at the periphery was frequently unable to avoid impacting the civilian population, further undermining the legitimacy of the government and provoking a series of counterattacks.[78] With the rising number of terrorist attacks, U.S. officials frequently viewed the violence through the lens of al-Qaeda's transnational jihad and increased pressure on their counterparts in partner states to expand their military efforts in the periphery, starting this cycle of violence anew.

There has been a perception that relying on partner states' militaries as a surrogate force to conduct counterterrorism operations was a means of protecting U.S. national security interests abroad while avoiding the high costs of unilateral U.S. military action. Soldiers operating within their own borders were expected to be more familiar with the local language, culture, and terrain and more effective in gathering intelligence and targeting terrorists. Further, it was often assumed that domestic military deployments would be viewed as more legitimate by local communities and, thus, avoid the danger of a violent backlash that a foreign military intervention would provoke, as occurred with U.S. and Coalition forces in Afghanistan and Iraq. Before the war on terror, the U.S. government already recognized the importance of working with local authorities in confronting the issue of international terrorism as they possessed local knowledge, proximity, and greater perceived legitimacy within a target community.[79] Even "the best-behaved foreigners," as many U.S. officials thought, can provoke a negative reaction.[80] Besides the invasions of Iraq and Afghanistan, research suggests that the United States has in fact been less likely to engage in direct military interventions abroad for security reasons than for humanitarian ones.[81]

These arguments, however, do not consider domestic variations in geography, language, culture, ethnicity, and government capacity, nor do they take account of the existing tensions between center and periphery. Due to these factors, partner states' military forces faced several challenges undermining their effectiveness during counterterrorism operations at the periphery. Military units deployed for these operations often consisted of soldiers from the given state's dominant population, whose language, ethnicity, and sometimes religion were often different from the local population. Many of the soldiers deployed to FATA for counterterrorism operations, the first significant military presence in the region since the British garrisons were removed in 1947, were unfamiliar with the local Pashtun customs, language, and social structures.[82] Even many of the Pashtun soldiers used in these operations were from the settled, or less tribal, areas of the North-West Frontier Province and were disconnected from the tribal customs and social landscape of FATA. Viewed by the locals as outsiders, the military faced difficulties in extracting accurate information on terrorist activity as the troops had fewer contacts with local communities. Members of the military were at times even unwilling to use what information was available from the local population due to suspicions over their loyalties.[83] As a result, military forces often lacked key information and intelligence about the conflict environment, especially concerning who was and wasn't involved with or supportive of local terrorist groups. The difficulty of the terrain in many of these isolated peripheral regions, combined with the generally poor suitability of military forces vis-à-vis the operating environment, exacerbated many of these issues and undermined the effectiveness of U.S.-backed counterterrorism efforts.

Given the difficulties of operating in the periphery, military forces frequently relied on indiscriminate violence, particularly the use of air power and artillery, which resulted in high civilian causalities. While U.S. officials pressured partner states to target al-Qaeda operatives, the resulting counterterrorism operations and use of indiscriminate violence often targeted local communities suspected of harboring these militants, shifting the costs of the conflict onto the local civilian populations. Combined with a historical pattern of political tensions and conflict with the central government, the indiscriminate violence fed into the perception among local communities that the U.S.-backed counterterrorism operations constituted an outside and unwelcome invasion of their territory. Despite the stated goal of intervening in the periphery to fight al-Qaeda and international terrorism, partner states quickly became bogged down fighting local groups spurred to action by this very intervention.

Domestic terrorism rapidly increased as local groups attempted to force the military out of the periphery and sought revenge against the state.[84] The use of indiscriminate violence also frequently led to internal displacement of local populations, which has been shown to contribute to an increase in suicide terrorism.[85] Terrorist groups highlighted indiscriminate violence against civilian populations and the necessity of revenge in their public messaging and appeals for support. This helped drive recruitment and support for local terrorist groups, much as "accidental guerillas" took up arms in response to the military invasions of Iraq and Afghanistan.[86] Individuals seeking revenge against the government commonly joined local groups whose fight was primarily directed against the "near enemy," in contrast to al-Qaeda's focus on the "far enemy" of the United States, with recruitment patterns often based on personal relationships and social, ethnic, or tribal affiliations.[87]

These groups soon found themselves in the crosshairs of the U.S. government as officials were quick to frame the attacks as part of al-Qaeda's international struggle. They interpreted the increase in violence, despite mostly occurring within a domestic or regional context, as a threat to the United States and its national security interests. This led to increased U.S. pressure on partner states to expand their efforts in challenging these groups through strong military measures. Many groups even encouraged this level of international attention with their bombastic and internationalized rhetoric, a move that Pakistani general Abdullah Dogar, a former brigade commander in Waziristan, referred to in a discussion of the Pakistani Taliban group the Tehreek-e-Taliban Pakistan as "delusions of grandeur."[88] Despite their focus on domestic terrorist attacks, many of these groups did attack international targets within their state or region of origin. These attacks were often in response to the behavior of foreign actors within their conflict environment, such as their backing the government's military operations or militarily intervening themselves. Attacks against international targets were also a means for groups to demonstrate their own strength and resilience in support of their domestic political agendas.[89] Yet, the expanded military operations in the periphery served as a further catalyst for increased violence as groups sought to force the military to withdraw from the periphery and demonstrate their continued strength.[90] With expanded military operations provoking ever higher levels of domestic terrorism, partner states became trapped in a cycle of violence with targeted terrorist groups in which each military attack was met by a counterattack against the state—the terrorism trap.

A former senior Pakistani intelligence official, pointing to the numerous challenges facing Pakistan's military forces during their operations in the country's northwestern periphery, observed that "U.S. policymakers in their enthusiasm to vigorously pursue counterterrorism in partner states overlooked structural deficiencies in those countries." He argued that this was the "dilemma of the countries supporting the United States who went overboard in pursuing al-Qaeda."[91] Even al-Qaeda's leadership recognized this phenomenon and sought to exploit not only the historical struggle of communities at the periphery but also the increased grievances against the state stemming from the latter's cooperation with U.S.

counterterrorism efforts.[92] An internal al-Qaeda letter recovered in 2012 stressed the importance of finding allies among the beleaguered tribal communities targeted in U.S.-backed counterterrorism operations in the Middle East and Central Asia. "Many governments in the region," the letter argued,

> also made big mistakes when they ignored tribal attitudes. Those governments, and because of outside demands, would often kill their own countrymen without giving enough thought to the consequences of their actions. As outside pressure increased on those governments, those governments, in return, intensified their actions against their own tribes. That led many tribes in those countries to turn against the governments. If the Mujahidin treat the tribes well, the tribes will likely be on the Mujahidin's side. The tribal communities take the spilling of blood within its community very seriously.[93]

Al-Qaeda's leaders further observed that in Yemen "the depth of fanaticism and revenge with the Arabs is not hidden" and "blood has a huge effect on the individuals." They saw that "American pressure on the Yemeni Government made it make mistakes in dealing with the tribes and bomb the sons of the tribes in al-Mahfad and Shabwah." This "ongoing pressure," they argued, "makes it [the Yemeni government] vulnerable to bigger mistakes that will lead some of the tribes to gather against it. The US will continue its pressure on [Yemeni president] Ali Abdallah Salih to clash with his people until his card is completely burned with the people. . . . If the mujahidin improve their dealings with the tribes, most likely the tribes will lean toward them; the blood's effect on the tribal societies is great."[94] Aware of the potential backlash against al-Qaeda's forces as well, the group's leaders ordered its Yemeni affiliate to "avoid killing anyone from the tribes."[95]

Yet, the disparate affiliate groups comprising the wider al-Qaeda network often acted at odds with the leadership's orders to focus their efforts on the United States. Bin Laden and other al-Qaeda leaders advised the group's affiliates to avoid conflicts with local governments and instead work to "deplete the head of infidelity: the American enemy."[96] Despite such guidance, terrorist groups affiliated with al-Qaeda continued to target local governments in line with their locally focused goals, largely adapting their patterns of violence to their local conflict environments and frequently in response to the government's use of offensive military force.

In recent years, a growing body of research has pointed to offensive military operations as leading to an increase in violence while more conciliatory or defensive tactics are correlated with decreases in violence. In an examination of Russian counterinsurgency in the North Caucasus, for instance, Monica Duffy Toft and Yuri Zhukov identify two main strategies used: "(1) Denial, which operates by physically isolating insurgents and manipulating the costs of expanding fighting to new locations and (2) punishment, which uses offensive operations in contested areas to manipulate the costs of sustained fighting."[97] In testing these strategies, they find that denial, which does not involve offensive operations and can be equated to a defensive approach, is the most effective of these two approaches given its ability to limit insurgent options, halt the spread of violence, and avoid punitive reprisals. Punishment, with its focus on killing the enemy, only serves to increase the risk of continued violence, especially as it promotes conflict contagion between different areas within the country. Mustafa Unal and Petra Uludag similarly demonstrate the ineffectiveness of offensive military action in an analysis of Turkey's operations against the Kurdistan Workers' Party (Partiya Karkerên Kurdistan, or PKK).[98] Turkey's wide-ranging military operations in the southeastern region of the country have focused on "incapacitating (killing, injuring, and capturing) PKK militants and containing the PKK ideology. . . . [It has vowed] to continue military operations 'until no terrorist remains.'"[99] The study found that these military efforts, however, did not reduce PKK violence overall.

Focusing specifically on the connection between government violence against civilians and terrorism, researchers have shown that indiscriminate killings by the government, the deployment of coercive offensive tactics during domestic operations, and the use of security forces with poor oversight over their behavior triggers subsequent increases in terrorist attacks, an act of resistance that requires less opportunity and planning than an organized insurgency and helps to fuel a cycle of domestic violence between the government and terrorist groups.[100] This outcome stems from the government's use of violence, which alienates the civilian population and raises the likelihood that it will become a base of support for terrorist groups. It also incentivizes groups to engage in particularly brutal acts of terrorism to demonstrate their continued capacity to wage war and to show the government the costs of continuing to fight, especially in targeting civilians supporting the government. In a study of Provisional Irish Republican Army (PIRA) bombings between 1970 and 1998, Paul Gill, James Piazza, and John Horgan show that discriminate counterterrorism operations had no impact on PIRA bombings. However, indiscriminate state violence, in which both PIRA members and civilians were killed, resulted in an increase in PIRA bombings.[101] In a study of Israeli counterterrorism, Henda Hsu and David McDowall argue that the use of indiscriminate violence during counterterrorism operations has similarly resulted in a backlash effect, leading to an increase in both the frequency and deadliness of terrorist attacks against the Israeli state.[102] These arguments are in line with studies that show statewide repression of civilian populations by the government can fuel domestic terrorism.[103] Supporting these findings, a psychological study finds that the narrative of revenge for group grievances permeates many terrorist groups' messaging and ideology, especially as a means of gaining support from affected civilian populations.[104]

With partner states' domestic counterterrorism efforts playing a key role in the war on terror, scholars have explored the reasons behind variations in the states' level of cooperation with the United States. Their arguments largely have taken three different approaches focusing on (1) U.S. policy and whether it is in line with international norms;[105] (2) the particular characteristics of a partner state that might limit its ability to cooperate, such as its political system and style of governance, low state capacity, and the government's relationship with religious institutions;[106] and (3) the interactions between the United States and partner states and whether or not the various parties' strategic calculations align.[107] However, these studies have for the most part not addressed the impact of this cooperation on partner states' domestic security environments and whether or not these efforts have been comprehensively successful in reducing terrorism.

On the other hand, studies of the effectiveness of U.S. counterterrorism have often only examined one part of a broader picture, without considering the role played by partner states' domestic military operations or the increasing prominence of domestic terrorism in global terrorist activity. Jesse Lehrke and Rahel Schomaker, for instance, argue that increasing defensive counterterrorism measures in the United States and Europe have been effective in reducing terrorism and redirecting attacks to the "frontline wars of the War on Terror," without distinguishing between domestic and international terrorism in their study.[108] Their interpretation of this empirical finding is premised on the assumption that al-Qaeda's affiliate groups, responsible for most of the al-Qaeda network's terrorist attacks after 2001, maintained al-Qaeda core's primary goal of striking at the "far enemy" of the United States.[109] It does not consider the impact of partner states' domestic military operations or the emergence of affiliates whose campaigns of violence were largely motivated by local political conditions and directed against domestic targets. Kyle Kattelman does recognize that counterterrorism cooperation with the United States leads to an increase in al-Qaeda-related terrorism, though without making any distinction between al-Qaeda core and its affiliate groups.[110] However, his analysis only examines the impact of partner states' troop deployments in Afghanistan and Iraq as evidence of cooperation with the United States, and he does not consider these states' domestic counterterrorism actions. In a study of the connection between counterterrorism cooperation and causalities from terrorism, Peter Henne demonstrates that partner states that have been more cooperative with the United States on counterterrorism experience fewer deaths from terrorist attacks. Yet, his analysis also does not distinguish between domestic and international terrorism or between military and nonmilitary approaches to counterterrorism.[111] *The Terrorism Trap* attempts to fill these gaps in the understanding of counterterrorism cooperation and the effectiveness of U.S. counterterrorism by connecting U.S. policy with the increase in domestic terrorism inside America's partner states.

## METHODOLOGY

To address the puzzle posed at the opening of this chapter, I employ a mixed-methods approach using both statistical analysis and case studies based on extensive archival research, in-depth interviews, and relevant secondary sources. A full description of the quantitative research design and the results of the statistical models are found in the appendix. I complement the quantitative analysis, which ultimately shows correlation rather than causation, with case studies employing process tracing to establish the causal process that undergirds the dynamic that interests us here—namely, an increase in domestic terrorist attacks within America's partner states. By elucidating the intervening steps in a hypothesized causal process, process tracing provides insights into two issues that are difficult to address through statistical analysis—establishing causal direction and potential spuriousness of results—with process tracing helping to "establish whether there is causal chain of steps connecting X and Y."[112] On its face, U.S. counterterrorism policy, focused as it is on al-Qaeda and international terrorism, does not necessarily have a clear and direct connection with domestic terrorism abroad. However, this policy focus impacted the levels of domestic terrorism through its influence on partner states' use of the military for domestic counterterrorism operations as the key intervening step. By using within-case process tracing to detail the sequence of events leading to the terrorism trap, I connect U.S. counterterrorism policy and partner states' domestic counterterrorism operations to an increase in domestic terrorist attacks.

In support of my argument, I present four case studies of key partner states during the war on terror, largely focusing on events during the Bush and Obama administrations.[113] First, I examine Pakistan, arguably one of the most important counterterrorism partners the United States has had given its strategic location on Afghanistan's border. I have selected Pakistan for several theoretical reasons as well. First, Pakistan experienced the war on terror as a critical juncture in its relationship with the United States. Beginning in 1990, the U.S. government suspended military assistance, and the vast majority of economic aid, to Pakistan due to its continued pursuit of nuclear weapons. U.S. financial support was reintroduced in 2002 as part of the war on terror, giving this bilateral relationship new life after a decade of neglect. Therefore, I am better able to isolate the U.S. influence on Pakistan's domestic security policy after 2001 as Pakistan deployed a significant military presence for the first time into its northwestern periphery in pursuit of al-Qaeda and other al-Qaeda-linked militants. Because of Pakistan's strategic position, it has been an important part of U.S. security policy, but the United States has relied largely upon the Pakistani government to conduct counterterrorism operations within that country's borders, especially as Pakistan "jealously guarded its sovereignty" and would not allow foreign troops to operate on its soil.[114] An in-depth analysis of Pakistan's interaction with the United States in the context of counterterrorism and the resulting domestic impact serves as an illustration of the terrorism trap's causal mechanism.

I further test this theory with case studies focusing on Yemen, Mali, and Egypt. Like Pakistan, all three states possess "ungoverned spaces" in which government control has been limited. Further, these states have been a key part of U.S. counterterrorism efforts as U.S. officials feared al-Qaeda and al-Qaeda-affiliated groups could exploit these states' peripheries as a safe haven for operations targeting the United States and its interests abroad. And, as with Pakistan, the U.S. government has largely relied upon these states' military forces for conducting counterterrorism operations within their borders. These three cases also display variation in their approaches to security within the periphery prior to the eventual adoption of an offensive military approach—specifically, the duplicity of the Yemeni government, Egypt's use of traditional law enforcement, and Mali simply not acting against terrorist groups within its borders given low state capacity. This helps to isolate the effects of domestic counterterrorism operations by the military on the levels of domestic terrorism.

I have structured the four case studies so as to show the sequence of successive steps underlying the terrorism trap theory. First, I provide a historical overview of the political and social issues underlying the conflict between the center and periphery dating back to colonial rule. This "scene setter" provides important historical background on the tensions with the central government and important context for understanding why partner states' military operations would provoke the violent backlash that they did after 2001. Next, I examine in detail the counterterrorism policies that U.S. officials promoted to partner states at the outset of the war on terror. This first step in the theorized causal process, focusing on the United States–partner state relationship, led to the initial deployments of military forces into the periphery. Then, I demonstrate the backlash to these initial operations as terrorist groups attempted to force the military from the periphery and take revenge for these U.S.-backed military operations. This second step, focusing on the center-periphery relationship, resulted in an increase in domestic terrorist attacks within partner states. Finally, with the third step, I show how the actions of both terrorist groups and partner states, under increasing pressure from U.S. officials to expand their counterterrorism operations, resulted in a deadly cycle of violence.

A foundation of process tracing is careful description.[115] I therefore relied on a wide range of primary sources for detailed evidence, poring over thousands of unclassified and declassified documents, including diplomatic cables, intelligence reports, briefing materials, internal memoranda, letters, speeches and other public statements, oral histories, and interview transcripts held by various governmental and nongovernmental archives. My qualitative research strategy was to approach the problem from three different perspectives, thereby mirroring the causal sequence of the terrorism trap theory: U.S. officials working on counterterrorism; officials within partner states shaping and implementing their governments' counterterrorism efforts; and the targeted terrorist groups. My primary source research was supplemented by fifty-six in-depth, semi-structured interviews with current and former government officials, military officers, journalists, and academics in the United States and Pakistan, with some interviewees requesting anonymity given the sensitivity of the subject being discussed. My interview strategy was to focus on decision makers who were involved in counterterrorism policy at multiple levels of government as well as individuals who were involved in the implementation of such policy or who witnessed the impact of these efforts on the ground. In addition to primary sources and interviews, I relied on media reports and relevant secondary sources.

The remainder of the book is organized as follows: chapter 2 examines the disconnect between al-Qaeda core and its affiliate groups to highlight the importance of understanding the affiliates' local political, economic, and social contexts as key influences on their motivations and behavior. In addition, the chapter's analysis helps to refute the argument that the increase in domestic terrorism after 2001 can be explained by the al-Qaeda leadership's guidance and the group's international goals. Chapter 3 focuses on overall U.S. counterterrorism policy, both before and during the war on terror, and reconstructs the process by which it shifted to pressure partner states to target safe havens within their borders with military force, a key factor and process essential for understanding the influence of U.S. counterterrorism on partner state's counterterrorism actions. Chapter 4 presents the in-depth case study of Pakistan, thereby illustrating the terrorism trap's causal mechanism. Chapter 5 contains the case studies of Yemen, Mali, and Egypt, while a final concluding chapter provides a discussion of the book's overall findings and implications.

# 2

## WHAT'S IN A NAME?

Al-Qaeda and Its Affiliates

I n his final year in office, President Barack Obama issued a letter to Congress asserting his authority under the nearly fifteen-year-old Authorization for the Use of Military Force (AUMF) to continue counterterrorism operations against al-Qaeda, the Taliban, and their "associated forces."[1] The letter was sent following the expansion of U.S. air strikes and support for regional military operations in Somalia, and it argued that these efforts were necessary to counter the continued threat from al-Qaeda and "associated elements of al-Shabaab." Obama had already used the broad authorization of the 2001 law to conduct military operations in Libya, Iraq, and Syria during the previous year. The Bush administration similarly used the law for a wide range of military deployments and actions—from Latin America to Southeast Asia.[2] Both administrations' use of the 2001 AUMF, which was quickly and overwhelmingly passed by Congress shortly after September 11, 2001, was premised on the assumption that al-Qaeda and its affiliate organizations presented a unified threat to U.S. national security.

Following the 9/11 attacks, al-Qaeda was thrust to the forefront of American consciousness as both an immediate and an existential threat, one that would fundamentally alter not just the United States' but many other governments' approaches to security. The group, however, was perceived to be only the tip of the spear of a broader international jihadist movement whose aim was to violently challenge the prevailing international order under American hegemony, a "struggle over global-ization."[3] Speaking at the rostrum before a joint session of Congress nine days after 9/11, President Bush announced that "Our war on terror begins with al-Qaeda, but it does not end there. It will not end until every ter-rorist group of global reach has been found, stopped and defeated. . . . But the only way to defeat terrorism as a threat to our way of life is to stop it, eliminate it, and destroy it where it grows."[4] Terrorists adopting the al-Qaeda brand were lumped together into a single, coherent enemy as the United States' definition of al-Qaeda changed over time to accom-modate the emergence of new groups.[5]

This international security framework, however, was divorced from the local political dynamics underlying the emergence of al-Qaeda's numerous affiliate groups. This misunderstanding of the nature of the al-Qaeda network and the relationship between al-Qaeda core and its affili-ates has resulted in a failure to understand fully how U.S. counterterror-ism policy has impacted the local conflict environments that shaped the actions of targeted terrorist groups. This chapter discusses the affili-ates' distinct and often contradictory motivations, rooted as they are in their local political and social contexts. This analysis is not intended to be a comprehensive account of al-Qaeda's history, leadership, or ideol-ogy, all topics already covered by other scholars with great thoroughness and expertise using a variety of methods and theoretical approaches.[6] Instead, it unpacks the troubled relationship between al-Qaeda core and its affiliate groups, a context that is necessary to understanding the dis-connect between the affiliates' domestic-oriented campaigns of violence and al-Qaeda core's guidance. In doing so, this chapter lays a key foun-dation for understanding the impact of U.S.-backed counterterrorism operations on affiliate groups' campaigns of violence.

## AL-QAEDA: "AMERICA'S GREATEST ENEMY"

There is perhaps no name more associated with terrorism today than al-Qaeda. In pursuing its war against the United States, al-Qaeda estab-lished itself in the American collective consciousness as one of the country's preeminent threats—"America's greatest enemy." In the 1990s, however, only a few members of the U.S. intelligence community closely tracked al-Qaeda's activities or considered it an imminent threat. The group, whose name means "the base" in Arabic, originally emerged in the wake of the Soviet Union's 1979 invasion of Afghanistan to back the country's communist regime and the formation of the anti-Soviet insurgency known as the mujahedeen.[7] In order to invigorate the Afghan fighters and help unify the many competing factions and tribes within its ranks, the various groups operating under the umbrella of the mujahedeen adopted a religious frame by taking up a call to jihad to protect a Muslim state from the atheist forces of the Soviet Union; this was a strategy with historic precedent dating back to the late nineteenth-century Afghan amir Abdur Rahman Khan.[8]

The mujahedeen's religious posturing was encouraged by their international backers—the CIA, Saudi intelligence, and, in particular, Pakistan's Inter-Services Intelligence (ISI) with the support of the Pakistani military dictator General Muhammad Zia-ul-Haq, a devoted follower of the Deobandi movement Jamaat-e-Islami. Zia only allowed those exiled Afghan political parties and militant groups who were committed to a religious-based struggle in Afghanistan to operate within Pakistan, a key safe haven and launching pad for their anti-Soviet activities. He also ensured that international funds were funneled into jihadist groups alone, especially to the seven leading religious groups based in the northwestern Pakistani city of Peshawar, known as the Peshawar Seven. He barred ethnic-based groups, given the long-standing suspicions of Afghan nationalists laying claim to the Pashtun areas of northwestern Pakistan in a united "Pashtunistan."[9] Such policies swelled religious-oriented groups' ranks and further encouraged militant groups active in Afghanistan to adopt jihad as a framework for their operations in order to gain external support.

This religious-based messaging not only resonated among numerous Afghans but among Muslims from many different parts of the world who found common cause in the fight against the Soviet forces or who used it as an outlet for their anger against repressive regimes in their home countries, such as the Soviet-backed Communist regime in South Yemen.[10] Among these foreign fighters, Osama bin Laden has become the most well-known individual who heeded this call. He was one of the fifty-six children of Mohammed bin Laden, an ethnic Yemeni construction baron in Saudi Arabia whose family originated from Yemen's

Hadhramaut region. During the 1980s, bin Laden used his family fortune to help establish the organization Maktab al-Khidamat (MAK) in Peshawar, where it would recruit, house, and train foreign recruits to the mujahedeen, especially fellow Arabs. He established twelve training camps in which as many as five thousand militants reportedly trained. In this role, he was able to connect with fighters from across the Muslim world, expanding his global network.[11]

However, MAK was just one organization of many through which recruits could join the fight against the Soviets, and it ultimately played a relatively minor role in the war. Besides the compulsions of hospitality according to local custom, the mujahedeen largely welcomed Arab fighters, who became known as Afghan Arabs and set up their own training camps in eastern Afghanistan, to gain access to their seemingly endless oil wealth and under the belief that the presence of fighters from Islam's heartland granted them some measure of religious legitimacy.[12] U.S. diplomats in Pakistan at the time, however, were aware of the contempt that many Afghans held for the Arabs operating in their midst, describing them as "high-grade tourists who were a lot more trouble than they were worth" and "completely useless" given their inexperience in combat.[13] Afghans reportedly kept many of them away from any real fighting, treating them with "kid-gloves."[14] This divide was deepened by Arab fighters' cultural insensitivity, condescension in the face of what they perceived as Afghans' limited understanding of Islam, and brutality toward local communities.[15] The term "Afghan Arab," according to a former Arab member of the mujahedeen, was originally intended as an insult.[16] Nonetheless, bin Laden and his fighters did win some renown, especially within the Arab world, through their victory over the Soviets in the Battle of Jaji in 1987, despite the engagement lacking broader strategic value.[17]

With the withdrawal of Soviet forces from Afghanistan in the late 1980s, bin Laden and other members of MAK who had volunteered in Afghanistan transformed the group into al-Qaeda, reportedly named after one of the guesthouses bin Laden had established to support the mujahedeen. They sought to use their existing recruiting network and assets to assist Muslims suffering in other regions around the world, and eventually joined with Egyptian Islamic Jihad, whose leader, Ayman al-Zawahiri, became al-Qaeda's second-in-command in 1998. In this effort, al-Qaeda's leadership, including bin Laden, was influenced by the writings of the Egyptian Sayyid Qutb of the Muslim Brotherhood. Writing in the 1950s and 1960s, Qutb argued the decline of Muslim society was caused by the decadence and corruption of secular governments adopting Western culture and backed by the United States.[18] For bin Laden, this was of particular relevance due to strong U.S. support for the government of his home country of Saudi Arabia and the deployment of American troops to the Saudi kingdom during the Gulf War. In 1994, bin Laden's openly critical position led the Saudi government to strip him of his citizenship and force the bin Laden family to cut him off financially. At this time, bin Laden and his followers took refuge in Sudan, which had an extremely open immigration policy for fellow Muslims under General Omar Hassan al-Bashir's Arab-dominated government. As a result of this policy, Sudan quickly became a haven for a number of extremist Islamic groups.

While operating from Sudan, bin Laden and al-Qaeda increasingly attracted the notice of the U.S. intelligence community. In 1996, the CIA established Alec Station, whose small staff of analysts, originally counting twelve, was specifically tasked with monitoring bin Laden's activities.[19] With al-Qaeda becoming more of a concern, the U.S. and Saudi governments were pressuring Sudanese officials to expel him. The U.S. government, according to the American ambassador to Sudan at the time, pushed for his expulsion rather than taking the al-Qaeda leader into custody as it did not yet have an indictment against him.[20] When the Sudanese government finally expelled bin Laden in May 1996, he and around fifty of his men relocated to Afghanistan, where the Taliban would shortly take Kabul amid the devastating civil war that erupted following the Soviet exit and the eventual collapse of the Soviet-backed Afghan government four years earlier. Bin Laden's son Omar reported that his father became "hugely embittered" and blamed the Americans for his expulsion.[21]

Three months after arriving in Afghanistan and much to the chagrin of his Taliban hosts, bin Laden made his first public statement declaring war against the United States in a text titled "Declaration of War Against the Americans Occupying the Land of Two Holy Places [i.e., in Saudi Arabia]." This declaration was based on three core grievances: (1) the stationing of U.S. troops in Saudi Arabia; (2) the negative impact of U.S. sanctions against Iraq; and (3) U.S. support for Israel.[22] Bin Laden in particular saw the stationing of hundreds of thousands of U.S. troops in the Middle East and the Horn of Africa over the previous decade as a new attempt at colonizing the Muslim world. In response, al-Qaeda operatives began to launch increasingly brazen attacks against U.S. targets within the region—such as the 1998 U.S. embassy bombings in Kenya and Tanzania and the 2000 USS *Cole* attack in Yemen—and attracted more international attention as a result. By 2001, the U.S. intelligence community reported to the White House that bin Laden hoped to retaliate with attacks in Washington, DC, following the 1998 U.S. missile strikes against al-Qaeda bases in Afghanistan, with al-Qaeda cells attempting to recruit Muslim youth from the United States.[23] As al-Qaeda's activities increased in the late 1990s, the State Department dispatched a group of officials to Kandahar and Kabul to reiterate to the Taliban the importance of giving up the al-Qaeda leader.[24] In meetings with various Taliban leaders, the visiting U.S. officials implied that harboring bin Laden was an obstruction to any constructive engagement with the United States. At the time, the State Department's goal was to "induce the Taliban to expel Bin Laden to a jurisdiction where he will face justice."[25] While the Taliban were focused on consolidating their control within Afghanistan and had little interest in picking a fight with the United States, they nevertheless refused the visiting officials' request, citing the imperative of Pashtun hospitality.[26]

Al-Qaeda's attacks in East Africa and the Middle East were but a lead-up to the September 11, 2001, attacks against New York's World Trade Center and the Pentagon just outside of Washington, DC, which propelled the group onto the global stage. The selected targets symbolized the economic and military strength of the United States, which were used, in the view of al-Qaeda leadership, to extend American influence over Muslim societies. In describing the motivations for attacking the United States, bin Laden cited the need to take revenge against American oppression within the Islamic world, explaining, "The enemy invaded the land of our umma, violated her honor, shed her blood, and occupied her sanctuaries."[27] He interpreted the international order under American hegemony as a continuation of Western colonialism over the Muslim world, underpinning the group's operational focus on challenging the United States and its global influence. A 2003 al-Qaeda statement declared, "The Muslim countries today are colonized. . . . The ruler of a country is the one that has the authority in it. . . . The real ruler is the Crusader United States. The subserviency of [Muslim] rulers is no different from the subserviency of the amirs or governors of provinces to the king or president. The rule of the agent is the rule of the one who made him his agent."[28] In order to affect any meaningful political change within Muslim-majority states, al-Qaeda's leaders believed it was first necessary to cripple the "far enemy" of the United States and remove its support for the regional governments doing its bidding. Only after this was accomplished could al-Qaeda and its supporters direct their attention to challenging the "near enemy" of their own, Western-influenced governments within the Muslim world and eventually replace their rule by establishing a caliphate in line with their Salafist ideology.

This strategy of focusing on the "far enemy" had the further advantage of uniting Muslims of different nationalities and sects against a single enemy, with the group's leadership concerned that intra-religious fighting would alienate potential supporters. As bin Laden's successor, Ayman al-Zawahiri stated in a 2014 interview with *As-Sahab*, al-Qaeda's media branch, "We would like to advise our brothers that in order to succeed any armed opposition must mobilise public support. Experience has shown that without this support combat does not turn into victory or success. Thus they must avoid any action, and even though it may be legal they should abandon it, if it should alienate the Ummah from them." He added that al-Qaeda's approach is "to bring together the Ummah and to unify it around the message of unity, and [to] work towards the return of the rightly guided caliphate which is founded on the consultation and agreement of Muslims. . . . We could not join the Ummah together if our vision was a vision [of] absolute power over it, the usurper of its rights, committing aggression towards it, or the overpowering of it."[29]

## THE GROWING AL-QAEDA NETWORK

For the United States, al-Qaeda was a new kind of enemy—an amorphous organization lacking the characteristics of a state and seemingly able to attack anywhere without warning, especially with its expanding network of affiliate groups swearing allegiance to al-Qaeda's core leadership. Prior to 2001, various intelligence agencies viewed al-Qaeda as a formal organization based out of Afghanistan with a clear leadership structure and membership ranging from only a few dozen to just under five hundred individuals.[30] Confronting coordinated international counterterrorism efforts, al-Qaeda core adapted their tactics. By 2006, the CIA's National Intelligence Estimate argued the "global jihadist movement" had evolved into three distinct categories: al-Qaeda and its core leadership; al-Qaeda affiliates; and "unaffiliated groups, cells, and individuals that have been inspired by the jihadist message and subscribe to a loosely defined global, anti-US agenda."[31] The CIA further argued that Osama bin Laden's "hands-on operational leadership has become less necessary" as "regional network leaders have proven themselves capable of functioning with limited direction."[32] In 2009, Harun Fazul, who was responsible for planning al-Qaeda's 1998 U.S. embassy bombings in Kenya and Tanzania, asserted, "We have become an idea and we are no longer a group."[33] In an interview five years later, al-Zawahiri further stated that the group was "a mission before it is an organization or group and, in this sense, it is expanding more."[34]

Al-Qaeda's leadership increasingly shifted to relying on mobilized affiliate groups such as the various Pakistani Taliban groups and other terrorist groups operating in South and Southeast Asia, the Middle East, and North and West Africa—many of whom had members with links to bin Laden and other al-Qaeda leaders from their time in Afghanistan—as well as inspiring unaffiliated but radicalized individuals or cells, especially within Western countries, over the Internet to commit terrorist attacks independently, even if they had "little or no direct physical contact" or specific "direction" from al-Qaeda core.[35] This was part of the group's franchising strategy and its attempt to spark a global jihad, or, as David Kilcullen has argued, a "globalized Islamist insurgency" against the prevailing world order defined by U.S. hegemony.[36] Kilcullen identified a wide range of theaters into which al-Qaeda wished to expand its network: the Americas, western Europe, Australasia, the Maghreb, the so-called Greater Middle East (encompassing countries like Egypt and Turkey), East Africa, the Caucasus and European Russia, South and Central Asia, and Southeast Asia.[37] In his argument, al-Qaeda core linked different groups and individuals using the tools of globalization—global communications, financial tools, and the Internet—to coordinate their efforts and advance a shared ideology. As a unifying organization, al-Qaeda core relied on a fundamentalist interpretation of Islamic theology, cultural links in Islam and the Arabic language, personal history through participation in the Afghan mujahedeen, family relationships (many al-Qaeda operatives married into local populations), financial connections, operational and planning links, and propaganda.

Over time, al-Qaeda core relied on increasingly sophisticated yet undirected broadcasts and web postings to inspire attacks as well as suggest types of targets and provide general motivation for recruitment efforts.[38] In May 2008, the United Nations Security Council's 1267 Committee, the UN's vehicle for monitoring and implementing global sanctions against al-Qaeda, reported, "The inclusiveness of the Al-Qaida message, as disseminated through the internet, allows a wide range of potential supporters to see in it a reflection of their own personal grievances."[39] Leading al-Qaeda ideologues, foremost among them the Yemeni American cleric Anwar al-Awlaki, who joined AQAP in 2009 and was killed in a 2011 U.S. drone strike, spread the group's anti-American message and sought to inspire individual adherents to its cause through recorded lectures and even direct messages to individuals, such as the November 2009 Fort Hood shooter Nidal Hassan in Texas. According to scholar of extremism Alexander Meleagrou-Hitchens, al-Awlaki in particular helped to "develop and codify jihadist lone-actor terrorism" by conveying "a stark sense of Muslim victimhood ... among Western, English-speaking Muslims." In his stirring sermons and messages, al-Awlaki portrayed a "war on Islam" that was "more relevant to their lives, framing disparate events involving Muslims as part of a wider conspiracy. No longer would this Western, secular 'plot' to destroy Islam and oppress Muslims be presented only in terms of foreign wars and occupations in distant lands. It was, according to Awlaki, taking place right under their noses."[40]

Debates quickly emerged among scholars as to the implications of al-Qaeda's strategic shift and what it meant for the strength of the organization. Some argued that this franchising strategy was a demonstration of the group's continued strength and relevance, giving it "more members, greater geographic reach, and a level of ideological sophistication and influence it lacked ten years ago"; others pointed to a change in the nature of the threat itself.[41] Journalist Peter Bergen, who made his name by conducting the first television interview with bin Laden in 1997, began speaking of "Al-Qaeda 2.0" to describe the expanding terrorist network. In his 2011 book *The Longest War: The Enduring Conflict Between America and al-Qaeda*, Bergen quotes from Albert Camus's *The Plague* to capture the al-Qaeda threat: "The plague bacillus never dies or vanishes entirely . . . it can remain dormant for years and years in furniture and linen chests . . . it waits patiently in bedrooms, cellars, trunks, and bookshelves and . . . perhaps the day will come when, for the instruction of mankind, the plague will rouse its rats again and send them forth to die in a well-contented city."[42]

Former CIA officer Marc Sageman classified the shifting and decentralized al-Qaeda threat as a "leaderless jihad," especially in its ability to inspire attacks within the West. Pushing against the idea of an organized terrorist network, Sageman, a trained psychiatrist, focused on assessments of individual motivations. He argued that

The present threat has evolved from a structured group of al Qaeda masterminds, controlling vast resources and issuing commands, to a multitude of informal local groups trying to emulate their predecessors by conceiving and executing operations from the bottom up. These "homegrown" wannabes form a scattered global network, a leaderless jihad. Although physically unconnected, these terrorist hopefuls form a virtual yet violent social movement as they drift to Internet chat rooms that connect them and provide them with inspiration and guidance.[43]

In a written exchange with Sageman, one covered even by the *New York Times*, Georgetown professor and terrorism expert Bruce Hoffman rejected this assessment.[44] He dismissively summed up Sageman's description of a "leaderless jihad" as simply "bunches of guys" and criticized his argument as too focused on individual motivations to the neglect of organizational dynamics. In an article in *Foreign Affairs*, Hoffman went on to call Sageman's analysis a "fundamental misreading of the Al Qaeda threat" and stated that his "historical ignorance is surpassed only by his cursory treatment of social-networking theory." Hoffman argued that al-Qaeda core under the leadership of bin Laden is a "remarkably agile and flexible organization" and still very much the main threat to the United States. "Only by destroying the organization's leadership and disrupting the continued resonance of its radical message," he emphasized, "can the United States and its allies defeat al Qaeda."[45]

A handful of scholars, by contrast, argued that al-Qaeda core's franchising strategy, which the group adopted only gradually after 2001, was a sign of its growing weakness, especially as its affiliates pursued local agendas independent of and often contradictory to al-Qaeda core's transnational goals.[46] Political scientist Barak Mendelsohn identified three factors that limit the effectiveness of transnational terrorist organizations in achieving any of their internationally focused goals: (1) the strength of local nationalism and tribalism in defining the motivations and conflict agendas of affiliates and potential recruits; (2) overly ambitious goals without realistic strategic plans to back them up; and (3) schisms within the transnational movement over divergences in preferences and strategies, particularly between foreign and local fighters.[47] Jacob Shapiro further pointed out that terrorist groups are bound by their operational environments. The actions terrorist leaders take to manage their organizations and control their followers' violence, he argued, inherently create risks that can undermine the group's effectiveness. He particularly highlighted the divide between leaders and the agents they delegated to commit attacks. Shapiro writes, "Operatives' views of how to use violence almost always deviate somewhat from those of their leaders. When the preferences of leaders and agents are not completely aligned, the covert nature of terrorist groups necessarily implies that agents can take advantage of the situation to act as they prefer, rather than as the principals would like."[48]

Though al-Qaeda increasingly shifted to a franchising strategy and spread their anti-American propaganda ever wider to lone actors in Western countries, it was the mobilized affiliate groups embracing the al-Qaeda brand that accounted for the lion's share of the movement's attacks and drove the perception of al-Qaeda's continued activities and capacity.[49] Yet, the affiliates often acted without operational control or influence from al-Qaeda core. As clearly demonstrated in al-Qaeda's internal communications, there was a growing frustration within the group's core leadership concerning affiliates' locally oriented attacks against the "near enemy." The 1267 Committee recognized that al-Qaeda core was unsuccessful in asserting its influence over affiliates and "unable to focus their supporters on key operational issues or guide them towards specific action."[50] With the expanding al-Qaeda network, the group "increasingly represented an idea of violent opposition to a whole range of local and global circumstances rather than a coherent group with fixed goals."[51] Local dynamics frequently overshadowed any meaningful influence or direction from the core leadership as affiliates saw "no need to see their actions as part of a wider political programme."[52] The al-Qaeda brand had become a catch-all for affiliate groups with little operational control from the core leadership and who pursued terrorist attacks according to autonomous agendas shaped by their local political and social contexts, agendas that were often at odds with al-Qaeda's focus on the United States.

Using data from the Global Terrorism Database, table 2.1 lists fifteen al-Qaeda affiliate groups and provides a basic breakdown of all terrorist attacks attributed to them from their founding to 2017.[53] It divides terrorist attacks first by location—whether within the group's country of origin or abroad—and then by target type—whether against domestic, regional, or U.S. targets. While international attacks have drawn global attention, it is evident from table 2.1 that domestic targets bear the brunt of al-Qaeda affiliates' attacks, accounting for 85.1 percent of these groups' total attacks. Attacks or attempted attacks within the United States or Europe or against U.S. targets abroad account for only 0.5 percent of affiliates' total attacks. Most of the attacks directed against U.S. targets (95.8 percent) occurred within the groups' home state or region of origin. The Taliban had the highest number of attacks targeting the United States. However, the vast majority of these were against U.S. military forces and other U.S. targets within Afghanistan and, therefore, related to the 2001 military invasion. Of the affiliates' other international terrorist attacks, 96.4 percent were directed against regional targets, both within the groups' state of origin or within neighboring states. The large number of international terrorist attacks by al-Shabaab, for instance, were directed against Kenyan, Ethiopian, and Ugandan targets in response to these states' military operations in Somalia. Al-Shabaab also recruited heavily from marginalized Somali populations on the Kenyan and Ethiopian peripheries. Similarly, many of the international terrorist attacks perpetrated by al-Qaeda in the Islamic Maghreb (AQIM) were connected to the anti-AQIM operations by French and African Union

TABLE 2.1 Terrorist Attacks by al-Qaeda Affiliates (up to 2017)

| Group Name (Country of Origin) | Year Founded | Domestic Targets | International Targets | U.S. Targets | Regional Targets | Domestic Attacks U.S. Regional Targets | International Attacks Targets in U.S./Europe |
|---|---|---|---|---|---|---|---|
| Taliban (Afghanistan) | 1994 | 6,799 | 624 | 46 | 55 | 2 | 0 |
| Tehreek-e-Taliban Pakistan | 2007 | 1,322 | 66 | 2 | 0 | 0 | 1 |
| Haqqani network (Afghanistan) | 1980 | 58 | 26 | 5 | 2 | 0 | 0 |
| Al-Qaeda in Iraq/Islamic State (Iraq; up to 2014) | 2004 | 1,088 | 29 | 9 | 36 | 2 | 1 |
| Al Nusrah Front (Syria) | 2012 | 228 | 23 | 4 | 27 | 0 | 0 |

| Organization | | | | | | | |
|---|---|---|---|---|---|---|---|
| Al-Qaeda in the Arabian Peninsula (Yemen) | 2009 | 974 | 45 | 5 | 11 | 3 | 2 |
| Al-Shabaab (Somalia) | 2006 | 2,196 | 697 | 2 | 419 | 2 | 0 |
| Ansar Dine (Mali) | 2012 | 33 | 21 | 0 | 0 | 0 | 0 |
| Al-Qaeda in the Islamic Maghreb (Algeria) | 2007 | 174 | 6 | 0 | 82 | 2 | 0 |
| Boko Haram (Nigeria) | 2002 | 2,065 | 25 | 0 | 82 | 0 | 0 |
| Ansar al-Sharia (Libya) | 2011 | 57 | 8 | 2 | 0 | 0 | 0 |
| Caucasus Emirate (Russia) | 2007 | 44 | 0 | 0 | 0 | 0 | 0 |
| Imam Shamil Battalion (Russia) | 2017 | 2 | 0 | 0 | 0 | 0 | 0 |
| Jemaah Islamiyah (Indonesia) | 1993 | 50 | 7 | 2 | 19 | 0 | 0 |
| Abu Sayyaf (Philippines) | 1991 | 464 | 46 | 5 | 17 | 0 | 0 |

*Source:* National Consortium for the Study of Terrorism and Responses to Terrorism, Global Terrorism Database [data file], 2018, http://www.start.umd.edu/gtd.

military forces after the group moved into northern Mali. Observing the local nature of affiliates' operations, the 1267 Committee reported in 2014 that these groups posed the greatest threat "towards people either under their control, as with ISIL [Islamic State of Iraq and the Levant] and Boko Haram, or close to their operating areas. The vast majority of killings, atrocities and kidnappings are committed in Member States where Al-Qaida-associated groups are active."[54]

In discussing the importance of the local context for understanding al-Qaeda's affiliate groups, a senior Yemeni diplomat explained that "al-Qaeda is not the same everywhere. They operate according to the environment." In particular, he saw AQAP as a local group focused on acquisition of territory, raising revenue, dealing with issues of governance, and contesting the sovereignty of the Yemeni government. He described the group as operating like a Yemeni tribe, making business deals and tribal alliances, and driven by various political and economic grievances in southern Yemen.[55] A Nigeria-based journalist similarly noted that Boko Haram's "grievances were always deeply rooted in the local politics of [the group's] native Borno State," and that it was "hardly the stuff of global jihad."[56] In 2012, Boko Haram leader Abubakar Shekau released a video stressing that the group's main motivation was revenge for the brutality of Nigerian counterterrorism operations. He demanded that the government withdraw the military from the country's northeastern periphery, repair destroyed mosques, and provide compensation to local families affected by the fighting.

In discussing the outbreak of violence in the Pakistan-Afghanistan border region, Akbar Ahmed, who served as political agent in FATA's South Waziristan and Orakzai Agencies, pushed back against the idea of al-Qaeda core's international goals serving as the primary motivation of the various Taliban groups operating within the country's northwestern periphery. "Nobody is thinking about that in Waziristan," Ahmed explained. "They are thinking, 'You attacked our mosque so we will take revenge.' It's purely local."[57] General Abdullah Dogar similarly argued that the TTP emerged because of "internal problems" within FATA rather than being primarily motivated by a transnational jihad. The group, he explained, only moved out of Waziristan when the military moved into the region. As the TTP was unable to fight the Pakistani army "head-on," they targeted Pakistan's "soft spots," especially soldiers' homes, in revenge for their own homes being targeted in counterterrorism operations.[58] A survey conducted between 2016 and 2018 in North Waziristan found "that the initial and current major causes of conflict are internal factors," with respondents pointing to the "bad governance system" within FATA, local injustices committed by both nonstate groups and government institutions, the prevalence of "jihadi culture" among the local population, and cultural obligations under the tribal code of honor. On the other hand, respondents acknowledged that various international factors did influence patterns of local violence, "but mainly through exacerbating internal factors."[59]

## THE TENSIONS BETWEEN AL-QAEDA CORE AND ITS AFFILIATES

While affiliates focused their efforts on domestic targets, al-Qaeda core remained committed to its internationally oriented mission and maintained the view that any premature action against the "near enemy" was a waste of vital resources and a distraction from its primary goal of toppling the "far enemy"—the United States and American hegemony within the Muslim world. Only after exhausting "the greatest enemy," bin Laden advised, can the al-Qaeda network "start exhausting the local enemy. . . . It is in our interest to stick to, and not skip, the steps and stages."[60] Bin Laden elaborated on this point in a 2010 letter that was subsequently recovered from the Abbottabad compound in northern Pakistan where he had been in hiding until he was killed in a May 2011 U.S. Navy SEAL raid:

> The plague that exists in the nations of Muslims has two causes: The first is the presence of American hegemony and the second is the presence of rulers that have abandoned Islamic law and who identify with the hegemony, serving its interests in exchange for securing their own interests. The only way for us to establish the religion and alleviate the plague which has befallen Muslims is to remove this hegemony which has beset upon the nations and worshippers and which transforms them, such that no regime that rules on the basis of Islamic law remains.

The way to remove this hegemony is to continue our direct attrition against the American enemy until it is broken and is too weak to interfere in the matters of the Islamic world. . . . The focus must be on actions that contribute to the intent of bleeding the American enemy. As for actions that do not contribute to the intent of bleeding the great enemy, many of them dilute our efforts and take from our energy.[61]

A letter from al-Qaeda core to its affiliates in Yemen further described this strategy through the metaphor of a tree:

The Ummah's enemies today are like a wicked tree. The trunk of this tree is the US. The diameter of this trunk is 50 centimeters. The branches are many and vary in size. . . . We want to bring this tree down by sawing it while our abilities and energy are limited. Our correct way to bring it down is to focus our saw on its American trunk. . . . If sawing continued into the depth of the American trunk until it falls, the rest will fall, with Allah's permission. . . . Therefore, concentration should be given to actions that focus on depleting the American enemy. Many of the actions that do not focus on depleting the biggest enemy distract our efforts and deplete our energy.[62]

According to a Libyan who worked with them, bin Laden and other al-Qaeda leaders guided their affiliates to "forget about the 'near enemy'; the main enemy is the Americans," and to avoid confrontations with local security forces.[63]

Yet, with the rising levels of domestic terrorism, al-Qaeda core's weakened leadership was unable to exert its operational influence and became increasingly alarmed by affiliate groups ignoring its directives and escalating local conflicts that were "spreading their efforts too thin and opening up less important fronts." Al-Qaeda leaders communicated the need to distinguish between "A—Jihad for which we prepared all the requirements, identified its time and place, considering all the local, regional, and international powers. [And] B—Some operations that our brothers conducted as an act of self-defense and in response to some operations that the government conducted against them." In making this distinction, they were concerned "to avoid finding ourselves drawn into a full war for which we did not plan to on this particular day or that we haven't prepared elements for its success."[64]

In a letter to AQAP leader Nasir al-Wuhayshi, for example, al-Qaeda core argued that the group needed to avoid directly targeting or fighting with the Yemeni government and its security forces, stating, "We do not see escalation as necessary at this point . . . [as] it is not in our interest to rush in bringing down the regime." They further pressed,

> Regarding the idea that calls for removing the apostate government and leaving the country in a state of chaos, our call cannot be spread in chaos. . . . A country without a ruler to make the security rules between people will allow people's viciousness to show on a large scale, and the people's main goal would be protecting their blood and honor. . . . We should be careful not to remove one evil only to allow a bigger evil to replace it.[65]

As their Yemeni affiliate increasingly launched deadlier and deadlier retaliatory attacks against Yemen's security forces, al-Qaeda leadership explicitly ordered it "not [to] target military and police officers in their centers unless you receive an order from us. Our targets are Americans, who kill our families in Gaza and other Islamic countries."[66] Instead, they argued that AQAP needed to minimize its domestic operations and work to establish a truce with the Yemeni government.[67] In reference to former Yemeni president Ali Abdullah Saleh, bin Laden justified his position by writing,

> We should distinguish between they who have an enmity against us because of a deep belief, and the others who have enmity that is based on finance and politics. It is in our interest to reduce our enmity to the latter to the lightest degree possible. Ali Abdallah Salih is not an obeying agent and does not do what he does out of conviction and reaction, but most of his actions are "by force not by choice". . . . In addition, his interest dictates that he prolong his war against al-Qa'ida without extracting it because "it is a gold mine" and an important source of income to him.[68]

Al-Qaeda core stressed to AQAP that it should instead focus on operations against the United States, a position it had previously stressed to the affiliate group. "We need to extend and develop our operations in America and not keep it limited to blowing up airplanes," al-Qaeda leaders urged. "Al-Qaida concentrates on its external big enemy before its internal enemy."[69] Bin Laden further reasoned, "Escalation in Yemen would siphon off a large portion of the energy of the Mujahidin without doing the same to the head of the infidels (America) directly."[70] Similarly, in Africa's Maghreb region, al-Qaeda core stressed to its affiliates that they should avoid antagonizing and fighting with local security forces and instead sign truces with local governments in order to focus their efforts on the "far enemy." Bin Laden stated, "The goal of the noble mujahideen in the mountains and deserts of the Islamic Maghreb is not to topple the apostate regime."[71]

Al-Qaeda core similarly had difficulties in directing the operations of its affiliate al-Qaeda in Iraq (AQI) under the leadership of Jordanian Abu Masab al-Zarqawi. The group initially swore allegiance to al-Qaeda in 2004 and quickly became a major concern for U.S. military leadership as it sought to destabilize Iraq amid U.S. military operations. Zarqawi, who had fought with bin Laden in Afghanistan, saw the advantages of joining with al-Qaeda but also was initially reluctant to become the group's affiliate out of a concern that he would lose operational autonomy and the ability to remain focused on his regionally defined goals.[72] Zarqawi, along with his influential deputy Abi Ali al-Anbari, viewed his group's fight through the prism of sectarian politics and rivalries within Iraq and the broader Middle East.[73] After pledging allegiance to al-Qaeda core, AQI continued to indiscriminately target both Shia and Sunni communities in the hopes of inciting a sectarian war in support of its political agenda, especially to demonstrate the weakness of the U.S.-backed and Shia-dominated Iraqi government. Many of these attacks involved increasingly high levels of brutality, including torture, mutilation, rape, beheadings, and the killing of children. In this way, AQI was hoping to give the Sunni population little choice but to back them.[74]

Al-Qaeda core expressed its frustration with this focus on the "near enemy" as well as the brutality toward fellow Muslims whom AQI had branded as apostates in line with the Iraqi affiliate's *takfiri* ideology.[75] Al-Qaeda leadership saw such intra-religious conflict as detrimental to its primary goal of uniting Muslims against the United States and American hegemony. In letters intercepted by U.S. forces in July 2005, al-Zawahiri urged Zarqawi to refrain from targeting Shia Muslims and executing hostages on television, "which won't be acceptable to the Muslim populace." The al-Qaeda leader wrote, "Many of your Muslim admirers amongst the common folk are wondering about your attacks on the Shia. . . . Among the things which the feelings of the Muslim population who love and support you will never find palatable are the scenes of slaughtering the hostages."[76] Atiyah Abd al-Rahman, al-Qaeda core's primary liaison with its affiliates in Iraq, also wrote to Zarqawi, emphasizing that "among the most crucial things involved is exercising all caution against attempting to kill any religious scholar or tribal leader who is obeyed, and of good repute in Iraq from among the Sunnis, no matter what. . . . We warn against all acts that alienate, from killing to any sort of other treatment." He further pushed him to "abstain from making any decision on a comprehensive issue," such as "announcing a war against the Shi'ite turncoats and killing them," until first consulting with al-Qaeda core leadership. "Do not act alone," Atiyah urged, "and do not be overzealous."[77]

Bin Laden further ordered AQI fighters in Iraq "to stay away from anyone who is fighting the crusaders during this phase, regardless of whether they are atheists, secular Ba'thists, or infidels." He specifically ordered Zarqawi's group to refrain from targeting fellow Muslims, stating that Zarqawi "had clear instructions to focus his fighting against the invader occupiers, starting with the Americans."[78] On the other hand, according to U.S. interrogations of captured al-Qaeda members, affiliate groups were perturbed by bin Laden commandeering their operatives to engage in operations against the "far enemy," which distracted them from their local goals.[79] With AQI continuing to act contrary to such directives, al-Qaeda core wished to "sever its ties" with its Iraqi affiliate.[80] They would eventually disassociate with the group after it moved into Syria against the orders of al-Qaeda core and adopted the mantle of the Islamic State in Iraq and Syria. An al-Qaeda spokesperson stated in 2014 that the Islamic State "is not a branch of the al-Qaeda group . . . does not have an organizational relationship with it and [al-Qaeda] is not the group responsible for their actions."[81]

Broader than AQI's sectarian brutality, al-Qaeda core remained concerned with many affiliates' continued attacks against fellow Muslims, which comprised the overwhelming bulk of their victims. According to documents found at the Abbottabad compound, bin Laden was increasingly burdened by what he saw as "the incompetence of the 'affili-ates,' including their lack of political acumen to win public support, their media campaigns and their poorly planned operations which resulted in the unnecessary deaths of thousands of Muslims."[82] The core leadership argued that the affiliates' intra-religious violence would alienate local bases of support and undermine al-Qaeda's long-term goal of politically uniting Muslims against the United States. Al-Qaeda core even warned that affiliates' efforts to generate local sources of revenue was "very dangerous and contradictory to the mission" as it could result in the profit-seeking groups to engage in corrupt behavior and alienate local communities. Affiliate groups "should be concerned only with security and justice," a 2010 letter from al-Qaeda core explained. They "should not compete for trade because this can destroy the Islamic state and movement and create a gap between the state and the people."[83] Despite this warning, affiliates increasingly engaged in various criminal activi-ties to raise funds, such as drug trafficking, kidnapping, and extortion.[84] David Rohde, a journalist held captive by the Haqqani network for seven months in Pakistan's FATA, observed, "During my time in captivity, I grew to see the Haqqanis as a criminal gang masquerading as a pious religious movement. They described themselves as the true followers of Islam but displayed an astounding capacity for dishonesty and greed."[85]

In orders to its affiliates to refrain from violence against fellow Mus-lims, al-Qaeda core cited restrictions within Islamic law against the killing of innocent Muslims and chastised the affiliates for their poor understand-ing of sharia and religious doctrine. An undated letter recovered from the Abbottabad compound stated,

We remind our brethren, the Mujahidin, everywhere, May God bless them all, to disseminate and spread the word about the significance of forbidding the shedding of Muslim blood. We must be cautious not to shed it and to protect and defend it from being shed unjustly. It is a must to stop any reason that might lead to the spilling of Muslim blood, the plundering of their property, or the ravaging of their honor. . . . I call them to issue orders to all battalions and companies fighting in the field to prevent explosions and using methods that kill generally and indis-criminately in Muslim mosques or similar, general gathering places, such as markets, streets, playgrounds, or whatever the target it may be, so as to control the situation, as a precaution, and to avoid mistakes and [collateral] damage.[86]

In 2010, bin Laden further wrote, "You may have recently heard on the news about the targeting of worshippers in mosques and markets, especially in Pakistan and Afghanistan. According to the news, the most recent attacks had been attributed to some mujahidin groups in those two countries. Per Islamic Law, it is unlawful to target mosques or public places. Hence, one cannot justify the killing of many innocent people in mosques and public places for the sake of killing one enemy."[87]

In December 2010, al-Qaeda core sent a letter to TTP leader Hakimullah Mehsud stressing this message and stating that the group's attacks against Muslims was a "negative deviation from the set path of the Jihadists Movement in Pakistan" and clear deviations from al-Qaeda core's operational guidance. The letter further claimed that the TTP's religious justification was "unacceptable" and "contains political and Shari'a mistakes." Al-Qaeda core leadership in particular denounced the fact that the TTP was "killing more people, taking them as shields without basing their action on the Shari'a, killing the normal Muslims as a result of martyrdom operations that takes place in the marketplaces, mosques, roads, assembly places, and calling the Muslims apostates."[88] An August 2010 letter from al-Qaeda core concerning al-Shabaab included a similar message: "Please talk to the Somali brothers about reducing the harm to Muslims at Bakarah Market as [a] result of attacking the headquarters of the African forces."[89] The previous year, al-Qaeda core chastised the leadership of al-Shabaab and AQIM for targeting Muslims and encouraged them to conduct operations against Western targets "in non-Islamic African countries to avoid Muslim casualties," though recognizing the need to "be careful not to injure non-targeted Crusaders and idolaters."[90]

This divide between al-Qaeda core and its affiliates had been a lingering issue from the earliest years of the war on terror. A member of al-Qaeda's longtime Indonesian affiliate Jemaah Islamiyah (JI) stated as early as 2002 that its relationship with al-Qaeda core was "that of an NGO with a funding agency. The NGO exists as a completely independent organization, but submits proposals to the donor and gets a grant when the proposal is accepted. The donor only funds projects that are in line with its own programs. In this case, al-Qaeda may help fund specific JI programs but it neither directs nor controls it."[91] Another JI member stated, "We can ask [al-Qaeda] for an opinion, but they have no authority over us. We are free. We have our own funds, our own men. We are independent, like Australia and the U.S. But when it comes to an operation, we can join together."[92]

Even before the 9/11 attacks and the resulting increase in international counterterrorism efforts, the CIA observed in February 2001 that bin Laden was increasingly allowing al-Qaeda's various cells to operate and plan attacks "more independently of the central leadership" in order to avoid implicating the group or its Taliban hosts, while also seeking to gain support outside the group. The CIA attributed a "spike" in the al-Qaeda network's activities over the previous two years to this growing compartmentalization.[93] After 2001, this disconnect was heightened with the increased seclusion of al-Qaeda leadership, especially bin Laden, to avoid detection. Beginning in 2005, when bin Laden reportedly moved into the Abbottabad compound in northern Pakistan, he lived without Internet or phone access, wary of using any kind of technology that could allow signals intelligence to track his location. He relied on an intricate system of couriers to send messages and, as a result, had limited communications and limited access to funds to share with affiliates and his supporters.[94] Other al-Qaeda leaders found refuge in Pakistan's isolated and mountainous FATA. Robert Dannenberg, the former head of CIA counterterrorism operations, stated that al-Qaeda members "retreated to the tribal areas because they felt safer there and they were willing to sacrifice the ability to communicate efficiently with their networks for their own safety."[95] In a 2012 letter to a breakaway faction of AQIM that sought closer ties to al-Qaeda leadership, AQIM's Shura Council complained of the lack of communication and support from al-Qaeda core:

Our dear brothers, we find it a strange contradiction in your message, the idea of separating from the leadership of the Islamic Maghreb and instead connecting with the leadership in Khorasan [Afghanistan and Pakistan]. The great obstacles between us and the central leadership are not unknown to you. They are far greater than any obstacles imaginable with the closer, local leadership that borders you. For example, since we vowed our allegiance up until this very day, we have only gotten a few messages from our emirs in Khorasan, the two sheikhs, bin Laden (God rest his soul) and Ayman (God preserve him). From time to time we also received messages from the two sheikhs Attiyat Ullah and Abu Yahia al-Libi (God rest their souls). . . . We only bring this up so that our brothers understand that the idea of adhering to the central leadership rather than the local leadership is not realistic.[96]

By December 2012, the 1267 Committee recognized that the al-Qaeda group responsible for the 9/11 attacks had "disappeared" as the fractured movement underwent geographic and generational change and now had a "greater focus on local issues and less capability and motivation to mount attacks on a global scale."[97] In May 2013, a senior official in the Obama administration similarly stated that the "core of al Qaeda in Afghanistan and Pakistan" had been "greatly damaged" and was "on a path to defeat." Yet, the official warned, the threat had changed "significantly" with new threats emerging from al-Qaeda affiliates.[98] Nevertheless, affiliates still saw an advantage in pledging allegiance to al-Qaeda core given issues of perception and legitimacy. With international attention fixed on al-Qaeda, its brand could lead to more global media exposure, greater perceived effectiveness or legitimacy, and, therefore, a strengthening of both internal and external support, increasing its chances of survival.[99] A former member of al-Shabaab explained, "Essentially, al-Shabaab wanted to remain important in the global jihad arena, and Al-Qaeda gave them the brand approval, despite Al-Shabaab having no real ties to the AQ core [as of 2015] aside from general guidance and advice."[100]

Some U.S. policy makers did voice support for the conclusion that the al-Qaeda organization had been largely decimated by counterterrorism efforts, undermining its capacity and global reach, with continuing violence the result of locally oriented affiliates operating autonomously from al-Qaeda core.[101] In 2011, Secretary of Defense Leon Panetta publicly acknowledged that there were perhaps only ten to twenty al-Qaeda leaders remaining, adding, "we're within reach of strategically defeating al Qaeda."[102] However, the following year he stated at the Center for a New American Security in Washington, DC, that even though "al-Qaeda's leadership . . . [has] been decimated . . . the threat from al-Qaeda has not been eliminated." His diagnosis of this "cancer" focused on al-Qaeda's affiliate groups: "We have slowed a primary cancer but we know that the cancer has also metastasized to other parts of the global body." He specifically cited the "spreading al Qaeda presence" in Pakistan, Yemen, Somalia, Mali, and Nigeria.[103]

---

As the perceived threat from al-Qaeda increasingly shifted onto the shoulders of its affiliate groups, policy makers did not fully grasp the domestic focus of affiliates' operations and the resulting implications for U.S. counterterrorism efforts. Despite the overwhelming attention al-Qaeda has garnered over the past two decades, there has been a general misunderstanding of its relationship with its network of affiliates, as well as the kind of threat that these groups pose. There has been a tendency to rely too often on the broadest conception of al-Qaeda, especially to justify particular policies, to score political points with fear-inducing rhetoric, or simply because government officials fear being wrong. With the advent of the war on terror, even the smallest whiff of an al-Qaeda connection was enough to steer the many, sweeping tools of the U.S. government against countless groups around the world, often without appreciating the local political environment. Many governments further fed into this perception for a variety of strategic reasons, such as legitimizing the use of domestic military force, distracting from human rights abuses by government forces, or gaining U.S. support.[104]

For instance, senior Russian officials, including Russian president Vladimir Putin, stressed the operational and financial ties between Chechen rebels and al-Qaeda leadership, creating a "terrorist enterprise" in Chechnya partially funded by al-Qaeda.[105] China similarly began to frame unrest among its persecuted Uighur population in Xinjiang Province as al-Qaeda-linked international terrorism in order to justify highly repressive state actions within its vast western periphery.[106] Even Myanmar's military government saw the war on terror as an opportunity to "bolster relations with the United States by getting credit for cooperation on the [counterterror] front."[107] Myanmar claimed two organizations representing the Muslim Rohingya, considered one of the most persecuted minority groups in the world, were "a fifth column of dangerous Islamist extremists with links to al-Qaeda" in order to give the Myanmar military a freer hand in ongoing operations against the

Rohingya, which the U.S. government publicly declared a genocide in March 2022.[108]

Lawrence Wilkerson, the former chief of staff to Secretary of State Colin Powell, recounted one CIA briefing on al-Qaeda he attended in which the analyst "threw up this butcher board with hundreds of other groups. I mean, localized terrorists with no global capabilities to speak of and no global intent, like al-Qaeda did."[109] Wilkerson recognized that the U.S. intelligence community, after being "burned" over the 9/11 attacks, "assumed what I would call a military posture toward intelligence." He further explained that

> Military posture is to worst-case everything. It's understandable for the military. They're going to have to bleed and die over it so they're going to worse-case it. The intelligence community—mainly the CIA—is supposed to tell the president or other people they advise, "This is probably what's happening or going to happen." And this is with an 80 percent surety, 85 percent surety. Not this is the worst thing that can happen. That's the military's outlook. So what was thrown into the White House, in Vice President Cheney's office, as raw intelligence were worst-case threats from all over the world. I mean, there was somebody in almost every country in the world that looked like, smelt like, felt like al-Qaeda. And they were going to attack the United States.[110]

With this approach, the CIA began to include with the Presidential Daily Brief any intelligence picked up over the previous twenty-four hours concerning potential or suspected al-Qaeda attacks, plots, or sightings—a compendium of raw intelligence known as the Threat Matrix. Former CIA director and secretary of defense Robert Gates stated, "After 9/11, all the filters came off the information. So anybody anywhere in the world who made some comment about bombing the United States or getting a weapon of mass destruction—all those reports came straight into the leadership of the country and I think it scared the hell out of them."[111] He further observed, "We didn't know jack shit about al-Qaeda. . . . If we'd had a great database and knew exactly what al-Qaeda was all about, what their capabilities were and stuff like that, some of these measures wouldn't have been necessary. But the fact is that we'd just been attacked by a group we didn't know anything about."[112]

As a result, senior officials within the Bush administration viewed any suspected al-Qaeda operatives as imminent threats that needed to be taken out before they could strike against the United States.[113] According to Alan Eastham, the former principal deputy assistant secretary of state for South Asian affairs, "Before September 11, there was a pretty high threshold that had to be achieved before we would shoot a missile. We would hesitate before action. Now, we would take action in a second."[114] Steve Kashkett, a former senior advisor to the State Department's coordinator for counterterrorism, also observed that the designation process for identifying terrorist groups was quickly expedited following the 9/11 attacks, and that "entities that had previously been undesignated were quickly designated. The [U.S. government] concluded that it was vital to designate any entity remotely related to Al Qaeda."[115] Even bin Laden recognized the tendency for the U.S. government to overreact to the perceived threat of al-Qaeda, stating in December 2004,

> All that we have mentioned has made it easy to provoke and bait this [U.S.] administration. All we have to do is to send two Mujahideen to the furthest point East to raise a piece of cloth on which is written al-Qaeda, in order to make the [U.S.] generals race there to cause America to suffer human, economic, and political losses without achieving for it anything of note. . . . So we are continuing this policy of bleeding America to the point of bankruptcy.[116]

Yet, despite their established links with al-Qaeda core, the various affiliates represented a distinct, localized threat and largely operated in response to the dynamics of their local political, economic, and social contexts. While affiliates "position themselves strategically within a globalized discourse," it would be wrong to focus solely upon their links with al-Qaeda core without considering how their local conflict environments have directly and demonstrably impacted their motivations and behavior.[117] The focus on bin Laden and al-Qaeda eventually shifted to the group's wide range of affiliates, with U.S. officials pushing partner states to confront the terrorist threat in the "ungoverned spaces" of the periphery. However, many officials within the U.S. government did so without fully grasping the complex political situations in which they would quickly entangle themselves and the resulting impact of their actions.

# 3

## THE UNITED STATES AND ITS COUNTERTERRORISM PARTNERS

With the 9/11 attacks representing a critical juncture for the United States, counterterrorism quickly became the organizing principle of U.S. foreign policy.[1] The White House deputy chief of staff under President Bush, Joel Kaplan, remarked that the war on terror was "just omnipresent. It was the purpose of the administration, protecting the country. It infused everything we did."[2] The U.S. government's focus on counterterrorism—what former CIA director Michael Hayden described as a "CT obsession"[3]—quickly overwhelmed other priorities. Many policy areas were soon securitized and drafted into the fight against terrorism, with U.S. officials embracing an "all-consuming focus" to prevent another catastrophic attack against the United States.[4] Former national security advisor and secretary of state Condoleezza Rice wrote in her 2011 memoirs, "Every day since has been September 12. No security issue ever looked quite the same again, and every day our overwhelming preoccupation was to avoid another attack."[5] U.S. officials recalled that nobody in the administration "wanted to appear to be not putting security first," seemingly without concern for the long-term implications of such actions as there was no time "to focus on larger, strategic considerations."[6] President Obama's deputy national security advisor, Ben Rhodes, even described a sign reading "Every day is September 12" hanging in CIA headquarters, instilling this same sentiment into intelligence officers tasked with hunting down al-Qaeda and protecting the homeland.[7]

In the early days of the war on terror, with the fear of future attacks looming large in the minds of senior leaders in the White House, Bush set the tone for the United States' interactions with its future counterterrorism partners. As a forewarning of the invasions of Afghanistan and Iraq, Bush declared in his September 20, 2001, speech before a joint session of Congress, "We will pursue nations that provide aid or safe haven to terrorism. Every nation in every region now has a decision to make: Either you are with us or you are with the terrorists."[8] In preparations for the invasion of Afghanistan, General Tommy Franks, the commander of U.S. Central Command, pointed to Bush's position as setting the stage for winning the cooperation of key partners in the region. He later recounted,

> When I went into Saudi Arabia, when I went into Pakistan, when I went into you-name-it in the Middle East, and said, "Here's what I want. We can do this the easy way or we can do this the hard way," the relationships that we were operating with were all influenced by George W. Bush's comments. They believed him. So when I told the President of Tajikistan that I wanted to stage some people in there, he walked down the hall, got a map, came back, laid it on the desk in his office and showed me every old Soviet installation in Tajikistan, and said, "Whatever you want."[9]

Yet, as the war on terror progressed, the U.S. government's working definition of safe havens shifted away from state sponsorship to a primary focus on the "ungoverned spaces" of the periphery where terrorists could operate outside of government control. With the increased focus on the periphery, U.S. officials understood the difficulty of pursuing direct military action in states with which the United States was not at war. Therefore, the United States sought the cooperation of key partner states to assist with and support U.S. counterterrorism priorities, leveraging key bilateral relationships to protect U.S. national security and, when needed, applying pressure on these governments to support U.S. interests. This cooperation encompassed a wide range of activities— from policing and military actions to security reforms and intelligence sharing—under the framing of a global war with al-Qaeda and its network of supporters.

To understand the motivations and progression of the U.S. government's overarching counterterrorism policy and the role played by partner states' cooperation, this chapter reconstructs the process by which U.S. counterterrorism policy changed over the course of the war on terror. It first compares the United States' approach to counterterrorism before and after 9/11, helping to show how it shifted from primarily a law enforcement focus to a military one. It then discusses how the war on terror expanded outside of Afghanistan and Iraq, with U.S. attention increasingly focusing on the threat posed by terrorist groups operating in "ungoverned spaces" as senior U.S. officials adopted a "disaggregation" strategy, a key mechanism underlying the causal process connecting U.S. counterterrorism to the increase in domestic terrorism within partner states.

## COUNTERTERRORISM BEFORE
## THE WAR ON TERROR

The problem of terrorism is one the U.S. government had been working to address for decades prior to September 11, 2001; the Nixon administration introduced the first federal counterterrorism measures after Palestinian terrorists attempted to hijack four airplanes in September 1970.[10] Before 2001, however, the U.S. government classified terrorism primarily as a criminal act with limitations on the level of permissible force with which it could be met.[11] The opening lines of the FBI's 1999 *Terrorism in the United States* report, for example, read, "In accordance with U.S. counterterrorism policy, the FBI considers terrorists to be criminals. . . . Terrorists are arrested and convicted under existing criminal statutes. All suspected terrorists placed under arrest are provided access to legal counsel and normal judicial procedure, including Fifth Amendment guarantees."[12] Terrorism investigations by law enforcement agencies were narrower in scope and aimed at uncovering specific details about those directly responsible for attacks in order to arrest and prosecute them. Like other crimes, each attack was usually responded to "on its own," often without making broader connections to an overarching strategy.[13] Terrorism was something to be managed, not defeated, with counterterrorism measures focusing on bringing responsible individuals before a court of law.

Following a string of high-profile terrorist attacks in the early 1990s in the United States and abroad, including the 1993 World Trade Center bombing, the 1995 Tokyo subway attack, and the 1995 Oklahoma City bombing, President Bill Clinton issued the classified Presidential Decision Directive 39 for "U.S. Policy on Counterterrorism" on June 21, 1995, which defined terrorism as both "a criminal act" and a "threat to national security."[14] This document outlined the counterterrorism roles of various government agencies and expanded the capabilities of the government by enhancing protections and deterrence domestically and abroad and by strengthening the government's ability to both respond to and prevent attacks. While this directive made clear that it was not the U.S. government's policy to "make concessions to terrorist," it fundamentally maintained a law enforcement approach to counterterrorism by emphasizing that the "return [of wanted terrorists] for prosecution shall be a matter of the highest priority and shall be a continuing central issue in bilateral relations with any state that harbors or assists them."[15] Clinton also sought from Congress an expansion of the administration's legal authorization to increase its ability to deport individuals accused of terrorist activity and target terrorist funding. The following year, Congress passed the Antiterrorism and Effective Death Penalty Act granting the secretary of state the authority to designate groups as Foreign Terrorist Organizations and block their assets within U.S. financial institutions, as well as authorizing other legal tools to fight terrorism, such as increased criminal penalties, prohibition on U.S. assistance to state sponsors of terrorism, and the authority to deny entry and deport "alien terrorists."[16] In October 1997, Secretary of State Madeleine Albright placed thirty groups on the new Foreign Terrorist Organizations list.

Despite defining terrorism primarily as a crime, government officials at the time still recognized the utility of limited military force as a deterrent, while recognized the accompanying risks. The 1986 *Public Report of the Vice President's Task Force on Combatting Terrorism*, which defined terrorist attacks fundamentally as criminal offenses, argued, "Military actions may serve to deter future terrorist acts and could also encourage other countries to take a harder line. Successful employment, however, depends on timely and refined intelligence and prompt positions of forces. Counterterrorism missions are high-risk/high-gain operations which can have a severe negative impact on U.S. prestige if they fail."[17] The White House's 2000 *National Security Strategy* described terrorism as a crime at its core with military force an option of last resort. "Whenever possible," the strategy document stated, "we use law enforcement, diplomatic, and economic tools to wage the fight against terrorism. But there have been, and will be, times when those tools are not enough. As long as terrorists continue to target American citizens, we reserve the right to act in self-defense by striking at their bases and those who sponsor, assist, or actively support them, as we have done over the years in different countries."[18]

However, these discussions of military force were often based on the use of isolated, "one-off" operations, rather than an overarching war against nonstate actors.[19] This was the case for Operation Infinite Reach, launched in response to the 1998 U.S. embassy bombings in Kenya and Tanzania by al-Qaeda. The military operation involved cruise missile strikes against the Al-Shifa pharmaceutical factory in Khartoum, Sudan, and al-Qaeda bases in Khost, Afghanistan. Counterterrorism at this time was largely a niche issue for the military that concerned special forces in an "adjunct and supporting role providing support as needed to law enforcement," according to former State Department coordinator for counterterrorism Phillip Wilcox.[20] Conventional military forces did not play a significant role in counterterrorism operations given concerns they would be ineffective in discriminately targeting terrorist groups.[21]

Within the halls of the CIA, on the other hand, counterterrorism before the war on terror was considered "first among equals." Counterterrorism weathered the budget and personnel cuts that the intelligence community faced at the end of the Cold War better than other areas in terms of resource allocation, in part because of its clearer focus.[22] Despite this, the CIA never formulated a comprehensive counterterrorism strategy prior to 2001.[23] Similarly, counterterrorism efforts of the Defense Intelligence Agency (DIA) at this time were "rather ad hoc," according to the director of DIA's Joint Intelligence Task Force Combating Terrorism.[24] During the early 2001 quadrennial intelligence community review process, a strategic planning exercise, the deputy secretary of defense told Joan Dempsey, then serving as the deputy director of central intelligence for community management, that "counterterrorism would never be an issue and that no money would be available for it."[25] At the time, terrorism was simply one concern among many facing the new Bush administration.

This view was not shared by everyone within the U.S. government. On December 4, 1998, four months after the al-Qaeda attacks in East Africa, CIA Director George Tenet sent a memorandum to his deputies arguing that the government "must now redouble our efforts against Bin Ladin himself, his infrastructure, followers, finances, etc. with a sense of enormous urgency. . . . We are at war. I want no resources or people spared in this effort, either inside CIA or the Community."[26] However, there was little follow-through with senior leadership in the White House and the broader intelligence community, as various agencies were unable to "redirect resources for counterterrorism because they have other priorities."[27] Tenet continued to raise—both publicly and privately—the threat posed by al-Qaeda and Osama bin Laden in the years leading up to 2001.[28] In 1998, a memorandum was informally circulated within the Pentagon written by Tom Kuster, the deputy director of the counterterrorism division under the assistant secretary of defense for special operations and low intensity conflict. This document similarly pushed for a "more proactive and offensive strategy by the Department of Defense in combating international terrorism."[29] In particular, it argued for the potential need for "large-scale operations across the whole spectrum of U.S. military capabilities . . . to take up the gauntlet that international terrorists have thrown at our feet."[30] This strategy was considered "too aggressive" by the assistant secretary, and the proposal went no further.[31]

From a broader national security perspective, counterterrorism during this period was generally of secondary concern to more traditional, state-based security threats to the United States.[32] A former U.S. military intelligence officer stated that prior to al-Qaeda's 9/11 attacks, "Terrorism was nothing we were thinking about or even looking at, at that time. . . . We were focused on state actors."[33] According to White House counterterrorism advisor Richard Clarke, he had never even conducted a briefing on terrorism directly with the president before September 11, 2001.[34] With respect to Osama bin Laden, even Bush admitted that neither he nor his national security team prioritized the terrorist leader before the 9/11 attacks. "I was prepared to look at a plan that would be a thoughtful plan that would bring him to justice, and would have given the order to do that," Bush told journalist Bob Woodward. "But I didn't feel that sense of urgency, and my blood was not nearly as boiling."[35]

## THE ENDLESS WAR

The war on terror flipped national security on its head. No longer were the strongest states the threats with which the U.S. government was most concerned. Rather, nonstate actors, emerging from and operating in the weakest states, became the greatest perceived danger to U.S. national security. As the 9/11 Commission observed in its report, "In the twentieth century, strategists focused on the world's great industrial heartlands. In the twenty-first, the focus is in the opposite direction, toward remote regions and failing states."[36] Nearly five years into the war on terror, the 2006 *Quadrennial Defense Review Report* further argued that the twenty-first-century military was "shifting emphasis . . . [f]rom nation-state threats—to decentralized network threats from non-state enemies. From conducting war against nations—to conducting war in countries we are not at war with."[37]

With a new understanding of the looming threat posed by terrorist groups, the U.S. government rejected a traditional law enforcement approach to counterterrorism and embraced a war footing to confront the al-Qaeda network and deter future attacks. Senior officials in the Bush administration immediately pushed for a decisive military response to the 9/11 attacks. On Air Force One, just hours after the second World Trade Center tower collapsed, the president reportedly said, "We're going to find out who did this and we're going to kick their asses."[38] Rumsfeld recalled his advice to the president in the coming days:

> I believed our nation's response should not primarily be about punishment, retribution, or retaliation. Punishing our enemies didn't describe the range of actions we would need to take if we were to succeed in protecting the United States. The struggle that had been brought to our shores went beyond law enforcement and criminal justice. Our responsibility was to deter and dissuade others from thinking that terrorism against the United States could advance their cause. In my view, our

principal motivation was self-defense, not vengeance, retaliation, or punishment. The only effective defense would be to go after the terrorists with a strong offense.[39]

Then deputy secretary of defense Paul Wolfowitz later recalled that Bush at the time believed that the United States' military response first needed to be "decisive," not a "pinprick" like Operation Infinite Reach, and more broadly needed to focus "most of all on prevention."[40] The U.S. government also had the political backing to pursue the military option. An NBC News poll on September 12, 2001, found that 83 percent of the American public supported "forceful military action," and *Newsweek* polling from October to December 2001 averaged 88 percent positive support for a military response.[41]

On September 18, 2001, Bush signed into law the Authorization for the Use of Military Force (AUMF), which had passed both houses of Congress four days earlier with only one vote against the bill. Totaling only 243 words, the law authorized the president "to use all necessary and appropriate force against those nations, organizations, or persons he determines planned, authorized, committed, or aided the terrorist attacks that occurred on September 11, 2001, or harbored such organizations or persons, in order to prevent any future acts of international terrorism against the United States by such nations, organizations or persons."[42]

The AUMF does not specify any geographic or temporal bounds to these actions or specifically name al-Qaeda, purposefully leaving the language vague enough to authorize the U.S. government to target the Taliban in Afghanistan and any other organizations or governments affiliated with al-Qaeda. (In October 2002, Congress passed a separate authorization for the 2003 military invasion of Iraq.) With its broad language, the AUMF has been used as legal authorization for military deployments or military strikes in over twenty countries, with U.S. political leadership framing these operations as self-defense against impending attacks, a justification repeated by the Bush, Obama, and Trump administrations.[43] The ambiguity within the 2001 law essentially provided the framework for an open-ended war, and it was still in effect at the time of writing; the "over-the-horizon" U.S. counterterrorism efforts within

Afghanistan that followed the August 2021 Taliban takeover were authorized under the auspices of the AUMF.[44]

The U.S. government's policy framework and rhetoric militarized the counterterrorism response to the 9/11 attacks, with many government officials remaining focused on a military-centric approach as "the silver bullet against terrorism."[45] With U.S. forces beginning to hunt down and capture suspected al-Qaeda operatives around the globe, terrorists were now considered enemy combatants, a status with implications for how they would be treated following their capture, including indefinite detainment at Guantanamo Bay and trial by military courts.[46] According to a July 2004 congressional hearing recommendation memo to Secretary Rumsfeld from Assistant Secretary of Defense for Legislative Affairs Powell Moore, one of the Bush administration's key messages was that "law enforcement approaches will not work against an enemy who has declared war and who has the means to visit war upon us *and* our allies."[47] Rumsfeld signaled his agreement with the memo's arguments by scrawling "Good" on the document. During a 2006 speech at the Council on Foreign Relations, then CIA director Michael Hayden also emphasized that the United States was "without ambiguity" in a "state of war. . . . The fight against international terrorism cannot be mastered by the classic methods of the police."[48]

In the early years of the war on terror, a string of high-profile world leaders, journalists, and scholars touting their expertise on the Middle East and the broader Islamic world, helped to shape public debates and push this military-centric approach to the fight against al-Qaeda. Mere days after the 9/11 attacks, Pulitzer Prize–winning journalist Thomas Friedman, noted for his past reporting from the Middle East, wrote in the pages of the *New York Times* that, much like the Japanese forces at Pearl Harbor, al-Qaeda had struck the first blow of "World War III," which "will be a long war" against "terrorists who hate our existence, not just our policies."[49] Two years later, on the *Charlie Rose Show*, Friedman again justified the United States' military response by stating, "We needed to go over there basically and take out a very big stick right in the heart of that world. . . . What they needed to see was American boys and girls going house to house from Basra to Baghdad and basically saying, 'Which part of this sentence don't you understand; you don't think we care about our open society . . . well suck on this.' "[50] In September 2002, Israeli prime minister Benjamin Netanyahu, testifying before Congress, said that "the way to deal with terror was to deal with terrorist regimes and the way to deal with terrorist regimes among other things was to apply military force against them. . . . The application of power is the most important thing to winning the war on terrorism."[51] Bush also frequently met with former secretary of state Henry Kissinger, who offered his support for a military response to the 9/11 attacks, including the invasion of Iraq, and argued for the necessity of achieving an outright military victory, reinforcing the president's own convictions.[52]

In particular, senior U.S. officials were influenced by historian of the Middle East Bernard Lewis. While Lewis advocated for a policy of democracy promotion in the region, which he believed would bring it closer to Western values—a strategy echoed in Bush's foreign policy objectives—he also stressed the need to use overwhelming military strength to achieve American objectives. The *Wall Street Journal* dubbed this approach the "Lewis Doctrine."[53] Brent Scowcroft, the national security advisor under Presidents Gerald Ford and George H. W. Bush and chair of the President's Foreign Intelligence Advisory Board from 2001 to 2005, summed up Lewis's advice as the "idea that we've got to hit somebody hard. And Bernard Lewis says, 'I believe that one of the things you've got to do to Arabs is hit them between the eyes with a big stick. They respect power.' "[54] This advice was based on Lewis's understanding of Arab culture as historically responsive only to force and resistant to political change. The application of military force, in his view, would help bring Arabs and the broader Middle East in line with Western modernity and secularism; in so doing, the administration could resolve the instability and disorder of the region, which had thus far been buttressing al-Qaeda's war against the United States. Democratization backed by force, he surmised, would lead the region away from the fundamentalist ideology espoused by bin Laden and his acolytes and stymie the threat against the United States.

Lewis saw modernity and secularism—which he claimed had been introduced to the region by European colonialism in the eighteenth and nineteenth centuries—as slowly transforming the Middle East while provoking a counterresponse from local fundamentalists. In his 2002 book *What Went Wrong: The Clash Between Islam and Modernity in the*

*Middle East,* he forewarned that "If the peoples of the Middle East continue on their present path, the suicide bomber may become a metaphor for the whole region, and there will be no escape from a downward spiral of hate and spite, rage and self-pity, poverty and oppression, culminating sooner or later in yet another alien domination."[55] Moreover, Lewis saw the war on terror as the end of a centuries-old struggle between Western and Islamic civilizations—the clichéd "clash of civilizations." He argued, "I have no doubt that 11th September was the opening salvo of the final battle."[56] Bin Laden and al-Qaeda, viewed through the frame of a civilizational clash, represented a post–Cold War Islamic challenge to American power and dominance in the world, with the 9/11 attacks an attempt to force the Western "crusaders" out of the Islamic world. Therefore, from this perspective, it was necessary to demonstrate American military strength, without which the United States would only be inviting future attacks.

In private dinners with Vice President Cheney and meetings with and lectures to the highest officials within the Bush administration, Lewis laid out this approach and helped justify a policy that already had strong support among leading political figures in Washington, DC. Paul Wolfowitz stated in 2002, "Bernard has taught us how to understand the complex and important history of the Middle East, and use it to guide us where we will go next to build a better world for generations to come."[57] On NBC's *Meet the Press* the following year, Cheney echoed this sentiment: "I firmly believe, along with men like Bernard Lewis, who is one of the great students of that part of the world, that a strong, firm response to terror and to threats to the United States would go a long way, frankly, toward calming things in that part of the world."[58]

Despite viewing itself at war, the United States also leveraged a wide range of tools on multiple fronts to deal with the problem of terrorism—humanitarian and economic assistance, public outreach and diplomacy, education reforms, and police actions. The 2006 *Quadrennial Defense Review Report* recognized that there was "no 'one size fits all' approach, no 'silver bullet'" to defeat terrorism.[59] Like the Bush administration, the Obama administration also discussed a comprehensive, "whole-of-government effort" as a necessary framework for combating terrorism. This "whole-of-government" rhetoric, according to American University professor and counterterrorism expert Stephen Tankel, was simply "boilerplate language" that found its way into all policy discussions and strategies.[60]

Nevertheless, the military option remained a central part of U.S. counterterrorism efforts, especially with the key role played by the Department of Defense in policy planning for the war on terror. With its higher budget and influence over the White House, the political leadership in the Pentagon had "the stronger hand" and took "the lead role" in many areas of counterterrorism, including encroaching on the responsibility of other departments, especially the State Department; in July 2002, for instance, Rumsfeld pushed for senior Pentagon leadership to be involved in the selection process for candidates to ambassadorial posts in key partner states such as Afghanistan, Pakistan, the Philippines, and Yemen.[61] General Stanley McChrystal, the former commander of the Joint Special Operations Command (JSOC) and the International Security Assistance Force (ISAF) in Afghanistan, further argued, "One of the reasons people use the military is because it's quick." Given the immediacy of the terrorist threat for senior U.S. officials, he explained, "You can't get sometimes the legal system or the State Department or those other things to move that quickly, and they're not designed to. The military becomes the easy button. So it's not evil or stupid, it just becomes expedient."[62]

## LOOKING BEYOND AFGHANISTAN AND IRAQ

Almost immediately after the 9/11 attacks, senior members of the Bush administration pushed for a broadening of U.S. counterterrorism efforts beyond Afghanistan and al-Qaeda's core leadership. Then undersecretary of defense for policy Douglas Feith, who played a key role in constructing the early policy framework for the war on terror, recalled that a major strategic challenge was defining the enemy.[63] On September 11, 2001, Feith was in Moscow to discuss a missile treaty with the Russian government. He was soon aboard a military aircraft heading back to Washington, DC, the only method of travel available given the grounding of commercial flights. He was joined by other senior Pentagon officials caught abroad, including the head of strategy and plans for the Joint Chiefs of Staff, Lieutenant General John Abizaid, and the assistant secretary of defense for international security, Peter Rodman. During the long flight, Feith and the other officials huddled together and began to map out a strategic policy response to the al-Qaeda attacks.

Aware that Bush had already informed his administration that the United States was at war, they focused on the question of with whom the country was at war. Given the unpredictability of future events, they saw it necessary to define the enemy as an activity as opposed to a specific organization so as to avoid limiting the government's potential actions, a consistent point of emphasis for Rumsfeld. Feith argued that "part of the reason it was called the war on terrorism and not the war on al-Qaeda was that we saw the network of enemies as broader than al-Qaeda."[64] He wrote in a policy memo that the U.S. government had to confront

> the entire network of states, non-state entities, and organizations that engage in or support terrorism against the United States and our interests, including the states that harbor terrorists. All those organizations and states constitute a threat, joint and severally. The United States cannot tolerate continued state support for terrorism, regardless of whether a specific tie can be established to the perpetrators of the World Trade Center and Pentagon outrages. The objective is not punishment but prevention and self-defense.[65]

He submitted these ideas to an approving Rumsfeld, helping to inform the Department of Defense's initial operational planning for the war on terror.

There was initial pushback within the Bush administration, such as from Secretary of State Colin Powell, Deputy Secretary of State Richard Armitage, and Richard Clarke, about the scope of America's response, especially when the subject of invading Iraq as a state sponsor of terrorism first came up. Powell and the senior leadership in the State Department opposed expanding the scope of the war on terror against an overly ambiguous enemy and advocated for a focused military campaign against only those individuals responsible for the 9/11 attacks. Powell argued that a narrower, yet decisive, campaign limited to al-Qaeda targets in Afghanistan would be more acceptable to U.S. partners, and that an unnecessarily expansive response, especially a military invasion of Iraq, could undermine the U.S. government's ability to assemble an international coalition and generate international support.[66]

This limited scope of engagement ultimately lost out to the more comprehensive military strategy against the full spectrum of terrorists and their supporters that was advocated by Cheney, Rumsfeld, and senior officials within the White House and Pentagon. An October 2001 White House briefing memo on the Afghanistan strategy had already warned against long-term military commitments there "since the U.S. will be heavily engaged in the anti-terrorism effort worldwide."[67] Key members of the president's national security team were committed to a broad interpretation of the war and its aims, in part due to memories of the Gulf War in the early 1990s and the limiting effect of its coalition-based planning and operations.[68] In early policy planning discussions after September 11, 2001, as Feith stated,

> One of the thoughts at the fore of Rumsfeld's mind—and I assume this was true also for Cheney and ultimately President Bush—related to the Gulf War of 1990–1991. The aim of the Gulf War had been negotiated. It was the basis of the U.S.-led coalition. That war aim was limited to the expulsion of the Iraqi force from Kuwait. When the issue arose whether the coalition should destroy Saddam's army, U.S. officials argued that that went beyond the coalition's limited war aim.

Feith explained that this concern over any potential future constraints was also "at the fore of the minds of U.S. officials ten years later, after 9/11. Officials didn't want to tie our own hands by trying to predict in this post-9/11 world of uncertainty what was going to happen next and how things were going to unfold and how we might have to adjust our war aims." As a result, many U.S. officials "were conscious of uncertainty. Rumsfeld did not want to define our war aims or define our specific operations so precisely that it would create commitments to Congress or to our allies that would tie our hands and make it harder to take appropriate action if and when things happened that we couldn't anticipate."[69]

As U.S. and Coalition military operations degraded al-Qaeda's Afghanistan operations and its ability to exploit the country as a safe haven, U.S. officials soon realized that the terrorist group could reorganize in other weak states and attract new supporters.[70] On the ground in Afghanistan, U.S. military leaders were aware by spring 2002 that al-Qaeda fighters were leaving the country and finding safe haven in

"under-governed areas" elsewhere.[71] CIA and FBI interrogations of captured al-Qaeda members at this time focused on uncovering the networks
used to smuggle al-Qaeda operatives out of Afghanistan to potential
bases of operation in other weak states from which they could plan and
commit attacks against the United States and its interests abroad.[72]

As al-Qaeda members spread outside of Afghanistan, the U.S. government eventually saw the organization connecting many disparate terrorist groups around the world in a "global Salafi jihadist movement." The
CIA's 2006 National Intelligence Estimate outlined four factors leading to
the spread of this movement: "(1) Entrenched grievances, such as corruption, injustice, and fear of Western domination, leading to anger, humiliation, and a sense of powerlessness; (2) the Iraq jihad; (3) the slow pace of
real and sustained economic, social, and political reforms in many Muslim majority nations; and (4) pervasive anti-US sentiment among most
Muslims—all of which jihadists exploit."[73] In particular, it identified the
costly U.S. military invasion of Iraq as a "cause celebre for jihadists,
breeding a deep resentment of US involvement in the Muslim world and
cultivating supporters for the global jihadist movement" and helping
"foster a perception that US counterterrorism policies are a cover for
efforts to subjugate Muslims."[74] There also were heightened fears of the
ramifications of foreign fighters beginning to return home from Iraq and
terrorist groups shifting operations outside of the country.[75] With this
expanding threat, the CIA warned of the negative repercussions of any
further U.S. or Western military intervention into predominately Muslim states over the next five years. Such military operations would likely
"ratchet up sympathy for jihadists and could produce another jihadist
conflict" and place further public pressure on partner states to reduce
their cooperation with the United States.[76]

With the dispersal of al-Qaeda operatives, the military invasions of
Afghanistan and Iraq were seen as sunk costs that would bolster the
credibility of U.S. threats and convince key leaders abroad, fearful of
U.S. military action against their own governments, to cooperate with
the United States.[77] This sunk cost approach was built into the planning
of the war on terror from its very beginning. In the run-up to the
Afghanistan invasion, Rumsfeld argued to President Bush that "a key
war aim would be to persuade or compel States to stop supporting terrorism. The regimes of such States would see that it will be fatal to host

terrorists who attack the U.S. . . . If the war does not significantly change the world's political map, the U.S. will not achieve its aim."[78] The following month, a White House briefing memo on the U.S. strategy for Afghanistan further stressed that one of the main aims of a military invasion was to "end the use of Afghanistan as a sanctuary for terrorism. Do so in a manner that signals the world that harboring terrorism will be punished severely. . . . Making an example of the Taliban increases U.S. leverage on other state supporters of terrorism." In a nod to the tactics to be relied upon, the briefing document unequivocally stated, "Al-Qaida's and the Taliban's main assets are people. They must be destroyed."[79] During planning for the 2003 Iraq invasion, a White House briefing document similarly stated, "Regime change will remove a source of support for international terrorism, and will serve as an object lesson to other state supporters of terrorism. After Afghanistan, many states that had supported terrorism started to indicate willingness to cooperate with us. The salutary effect of our victory of Afghanistan has begun to wear off, however. Success in Iraq will re-invigorate it."[80] The National Intelligence Council further argued that regime change in Iraq would "highlight the inability of existing regimes to stand up to US power" and help to "encourage" governments to cooperate with the United States on security issues.[81]

The cooperation that U.S. officials sought can be broadly classified into foreign and domestic cooperation. On the foreign front, the U.S. government made efforts to build a coalition of international partners to target Taliban and al-Qaeda forces in Afghanistan, aided by invoking Article 5 of the North Atlantic Treaty,[82] and support the Iraq invasion. This was meant to bolster the perceived legitimacy of these operations as collective actions in line with international norms.[83] The U.S. government also focused on procuring rights of access in key regional states for troop and supply movements through these territories, such as Uzbekistan, Turkey, and Pakistan. By June 2002, there were sixty-nine states contributing varying levels of support to this front of the war on terror, with a military coalition of twenty states deploying a combined sixteen thousand troops for combat, combat support, and combat service operations.[84] The domestic front, on the other hand, focused on partner states' counterterrorism cooperation within their own borders. U.S. officials pressed their counterparts to pass new and strengthen existing antiterrorism laws, arrest and turn over suspected al-Qaeda operatives, share intelligence, counter extreme ideologies, target terrorist financing, increase border security, and conduct offensive counterterrorism operations.[85]

## "UNGOVERNED SPACES" IN THE CROSSHAIRS

With the growing costs and unpopularity of unilateral U.S. military action, coupled with the spread of the perceived "global Salafi jihadist network," U.S. counterterrorism shifted at the outset of Bush's second term to a new strategy based in "disaggregation."[86] This new strategy focused on dismantling the growing al-Qaeda network into smaller and disconnected groups that could be targeted by partner states' security forces. In August 2005, Rumsfeld met with the president at his ranch in Crawford, Texas, to brief him on recommendations for how the U.S. approach to the war on terror needed to change, relying on new ideas gleaned from traditional deterrence theory. A key aspect of this was expanding U.S. focus beyond targeting bin Laden and al-Qaeda's senior leadership to the rapidly growing network of al-Qaeda affiliates around the world in an attempt to deter and degrade their ability to operate and plan attacks. In particular, this meant supporting partner states' militaries to target al-Qaeda safe havens within their borders.[87]

Following a December 2001 meeting, British prime minister Tony Blair sent Bush a top secret paper—"The War Against Terrorism: The Second Phase"— already outlining the need to pressure key states to deploy their military forces domestically, bolstered by support from the United States and the United Kingdom, to target al-Qaeda and other affiliated terrorist groups. In the Philippines, Blair argued that "the key policy should be to provide equipment, CT training and . . . to improve the capacity of the Philippines armed forces to deal with Islamic extremist groups in the south. We should be ready to join them in hitting terrorist concentrations and terrorist camps in . . . air operations." Similarly in Yemen, he wrote, "We need to set out clear expectations for Yemeni action against terrorism. There may be a scope for practical assistance on CT and defence cooperation if we are sure the Yemenis are genuinely committed to this. We should offer to mount . . . air operations against terrorists. Our strategy should be to work with the Yemenis if we can, but to leave them in no doubt if they fail to take the necessary action, they run the risk of others doing it for them." In Indonesia, Blair stated, "We should help [the government's] efforts to deal with Lashkar Jihad through CT assistance and intelligence cooperation. We should also be ready, with Indonesian support/collaboration, to take military action against known terrorist training camps."[88]

Senior U.S. officials' awareness of the expanding al-Qaeda network and its use of "ungoverned spaces" in the periphery as safe havens was "gradual," Lawrence Wilkerson argued, and "then the policy caught up with it and shifted." He continued, "I think the principal impetus for that was not just clearer strategic thinking. It was the physical cost of the unilateralism."[89] This shift in strategy would rely heavily on gaining the cooperation of key but often difficult partner states, like Yemen and Pakistan. Undersecretary of Defense for Intelligence Steve Cambone wrote in a May 2004 memo to Rumsfeld, which was shared with Bush,

> For now, the United States has no choice but to continue the tactical engagement against Al Qaeda and other terrorist networks. But it is time for us to realize that we have a larger problem than Al Qaeda, and that its solution will require a multi-variant approach. That approach ought to allow for the creation of "alliances of convenience" between the United States and other states such that those states can address their domestic problems in ways conducive to their own political realities while, at the same time, and without attribution, contribute to the overall objectives of the United States.[90]

This strategy gained further weight after the 2006 midterm elections, in which the Democratic Party won control of both the House and the Senate, and the 2008 presidential election, during which Democrats campaigned against the increasingly unpopular war in Iraq.[91] The political rhetoric that had characterized both elections helped to turn public opinion away from support for U.S. troop deployments and increased domestic political pressure on the government to rely on partner states to help confront terrorist threats abroad.

With the new "disaggregation" approach, the U.S. government increased its support for partner states' militaries through financial assistance, equipment, and training. This would develop into the U.S. military's "by-with-through" operational approach, an approach originating with U.S. special forces and adapted for use with conventional military forces. U.S. Central Command defined this as operations that are "led *by* our partners, state or nonstate, *with* enabling support from the United States or U.S.-led coalitions, and *through* U.S. authorities and partner agreements."[92] The 2006 *Quadrennial Defense Review Report* explained that "recent operations demonstrate the critical importance of being organized to work with and through others, and of shifting emphasis from performing tasks ourselves to enabling others. They also underscore the importance of adopting a more indirect approach to achieve common objectives. The Department must help partners improve their ability to perform their intended roles and missions."[93]

The U.S. government relied on a number of existing and newly created programs and funding authorities to support partner states' domestic counterterrorism efforts, with various military assistance programs also serving as a signal that these states should rely on military force to target terrorist groups within their borders.[94] According to a former U.S. military intelligence officer, "We were expecting them to take the strong, hard approach that we were taking. . . . We were expecting that harder stance via military force."[95] In reference to the February 2002 Acquisition and Cross-Servicing Agreement (ACSA) with Pakistan, for instance, officials with the Departments of Justice and Defense interpreted the ACSA, a vehicle for reimbursing countries for their logistical support of U.S. military operations, to also allow the Department of Defense "to pay a supplying country for logistic support, supplies, and services that the country provides to *its own* forces in carrying out military operations for [the Department of Defense], *if* U.S. forces benefit by not having to provide the support, supplies or services to conduct the operations themselves."[96] On March 4, 2003, Rumsfeld authorized the use of the ACSA for the reimbursement of partner states' military activities "in connection with the continuing war on terrorism," including a payment of $530 million to Pakistan for its actions taken in support of the war on terror over the previous year.[97]

In 2002, the U.S. government also established the Coalition Support Funds (CSF) to reimburse partner states for their logistic and military support of U.S. military operations in Afghanistan and Iraq. These funds were also drawn upon to support regional partner states for their military operations in support of U.S. counterterrorism objectives, such as Pakistan's military operations in FATA (the majority of U.S. assistance provided to Pakistan came from the CSF). In addition, the Pentagon created the Regional Defense Combating Terrorism Fellowship Program to "provide coalition counterparts with the training and education necessary to establish and maintain effective counterterrorism programs in their home countries."[98] Through the State Department, the U.S. government relied on the Foreign Military Financing Program, authorized under the Arms Export Control Act of 1976, to provide grants and loans to partner states to procure weapons and other military equipment. This program, according to the White House's *National Strategy for Combating Terrorism* (released in February 2003), provided "a direct infusion of badly needed resources used to combat terrorism."[99]

Under Section 1208 of the National Defense Authorization Act for Fiscal Year 2005, the secretary of defense was further authorized to disburse up to $25,000,000 per fiscal year to provide assistance to "foreign forces, irregular forces, groups, or individuals engaged in supporting or facilitating ongoing military operations by United States special operations forces to combat terrorism."[100] The level of authorized Defense funding for surrogate forces to combat terrorism was later increased to $100,000,000 under U.S. Code Section 127e.[101] While testifying before Congress, Major General James Hecker, the vice director of operations for the Pentagon's Joint Staff, remarked that this funding authority allowed the U.S. military to lessen "the need for large scale U.S. troop deployments" and "fosters an environment where local forces take ownership of the problem."[102] Yet, according to one army Green Beret, "It's less, 'We're helping you,' and more, 'You're doing our bidding.' "[103]

In addition to these programs and funding authorities, the U.S. government implemented several regional and country-specific counterterrorism programs and military task forces. The Combined Joint Task Force—Horn of Africa (CJTF-HOA) focused on bolstering the military capacity of Kenya, Ethiopia, and Djibouti, especially in confronting al-Shabaab after its emergence in 2006. In December 2004, the commander of CJTF-HOA, Major General Samuel Helland, explained that the task force's mission was not to lead counterterrorism efforts but to provide support to local security forces. He stated, "We by ourselves don't really pursue the threat of terrorism. Our job is to prevent it, deter it, and to support the host nations as they develop the capability that they require to fight the terrorist threat that is germane to their countries."[104] Colonel Bill Coultrup, the commander of the Joint Special Operations Task Force—Philippines, described his mission after arriving in country in 2007 as one of support for Philippine military operations in its southern periphery. "Help the Philippines security forces. It's their fight," he stressed. "We don't want to take over."[105] This model of U.S. military assistance, according to Lieutenant General Douglas Lute, the director of operations for U.S. Central Command from 2004 to 2006 and subsequently the deputy national security advisor for Iraq and Afghanistan, was meant "to deter terrorists by interacting with local nationals in an effort to help them help themselves without the burden of a large American military presence."[106]

In 2005, the U.S. government inaugurated the Trans-Sahara Counterterrorism Partnership, to replace the earlier Pan-Sahel Initiative, to assist Algeria, Burkina Faso, Cameroon, Chad, Libya, Mali, Mauritania, Morocco, Niger, Nigeria, Senegal, and Tunisia in "their immediate and long-term capabilities to address terrorist threats and prevent the spread of violent extremism" through "enabling and enhancing the capacity of North and West African militaries to conduct [counterterrorism] operations."[107] With the support of this program, the U.S. government's counterterrorism priorities within the Sahel region were "locating and eliminating the threat from Al-Qaida operatives and supporters in the short term, and improving border control and security in the medium term."[108] In 2009, the State Department also implemented the Partnership for Regional East Africa Counterterrorism "to build the capacity and cooperation of military, law enforcement, and civilian actors across East Africa to counter terrorism in a comprehensive fashion."[109] In the same year, Congress established the $3 billion Pakistan Counterinsurgency Capability Fund to provide support to and bolster the capacity of Pakistan's military as it battled the Pakistani Taliban groups on its northwestern periphery.[110]

The focus of U.S.-supported counterterrorism operations overwhelmingly fell on the "ungoverned spaces" of the periphery suspected of being terrorist safe havens. The 9/11 Commission identified a wide array of operational conditions that an "international terrorist operation" relies on, including

- time, space, and ability to perform competent planning and staff work;
- a command structure able to make necessary decisions and possessing the authority and contacts to assemble needed people, money, and materials;
- opportunity and space to recruit, train, and select operatives with the needed skills and dedication, providing the time and structure required to socialize them into the terrorist cause, judge their trustworthiness, and hone their skills;
- a logistics network able to securely manage the travel of operatives, move money, and transport resources (like explosives) where they need to go;
- access, in the case of certain weapons, to the special materials needed for a nuclear, chemical, radiological, or biological attack;
- reliable communications between coordinators and operatives; and
- opportunity to test the workability of the plan.[111]

The key underlying factor that makes these possible is the presence of a safe haven as a base for necessary support operations, which "ungoverned spaces" provide. When terrorist groups can operate outside of government control in weak or failing states, they have greater opportunities to recruit, coordinate, and train their members to commit acts of violence, making their operations more efficient and more deadly.[112] In particular, terrorist groups have been able to exploit the absence of government control in the periphery—whether the absence of government control is due to capacity limitations, institutional design, or lack of political will.[113]

Even before the war on terror, senior officials in the Bush administration were aware of the variable levels of control that foreign governments held within their territories, along with the potential problems stemming from the lack of effective or uniform governance. Rumsfeld noted after a May 21, 2001, meeting with former secretary of state George Shultz, "There are a growing number of places that are not being governed. For example, Indonesia, Pakistan, half the Muslim world, Africa,

Ukraine, Colombia. This is a new type of issue we have to deal with."[114] The saliency of this concern was heightened after the 9/11 attacks with the fear that al-Qaeda could exploit these "ungoverned" regions to plan further attacks against the United States. The CIA director's 2003 *Worldwide Threat Briefing* stated, "We cannot lose sight of those national security challenges that, while not occupying space on the front pages, demand a constant level of scrutiny. Challenges such as the world's vast stretches of ungoverned areas—lawless zones, veritable 'no man's lands' like some areas along the Afghan-Pakistani border—where extremists find shelter and can win the breathing space to grow."[115] The 2004 *National Defense Strategy* further argued, "The absence of effective governance in many parts of the world creates sanctuaries for terrorists, criminals, and insurgents. Many states are unable, and in some cases unwilling, to exercise effective control over their territory or frontiers, thus leaving areas open to hostile exploitation."[116]

In the immediate aftermath of the 9/11 attacks, the U.S. government did not have a specific policy to address terrorist safe havens in these "ungoverned spaces" as distinct from state sponsorship; it was simply one issue among many at which officials were looking.[117] The Bush administration initially focused on the larger missions in Afghanistan and Iraq, along with the targeting of identified al-Qaeda operatives across the globe. With the toppling of the Taliban government and ongoing military operations in Afghanistan, however, senior U.S. officials were increasingly raising the alarm in internal communications that al-Qaeda was being squeezed out of the country and its operatives were seeking new safe havens from which to operate.[118] Douglas Feith summed this up as follows: "What we did by going into Afghanistan, as somebody put it, was stomp our foot into a pool of water. The water splashed out and we got a small pool over there and another over here."[119] A former U.S. intelligence official similarly explained, "After 9/11 the U.S. thought we'd squeezed the toothpaste in Afghanistan and these guys were just going to squirt into all these different ungoverned spaces."[120]

As U.S. officials increasingly recognized the extent of this problem, they worked to identify specific regions that al-Qaeda operatives were using or could use as safe havens. In December 2001, for instance, Colin Powell stated in an interview, "There are lots of al Qaeda cells around throughout the world that we're going after, and there are other countries that are of concern to us besides Iraq." He, in particular, pointed to Somalia and argued that its instability made the country "ripe for misuse by those who would take that chaos and thrive on the chaos. That's why we're really looking at Somalia—not to go after Somalia as a nation or a government, but to be especially sensitive to the fact where Somalia could be a place where people suddenly find haven."[121] A January 2003 DIA report further found that after al-Qaeda members had lost Afghanistan as a base of operations, they "attempted to re-deploy to the Sahel and Maghreb regions of Africa." As evidence, DIA analysts cited the killing of the Yemeni Imed Abdelwahid Ahmed by Algerian security forces in September 2002, arguing he had been dispatched by al-Qaeda core to assess the suitability of this desert area as a new base of operations. In addition to visiting southeastern Algeria, Ahmed reportedly traveled to Mauritania, Niger, Nigeria, and Chad. The intelligence report also discussed two members of al-Qaeda with a Mauritanian background, hinting that this connection could make Mauritania's empty deserts a potential al-Qaeda base.[122] U.S. officials also expressed concern with al-Qaeda's links to militant groups in the Muslim-majority southern periphery of the Philippines, especially Abu Sayyaf (a splinter group of the Moro National Liberation Front).[123]

The 2004 *National Military Strategy* identified an "arc of instability stretching from the Western Hemisphere, through Africa and the Middle East and extending to Asia." It continued, "There are areas in this arc that serve as breeding grounds for threats to our interests . . . [and where] adversaries take advantage of ungoverned spaces and under-governed territories from which they prepare plans, train forces and launch attacks."[124] The strategy document further stated that the U.S. military would "work to deny terrorists safe haven in failed states and ungoverned regions. Working with other nations' militaries and other governmental agencies, the Armed Forces help to establish favorable security conditions and increase the capabilities of partners."[125] U.S. officials wanted to prevent al-Qaeda from shifting to new safe havens and "re-creating in a new location what they had had in Afghanistan."[126] David Kilcullen also argued that this approach was intended to limit the ability for al-Qaeda to inject its cause into and exploit local conflicts, which could aggregate a wide range of actors into a "global jihad" movement.[127]

The report of the 9/11 Commission, released in July 2004, recommended expanding U.S. counterterrorism efforts to target safe havens through cooperation with partner states. The report stated, "The U.S. government must identify and prioritize actual or potential terrorist sanctuaries. For each, it should have a realistic strategy to keep possible terrorists insecure and on the run, using all elements of national power. We should reach out, listen to, and work with other countries that can help."[128] The report identified several regions that al-Qaeda could use as safe havens:

- western Pakistan and the Pakistan-Afghanistan border region
- southern or western Afghanistan
- the Arabian Peninsula, especially Saudi Arabia and Yemen, and the nearby Horn of Africa, including Somalia and extending southwest into Kenya
- Southeast Asia, from Thailand to the southern Philippines to Indonesia
- West Africa, including Nigeria and Mali
- European cities with expatriate Muslim communities, especially cities in central and eastern Europe where security forces and border controls are less effective.[129]

To implement the 9/11 Commission's recommendation, Congress passed the Intelligence Reform and Terrorism Prevention Act, signed into law by the president on December 17, 2004. Regarding safe havens, this act required the government

(1) to identify foreign countries that are being used as terrorist sanctuaries; (2) to assess current United States resources and tools being used to assist foreign government to eliminate such sanctuaries; (3) to develop and implement a coordinated strategy to prevent terrorists from using foreign countries as sanctuaries; and (4) to work in bilateral and multilateral fora to elicit the cooperation needed to identify and address terrorist sanctuaries that may exist today, but, so far, remain unknown to governments.[130]

The law further required that the State Department's annual *Country Reports on Terrorism* (known from 1996 to 2004 as *Patterns of Global Terrorism*) provide an overview of efforts made by partner states in eliminating terrorist safe havens and how the U.S. government supported them.[131]

The 2005 *Country Reports on Terrorism* was the first to include a section on "Terrorist Safe Havens." It stated,

> The most intractable safe havens worldwide tend to exist astride international borders or in regions where ineffective governance allows their presence. . . . Denying safe haven to terrorists requires a regional approach based on coordinated action by partner governments working with the United States as well as with each other, and by regional and multilateral institutions. . . . Efforts to build partner capacity and encourage partner states to cooperate more effectively with each other at the regional level are key to denying terrorists safe haven.[132]

In outlining how terrorist groups were utilizing specific safe havens, the report identified Mali, Mauritania, Somalia, the southern Philippines, eastern Malaysia, Indonesia, the Mediterranean, the Caucasus, the Afghanistan-Pakistan border region, northern Iraq, southeastern Turkey, Yemen, the Colombia border region, Venezuela, and the Triple Frontier region between Brazil, Argentina, and Paraguay as areas of particular concern. It also provided an overview of efforts, or lack thereof, made by local governments in asserting control over these regions to mitigate their potential exploitation or efforts to directly challenge terrorist groups operating in these regions. The White House, in its updated *National Strategy for Combating Terrorism* released in September 2006, further stressed the need to "eliminate safe havens," which "can stretch across an entire sovereign state, be limited to specific ungoverned or ill-governed areas in an otherwise functioning state, or cross national borders." Outlining a new approach to counterterrorism, it stated the U.S. government would "strengthen the capacity of such War on Terror partners to reclaim full control of their territory through effective police, border, and other security forces."[133]

Through early 2006, senior officials in the Pentagon continued to prioritize planning to counter "any move by the al-Qaeda network" out of the Afghanistan-Pakistan border region.[134] The disbursement of military assistance and strengthening of military-to-military relationships were increasingly directed toward states where al-Qaeda operatives were currently operating or where it was feared they could potentially set up new bases of operations to plan further attacks. In Somalia, for example, the U.S. government sought the cooperation of the frontline states of Ethiopia and Kenya, given the absence of a viable Somali government following the Somali Civil War of the 1990s, to confront the terrorist threat. As the Islamic Courts Union (ICU) consolidated power in southern Somalia and promoted their interpretation of a sharia-based system of governance, U.S. diplomats feared the country would transform into a "jihadist state," much like Afghanistan under Taliban rule, and that al-Qaeda could exploit it as a safe haven, despite the fact that only a handful of the group's operatives were suspected of being in Somalia at the time.[135]

With the increasing unrest and fears of the ICU consolidating political control, along with the emergence of the ICU "youth" militia al-Shabaab in 2006, the United States backed an Ethiopian military invasion of Somalia in December 2006, which was subsequently supported by the African Union Mission to Somalia by early 2007. Ethiopian military operations lasted until the country's withdrawal from Somalia in January 2009, followed by a U.S.-backed Kenyan military invasion in 2011 (Kenya was already militarily engaged with its own northeastern, Somali-populated periphery with U.S. backing). One American official stationed in Addis Ababa in 2006 stated, "The idea was to get the Ethiopians to fight our war."[136] In response to the U.S.-backed Ethiopian invasion, terrorist attacks by al-Shabaab rapidly increased, both against domestic and international targets within Somalia. One member of al-Shabaab cited the Ethiopian invasion as his reason for joining the terrorist group. He explained,

> In 2006, the ICU came to power and, for the first time in my life, Mogadishu was quiet. I had grown up with nothing but clan warfare and brutal warlords. But a few short months after the ICU took over, the Ethiopians came. They removed the peace and butchered the people. I thought to myself, I am a man. I cannot just sit down and accept this. I had to make a choice and I chose Al Shabaab. It was the best option available to fight back against the Ethiopian invaders.[137]

Beginning in 2011, the Kenyan invasion also increased major terrorist attacks by al-Shabaab in an attempt to force Kenya to withdraw its military.[138] Following the April 2015 attack against Garissa University in northeastern Kenya, al-Shabaab stated, "We have repeatedly warned you that the actions of your government will not be without retaliation. Choices have consequences; you chose your government out of your own volition so endure the consequences of your actions for you will bear the full brunt of its follies. Not only are you condoning your government's oppressive policies by failing to speak out against them but [you] are reinforcing their policies by electing them. You will, therefore, pay the price with your blood."[139] Foreign groups like al-Qaeda, despite shaping many governments' perceptions of the emerging violence in Somalia, had limited influence over al-Shabaab's operations, whose motivations related more to the rapidly changing local security environment amid regional military interventions.[140]

CAMPAIGNING AGAINST BUSH'S WAR

Following the 2008 presidential election, newly elected Barack Obama publicly sought to recalibrate U.S. counterterrorism. His administration moved away from the ideological underpinnings of Bush's foreign policy and ended policies aimed at democratization in the Middle East and the broader Muslim world. He even eschewed the use of the phrase "war on terror." Mirroring the Democrats' electoral strategy in the 2006 midterm elections, he campaigned against Bush's Iraq invasion (the "bad" war), stating on the campaign trail, "There was no such thing as Al Qaeda in Iraq until George Bush and John McCain decided to invade. They took their eye off the people who were responsible for 9/11, and that would be Al Qaeda."[141]

The Obama administration narrowed its counterterrorism efforts back to Afghanistan (the "good" war) and other safe havens where al-Qaeda affiliates were operating, such as Pakistan's FATA, southern Yemen, southern Somalia, and the Maghreb region, understanding this to be the main terrorist threat against the United States. White House Communications Director Dan Pfeiffer stated that the policies of the former administration led to al-Qaeda "regenerated in places like Yemen and Somalia, establishing new safe-havens that have grown over a period of years."[142] In an interview with journalist Bob Woodward, President

Obama argued, "What you've seen is a metastasizing of al-Qaeda, where a range of loosely affiliated groups now have the capacity and the ambition to recruit and train for attacks that may not be on the scale of a 9/11, but . . . which could still have, obviously, an extraordinary traumatizing effect on the homeland."[143]

In the early months of the new administration, Obama dispatched senior officials to media roundtables and policy venues around Washington, DC, to emphasize the need to focus on al-Qaeda's safe havens and its growing network of affiliates.[144] Testifying before Congress, Secretary of State Hillary Clinton argued that the "persistent enemy" of al-Qaeda was spreading its "tentacles . . . far and wide."[145] Chairman of the Joint Chiefs of Staff, Admiral Michael Mullen, further noted that al-Qaeda sought to regenerate in numerous safe havens, "not unlike what they had in Afghanistan," specifically citing Yemen, Somalia, North Africa, the Philippines, and Indonesia.[146] The 2010 *National Security Strategy* stated, "Where al-Qa'ida or its terrorist affiliates attempt to establish a safe haven—as they have in Yemen, Somalia, the Maghreb, and the Sahel—we will meet them with growing pressure. We also will strengthen our own network of partners to disable al-Qa'ida's financial, human, and planning networks; disrupt terrorist operations before they mature; and address potential safe-havens before al-Qa'ida and its terrorist affiliates can take root."[147]

This was motivated not just by intelligence on al-Qaeda operatives' movements but also the perceived potential for such activities. During a July 2009 event at the Carnegie Endowment for International Peace in Washington, DC, Shari Villarosa, the deputy coordinator for regional affairs in the State Department's Bureau of Counterterrorism, stated that while her office didn't have any "concrete figures" or "travel data" concerning al-Qaeda fighters moving into Yemen, "our concern is the potential."[148] With the U.S. military conducting a troop surge in Afghanistan, officials in the Obama administration expressed the concern that hitting al-Qaeda hard in Afghanistan would increase the likelihood that the group would shift its operations to safe havens around the world. This underlined the need for a comprehensive and coordinated approach to address both current and potential safe havens. In June 2011, John Brennan, then serving as assistant to the president for homeland security and counterterrorism, outlined an increased focus on al-Qaeda's network of affiliates and its safe havens in his introduction to the administration's *National Strategy for Counterterrorism*. This was a position he had been pushing since the early months of Obama's presidency.[149] He stated,

> ultimately defeating al-Qa'ida also means addressing the serious threat posed by its affiliates and adherents operating outside South Asia. This does not require a "global" war, but it does require a focus on specific regions, including what we might call the periphery—places like Yemen, Somalia, Iraq, and the Maghreb. This is another important distinction that characterizes this strategy. As the al-Qa'ida core has weakened under our unyielding pressure, it has looked increasingly to these other groups and individuals to take up its cause, including its goal of striking the United States.[150]

A key aspect of this strategy was to continue to build up the military capacity of partner states "so they can take the fight to al-Qa'ida in their own countries."[151]

Even though Obama publicly moved away from the rhetoric of the Bush administration, his administration's counterterrorism policies were still premised on an understanding that the United States was at war with al-Qaeda. In many ways, the counterterrorism focus of the Obama administration would be a continuation of the policy shift implemented in Bush's second term. The focus of Obama's persistent criticisms of Bush's counterterrorism policies had been the direct application of U.S. military force in Iraq, a decision pushed during his first term. While Obama shifted the U.S. military's attention back to Afghanistan, he continued to rely on partner states' militaries to target terrorist safe havens in the periphery, as outlined in the 9/11 Commission's report and subsequently pushed by the Bush administration.

Obama made a cornerstone of his administration's counterterrorism strategy working with and through partner states to confront threats within their borders and increased assistance to improve partner states' military capabilities for counterterrorism operations. He viewed this as a means to promote the legitimacy of and ownership over counterterrorism by partner states and create a more sustainable security framework to confront continuing and future security threats. This focus on partnerships also allowed the United States to avoid further U.S. military deployments. In the 2010 *National Security Strategy*, the Obama administration stressed that "when we overuse our military might . . . or act without partners, then our military is overstretched, Americans bear a greater burden, and our leadership around the world is too narrowly identified with military force."[152] As the 2015 *National Security Strategy* would put it, "Specifically, we shifted away from a model of fighting costly, large-scale ground wars in Iraq and Afghanistan in which the United States—particularly our military—bore an enormous burden. Instead, we are now pursuing a more sustainable approach that prioritizes counterterrorism operations, collective action with responsible partners, and increased efforts to prevent the growth of violent extremism and radicalization that drives increased threats."[153] The Obama administration, though, reasserted the U.S. government's right to act directly and unilaterally "if necessary to defend our nation and our interests."[154] However, Obama shifted away from the reliance on public displays of force and put more emphasis on conducting covert operations and drone strikes in the "ungoverned spaces" when it was feared that partner states could not or would not act.

Successive presidents have framed U.S. counterterrorism efforts as preemptive acts of self-defense against imminent and evolving threats from al-Qaeda and its affiliate groups. In his 2002 commencement speech at West Point, Bush stated, "The war on terror will not be won on the defensive. We must take the battle to the enemy, disrupt his plans and confront the worst threats before they emerge. In the world we have entered the only path to safety is the path of action. And this nation will act."[155] In a 2013 speech at the National Defense University in Washington, DC, Obama similarly argued that "under domestic law, and international law, the United States is at war with al-Qaeda, the Taliban, and their associated forces. We are at war with an organization that right now would kill as many Americans as they could if we did not stop them first. So this is a just war—a war waged proportionally, in last resort, and in self-defense."[156] Following its first counterterrorism action, which took place in Yemen, the Trump administration likewise cited the need for self-defense in the face of the al-Qaeda threat.[157]

On August 31, 2021, as the final U.S. troops were withdrawn from Afghanistan, President Joe Biden again stressed the importance of continuing to defend the United States against the terrorist threat that had "metastasized across the world, well beyond Afghanistan. We face threats from al-Shabaab in Somalia; al Qaeda affiliates in Syria and the Arabian Peninsula; and ISIS attempting to create a caliphate in Syria and Iraq, and establishing affiliates across Africa and Asia."[158]

With U.S. focus pivoting to al-Qaeda's affiliates and key partner states increasingly conducting U.S.-backed counterterrorism operations to target this terrorist threat in the periphery, U.S. officials pushed this approach without fully appreciating the historic conflict between center and periphery in many of these states and the resulting ramifications for counterterrorism operations. Following this strategic shift, partner states' militaries quickly became bogged down fighting local groups as domestic terrorist attacks spiked abroad, with U.S. officials continuing to push the necessity of pursuing the terrorist threat emanating from safe havens in the periphery. As former assistant secretary of state for South and Central Asian affairs Richard Boucher argued, "If you look around the world, you see many places where the United States starts out chasing al-Qaeda and then it becomes a domestic problem for the locals."[159]

# 4

## OUR MAN IN ISLAMABAD

Pakistan and the War on Terror

On November 19, 2018, newly elected Pakistani prime minister Imran Khan responded to President Donald Trump's accusations that Pakistan had not done a "damn thing" to support U.S. counterterrorism by tweeting, "No Pakistani was involved in 9/11 but Pak decided to participate in US War on Terror." Imran Khan was clear about the costs of this cooperation. "Pakistan suffered 75,000 casualties in this war & over \$123 bn was lost to economy," he asserted. "Our tribal areas were devastated & millions of ppl uprooted from their homes."[1] Like so many partner states drafted into America's fight against al-Qaeda, Pakistan has experienced considerable turmoil as a result of the war on terror, with the previous two decades leaving an indelible mark on its domestic political landscape and created tensions between the U.S. and Pakistani governments. The many ups and downs of the U.S.-Pakistan relationship, both before and after 2001, have been thoroughly documented and analyzed by former diplomats, journalists, and scholars of South Asia.[2] These accounts all convey a similar sentiment: this was no easy relationship, but it has been a necessary one.

This chapter presents an in-depth case study of U.S-Pakistani relations during the war on terror as an illustrative example of the terrorism trap's causal mechanism. It opens with a "scene setter" providing important historical and ethnographic context for understanding relations between center and periphery in Pakistan dating back to the British Raj. These interactions between the center and periphery under British colonial rule are key to understanding how Pakistan subsequently governed the border region with Afghanistan as officials in the postcolonial state maintained colonial-era institutions and policies within the Tribal Areas. By maintaining this colonial approach, the Pakistani government fostered the political conditions that underlay the subsequent trajectory of events in FATA and the pattern of violence pursued by the Pakistani Taliban after 2001. The case study then demonstrates in detail how U.S. counterterrorism policy shaped Pakistan's domestic security after 2001, shifting the Pakistani government's attention to the country's northwestern periphery.[3] U.S. officials pressed their Pakistani counterparts to deploy their military assets to target al-Qaeda and the Taliban groups operating in this region, leading to a violent backlash against the Pakistani state. As domestic terrorism intensified, U.S. officials continued to press Pakistan to "do more," with the resulting military operations contributing to the dramatic rise in domestic terrorism and further trapping the country in a deadly cycle of violence with the Pakistani Taliban.

## THE FEDERALLY ADMINISTERED TRIBAL AREAS: A SCENE SETTER

It is the nature of the current security environment that little-known places—whose names evoke images of dusty old books recounting the historical exploits of colonial officers in faraway and forgotten frontiers— have become the focus of international politics. Among such regions, Pakistan's mountainous and inaccessible FATA has stood at the forefront— the "ungoverned space" par excellence. The region is known within Pakistan as Illaqa-e-Ghair, an Urdu phrase meaning "Foreign or Unknown Land" with connotations of backwardness and wildness. FATA's association with al-Qaeda and the war on terror has become engrained in the world's consciousness, with Bush calling the region "wilder than the Wild West"[4] and Obama singling it out as "the most dangerous place in the world."[5]

This perspective echoes the security concerns of British colonial authorities a century earlier. During the days of the so-called Great

Game, a geopolitical chess match between the British and Russian Empires among the mountains and steppe of Central Asia in the nineteenth and early twentieth centuries, British India's frontier policy focused on stymieing Russian influence among those tribes residing beyond government control astride the newly demarcated border with Afghanistan known as the Durand Line. The arch-Russophobe Lord George Curzon, installed as the viceroy of British India in 1899, viewed St. Petersburg's machinations in the broader region with trepidation. With the tsar's ultimate ambition to dominate Asia, he was fearful that the increasing rebelliousness of the Pashtun tribes and unrest on the frontier would be exploited by the Russians to sow political discord within India and threaten Britain's hold over its colony—the "jewel in the crown" of the vast British Empire. Curzon warned in a 1904 speech at Guildhall, London (given one year before departing his position as Viceroy) that with "a land frontier 5,700 miles in length, peopled by hundreds of different tribes . . . a single outbreak at a single point may set entire sections of that frontier ablaze. Then, beyond it . . . are the muffled figure of great European powers, advancing nearer and nearer, and sometimes finding in these conditions temptations to action that is not in strict accordance with the interests which we are bound to defend."[6] The central question that Curzon faced was how to protect British interests in what was seen at the time as a lawless and violent land that offered little economic return.[7]

The Pashtun tribes ensconced in the towering and inhospitable peaks of the Hindu Kush had long lived outside of the political control of the great South Asian empires and governed themselves according to local customs. As a means of regulating behavior outside of state institutions, the people historically lived according to the Pashtun code of honor, or *Pashtunwali* (the way of the Pashtun), as the organizing principle of social interactions, with its idealized demands for courage (*tora*), revenge (*badal*), hospitality (*melmastia*), equality (*barabari*), providing sanctuary to fugitives (*nanawatai*), and the protection of honor (*nang*).[8] Whenever an individual conducted a criminal act or transgressed against another's honor, he did so knowing the compulsion for the victim or the victim's clan to take revenge against the aggressor or their clan. With such a process potentially sparking lengthy and violent reprisals, it provided incentives to keep behavior in check through intervention by *maliks* (elders) and ongoing negotiation within the *jirga* (council of elders), which could be an "arduous process" requiring "quick wits and physical stamina."[9]

Despite the ideals of *Pashtunwali* in maintaining law and order, the region was plagued by long-standing blood feuds between rival clans. Often, local violence could spill into adjacent areas, especially as tribes raided into neighboring communities as demonstrations of honor, to resist outside influence, or simply as a means of procuring meager resources.[10] In the 1890s, Winston Churchill, the future British prime minister, observed in one of his dispatches as a young press correspondent attached to the Malakand Field Force, "Tribe wars with tribe. The people of one valley fight with those of the next. To the quarrels of communities are added the combats of individuals. Khan assails khan, each supported by his retainers. Every tribesman has a blood feud with his neighbor. Every man's hand is against the other, and all against the stranger."[11]

Within the Tribal Areas, Curzon was aware of the limitations of a purely military approach that had been the cornerstone of the colonial government's frontier policy throughout the nineteenth century, limitations that stemmed from similar challenges that the Pakistani army would face in the region over a century later. The tribes of this far-flung but strategically important border region fiercely protected their independence from any external intervention, with tribesmen exploiting the rough terrain, absence of local administrative structures, and the porous international border to evade the reach of authorities; anthropologist Kalyanakrishnan Sivaramakrishnan described these "zones of anomaly" as "blank spots in the cultivated vistas of British sovereignty."[12] Even before Curzon's arrival to the subcontinent in the late 1890s, there was a growing recognition in Calcutta (the capital of British colonial rule at the time) that the army's presence contributed to unrest on the frontier as local tribesmen saw the garrisons' encroachment into their territory as a provocation stoking violent resistance, such as the 1897 Frontier Revolt during which the British lost control of the strategically vital Khyber Pass. The quelling of this revolt required the largest military operation in India since the 1857 rebellion against British rule.[13] In recognition of the Pashtun tribesmen historically protecting their independence and resisting any external interventions into their territory, a

Pashtun army officer in Pakistan imparted the following proverb with a hearty laugh: "You cannot take a Pashtun by force to heaven but you can take him willingly to hell."[14]

In 1898, Calcutta issued new orders to local military units aimed at minimizing the negative impact of their presence. "No new responsibility should be undertaken on the frontier," the viceroy ordered, "which was not rendered obligatory by actual strategical requirements; that unnecessary interference with the tribes should be avoided; and that concentration of the troops should be effected."[15] The India Office in London concurred that a change in British frontier policy was needed, writing shortly after the revolt that it had "always been an axiom that the goodwill of the tribesmen affords the best guarantee for the success of a frontier policy—the friendly attitude of the frontier tribes would be of much greater moment than the absolute safety of any single pass, however important."[16]

Understanding the need for a new approach to contain the tribes, minimize disruptions throughout the frontier, and assert British control, Curzon replaced the Indian Army with "a policy of employing the tribes themselves as far as possible to protect our military interests."[17] In 1901, the British government created the North-West Frontier Province (NWFP) out of the old Punjab Province and introduced a new administrative framework for the Tribal Areas—the Frontier Crimes Regulation (FCR)—which superseded earlier, less comprehensive laws; the Pakistani government retained this law following independence in 1947.[18] Curzon argued that the new policy, built on existing tribal customs and emblematic of the administrative approach to indirect rule, was intended to "promote a spirit of local harmony and co-operation by the enlistment, in the service of the British Government, but in the defence of their own country, of the wild but not intractable inhabitants of these regions."[19] With the FCR, the British recognized the political authority of local maliks and provided them "allowances for keeping open the roads and passes, such as the Khyber and Kohat Passes and the Chitral Road, for the maintenance of peace and tranquility, and for the punishment of crime."[20] These formally recognized maliks—whose authority was now dependent on British recognition—also served in jirgas as a kind of jury system to decide matters of law and order and, in this role, were responsible to "no one except to their own consciences and to the officer who receives their verdict."[21] Under the law, local tribesmen were also subjected to collective punishment and denied access to the regular judicial system, with the maliks' decisions often swift and decisive.

Historian Benjamin Hopkins argues that the FCR treated the Pashtun tribesmen of the northwestern frontier as imperial objects and targets of imperial control rather than participatory colonial subjects with access to political or civil rights. "They were subject to the law," Hopkins writes, "not subjects of the law."[22] Under the shadow of Russian movements in Central Asia and ongoing hostilities with Afghanistan, the FCR's sole aim was to isolate the region and maintain law and order with minimum administrative and government presence, essentially blocking the region's inhabitants from the broader colonial sphere in the subcontinent. In 1893, British officials had similarly intended for the settlement of the Durand Line dividing British India and Afghanistan to define a frontier in which the British imperial machine could contain the Pashtun tribes and assert political influence over them. This served British interests by creating a buffer zone against Russian encroachment absent the high costs of establishing direct control.[23] Therefore, the Tribal Areas' status as "ungoverned spaces" was essentially by design.

Under the FCR, the local representative of British, and later Pakistani, authority was the political agent (PA), a position originally established with the creation of the tribal agencies in the late 1890s along the Durand Line. To protect British interests under the FCR, the PA worked through local tribal structures. It was famously said that British authority only extended to a hundred yards on either side of the agency's main road, beyond which lay the land of *riwaj* (tribal custom). The PA's authority was ultimately based on his personal reputation and influence among the tribes and his ability to negotiate with them. In pursuit of criminals within his agency, for instance, the PA—the proverbial "man on the spot"—would, ideally, use his intimate knowledge of tribal customs and local personalities to apply pressure to the maliks to hand over the wanted men. The maliks, in turn, used their own standing within the tribe, lengthy negotiations, and appeals to honor to convince wanted men to surrender.

Yet, this approach to tribal administration frequently failed to prevent the outbreak of violence. Military historian Christian Tripodi argued, "Such shortcomings are better explained by acknowledging a far more influential factor, namely the fact that for all their clever designs and often elevated intentions, this political cadre were caught in the midst of an elemental competition between tribe and government—between independence and control—that dominated the narrative at play."[24] Even with negotiation being the ideal method of handling problems on the frontier, the PA at times resorted to force in the face of widespread unrest or violent opposition to the central government. In April 1902, Curzon warned a *durbar* (tribal court) of over three thousand tribal leaders in Peshawar,

> We have no wish to seize your territory or interfere with your independence. If you go on worrying and raiding and attacking, there comes a time when we say, This thing must be put an end to: and if the tribes will not help us do it, then we must do it ourselves. The matter is thus almost entirely in your own hands. You are the keepers of your own house. We are ready enough to leave you in possession. But if you dart out from behind the shelter of your door to harass and pillage and slay, then you must not be surprised if we return quickly and batter the door in.[25]

The PA possessed the authority to deploy the Frontier Corps, a paramilitary organization under the command of civil authorities and recruited from among the local Pashtun population, or pressure maliks to form local tribal militias, known as *lashkars*. Yet, PAs recognized that these local forces' interests as tribesmen often conflicted with the interests of the government, and they could be wary of acting decisively, especially if it led to the deaths of fellow Pashtun, which could spark blood feuds.[26] While the government reserved the right to deploy regular military forces if British officials felt circumstances dictated it, which did occur, they hesitated to do so and preferred to rely on local militias when possible to avoid a violent backlash.

Curzon hoped the creation of a tribal militia system would diminish the need for outside intervention when the use of force was deemed necessary, a policy supported by political officers operating on the frontier. In 1923, the General Staff in British India stressed the importance of using irregular militias, even with their general ineffectiveness as a fighting force, and avoiding regular military deployments if possible. "Irregulars are under the political authorities and as such their action is quite

distinct from military action," a General Staff note read. "This undoubt-
edly is understood by the tribesmen who accept, with comparative equa-
nimity, action by [the Frontier Corps] or other political bodies which
they would oppose more strenuously if attempted by an equal number of
regulars. . . . This reserve power, unnecessarily used or unnecessarily
displayed, acts as an irritant."[27] The following year, the Army Department recognized that military deployments into the Tribal Areas were
viewed by the local population as "a fresh invasion of tribal territory,
and, as such, will tend to consolidate the tribes in opposition against us."[28]
Moreover, the military often found it difficult to operate against the tribesmen's guerrilla tactics in the mountainous terrain. A British Army officer
who served during the Waziristan campaign of the late 1930s, which
involved the deployment of sixty-one thousand troops to respond to
rebellious tribes in the region, observed,

> The core of our problem in the army was to force battle on an elusive
> and mobile enemy. The enemy, while he retained any common sense,
> tried to avoid battle and instead fight us with pinpricking hit-and-run
> tactics. We had light automatic guns, howitzers, armoured cars, tanks,
> and aircraft. The Pathan [Pashtuns] had none of these things, yet when
> he tried to even up the disparity, and cumbered himself with stolen
> automatics or home-made artillery, he suffered heavily, because they
> constituted impediments, things that were difficult to move but were
> worth defending. And when he stayed and defended something, whether
> a gun or a village, we trapped and pulverized him. When he flitted and
> sniped, rushed and ran away, we felt as if we were using a crowbar to
> swat wasps.[29]

The PA was likewise reluctant to rely on force, even by the Frontier
Corps, as this was an admission of his lack of political acumen and ineffectiveness as a tribal administrator. This could harm his reputation
among the tribes and create future security challenges as it invited others to challenge his, and the government's, authority. If the military acted
against the tribes, according to former Pakistani PA Akbar Ahmed, who
consistently pushed back against the use of force during his postings,
"I've failed," and the introduction of the army brings "an unstable

element into the political arena of the agency."[30] With the application of force often provoking a string of retaliatory attacks from the tribes, the threat of force often was more effective than its actual use. The Mehsud of South Waziristan have a saying: "The Political Agent should brandish his sword but not use it."[31]

## CONTESTING POLITICAL AUTHORITY IN PAKISTAN'S FATA

Following Partition in 1947, Pakistan's founding father, Muhammad Ali Jinnah, reversed the British policy of forward defense. He withdrew the remaining military garrisons from the border region as a needless provocation and based Pakistani policy on the principles of frontier governance, which entrusted the tribes with dealing with cross-border challenges. Meeting with a grand tribal jirga in Peshawar, Jinnah told them, "Keeping in view your loyalty, help, assurances and declarations we ordered, as you know, the withdrawal of troops from Waziristan as a concrete and definite gesture on our part—that we treat you with absolute confidence and trust you as our Muslim brethren. . . . Pakistan has no desire to unduly interfere with your internal freedom."[32] He continued, "You expressed your desire that the benefit, such as your allowances and khassadari [militia stipend], that you have had in the past and are receiving, should continue. Neither my government nor I have any desire to modify the existing arrangement except in consultation with you so long as you remain loyal and faithful to Pakistan."[33]

The Pakistani government maintained the prevailing status quo under the FCR, including the position of the PA, and redesignated the tribal agencies as the Federally Administered Tribal Areas, or FATA, with direct administrative authority vested with the president of Pakistan.[34] Pakistani officials were wary of upsetting the precarious political balance within the region given its difficult relationship with Afghanistan due to disputes over the international border. Afghanistan refused to recognize the validity of the Durand Line following the withdrawal of British rule and subsequently laid claim to the Pashtun-populated regions of northwestern Pakistan. Pakistani authorities worried that the

Afghan government could use post-Partition instability to sow discord in the region and lay the seeds for a united "Pashtunistan."[35]

Given these concerns, the Pakistani government's focus was similarly to maintain law and order, and it used the FCR as a vehicle to suppress lawlessness and antigovernment activities in the border region. The structure of the FCR, which kept FATA under the partial control of the Pakistani government, as had been the case under British colonial rule, sustained a forced stagnation in the periphery. FATA remained outside of the country's broader political and economic evolution, resulting in chronic underdevelopment. This brought about a mass migration out of the region as tribesmen sought work elsewhere, particularly to the Persian Gulf region amid the oil boom of the 1970s. The FCR also denied FATA residents their basic constitutional rights, with universal suffrage only extended to FATA in 1996, though political parties were banned from campaigning in the region until 2013. Prior to this, government-recognized maliks were the only FATA residents allowed to vote. Contemporary civil and human rights organizations in Pakistan strongly critiqued the legal restrictions and discrimination of FATA residents under the FCR, which was repealed in May 2018, when FATA was merged into the neighboring Khyber Pakhtunkhwa Province (NWFP was henceforth renamed Khyber Pakhtunkhwa in April 2010) and the seven tribal agencies constituting FATA were redesignated as tribal districts.

The institutionalization of the maliks' authority under the FCR sharpened social and political inequalities and engendered intra-tribal conflict within this self-consciously egalitarian society. With their authority connected to external state power and the perpetuation of the *maliki* system, the maliks faced opposition from the disenfranchised *kashar* (youth), consisting of the tribe's youth, poor, and junior or powerless lineages, who saw little benefit from the British-instituted governing structures in FATA. Throughout the twentieth century, the kashar—or "political have-nots" according to one anthropologist—consistently expressed dissatisfaction with the political status quo under the FCR, which denied them a wide range of political rights and economic opportunities.[36] Members of the kashar class accused the appointed maliks of incompetence, corruption, and acting in their own interests rather than the interests of the broader community. A British political officer who served in Waziristan remarked,

> Of course, they prefer independence if they see that there is little or no benefit coming to them from "control".... We must remember that they are not willing that the pecuniary benefits should go only to the few, which is so often if not invariably the case when "control" is inadequate. They are certainly sturdier in their pleas for independence if they think we are not carrying out our side of the bargain. The young men are certainly hostile, if they see, as they often do see, that, owing to our refusal to extend "control," the benefits are not fairly distributed.[37]

In particular, the maliks' authority often was challenged by local religious leaders known as mullahs, who jockeyed for their own power and influence. Emerging from the kashar, mullahs were disadvantaged by the FCR's administrative structures as they had no position within the jirga, were customarily subordinate to maliks as they did not appear on the local genealogical charter, and were financially dependent on the maliks, who were dismissive of the mullahs playing any role in tribal politics and often treated them with contempt. Political dynamics within the Tribal Areas were frequently defined by a balancing act between three "broad but distinct categories of leadership" within Pashtun society in these areas—the political agent, the maliks, and the mullahs—according to a leadership model developed by anthropologist Akbar Ahmed and known as the Waziristan model, which emerged from the colonial encounter but persisted after Pakistani independence as the central government maintained colonial-era institutions and policies in the periphery. Within the framework of the Waziristan model, Ahmed wrote, "Personnel from the three categories of leadership vie for power, status, and legitimacy in society."[38]

To bolster their own standing, mullahs attacked the maliks and the maliki system using religiously charged rhetoric, and they often accused the maliks of being "government toadies" who sold out their tribe and religion, with their hostility having the potential to spark violence.[39] In 1977, for instance, the PA in South Waziristan Agency warned of attempts by Mullah Noor Muhammad in Wana, the agency's headquarters, to undermine the maliks' authority. "His first target was the institution of Maliki," the PA wrote. "He started condemning the Maliks openly and at times when he abused them on the pulpit. The idea was to weaken the institutional arrangements so that he could bulldoze his way by shattering all the norms and forms of administration."[40] Mullahs, frequently using the language of jihad to unite traditional rivals against outside forces, at times found themselves at the head of rebellions against government authorities within the Tribal Areas; this was most famously the case with Mullah Powindah at the turn of the twentieth century (dubbed a "first-class scoundrel" by Lord Curzon) and the Faqir of Ipi during the 1930s and 1940s. Maliks often pressed the government to allow them to handle any unrest stirred up by the mullahs in order to avoid the deployment of military forces, which only served as a further provocation to the mullahs' followers and ultimately weakened the maliks' standing.[41]

Beginning with the Soviet invasion of Afghanistan in 1979, mullahs became ascendant in tribal politics as the international backers of the mujahedeen fostered a religious framing for Afghan resistance to the Soviets. As a result, Pakistan's ISI, working with the CIA, relied on, and expanded, FATA's madrassa network and used its *taliban* (students), largely drawn from the kashar class, as recruits to fight the Soviet forces in Afghanistan. Pakistani and American intelligence agencies provided the mullahs and their supporting forces with training, funding, and weapons. The mullahs now had the money, the guns, and the external support to usurp the maliks' authority and replace them as powerbrokers in the region. Following the Soviet withdrawal, the Afghan Taliban, following its emergence in southern Afghanistan in 1994, continued to rely upon these networks for recruiting fighters during the Afghan Civil War. This maintained the relationship between the Afghan Taliban and their network of fighters and supporters within FATA despite objections by the now weakened maliks. These links were encouraged by the Pakistani government, who supported the Afghan Taliban government after it took Kabul in 1996 to promote strategic depth in Afghanistan against India.[42] During the 1990s, however, the region quickly dimmed in importance for the United States and many other governments, and it remained largely a forgotten remnant of Cold War politics and rivalries until the 9/11 attacks and the United

States' invasion of Afghanistan brought the world's attention once again to this mountainous and isolated border region.

## OUR MAN IN ISLAMABAD: THE FIRST STEP

The war on terror is merely the latest phase of a long and often fitful bilateral relationship between the United States and Pakistan. U.S. interactions with Pakistan historically have been framed by broad international security paradigms—namely, the Cold War and the war on terror. The strength of this relationship rose and fell according to the saliency of U.S. security interests in South Asia. With the Soviet withdrawal from Afghanistan, the U.S. relationship with Pakistan was effectively put on hold, with the broader South Asian region falling victim to post–Cold War neglect as the U.S. government shifted its focus to former Warsaw Pact nations.[43] Abida Hussein, who served as Pakistan's ambassador to the United States in the early 1990s, stated that at this time the U.S. government "had about as much interest in Pakistan as Pakistan had in the Maldives."[44] No longer concerned with maintaining an effective working relationship with Pakistan, the U.S. government suspended foreign assistance in 1990 due to Pakistan's continued pursuit of nuclear weapons. Pakistan's first nuclear weapons test, held in May 1998 in response to an Indian test, was considered a "major sin" among U.S. leadership and resulted in the imposition of even tougher sanctions.[45] These sanctions "cut very deep" and bred further distrust of the United States among the Pakistani elite.[46]

After al-Qaeda's 1998 U.S. embassy bombings in Kenya and Tanzania, U.S. officials understood the importance of engaging with Pakistani authorities given their support of the Taliban in Afghanistan, where bin Laden and his organization were based.[47] Due to existing sanctions, the State Department recognized that the U.S. government needed "to understand the limits of its own influence in Pakistan and calibrate its policies accordingly."[48] In order to normalize relations with Pakistan, the Bush administration had already decided in its first year to begin working toward lifting the sanctions, even if it remained suspicious of

Pakistani support for the Taliban as well as various militant groups operating in Kashmir.[49] However, prior to September 11, 2001, Pakistan and the broader South Asian region were simply not a priority for senior leadership within the new administration.[50]

The U.S.-Pakistan relationship immediately shifted with the 9/11 attacks as national security interests overshadowed all other policy priorities. With the U.S. military invasion of Afghanistan, Pakistan's strategic importance loomed large, especially with U.S. and Coalition forces relying on Pakistan's land routes to resupply its troops, a fact that U.S. officials understood well from the 1980s.[51] Sanctions were quickly lifted to assist in gaining Pakistani cooperation, drastically accelerating a process that had already begun earlier in the year. Pakistan quickly changed from a pariah state to a "darling" of U.S. senior leaders, with Bush eventually describing his relationship with Pakistani president Pervez Musharraf as tight.[52] "With Pakistan before 9/11," according to scholar of South Asia and former State Department official Marvin Weinbaum, "counterterrorism didn't ring any bells. If we go back before 9/11 and say what has been the change in terms of American domestic demands on Pakistan, well we go from zero to ten because there was no real relationship beyond the normal diplomatic ties with Pakistan prior to 9/11. They were off the radar for us, and then we just dump it on them."[53]

U.S. official's immediate mission in the days after the al-Qaeda attacks was to gain without delay the full cooperation of the Pakistani government for any actions in Afghanistan against al-Qaeda and the Taliban and for broader U.S. counterterrorism efforts in the region. The White House understood the path toward this cooperation lay with President Musharraf, the army chief of staff who had taken power in a 1999 military coup. Despite drawing the public ire of Washington, DC, and a fresh round of sanctions following the coup, U.S. diplomats in Islamabad argued that with Musharraf, "someone was finally in charge in Islamabad," and that he would be a more effective executive than the civilian government under Prime Minister Nawaz Sharif.[54] Understanding Musharraf and his supporting generals' tight political control, U.S. officials pushed for total cooperation without conditions, with the early meetings and messages between U.S. and Pakistani officials setting both the tone and the priorities for future cooperation.

On September 12, 2001, Deputy Secretary of State Richard Armitage, a physically imposing former naval officer known for his direct speech, met with the director general of Pakistan's ISI, General Mahmud Ahmed, at the State Department; the Pakistani intelligence chief just happened to be in Washington at the time. During their tense meeting, Armitage told General Ahmed that the U.S. government strongly suspected that bin Laden and al-Qaeda, operating out of Afghanistan, were responsible for the attacks the previous day, and he would soon be providing a list of demands from the U.S. government to be shared with Musharraf. Armitage stressed "in no uncertain terms" that the country General Ahmed had arrived in on September 10 no longer existed. Armitage bluntly stated, "You have to get on board. We will be coming at you to get cooperation."[55] He added, without diplomatic nuance, "Pakistan faces a stark choice; either it is with us or it is not; this was a black-and-white choice, with no grey."[56] When General Ahmed began to waver, Armitage stopped the meeting and pulled him into a smaller room adjacent to the deputy secretary's conference room for a one-on-one chat. Armitage showed him his Sitara-e-Pakistan (Star of Pakistan), one of the highest civilian honors the Pakistani government awards to individuals for service to the country. Armitage had received it for his efforts during the 1980s for his support of anti-Soviet efforts in Afghanistan. He held up the award and told General Ahmed, "Do you see this? No American will ever accept this again if we don't get full cooperation. I'm going to give you a list of items and this is not a pick one. This is not a menu. You have to do all of these."[57]

Despite complaining about America's past "betrayals," Musharraf already was anticipating the coming U.S. invasion of Afghanistan and its potential to reshape the political order in South Asia. Fearful of India's ability to manipulate the developing situation in its favor, especially regarding the disputed territory of Kashmir, he saw the need to cooperate with the United States to manage the coming conflict to Pakistan's advantage, cooperation that would have the added advantage of restarting the flow of U.S. dollars into Pakistan's struggling economy. Musharraf told his close advisors, "We should offer up help and mark my words, we will receive a clean bill of health."[58] In a September 12 meeting between Musharraf and senior military and civilian leaders, according to the former foreign minister Abdul Sattar, who attended the meeting, "We agreed that we would unequivocally accept all U.S. demands, but then later we would express our private reservations to the U.S. and we would not necessarily agree with all the details."[59] The following day, the newly appointed U.S. ambassador to Pakistan, Wendy Chamberlin, held a forty-minute meeting with Musharraf in which she further pressed for his cooperation, explaining that there was "no inclination" in Washington for negotiation or dialogue with the Taliban.[60] Amid much prevarication and complaints, Musharraf assured an insistent Chamberlin, "I am with you and not against you."[61] In a follow-up telephone conversation with Bush, Musharraf repeated to the U.S. president, "The stakes are high. We are with you."[62]

On the same day as Chamberlin's meeting with Musharraf, Armitage again met with Ahmed and reiterated "the need for extraordinary action in this perilous time and the importance of Pakistan's stepping up to U.S. requests in the fight against terrorism."[63] During the meeting, he handed Ahmed a nonpaper (an informal diplomatic discussion paper) to be shared with Musharraf outlining seven action points that the U.S. government would expect of Pakistan. Hoping to avoid the delays involved in drafting and sending these demands for review through standard bureaucratic channels, Armitage and Powell wrote the points themselves without consulting anyone else in the administration. They had both served in combat, had long-standing relationships within the Pakistani government, and therefore "knew what we felt was right."[64] These points included the following:

- Stop al Qaida operatives at your border, intercept arms shipments through Pakistan and end all logistical support for Bin Ladin;
- Provide the U.S. with blanket overflight and landing rights to conduct all necessary military and intelligence operations;
- Provide as needed territorial access to U.S. and allied military intelligence, and other personnel to conduct all necessary operations against the perpetrators of terrorism or those that harbor them, including use of Pakistan's naval ports, airbases and strategic locations on borders;
- Provide the U.S. immediately with intelligence [redacted];
- Continue to publicly condemn the terrorist acts of September 11 and any other terrorist acts against the U.S. or its friends and allies;

- Cut off all shipments of fuel to the Taliban and any other items and recruits, including volunteers en route to Afghanistan, that can be used in a military offensive capacity or to abet the terrorist threat;
- Should the evidence strongly implicate Usama Bin-Ladin and the al Qaida network in Afghanistan and the Taliban continue to harbor him and this network, Pakistan will break diplomatic relations with the Taliban government, end support for the Taliban and assist U.S. in the aforementioned ways to destroy Usama Bin-Ladin and his al Qaida network.[65]

Armitage told Ahmed that "the noose was tightening around Bin Ladin's and al Qaida's neck . . . [and that] this involves not only Afghanistan, but would encompass terrorist groups elsewhere."[66] Following this meeting, so as to further cement the importance of cooperation, Powell called Musharraf and stressed that "terrorist attacks had to be dealt with directly by going after the organization responsible." He added, "As one general to another, we need someone on our flank fighting with us. And speaking candidly, the American people would not understand if Pakistan was not in this fight with the U.S."[67]

In a September 14 meeting with Chamberlin in Rawalpindi, which lasted an hour and half, Musharraf accepted all seven points "without conditions."[68] He also withdrew ISI personnel from Afghanistan as a clear signal that Pakistan was withdrawing its official support of the Taliban and made key personnel changes among senior military officers, including removing General Ahmed as head of the ISI, as a means of bolstering support for cooperation with U.S. counterterrorism efforts.[69] Five days later, Musharraf made a televised speech announcing Pakistan's intended cooperation with the United States in the war on terror. In a November 2001 memorandum to Bush in preparation for his upcoming meeting with Musharraf at the United Nations, Powell, who had visited Pakistan the previous month, wrote, "President Musharraf's decision to fully cooperate with the United States in the wake of September 11, at considerable political risk, abruptly turned our stalled relationship around. . . . Musharraf has abandoned the Taliban, frozen terrorist assets. . . . These moves open up bold new possibilities in our relationship."[70]

Officials at the highest levels of the U.S. government now publicly embraced their man in Islamabad, seeing Musharraf as the key to gaining and maintaining Pakistan's cooperation given his wide-ranging political and military authority and his ability, thanks to his popularity at the time, to generate Pakistani public support for the war on terror.[71] In place of what was perceived as chaotic and corrupt civilian leadership, some U.S. officials felt that Musharraf was "a person with whom we could do business."[72] During a February 13, 2002, press conference at the White House, Bush announced that "President Musharraf is a leader with great courage and vision, and his nation is a key partner in the global coalition against terror. . . . I am proud to call him my friend."[73] Armitage, who served as the point person for relations with Pakistan in the early years of the war on terror, said in a 2006 interview, "I have been from the beginning a big fan of President Musharraf, notwithstanding the extra-legal way in which he assumed power. I think he's genuine in trying to improve the lives of the people of Pakistan. . . . There's never been a taint of corruption to him."[74] There were also lingering fears among senior officials of the chaos that might result if Musharraf fell from power, and this further underlined the need to support his position.[75]

As U.S. funds increasingly flowed into Pakistani coffers, Musharraf began to move against extremist groups within Pakistan in line with U.S. demands. This included pursuing a crackdown on key militant groups with suspected links to al-Qaeda; the banning of Lashkar-e-Taiba and Jaish-e-Mohammad for their affiliations with al-Qaeda; and the carrying out of several high-level arrests.[76] In late November 2001, the CIA warned that bin Laden and al-Qaeda had developed "close ties to several Pakistani militant groups, particularly those with connections to the Taliban," and were assisting these groups in planning attacks against U.S. diplomatic and commercial facilities and U.S. citizens in Pakistan.[77] Musharraf also promised U.S. officials that Pakistan would turn over any Arabs captured at the Afghan border for joint interrogation.[78] By 2003, the White House reported in its *Progress Report on the Global War on Terrorism* that Pakistan had taken into custody "more than 500 extremists, including al-Qaida and Taliban members. These include senior al-Qaida operational leader Khalid Shaykh Muhammad, 9/11 conspirator Ramzi bin al Shibh, and USS *Cole* plotter Khallad Ba'Attash."[79]

However, in late 2003, the State Department reported that many individuals arrested as part of this crackdown were later quietly released.[80] At the time, DIA director Vice Admiral L. E. Jacoby began to question

Musharraf's resolve in targeting extremist groups, recognizing that he "probably fears that jihadis will turn on his government; they are angered at his support for the United States and have attempted to kill him several times. . . . Under pressure, he is prone to sacrifice long-term objectives for short-term advantage." He argued that "Pakistan must sustain and broaden its crackdown on extremist groups," as he told Secretary Rumsfeld. "These groups pose the greatest threat of sparking conflict and directly threaten U.S. forces in Afghanistan. Musharraf will be cognizant of the threat they pose to his government and his life."[81] Two months prior to this, Brigadier General Doug Stone, then the U.S. defense representative in Pakistan, stated in his interview with the 9/11 Commission that within Pakistan, "Al-Qaida and other extremists are a cancer metastasizing all over this country. By not addressing this, we are effectively spraygunning them into new areas. They are breeding faster than we can take them down."[82] Nevertheless, the U.S. intelligence community remained optimistic in the long run, with a DIA report stating that "removing highly-visible leaders, prohibiting widespread public fundraising, and restricting the flow of new recruits will eventually reap large dividends." Yet, there was also a worry that these efforts would have a limited, short-term impact on terrorist threats against the United States emanating from Pakistan.[83]

Moreover, early counterterrorism successes, such as the arrests of key al-Qaeda figures, were concentrated in Pakistan's urban areas. With the Afghan Taliban regrouping and launching an insurgency against U.S. and Coalition forces in 2003 as the U.S. government and international community sought to rebuild Afghanistan's security forces and governing institutions, there was a growing awareness among U.S. officials that FATA was being used as a safe haven for both al-Qaeda and Taliban fighters outside the reach of military forces in Afghanistan. General Stanley McChrystal, who first arrived in Afghanistan in May 2002, stated at the time that "We were already heavily focused on the idea that almost all of the leads on al Qaeda were focused into Pakistan."[84] Marin Strmecki, a civilian advisor to the secretary of defense, also observed that in late 2002 and early 2003, security incidents in Afghanistan began to go up due to operations launched "out of the safe havens" in Pakistan. This was an issue that Afghan president Hamid Karzai and other senior Afghan leaders were "constantly" bringing up in meetings with their

U.S. counterparts beginning in early 2002, but it was initially met with "unsympathetic ears because of the belief that Pakistan was helping us so much on al-Qaeda."[85] Richard Armitage further recalled that there was a "steady stream of reporting" from the U.S. consulate in Peshawar that the border area was ripe with "jihadists" and "troublemakers." However, he noted that the reporting was often unclear about "who came from Afghanistan and who were homegrown Pakistani."[86] There were varying accounts of the number of Arabs, Uzbeks, Chechens, and other foreign fighters in FATA, ranging from a few hundred to almost two thousand—and all with potential links to al-Qaeda.

Not willing to take any chances, the CIA began to monitor the cell phones of any suspected foreign fighters in Pakistan, a number that grew exponentially.[87] CIA officers pressured Pakistani officials to arrest anyone they considered to be working with al-Qaeda and turn them over for interrogation. Given conditions within FATA, however, Pakistani authorities' ability to reach into the tribal agencies and apprehend fighters taking shelter among the local population was limited. As a result, this periphery remained essentially untouched by Musharraf's early crackdowns. With U.S. counterterrorism shifting to targeting terrorist safe havens in the periphery, U.S. officials grew increasingly concerned that Pakistan had not taken appropriate action to challenge the al-Qaeda threat within FATA. With limitations on the U.S. ability to pursue leads across the Durand Line into FATA, the unambiguous message delivered to the Pakistani government was to "get control" of its periphery. To ensure Pakistan's cooperation on this front, Rumsfeld communicated the need for increased U.S. support, "a chunk of money" in the defense secretary's words, "if we are going to get the Paks [Rumsfeld's term] to really fight the war on terror where it is, which is in their country."[88]

Musharraf at first resisted this pressure, glossing over FATA in meetings with U.S. officials and quickly moving on to the next subject. Armitage recalled, "I can remember a conversation with Musharraf about stopping the border. He responded it's not possible. He said there are thousands of years that people have been moving back and forth. He wasn't wrong."[89] Pakistani officials expected a low probability of success for any military efforts in FATA, and that the inevitably difficult counterterrorism operations would divert Pakistan's limited resources from its perceived primary threat from India. Former CIA director Michael

Hayden observed that "when al-Qaeda settled in the distant tribal regions, the Pakistanis were less interested and, frankly, far less capable of helping us." Aware of the "threat of violent blowback" to any government action in the northwestern periphery, Hayden recalled that Pakistani officials "always made it clear that if bin Laden or Zawahiri were ever located, for example, the potential blowback might prohibit a Pakistani response."[90] While there was hope that Pakistan would send its military into FATA and "more or less clean up," Armitage reflected, "I don't think any of us expected 100% cooperation from the Pakistanis. We would, by cajoling, threatening, pointing out certain anomalies, sometimes get them to move on things, but you had to have real follow through if you made a threat, and this was a problem."[91] Stone similarly stated, "The army is the least corrupt, most honorable institution in Pakistan. They can help us but we have to exert maximum pressure on Musharraf to get him to give the order."[92]

## LIGHTING THE POWDER KEG: THE PAKISTANI MILITARY ENTERS THE SCENE

U.S. officials were increasingly concerned with Pakistan's limited ability to challenge al-Qaeda-linked terrorist groups operating within FATA, especially with the worsening Taliban insurgency in Afghanistan. Therefore, there was growing pressure on Musharraf and other senior Pakistani leaders to directly confront militant groups operating within FATA and to use the country's military to act as a blocking force against cross-border movements. As early as September 15, 2001, at a meeting with Chamberlin, Musharraf argued that relying solely on the ill-equipped Frontier Corps and other tribal militias to seal the international border or target al-Qaeda or al-Qaeda-linked terrorists moving through the region would be insufficient for the task.[93] Pakistani officials feared that the Pashtun tribesmen comprising the local paramilitary force might be unwilling to act strongly against the Taliban due to fear of revenge killings, pro-Taliban sentiments, or the financial benefits of hosting foreign fighters.[94] U.S. troops in Afghanistan reported observing Frontier Corps posts allowing groups of Taliban fighters to cross the international border without interference. Zalmay Khalilzad, the U.S. ambassador to

Afghanistan from 2003 to 2005, saw the presence of the Taliban in FATA as evidence of Musharraf and the ISI's duplicity and sought to increase pressure on the Pakistani government to challenge the Taliban presence.[95] General David Barno, the Coalition commander in Afghanistan, argued that the Pakistanis were not necessarily acting duplicitously but "basically tolerated the Taliban in the tribal areas" as their "ability to control these areas was negligible."[96] From the other side of the Durand Line, the U.S. ambassador to Pakistan, Ryan Crocker, similarly argued that the presence of the Taliban in FATA was "not simply Machiavellian deviousness" on the part of Pakistani authorities but stemmed from an absence of effective government control. Crocker recounted Musharraf saying, "How many enemies do you want me to take on before those enemies outweigh me?"[97]

As the terrorist threat increasingly shifted to Pakistan's northwestern periphery, the unreliability of the FATA militia system and its inability to act quickly and decisively against threats within the border region highlighted the need to rely on the regular Pakistani army for counterterrorism operations in order "to just squash [the militants]," according to one Pakistani army officer.[98] Pakistan used the U.S. invasion of Afghanistan and the potential for U.S. military incursions into FATA as an opportunity to deploy the regular military into the region for the first time since the government withdrew the military garrisons in 1947—barring a brief and limited deployment into Bajaur Agency in 1961 to counter the infiltration of Afghan troops, to which local tribesmen "violently objected."[99] Army officials now told Pashtun leaders, "You have a choice. Either we guard our borders and check foreign fighters or you accept the risk of a spillover from Afghanistan."[100] Muhammad Amir Rana, a member of the steering committee for Pakistan's National Counterterrorism Authority, explained that before the war on terror Pakistan primarily relied on the country's police forces for counterterrorism operations as they were largely focused on sectarian groups operating within urban areas. However, after 2001, the focus of counterterrorism shifted to FATA, with the military taking the lead. Rana further observed that "U.S. perception is quite narrow, very strict," and as a result of this pressure, Pakistan "didn't have this luxury of time" to rely on traditional mechanisms through the weakened maliki system. Therefore, "the U.S. was dependent on the Pakistan military" as it entered FATA "in full force."[101]

The first small-scale operation, Operation Kazha Punga, conducted on June 25, 2002, was a raid on a South Waziristan village suspected of housing around thirty al-Qaeda fighters. The CIA passed the intelligence on to the Pakistani army, which quickly dispatched a company to attack the compound. The raid was a failure, with intense tribal resistance resulting in the deaths of two officers and ten soldiers. Afterwards, a senior Pakistani official told Richard Haass, the State Department's director of policy planning, that the army's initial action into FATA "showed no reservations, [having] taken risks and ignored the sensitivities of the local people," which left them "alienated." Wary of committing Pakistani troops to difficult counterterrorism operations in the region, the senior official reiterated that Pakistan had no specific information about an al-Qaeda presence in FATA and that the real issue was the ongoing conflict between the maliks and mullahs, who he described as "al Qaeda sympathizers" who were nonetheless unable to shelter foreign fighters for more than a day or two. Haass responded that the "U.S. believed that al Qaeda and Taliban had been pushed out of Afghanistan and al Qaeda's core was in Pakistan today. . . . Al Qaeda had reconstituted and posed a threat as large as it had been on September 10. The al Qaeda presence in Pakistan was the single largest concentration anywhere."[102]

Despite hesitation on the Pakistani side, the Pakistani military launched its next operation the following year, in June 2003, after the CIA had come to suspect that al-Qaeda fighters had gathered at a camp in Mohmand Agency. This operation, under the command of General Ali Jan Orakzai, further antagonized local communities and immediately led to clashes with the agency's tribes. Three months later, the army's XI Corps, backed by the Frontier Corps, launched Operation Angoor Adda against a suspected al-Qaeda hideout in South Waziristan, based on intelligence from the CIA operating from across the border. While nominally targeting al Qaeda, the army attacked members of the Ahmadzai Wazir tribe thought to be harboring foreign fighters. The corps commander, Lieutenant General Safdar Hussain, declared, "We are going to sort out the Ahmadzai Wazirs."[103] General Hamid Khan, then the inspector general of the Frontier Corps, opposed these operations, fearing they would only stir antigovernment violence in the region, and he pushed to have responsibility for clearing FATA left to his paramilitary forces. He later stated, "You have to know when to send a tough signal. It is important to be firm, but you must not get into a cycle of violence. If you belittle the local people, or are too oppressive, antagonism towards the Army will grow."[104]

The reaction of U.S. officials to these initial operations, according to Armitage, "was one largely of satisfaction that they were finally getting off their ass, but we didn't realize they were going to get their ass kicked so badly."[105] Following the military's early failures, Pakistani officials attempted to work through the maliks and local tribal structures to capture foreign fighters in the region, yet this approach found little success. Under U.S. pressure, Pakistani officials quickly abandoned it given the slow response from the weakened maliki system and again shifted to the use of direct military force.[106] Nevertheless, maliks warned that any further operations would be a violation of tribal customs and tantamount to a declaration of war on the Pashtun tribes. An Ahmadzai Wazir malik stated, "We were stabbed in the back. We were promised dialogue and development funds, but all the time plans for military operations against our tribes were well under way."[107] There also was a sense of "betrayal" among the local tribes who extended hospitality to many of the foreign fighters in the 1980s and 1990s at the behest of Pakistani officials. As the prominent Pakistani journalist Imtiaz Gul found in speaking with locals in South Waziristan after these early operations, foreign fighters were considered "Muslim brothers and mujahedeen," but, after 9/11, they were abruptly labeled "terrorists." Gul continued, "The same state that had put them on track to tag them along for jihad against the Russians and had been telling them you have to take care of them, now had turned against them. So they could not internally reconcile that."[108]

By early 2004, Musharraf was ready to drastically expand military operations in FATA. In December 2003, he had survived two assassination attempts that the government had pinpointed as originating in South Waziristan.[109] It was suspected that the bombings were committed by Taliban supporters angry at the military presence in the region and in response to al-Zawahiri's fatwa ordering Musharraf's death for cooperating with the United States. Following the assassination attempts, the CIA station chief in Islamabad, Rich Blee, repeatedly told Musharraf and other Pakistani officials, "You have to kill them or they're going to kill us."[110] At the same time, the CIA discovered an al-Qaeda operative's notebook in Iraq, from which it was determined that al-Qaeda was operating out of South Waziristan. In response, the U.S. government offered Pakistan increased military assistance, including helicopters necessary for troop movements, to expedite its operations in FATA. In March 2004, the U.S. government also granted Pakistan the status of a major non-NATO ally, allowing the government to purchase advanced U.S. military technology for use in its counterterrorism efforts.

In January 2004, after receiving intelligence reports of around 200 Uzbek fighters near Wana in South Waziristan, Pakistan's Special Services Group (SSG) mounted a raid on a compound in the area. The troops took around 30 people into custody and found no Uzbeks present, blaming an intelligence failure. That evening, however, local tribesmen attacked the Wana garrison in retribution, killing eight soldiers. A lieutenant general stated of the raid, "We made a mess of the whole thing. Our source was flawed and none of the troops acquitted themselves particularly well, including the SSG. Then our people made the attack on Wana even worse than it was. The Pakistan Army was trigger-happy. They opened up out of fright. But good trigger control is the sign of a professional army."[111] Fighting intensified in the Wana area three months later as the Pakistan army launched Operation Kalosha, supported by helicopter gunships and artillery. Musharraf went on television and mentioned a high-value target, alluding to al-Qaeda's number two, al-Zawahiri, as the target of the operation.[112] After facing stiff resistance, the army shifted to indiscriminate bombing of villages and tribal compounds, resulting in high civilian casualties.[113] One hundred thirty people were killed, including 46 soldiers. During the operation, the military also bulldozed to the ground the homes of tribesmen suspected of providing shelter to foreign fighters, legally permissible under the FCR. However, there were no high-value al-Qaeda leaders killed or captured as a result of these operations. By 2004, all the key al-Qaeda operatives arrested were apprehended in Pakistan's major cities, such as Karachi, Peshawar, Quetta, Faisalabad, and Rawalpindi, but none as result of counterterrorism efforts in FATA.[114]

With the military operations creating tensions with local militant groups, a peace deal known as the Shakai Agreement was brokered on April 24, 2004, in a ceremony between General Safdar Hussein and the local Taliban leader Nek Muhammad Wazir of the Ahmadzai Wazir, who was educated in madrassas in FATA and returned home to South Waziristan in the early 2000s after fighting with the Afghan Taliban.

This agreement allowed Pashtun militants to remain in FATA without government interference if they turned in their weapons and renounced terrorism. The government also promised to pay reparations to local communities affected by the recent fighting. The peace deal was signed in a madrassa, rather than a public forum, with Wazir's men offering AK-47s to the Pakistani army, a traditional sign of surrender. Hussein, in turn, bestowed garlands around Wazir's neck. The two men, in a sign of reconciliation, hugged. However, the militants under Nek Muhammad Wazir saw themselves bringing the Pakistani army to its knees. From their perspective, the army came to Wazir's territory to negotiate the agreement, another sign of surrender in the tribal context. Wazir stated, "I did not go to them; they came to my place. That should make it clear who surrendered to whom."[115] After the agreement, however, the Pakistani army did not exit FATA and maintained a presence in the region, though largely within fortified barracks. While not directly challenging local militants and conducting few patrols, the military's continued deployment was enough to stoke the anger of local communities. The peace deal quickly fell apart, particularly with the government forcing over six thousand merchant shops to close to leverage economic pressure on "uncooperative" tribesmen and with reports of a "massive mobilization" of troops in the area.[116]

In June 2004, Pakistan suspended the short-lived peace agreement and launched air operations against three militant compounds in South Waziristan, followed by a sweep operation involving over twenty thousand troops. That month, General Barno publicly praised Pakistani efforts, telling reporters, "I would give strong commendation to the ongoing aggressive efforts of the Pakistani government and military to eliminate terrorist sanctuaries."[117] Yet, Musharraf was aware of the impending backlash to these operations and the potential for violence to spread to other areas. He explained that such actions "can have a fallout—these people have contacts elsewhere in the country and they can retaliate in the rest of the country in the form of bomb blasts, attacks on important persons and installations—and so we have to guard against that."[118] In 2004, there were altogether 35 military operations resulting in over 250 deaths and 600 individuals captured without any high-value targets among them but with reports that air strikes resulted in large numbers of civilian casualties.[119] A spokesperson for the Pakistan Army, Major General Shaukat Sultan, announced that the military operations in South Waziristan provoked a series of bombings and other terrorist attacks in Karachi and other parts of the country, including a suicide bomber killing an intelligence officer in Kohat, an attack on a Pakistani army commander's motorcade, and a suicide bombing attempting to kill the prime minister–designate.[120]

U.S. officials expressed their appreciation of the Pakistani government's willingness to put troops into the field at great cost to its military, but no high-level meetings between the two countries occurred without "encouragement to do more in the Tribal Areas." Senior U.S. officials came to believe that Pakistani military efforts were for show, with operations being conducted in anticipation of U.S. delegation visits to "pre-empt the conversation" and demonstrate cooperation.[121] In early 2005, with attacks against U.S. and NATO forces in Afghanistan increasing, the White House kept pressure on Musharraf to expand military operations in FATA. A series of phone calls between the two heads of state and official visits to Pakistan hammered home this point.[122] In the coming months, senior U.S. officials increasingly connected the rising violence in Afghanistan with the Taliban's ability to exploit Pakistan's periphery beyond the reach of either the Afghan or Pakistani governments. In February 2006, the U.S. ambassador in Kabul, Ronald Neumann, warned that if the safe havens in Pakistan's border region were not adequately addressed then this could "lead to the re-emergence of the same strategic threat to the United States that prompted our [Operation Enduring Freedom] intervention over 4 years ago."[123]

In 2005 and 2006, the fighting increasingly shifted into North Waziristan, with the Pakistani army targeting camps believed to be used by al-Qaeda, as well as conducting limited operations in Bajaur and Khyber Agencies. In March 2006, the Pakistani army launched an operation to target training camps outside of Miranshah, North Waziristan, from which it was feared al-Qaeda-linked foreign fighters, including Arabs and Chechens, were operating.[124] During the operation, which according to Pakistani officials resulted in the deaths of around 140 militants, helicopter gunships destroyed the Darul Uloom Faredia Gulshan-e-Ilum madrassa led by Maulvi Abdul Khaliq, thought to be a local al-Qaeda supporter and facilitator.[125] Khaliq ordered immediate retaliation against the military and its camps, leading to a string of revenge attacks within the area.

Shortly after, U.S. diplomats in Islamabad warned of the potential for a violent backlash out of FATA. Ambassador Crocker told David Kilcullen, who was dispatched by Secretary of State Condoleezza Rice to assess the counterterrorism situation in Pakistan and find ways to increase support for the Pakistani military to expand their operations within the border region, "Dave, I'm sitting on a powder keg here, and you're lighting matches."[126] At this time, visiting U.S. officials also heard similar warnings from Pakistani military leadership, who pointed to widespread opposition among the tribal communities to the military deployments. Civilian causalities during counterterrorism operations, according to Pakistani officials, exacerbated this tribal opposition, which was then exploited by Taliban groups to gain support within the region. "Once the army comes in," a Pakistani security official explained, "these Taliban fire at the army, and the whole thing escalates."[127]

In the face of such warnings, U.S. officials in Washington continued to push for offensive action and worked to increase Pakistan's offensive military capabilities, including through the sale of eighteen F-16s with associated support equipment to the Pakistani government in 2006—a transaction that Rumsfeld had pushed forward to avoid any impediments or delays. This was followed up with a further fourteen U.S.-supplied F-16s designated as Excess Defense Articles.[128] The U.S. government's justification for the sale was that the fighter jets would be used in Pakistan's counterterrorism operations. "Given its geo-strategic location and partnership in the Global War on Terrorism (GWOT), Pakistan is a vital ally of the United States," the Defense Security Cooperation Agency announced, and "this proposed sale will contribute to the foreign policy and national security of the United States by helping an ally meet its legitimate defense requirements. The aircraft also will be used for close air support in ongoing operations contributing to the GWOT."[129] A Pakistani air force officer explained that after their delivery to Pakistan, the F-16s were used in operations along the country's border "to stop the terrorists"; in September 2008, the State Department confirmed that the U.S.-provided F-16s provided "a critical counterterrorism capability to Pakistan and the Pakistan Air Force" and had been used extensively in Pakistani military operations in the Swat Valley and FATA's Bajaur Agency. [130]

At this time, however, Musharraf and Pakistani military leadership continually expressed their consternation that the United States did not properly recognize Pakistan's counterterrorism efforts, and they communicated to U.S. officials their hesitance to continue the use of regular military forces due to the violent backlash it provoked across the country.[131] Musharraf and his supporting generals hoped to increase the reliance on the Frontier Corps (which gained U.S. support from the Department of Defense–managed Frontier Corps Authority beginning in fiscal year 2008, with $75 million in funding to bolster its capacity for counterterrorism operations) and tribal allies within FATA by reestablishing the authority of the maliks, harkening back to British colonial strategies.[132] On September 5, 2006, the Pakistan Army signed another peace agreement, the Waziristan Accord, with local Taliban forces in North Waziristan. A week later, a grand jirga of tribal elders from Bajaur, Mohmand, Khyber, Orakzai, North Waziristan, and South Waziristan met in Peshawar and pushed for the government to withdraw the entirety of its military forces in FATA and replace it with a local force raised from the Pashtun tribes. The elders argued that the security situation in FATA had worsened because of the "unnecessary military operations" against foreign fighters, stressing, "In our customs and traditions, we can die but never even think of handing over our guests to their enemy. Tribal people fought against their own security forces for almost three years in North Waziristan Agency but did not compromise on their traditions."[133] Ali Jan Orakzai, now governor of the NWFP, championed the appeasement of militant groups in FATA as the only means of containing the violence. Orakzai argued that once peace was established and tribal autonomy restored, he could win the tribe's long-term loyalty by providing jobs and other government services severely lacking in the region.

Shortly after the September 2006 peace deal, Bush told Musharraf during a private dinner at the White House, "We got real concerns about this, whether it's going to work." The Pakistani president responded, "I want to try it. If it doesn't work, I'm prepared to end it."[134] U.S. officials remained skeptical. In an October 13, 2006, message to National Security Advisor Stephen Hadley, Rumsfeld wrote, "I think someone needs to talk to Musharraf—either the President, Abizaid, or I should tell him the deal made in north Waziristan isn't working and is not likely to work. The level of activity has gone up, not down."[135] There were reports that cross-border attacks against NATO forces in Afghanistan had risen by 300 percent since the implementation of the peace deal.[136] In fall 2006, Ambassador Neumann transmitted his assessment and recommendations for ongoing U.S. operations. As part of his recommendations for "important big things we need to do now," he included "Make sure we see real progress in Pakistan to stop the Taliban and take out Taliban leadership."[137]

By the following year, the White House continued to connect attacks in Afghanistan with the Taliban's safe haven in FATA, publicly stating that "more aggressive steps need to be taken" by Pakistan.[138] In late February 2007, Vice President Cheney and CIA deputy director Stephen Kappes visited Islamabad in order to apply further pressure on the Pakistani government to increase its efforts combating terrorist groups in FATA.[139] Cheney's trip was bolstered by visits from Defense Secretary Robert Gates and several U.S. military commanders bearing the same message; the U.S. government expected "strong Pakistani action against Taliban safe havens within Pakistan" and offered its continued support.[140] Gates told reporters after his February 2007 meeting with Musharraf in Rawalpindi, "If we weren't concerned about what was happening along the border, I wouldn't be here."[141] At this time, Michael Vickers, the Pentagon's assistant secretary for special operations and low intensity conflict, stated that Pakistan was "Job One . . . for me and among the [counterterrorism] guys," a focus that required trips to Islamabad every two to three months to keep tabs on Pakistani actions in FATA.[142]

The international condemnation of the peace deal, along with an increase in terrorist attacks in the wake of the Lal Masjid raid by Pakistani commandos (of which more below) led Musharraf to relaunch expansive military operations in July 2007, with over a hundred thousand Pakistani troops now operating within FATA. These operations faced numerous challenges. Many of the soldiers were Punjabis from the country's most populous province who dominated both the military hierarchy and political and economic systems within Pakistan. They did not know the local language and were unfamiliar with the cultural landscape. As a result, their deployment was seen by local communities as an unwelcome invasion by outsiders. A Pashto saying asserts that "Intruders are always unwelcome."[143] As one Pakistani diplomat explained of the militant groups operating in FATA, "Being tribal they see things in black and white. For them any outsider is the infidel. It is incumbent on them to fight the infidel."[144] A Punjabi major stationed in FATA further stated, "You know, we Punjabis are the foreigners here on the frontier. . . . It's almost impossible for outsiders, including the Pakistan army, to tell the terrorists apart from anybody else in the tribal areas, except by accident."[145] Another officer observed, "It is difficult to identify friend or foe" during these operations as everyone possesses the "same language, same dress," and goes about armed.[146] "Carrying guns is a common fashion around here," a Pashtun politician explained. "Like a woman wears her necklace, this is our jewelry."[147] An army officer that served in FATA even reported that he did not receive "detailed intelligence briefings with profiles of the tribes" in the areas where his unit operated and therefore was unprepared for the cultural and social landscape that he faced.[148] The Pakistani troops deployed to the frontier were essentially fighting an invisible enemy—"We never know where the next bullet is coming from."[149]

As an intervening force in the region, the army was also disconnected from the weakened administrative structure under the FCR. A former PA explained, "The political agent has been replaced by the army. Captains, majors, and colonels are dealing directly with the tribes, who don't know the ABCs of the tribal area. They don't know how to deal with them, with the result that it is a mess."[150] Bypassing tribal customs in this way further weakened the maliki system and the standing of the PA, cutting off "the only vehicle for a dialogue with the tribes."[151] With an over-reliance on the military to handle law-and-order challenges in the border region, a retired military officer observed, "We are doing what the police or the government should be doing."[152] Moreover, the Pakistan Army was primarily designed for land warfare against India in the broad Punjabi plains and was unprepared for the difficult operations in FATA's unfamiliar mountains and harsh climate. It was a region severely lacking in roads, which further limited troop movements. A former brigade commander in Waziristan said that the terrain is so difficult that "you couldn't see a man five meters away."[153] Traditionally, Pashtun tribesmen in the region exploited the mountainous terrain with adaptive guerilla tactics, skirmishes, and ambushes rather than directly confronting the military with its superior firepower in pitched battles.

The combination of these factors led the military to rely heavily upon indiscriminate air power and artillery during counterterrorism

operations. These "scorched-earth" tactics—likened to "shooting in the
dark"—often led to high civilian casualties.[154] A former U.S. diplomat
recounted one FATA resident telling him that "when the Punjabis [i.e., the
Pakistan Army] come through they just wipe out the entire village."[155] As
journalist Steve Coll wrote after interviewing Musharraf, "The campaign's
tactics reflected Musharraf's neocolonial attitude toward Waziristan's
Pashtuns: The only way to get their attention, he told the Americans repeatedly, was to hit the tribes ruthlessly."[156] A common tendency among some
Pakistani army officers was to treat civilian casualties as an unavoidable
part of the military's efforts to eradicate terrorists, simply the result of
"God's will."[157] A retired Pakistani military official further explained,
"There is also a risk [associated] with not targeting some civilians in these
areas . . . [as] militants escape amongst them into the mainstream society.
The TTP are a part and parcel of these civilian populations."[158]

Pakistani officials, under consistent pressure and facing high expectations from U.S. officials, also felt they didn't have the luxury of time to rely
upon more traditional and discriminate methods that would help avoid
civilian casualties. With tensions mounting between center and periphery,
the "hurried and forceful policy led to a lot of resentment," according to a
former senior ISI official, as "indiscriminate" attacks by the military stoked
the anger of local tribes.[159] A malik in Waziristan warned, "The more you
bomb, the stronger will become the sentiments against the Army."[160] Pakistan's continued military operations in the northwestern periphery led to
escalating violence from the various Taliban groups emerging from FATA's
tribal landscape, who targeted the military and other symbols of the Pakistani state. With the emergence of the TTP (known in English as the
Movement of the Pakistan Taliban) in 2007, however, domestic terrorism
within Pakistan would increase exponentially.

## PAKISTAN AND DOMESTIC TERRORISM: THE SECOND STEP

In December 2007, the most prominent and deadly Pakistani Taliban
group, the Tehreek-e-Taliban Pakistan, took center stage. The TTP
was formed as a movement of twenty-seven local Taliban groups in

northwestern Pakistan that joined together under the leadership of Baitullah Mehsud, a member of the Shabi Khel clan of the Mehsud tribe and
a mullah within his village in South Waziristan. In Pakistan, there was
not a single and unified Taliban but a nebulous assemblage of vari-
ously aligned and opposed groups that emerged predominately at the
tribal level and converged around tribal identities.[161] While many TTP
members were active in Afghanistan during the 1990s and early 2000s,
the Afghan Taliban, whose leadership in exile—known as the Quetta
Shura—was based in Balochistan's capital city, was a distinct organization and often had little influence over the formation or operations of
Pakistani Taliban groups in the northwestern border region.[162] The TTP's
formation and campaign of violence against the Pakistani state under
Baitullah Mehsud and his successors were quickened by the Pakistan
Army's heavy-handed intervention into FATA, which served to unite different tribal groups against it, just as British generals had warned a century before.

The Mehsud, particularly the Shabi Khel, were long considered one of
the toughest of the Pashtun tribes in isolated Waziristan, a region that
had pride of place in the annals of British frontier history as its tribes
proved to be the most resistant to government control. A British general
in the late nineteenth century remarked of the "most inveterate and most
incorrigible" Mehsud that "it was their boast that while kings and dynas-
ties had passed away, they alone of all the Afghan tribes had remained
free and that the armies of kings have never penetrated their strong-
holds."[163] A 1901 frontier report conceded, "We exercise control over the
Mahsud country and the tribe only from the outside and do not enter
the country to carry out police duties there."[164] The British General Staff
in the 1920s and 1930s further observed that the Waziristan tribes "can
be classed among the finest fighters in the world" and were "the best
umpires in the world as they seldom allow a tactical error to go unpun-
ished."[165] Sir Olaf Caroe, the former British governor of the NWFP, used
the imagery of the panther and the wolf to capture the character of the
two main Waziristan tribes—the Wazir (divided between the Ahmadzai
Wazir in South Waziristan and Utmanzai Wazir in North Waziristan
with ethnic kin across the border in Afghanistan) and the Mehsud (only
of South Waziristan). "The nearest I can get to it is to liken the Mahsud
to a wolf, the Wazir to a panther," he wrote. "Both are splendid creatures;

the panther is slier, sleeker and has more grace, the wolf-pack is more purposeful, more united and more dangerous."[166] Caroe further observed that the Mehsud would fiercely defend their lands from any outside invasion and would never consider submitting to an external power. Within weeks of Pakistan's creation, as the new government in Islamabad sought to consolidate its territorial control, the first Pakistani governor of the NWFP, Sir George Cunningham, expressed his concern over raiding out of the Tribal Areas by "Mahsud gangs."[167]

This assessment of the Mehsud and the Wazir has been repeated by contemporary Pakistani scholars with extensive experience working among and studying the Pashtun tribes of the country's northwest frontier.[168] A Pashtun soldier serving with the Pakistani army observed in the late 2000s, "The Waziristan tribes, the Mehsuds and the Wazirs, were the fiercest under the British and they still are the fiercest now. These people are different from the others. They even speak a Pashtu very different from the rest of the Frontier."[169] General Abdullah Dogar referred to the Mehsud as "the fiercest fighters and a free-spirited people which caused the most problems," and pointed particularly to the difficulties emanating from the Shabi Khel Mehsud.[170] By 2009, it was estimated that over 70 percent of suicide bombings in Pakistan were committed by individuals from the Mehsud tribe.[171]

Baitullah Mehsud and his militia originally emerged to fill the vacuum left after Nek Mohammad Wazir's death in the first U.S. drone strike in the region in 2004. Following clashes with the army, he signed a February 2005 peace agreement with the Pakistani government in which he pledged to refrain from attacking government forces in exchange for amnesty for him and 120 of his men and the withdrawal of regular army checkpoints from Mehsud territory. At the signing ceremony, he remained defiant and proclaimed, "My head can be chopped off but it will not bow to anybody. My head only bows to God five times a day."[172] Despite signing this agreement, he continued to target pro-government maliks, including former federal minister and senator Faridullah Khan. The following year, Musharraf announced that Baitullah was a terrorist and that military forces would kill him if presented with the opportunity. In summer 2007, Baitullah officially withdrew from the agreement after the Pakistani military reestablished military garrisons within Mehsud tribal territory.[173] He quickly directed attacks against military forces stationed in FATA, especially in the wake of the Lal Masjid (Red Mosque) raid in Islamabad.

The July 2007 Lal Masjid raid by Pakistani commandos served as a catalyst for the acceleration of domestic terrorism in Pakistan and the subsequent formation of the TTP. While located in the heart of Pakistan's capital city, a mere stone's throw from the president's house and around the corner from ISI headquarters, the mosque and its attached madrassas maintained strong links with the tribes and militants of the northwestern border region; it had served as a key recruiting center for the Afghan mujahedeen during the 1980s and 70 percent of the madrassa students were Pashtun. The leadership of Lal Masjid also played an influential role in stirring up antigovernment protests. In the preceding years, there had been increasing clashes between madrassa students and local Islamabad police. In 2005, for example, burqa-clad and stick-wielding female students, known as the "Burqa Brigade," from Lal Masjid's girls' school, Jamia Hafsa, hit the streets in protest after British prime minister Tony Blair pushed Pakistan to crack down on its madrassas following the 7/7 bombings in London.

Two years later, Jamia Hafsa students again drew the ire of authorities when they occupied a neighboring children's library to protest the destruction of illegally constructed mosques on state land. This came at a time when the mosque's clerics announced their charter for the implementation of a new legal system based on their interpretation of sharia. Shortly after this announcement, the mosque formed its own sharia courts, which leveraged public opinion against Tourism Minister Nilofer Bakhtiar after it was reported she hugged a male parachuting instructor in France, forcing her to resign. Shortly after, the madrassa students began detaining individuals they deemed to be "un-Islamic." Following clashes with police, teachers and students barricaded themselves inside the mosque complex, with the imam warning that an attack by the government would lead to an "appropriate response" from the Taliban.[174] "If the government tried to attack Lal Masjid," a Taliban commander in Waziristan declared in early 2007, they would take "revenge."[175]

Musharraf and his government were under mounting international pressure to contain the situation, which came amid broader concerns with Pakistan's madrassas preaching and spreading extremist ideas. Added to this was Chinese pressure following the abduction of several Chinese workers at a nearby massage parlor in late June.[176] In a July 1 meeting with senior advisors, Musharraf stated, "There is no way we can tolerate these kinds of activities."[177] Shortly after, he issued a public ultimatum to those barricaded in the Lal Masjid complex: "We have been patient. I want to say to the ones who have been left inside: they should come out and surrender, and if they don't, I am saying this here and now: they will be killed."[178] In explaining this call to action, Information Minister Muhammad Ali Durrani announced, "There was growing pressure from the media and the international community to contain it. The government was forced, compelled to do it."[179] On July 10, Pakistani commandos launched Operation Silence, storming the compound with mortar fire and a helicopter gunship flying overhead, an action captured on live television. Over the next thirty-five hours, they engaged in intense room-to-room fighting. According to the Lal Masjid Commission, a body formed by the Pakistani Supreme Court to investigate the operations, 103 individuals were killed, including 92 civilians and 11 members of the security forces.[180]

The response was immediate. On July 12, 20,000 tribesmen in Bajaur Agency protested the government action, chanting "Death to Musharraf."[181] Taliban leader Maulana Faqir Mohammed of Bajaur's Mamund tribe, who later joined the TTP, stated, "We beg Allah to destroy Musharraf, and we will seek revenge for the atrocities perpetrated on the Lal Masjid."[182] On July 14, there was an attack against a military convoy in North Waziristan, killing 26 soldiers and wounding 54. The following day, a suicide bomber attacked a convoy in Swat, killing 16 soldiers and wounding 47, with a second attack on a police station in Dera Ismail Khan killing 28 police and wounding 35. On July 17, there was another suicide bombing at a courthouse in Islamabad, killing 13 and wounding another 50 people. Later that month, a group of tribesmen in Mohmand Agency besieged a mosque and renamed it Lal Masjid. To distance the group from any suspected links with al-Qaeda, the group's leader, Omar Khalid, who became the local TTP commander, stated, "We are local. There is no single non-local in our ranks. Our struggle is to carry on the Ghazi Abdur Rashid [Lal Masjid's imam] mission."[183]

On July 19, 2007, the Pakistani military officially relaunched operations in FATA, provoking further retaliatory attacks against military and government targets. In early September 2007, a suicide bomber struck a military bus near Army General Headquarters in Rawalpindi, killing 26 soldiers and wounding another 66. Just a few days later, Baitullah Mehsud and his followers attacked a military convoy in South Waziristan and captured 247 soldiers, a humiliating blow for the army. This attack was preceded by fellow Mehsud kidnapping 213 Pakistani soldiers and demanding an end to military operations in South Waziristan and the removal of all troops and checkpoints. The military responded with air strikes and ground attacks resulting in 257 deaths—175 militants, 47 soldiers, and 35 civilians.[184] That same month, an eighteen-year-old suicide bomber targeted the Tarbela Ghazi mess south of Islamabad and killed 22 commandos of the SSG's Kararr Company, which had conducted the Lal Masjid raid. It was later revealed that the suicide bomber's sister had been one of the Jamia Hafsa students killed by the elite counterterrorism unit.[185] In Orakzai Agency, former Lal Masjid madrassa students formed the so-called Ghazi Force, which later allied with the TTP, to "avenge" the Lal Masjid raid with several suicide bombings.[186] Hakimullah Mehsud, the leader of the TTP following Baitullah Mehsud's death in a 2009 U.S. drone strike, later declared that he "would never forgive the government for committing excesses against students at Lal Masjid and Jamia Hafsa." He followed this declaration not with a religious incantation but with the recitation of a poem by the seventeenth-century Pashtun warrior-poet Khushal Khan Khattak: "Warriors had no other wish in life but to sacrifice their lives or emerge victorious."[187]

In the wake of the Lal Masjid raid, Maulana Fazlullah, a Babukarkhel Yusufzai Pashtun known as the "Radio Mullah" (and former chairlift operator at a ski resort), emerged as the head of a militant group in the former princely state of Swat, which had been formally incorporated into Pakistan in 1969. Formerly nicknamed the "Switzerland of the East," Swat was a mountainous region within the Provincially Administered Tribal Areas[188] of the NWFP. Since 2004, Fazlullah had been preaching a fundamentalist version of sharia on the radio. His vision of Islamic governance was in opposition to the prevailing political and economic system in Swat, dominated as it was by traditional landowners who were able to consolidate large amounts of land under the autocracy of the princely state's erstwhile ruler, known as the wali.[189] Following the Lal Masjid raid, Fazlullah explained his reasons for beginning to target Pakistani security forces. "I just told my followers to be prepared for *jihad*," he stated. "Whatever has started in Swat is not related to my announce-ment, but it is related to the government operation in Lal Masjid and Jamia Hafsa. . . . It is the responsibility of every Pakistani to rise up in arms against those who are bombing their own people."[190] In October and November 2007, Pakistani troops entered the Swat Valley to battle Fazlullah's forces. Over a thousand civilians were killed in the fighting and approximately two million people displaced. Fazlullah instructed his followers "to target two types of people: the Pakistan Army and their supporters."[191] He stressed that "the Pakistani Army also did cruelties and now people like the suicide bombers are targeting them."[192]

While suicide bombings had sporadically occurred before 2007, there was a dramatic increase in response to the Lal Masjid raid and sub-sequent military operations. In the year after the special forces raid in Islamabad, there were 88 suicide bombings, which resulted in the deaths of 1,188 people and 3,209 wounded.[193] In September 2007, the UN reported that Baitullah Mehsud and his forces were responsible for 80 percent of the suicide bombings inside Pakistan.[194] The perpetrators of these attacks were often young boys who were ill, "mentally challenged," or motivated by revenge, especially individuals whose family members had been killed in military operations, and were often abused by the group's leadership.[195] Pakistani journalist Zahid Hussain noted after vis-iting the bombed-out remnants of a suicide training center in South Waziristan, "Many of the boys in the camp had close relatives who had been killed in the Pakistani military's operations against the militants, and the tribal code of honor required them to avenge the death of their dear ones. The number of such volunteers swelled with the escalation in fighting."[196] During lectures at such training centers, a primary focus was the importance of revenge against the Pakistani military.[197]

Spurred by the escalating violence, the TTP announced its formation on December 14, 2007. Its purpose was to assert political control over the border region and extend the fight against the Pakistani military. It was a movement uniting all the disparate Taliban groups, including groups from traditional tribal rivals, throughout the seven FATA agen-cies and into the neighboring NWFP, with the "emir" Baitullah Mehsud and a forty-member Shura Council comprising its leadership. Their mission statement was largely grounded in local frontier politics and included the following points: "1) enforce Islamic law; 2) Unite against

NATO forces in Afghanistan and wage a defensive Jihad against Pakistani forces; 3) Abolish checkpoints in FATA and end military operations in Swat and North Waziristan; 4) No more negotiations with the government on any future peace deals; 5) Release Lal Masjid cleric Abdul Aziz."[198]

In line with their first goal, the TTP espoused an extremely harsh and fundamentalist ideology based on their interpretation of sharia as the core of a new governance system in FATA that would replace the maliki system under the FCR.[199] The TTP banned any activities they deemed un-Islamic, including the shaving of men's beards, the playing of music, Internet cafés, and holiday celebrations, and enforced these laws with brutal violence. The TTP's embrace of an Islamic system of governance was bound up with the tribal politics of FATA, especially the kashar's opposition to the maliks. Pakistani analyst Shuja Nawaz described the kashar leadership of the TTP as "tribal entrepreneurs" who sought to challenge and replace the maliki system with their own religious-based political authority.[200] The TTP presented the maliks with the choice of either publicly submitting to their authority or being killed, with many choosing to instead flee their agency. When General Abdullah Dogar arrived as brigade commander in South Waziristan, the mullah remained "supreme," with the PA "rendered ineffective" and maliks "driven underground."[201] By 2017, at least 1,100 maliks had been murdered in increasingly brazen attacks, including suicide bombings of entire jirgas.[202] Akbar Ahmed described this as a "virtual decapitation of the tribe," severing the link between the FATA tribes and the Pakistani government and creating a local power vacuum that the TTP could then fill.[203] Khalid Aziz, the former PA of North Waziristan Agency, stated, "The elders knew how to interact with the state. They knew the rules. They intellectually knew what statecraft is." The maliks' deaths, according to Aziz, "removed traditional management. And when it is removed it is very difficult for the chief administrator, locally known as political agent, to control the areas."[204]

As part of its "defensive jihad" against the Pakistani military, the TTP, now left unchecked thanks to the devastation of the maliki system, drew on distorted tenets of *Pashtunwali* for increasingly desperate and deadly acts of revenge. In particular, it exploited the obligation to take revenge for civilians killed by the military in their recruitment efforts and in justification for their acts of terrorism. A TTP recruitment video titled "Bloodshed and revenge" opens with the Urdu phrase *Napak fauj kai mezaalim* (The atrocity of the impure army). It next shows footage of destroyed madrassas, mosques, and other buildings alongside the bodies of civilians, including women and children, killed during Pakistani military operations in Bajaur, Mohmand, Swat, North and South Waziristan, and Orakzai.[205] In another statement, a TTP commander in Swat announced, "Wherever [the army] have gone, they have committed atrocities, killing children and the elderly, who have nothing to do with the Taliban. And they have looted their homes, stealing anything that is remotely valuable."[206] In 2011, the TTP further stated, "The Murtad [apostate] and Napak [impure] army of Pakistan is bombarding its own Muslims without any reasons. Locals: They acted very cruelly toward us, like an enemy army, brutally attacking and looting our houses. This is the madrassa of Sherakai [in Frontier Region Kohat, bordering Orakzai Agency], which was attacked in Ramadan by the Murtad and Napak army, killing and injuring scores of innocent people."[207] Muhammad Khurasani, a TTP spokesperson, explained, "Our war is not against Pakistan or people of Pakistan but against its government and army who has forsaken us from our religious right that is Islamic law. They are killing us massively and destroying our properties in return for this demand. We are not terrorists but we are fighting our religious war."[208] A Wana resident in South Waziristan argued that the actions of the Pakistani military only served to strengthen the local appeal of Baitullah Mehsud and the TTP, stating, "Mehsud is gaining the advantage of indiscriminate bombing and killing of common tribesmen. Sympathies are increasing for him with every passing day. I am not a literate person, or a security expert, but I know that no military operation will succeed against him. Those who are not supporters of Osama [bin Laden] or Baitullah, even they have been forced by the indiscriminate military operation to harbor sympathies for them."[209] Indeed, a survey conducted in North Waziristan found that the local Taliban's "most significant tactics for attracting the local communities" included "addressing their grievances against the state/government" and "addressing injustices among people-to-people and people-to-government."[210]

During 2008, the Pakistani government signed a series of ceasefire agreements with various groups in FATA, each of which quickly fell apart as the TTP launched a new wave of attacks targeting the Pakistani army in North Waziristan. In leaflets dropped from helicopters, the army blamed militants operating in North Waziristan for violating the peace agreement and threatened the local community if it did not cooperate in halting the attacks. The leaflets stated that "should an area experience an attack against the army, the government will use force against the perpetrators and their accomplices in the local population."[211] Militants, however, argued that the army's continued presence in FATA was a provocation and violation of the peace agreements. The Shura Ittehad-ul-Mujahideen, a Waziristan-based group aligned with the TTP, argued,

> Despite peace agreements dictating that the Pakistani government remove its army, it has strengthened its presence in Waziristan. More than 50 drone attacks have been carried out with the mediation of the army, and there is proof on CDs that they have been paid for it, plus 30 strikes in Mehsud areas and Wana. The Pakistani government also violates the agreement that they should allot specific days for army drills so that locals are not put unnecessarily at risk; instead activities have amplified to the extent of imposing curfews and children, women or old people are fired at. This may lead to new violence in Waziristan.[212]

The group pressed for the army to "leave all unnecessary areas and hand over responsibility to the locals, all army posts between Wana and Angoor Adda should be eliminated." The TTP further declared, "The U.S. and its allies want the bloodshed to continue on our soil. But we have made it clear that, if a war is imposed on us, we will take this war out of tribal areas and NWFP to the rest of the country and will attack security forces and important government functionaries in Islamabad, Lahore, Karachi and other big cities."[213]

The United States applauded Pakistan's aggressive military actions in Swat but pushed Musharraf to "follow up success in Swat with bold operations against al Qaeda and the Taliban in North and South Waziristan."[214] While the United States voiced support for economic development projects within FATA to combat extremism in the long term, it understood that "successful implementation of the development programs for the Tribal Areas hinges on the security element. To this end, we plan to robustly support the Frontier Corps and in the meantime are encouraging Pakistan's military to take aggressive and sustained efforts against the extremists, as it recently did in the Swat valley."[215] General McChrystal, while serving as JSOC commander, thought the emergence of the TTP could help push Pakistan to strengthen its counterterrorism cooperation with the United States.[216] With U.S. officials continuing to press Pakistan to "do more," General Ehsan ul Haq, the chief of Pakistan's Defence Staff, pushed back against this pressure and stated in a 2007 interview, "Tribal areas are 1/20th of the size of Pakistan but we have 85,000 Pakistani troops deployed in the tribal areas. It is double the troop deployment in Afghanistan."[217]

As domestic terrorism increased within the country, Pakistan focused its military efforts on countering the immediate threat from the TTP. The military conducted an undeclared troop surge within Waziristan, quietly redeploying tens of thousands of infantry troops from the Indian border and other parts of Pakistan, with the United States continuing to provide reimbursement payments to Pakistan for its military operations in FATA. In August 2008, the military launched an extensive bombing campaign into Bajaur Agency against TTP targets with helicopter gunships and American-provided F-16s. The air strikes destroyed entire villages, displaced over 250,000 people, and reportedly killed 900.[218] The military, however, provided no figures for civilian causalities, which local reports claimed were considerable. Pakistani military officials subsequently assessed that the September 20 suicide bombing of the Marriott Hotel in Islamabad, which killed 53 people, was an act of revenge for the military operations in Bajaur.[219]

While Pakistan focused on the domestic threat from the TTP, U.S. officials continued to press the Pakistani government to target groups active in Afghanistan that exploited FATA as a safe haven. They were in particular concerned with the al-Qaeda-linked Haqqani network (named after the ISI-backed mujahedeen commander Jalaluddin Haqqani and led by his son Sirajuddin Haqqani, who was raised in North Waziristan).[220] This group was active in targeting NATO forces in Afghanistan and relied on FATA as a safe haven to evade U.S. forces, primarily operating among the Mehsud's traditional rival, the Wazir, whose tribal territory straddled the Durand Line. At this time, the U.S. intelligence community was monitoring the presence of foreign fighters, including Afghans, Arabs,

Kashmiris, and Uzbeks, in Haqqani training camps in North Waziristan's Miranshah area.[221]

However, Pakistani officials were reluctant to target the Haqqani network as the group focused its efforts against U.S. and Coalition forces in Afghanistan and was not committing attacks against Pakistani targets. Pakistani military leaders wished to reserve their resources for the difficult campaigns against the TTP, which they deemed the more immediate threat. Lieutenant General Asif Yasin Malik, who previously served as the XI Corps commander overseeing military operations in FATA, explained in 2010, "Everyone who is challenging the writ of the government of Pakistan, he is a problem for me." But he recognized the limitations of his forces, saying, "I can't open three to four fronts. I don't have the resources."[222] DIA analysts further determined that the ISI was monitoring and supporting Haqqani training camps within FATA, in addition to broader Haqqani operations.[223] Under the expectation of a future U.S. exit from Afghanistan, it was thought that some ISI officials were hesitant to sever ties with militant groups active in Afghanistan given the importance of maintaining strategic depth against India, especially as they saw the Indian government's growing influence with the Afghan government. However, both the Pakistani military and Sirajuddin Haqqani denied such support.[224]

As the violence worsened in Afghanistan, senior officials in the waning days of the Bush administration grew increasingly frustrated with their South Asian ally and pushed Musharraf and the Pakistani military to "do more against the growing militancy in FATA or to allow the United States to do more."[225] At the end of his second term, Bush recalled that he was growing "tired of reading intelligence reports about extremist sanctuaries in Pakistan." While Bush relied on drones to "reach into the tribal areas," his administration also increased its support of the Pakistani military "to go after the extremists." It provided "money, training, and equipment, and proposed joint counterterrorism operations—all aimed at helping increase Pakistani capabilities," understanding the importance of targeting the Taliban safe havens in FATA for U.S. operations in Afghanistan.[226] U.S. officials largely advocated two positions at the time: essentially understand Pakistan as a lost cause and step up U.S. unilateral actions such as drone strikes or cross-border raids from

Afghanistan, or increase engagement and pressure on the Pakistani political and military leadership to expand their efforts in targeting terrorist groups in Pakistan's northwestern periphery. The U.S. government would soon take both paths.

## PAKISTAN FALLS DEEPER INTO THE TERRORISM TRAP: THE THIRD STEP

During the 2008 presidential campaign, then senator Barack Obama argued for the need to pull out of Iraq and redirect U.S. attention to "taking the fight to al Qaeda in Afghanistan and Pakistan." With the number of terrorist attacks in the region spiking, he emphasized the role FATA played as a safe haven for the Taliban in disrupting U.S. and Coalition military operations in Afghanistan, and he promised voters he would take a harder line. "The greatest threat to that security," Obama warned,

> lies in the tribal regions of Pakistan, where terrorists train and insurgents strike into Afghanistan. We cannot tolerate a terrorist sanctuary, and as President, I won't. We need a stronger and sustained partnership between Afghanistan, Pakistan and NATO to secure the border, to take out terrorist camps, and to crack down on cross-border insurgents. We need more troops, more helicopters, more satellites, more Predator drones in the Afghan border region. And we must make it clear that if Pakistan cannot or will not act, we will take out high-level terrorist targets like bin Laden if we have them in our sights.[227]

In one of Obama's first security briefings days after his November 2008 electoral victory, Director of National Intelligence Mike McConnell vindicated Obama's campaign rhetoric and informed the president-elect that the United States' top security priority had to be Pakistan's tribal regions, where al-Qaeda and the Taliban continued to operate.[228]

Obama and his senior foreign policy advisors came into office with the intention to bureaucratically link Afghanistan and Pakistan and appointed the hard-nosed, veteran diplomat Richard Holbrooke as the special representative for Afghanistan and Pakistan within the State

Department in January 2009 (though his bullish personality soon alienated many within the White House before his untimely death in December 2010). Many Pakistanis opposed the move to link the two countries,
arguing that it "made them a problem rather than a country."[229] Nevertheless, the Obama administration connected the violence in Afghanistan with conditions in the Pakistani periphery, with the upshot that
Pakistan increasingly was treated as simply the "ass end of the Afghan
war."[230] With U.S. officials pushing their Pakistani counterparts to "do
more" to increase the tempo and scope of the military's counterterrorism operations in FATA, the targeted Taliban groups increased the
tempo and scope of their own domestic attacks in kind. As the tit-for-tat
violence between the military and terrorists escalated in the coming
years, Pakistan fell deeper into the terrorism trap.

As Obama and his national security team prepared the details of its
new "Af-Pak" strategy, the White House enlisted the help of Bruce Riedel, a former CIA officer and National Security Council advisor then
serving as a senior fellow at the Brookings Institution in Washington,
DC, to conduct a strategic review of the situation in Afghanistan. One of
Riedel's core recommendations was "refocusing on al Qaeda as the
goal: disrupt, dismantle, and defeat al Qaeda and its safe havens in
Pakistan and Afghanistan and prevent its return to either country." To
achieve this, he further recommended "assisting Pakistan's capability
to fight extremists: It is vital to strengthen our efforts to both develop
and operationally enable Pakistani security forces so they are capable
of succeeding in sustained counterterrorism and counterinsurgency
operations." He stressed the importance of "engaging and focusing
Islamabad on the common threat: Successfully shutting down the Pakistani safe haven for extremists will also require consistent and intensive
strategic engagement with Pakistani leadership in both the civilian and
military spheres."[231] Riedel warned of al-Qaeda, "These guys are serious.
They are clever, and they are relentless. Until we kill them, they're going
to keep trying to kill us."[232] He also communicated that drones, despite
their attractiveness, were not the answer, likening the drone campaign in
FATA to trying to take out a beehive one bee at a time. What was needed
were Pakistani boots on the ground.

On March 27, 2009, Obama announced a comprehensive new security
strategy in Afghanistan and Pakistan. For Afghanistan, he announced

an increase in U.S. troop deployments and a renewed focus on expanding the Afghan security forces to target insurgents in the country's eastern border region. (In December 2009, he announced the next phase of the surge in U.S. forces, which would bring the total number of U.S. troops in Afghanistan to around one hundred thousand.) To target al-Qaeda in Pakistan's "vast," "rugged," and "ungoverned" tribal areas, Obama further stated that the United States would focus its military assistance to Pakistan on "the tools, training and support that Pakistan needs to root out the terrorists." He added, "Pakistan's government must be a stronger partner in destroying these safe havens, and we must isolate al-Qaeda from the Pakistani people."[233] To aid this effort, Congress established the Pakistan Counterinsurgency Capability Fund to support Pakistan's military efforts in FATA.

Success in Afghanistan would be inextricably linked with Pakistan. Deputy Director of National Intelligence Peter Lavoy argued in security briefings throughout the fall of 2009 that the U.S. military could not defeat the Afghan Taliban unless it was willing to invade Pakistan. Obama quickly ruled out this option. In the president's view, it was the Pakistani army that had to confront the Taliban and "wipe them out."[234] Chris Wood, the CIA station chief in Kabul and later director of the CIA's Counterterrorism Center, repeatedly stressed to visitors, "We either address the sanctuary and we win the war, or we don't and we lose the war. It's that simple."[235] The president agreed with this view. "Changing the Pakistan calculus," Obama urged in one briefing, was the "key to achieving our core goals." General David Petraeus argued that this change was occurring and recounted a recent meeting with General Ashfaq Kayani in which he was walked through new plans for additional ground operations in Swat and South Waziristan, which he called an "encouraging sign."[236] To bolster these operations, the White House increased U.S. military assistance to Pakistan, hoping they would help to assert government control over the border region and provide leverage for pressuring the Pakistani military to target al-Qaeda and the Haqqani network.

In February 2009, however, the Pakistani government signed a cease-fire agreement with Maulana Fazlullah following two years of heavy and costly fighting in Swat. As part of the agreement, the government agreed to allow sharia courts to operate within the Malakand region. This agreement lasted only months, with U.S. officials heavily criticizing it.[237]

Under mounting international pressure and with increasing clashes between the Pakistani Taliban and the military beginning to threaten Islamabad, the Pakistani government ordered over a million residents to evacuate the Swat Valley and launched further military operations against Fazlullah's forces. During these operations, Pakistani military units, in particular the army's 12th Punjab Regiment, were noted for their brutality and accused of the extrajudicial killings of at least 238 suspected Taliban fighters after taking them into custody, with many of the corpses reportedly bearing visible marks of torture.[238]

In a May 7, 2009, meeting with Pakistani president Asif Ali Zardari, elected to replace Musharraf following his August 2008 resignation, Obama again stressed the need to follow up these operations with expanded military action in FATA.[239] Richard Holbrooke told the Pakistani journalist Ahmed Rashid, "This progress is much appreciated, but there is a need now to do more, and the Pakistanis have proved they can do more."[240] In November 2009, John Brennan and National Security Advisor James Jones traveled to Islamabad to hand deliver a letter to Zardari from Obama proposing a paired escalation of military operations targeting al-Qaeda and the full range of al-Qaeda-affiliated militant groups operating within the northwestern periphery, including the TTP, Lashkar-e-Taiba, the Haqqani network, and the Afghan Taliban.[241] Later that year, Zardari pushed for new military offensives against the TTP in Waziristan, which the Pentagon supported with helicopters, aircraft, and other equipment paid for with Congressional approval.[242] In 2009 alone, it was reported that 1,150 civilians were killed in military operations that heavily relied on air power and artillery.[243]

U.S. intelligence estimates later questioned the effectiveness of these operations. U.S. officials saw Pakistan focusing its fight on the TTP and continuing to allow al-Qaeda and the Afghan Taliban to use FATA as a safe haven. At this time, Obama sought to replicate in Afghanistan the troop surge that had recently been brought to bear in Iraq, with a focus on key provinces in southeastern Afghanistan. The White House thought this troop increase would demonstrate U.S. resolve and, according to Admiral Mullen, would encourage the Pakistani government to continue its own efforts against the Taliban safe havens on its side of the international border.[244] Even before the official announcement of Obama's new Afghan strategy, senior U.S. officials were skeptical of the potential of its success given the unreliability of Afghanistan's security forces, the weakness of Afghanistan's political leadership, and the fact that Taliban forces could still exploit FATA as a safe haven. The enduring presence of an "ungoverned space" in FATA threatened to undermine any potential gains from the troop surge and the possibility of a successful conclusion to the war in Afghanistan. This necessitated an increased focus on the ability of Pakistan to address the al-Qaeda and Taliban-related security challenges emanating from its northwestern periphery.

The attempted Times Square bombing in early May 2010 by Faisal Shahzad, a Pakistani American who spent six weeks in Waziristan with the TTP, helped to put further pressure on Pakistan to confront the safe havens in FATA, stressed by a steady flow of senior U.S. officials flying into Islamabad to push the government to act. Holbrooke, for instance, was averaging a trip to Pakistan to confer with Zardari and other senior Pakistani officials once every six weeks.[245] In conversations with Pakistani leadership, U.S. officials continually alluded to the fact that if the Pakistani military failed to confront terrorist groups in FATA, the United States would do so, either with drone strikes or U.S. military operations.

While the drone program began under Bush with secret authorization from Musharraf and saw an uptick in activity during the final year of his presidency, Obama expanded its use, authorizing the same number of drone strikes in the first ten months of his presidency as Bush had in his entire eight years in office. Within policy circles and academia, a debate has raged over whether drone strikes have been effective in limiting terrorist groups' operations or merely provoked a violent backlash.[246] However, there has been broad recognition among U.S. officials that drones, regardless of any potential short-term successes or drawbacks, weren't enough in the long term to stymie terrorist activities, a point stressed by Bruce Riedel in his strategic review, in which he pointed to the need to have the Pakistani military present on the ground. General Stanley McChrystal similarly argued that "Done in isolation, I think drone strikes are counterproductive. They will . . . have some [near-term] effect in killing or stopping people. But long term, as we look in Pakistan, they can very rarely be decisive against an enemy because you just can't shoot enough drones. You don't have enough intelligence to do that."[247] In the "inhospitable land" of FATA, an officer for the Pakistan Army reiterated, "technology can't help," and there is "no substitute" for "boots on the ground."[248]

In late May 2010, Obama dispatched CIA director Leon Panetta, National Security Advisor James Jones, and Deputy National Security Advisor Douglas Lute to Islamabad to push for increased cooperation on counterterrorism, citing clear evidence of Pakistan's failure to adequately address the threat from groups like the Quetta Shura and the Haqqani network. During the trip, Jones warned Zardari, "The president wants everyone in Pakistan to understand if such an attack connected to a Pakistan group is successful there are some things even he would not be able to stop. Just as there are political realities in Pakistan, there are political realities in the United States." Panetta also told General Kayani, "We can't do this without some boots on the ground. They could be Pakistani boots or they can be our boots, but we got to have some boots on the ground."[249] During an October 2010 meeting in the White House, Obama escalated Jones's and Panetta's messages and directly warned senior Pakistani officials—including General Kayani and Foreign Minister Shah Mahmood Qureshi—that if Pakistan failed to take adequate action, then he could be forced to order major U.S. military action into Pakistani territory, a red line for senior Pakistani leaders.[250] The president further stressed to Cameron Munter, appointed U.S. ambassador to Pakistan in October 2010, "We have to stay tough with these guys," and he reiterated that his priority for Munter's new post in Islamabad was to ensure that no major attack on America's homeland originated from Pakistani soil.[251]

In the wake of the attempted Time Square bombing, the president explained, "[Pakistan] also ramped up their CT cooperation in a way that over the last 18 months has hunkered down al-Qaeda in a way that is significant," but this still wasn't enough.[252] In February 2011, Secretary Clinton publicly told the Asia Society in New York, "We've made progress, but the tribal areas along the border between Afghanistan and Pakistan remain the epicenter of violent extremism that threatens Americans and peace-loving people everywhere."[253] However, U.S. officials continued to express their frustration with Pakistan's continued failure to take adequate action against al-Qaeda and Afghan Taliban forces operating within Pakistan. The White House's suspicion of links between these groups and elements within the Pakistani government was so strong that Obama did not involve or even alert Pakistani authorities about the May 2011 Abbottabad raid out of fear the plans would leak to bin Laden and his network.[254]

With support from the Obama administration, Pakistan continued to respond to domestic terrorist attacks with new and expanded military operations, with U.S. reimbursements for Pakistani operations totaling nearly $1 billion a year by this time.[255] As of 2010, 2,300 Pakistani soldiers had been killed in domestic military actions (nearly all of these deaths occurring after 2006), a level that nearly matched the total number of U.S. servicepeople killed in action in Afghanistan from October 2001 to July 2020.[256] As the Pakistani military intensified its operations in the difficult terrain of the periphery, it fell back on the use of air strikes and artillery to pound TTP positions, leading to higher levels of civilian causalities and greater population displacement. The TTP responded to these operations with increased attacks against military, government, and civilian targets across Pakistan, citing revenge for counterterrorism operations and the resulting civilian casualties as its main motivation.[257]

Beginning in October 2009, Pakistan launched Operation Rah-e-Nijat, a three-pronged military invasion of South Waziristan involving 28,000 troops and described as the "mother of all battles." A number of towns were devastated in the fighting, particularly as the region was heavily bombed by jets and attack helicopters. A senior Pakistani official informed U.S. diplomats that the military intended to empty the area's population and separate "good Mehsuds" from "bad Mehsuds" by thoroughly screening any "South Waziri family attempting to flee the operations."[258] These operations displaced over 250,000 residents, adding to those already displaced by previous operations. In June 2009, Pakistan's National Database and Registration Authority reported a total of 1.73 million internally displaced individuals, with reports that the number, given the government's limited capacity for registering displaced persons, could be even higher.[259]

Many of those displaced as a result of the conflict resided in camps on the outskirts of Peshawar. A Pakistani intelligence report warned that these camps quickly became recruiting grounds for various Pakistani Taliban groups as young men sought to avenge the deaths of relatives in the ongoing military operations. A Pakistani intelligence official stated, "Taliban militants have been exploiting the deaths of women and children in both U.S. drone attacks and bombings by Pakistani forces to coax angry young men to join hands with them for revenge."[260] According to one resident of the camps who fled his home in Bajaur Agency following shelling by the Pakistan Army, hundreds of angry young men joined the Taliban, including his nineteen-year-old nephew, whose brother was killed by the army. "Our youths have become bitterly angry," he explained. "The courageous among them have joined Taliban, no matter whether they agree with their philosophy or not." He saw revenge as the clear motivation for his nephew's actions. "As far as I know him, he was a cool and calm boy who did not agree with Taliban philosophy. But he had no other force which could help him avenge the death of his brother."[261]

The Pakistani Taliban highlighted revenge for Pakistani military operations in the periphery as motivation for their domestic attacks. On August 21, 2008, suicide bombers from the TTP targeted the heavily fortified Pakistan Ordnance Factories—responsible for manufacturing ammunition, firearms, and explosives for the army—in Wah, twenty miles outside of Islamabad. The TTP announced that the suicide bombing, which killed sixty-four people, was in response to recent Pakistani military operations in Bajaur Agency, and it warned of additional attacks if the military continued its campaign in the Tribal Areas.[262] The following year, Amir Muawiya, a spokesperson for the Abdullah Azam Shaheed Brigade, claimed that the June 9 bombing of the Pearl Continental Hotel in Peshawar was in revenge for the deaths of innocent people in the military's counterterrorism operations.[263] During the TTP's December 2009 attack on Rawalpindi's Parade Lane Mosque, in which thirty-six people (including seventeen children) were killed, the assailants were heard shouting, "Now [you] know how it feels when other people are killed in the bombings!"[264] This mosque was only five minutes away from the army headquarters in a military cantonment area and frequented by senior military officials and their families, and six army officers, including two generals, were killed in the attack.[265]

In the coming years, the TTP targeted members of the Pakistani military in ever more gruesome assaults. In a January 2012 video released to the media, the TTP executed 15 Pakistani soldiers, explaining, "Twelve of our comrades were besieged and mercilessly martyred in the Khyber Agency. Our pious women were also targeted. To avenge those comrades, we will kill these men. We warn the government of Pakistan that if the killing of our friends is not halted, this will be the fate of you all."[266] Later that year, the TTP released another video of the severed heads of a dozen Pakistani soldiers executed in Bajaur and announced they had been killed in revenge for recent Pakistan army operations.[267] In

December 2012, the TTP, using ten suicide bombers, attacked the international airport in Peshawar, which served as a base for helicopter gunships used for counterterrorism operations in FATA. During a 2013 Independence Day speech, General Kayani announced, "The internal threat to Pakistan is now greater than any external one."[268]

In June 2014, the TTP attacked the Jinnah International Airport in Karachi, killing thirty-six people in revenge for the ongoing Pakistani air strikes in FATA and the drone strike that killed its leader, Hakimullah Mehsud.[269] In response, the Pakistan military launched Operation Zarb-e-Azb in North Waziristan the following week, which was intended as a "comprehensive operation . . . to eliminate these terrorists regardless of hue and color, along with their sanctuaries."[270] The operation involved nearly thirty thousand troops supported by air power and resulted in the deaths of hundreds and the displacement of tens of thousands of civilians. In revenge for these actions, the TTP conducted the highly publicized and widely condemned December 2014 attack on an army school in Peshawar that killed over 130 children, largely from military families. A TTP spokesperson, Mohammed Umar Khurasani, announced that the attack was specifically conducted in revenge for Operation Zarb-e-Azb. He explained, "We selected the army's school for the attack because the government is targeting our families and females. We want them to feel the pain."[271] In response to the Peshawar school attack, the Pakistani military launched further air strikes into Khyber Agency and increased military actions as part of the operation. By June 2015, the military was ready to declare victory in FATA. In the process, however, the military essentially emptied the region, resulting in the displacement of nearly a million people.[272] While the TTP's operational capacity was degraded by such efforts and further weakened by internal divisions leading to the formation of various splinter groups, domestic terrorism persisted, with the TTP continuing to clash with military forces within FATA and violence increasingly shifting to Pakistan's urban areas following the mass displacement of FATA's population.[273]

---

This in-depth case study of the U.S.-Pakistan counterterrorism relationship has detailed the three steps of the terrorism trap's causal process,

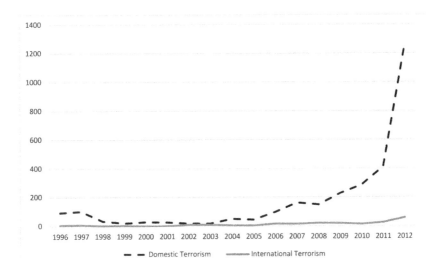

**FIGURE 4.1** Annual count of terrorist attacks in Pakistan, 1996–2012.

*Source:* Enders, Sandler, and Gaibulloev, "Domestic Versus Transnational Terrorism";
Gaibulloev, Piazza, and Sandler, "Regime Types and Terrorism."

connecting U.S. counterterrorism to an increase in domestic terrorism. While U.S. counterterrorism was nominally focused on al-Qaeda and international terrorism, it had a profound impact on the levels of domestic terrorism within Pakistan as it influenced the Pakistani government's decision to deployment of the military for domestic counterterrorism operations in the northwestern border region, leading to a violent blowback against the state. Under continued pressure from senior U.S. officials and with U.S. government support, the Pakistani military conducted fifty-seven separate domestic counterterrorism operations within FATA and neighboring areas of the Khyber Pakhtunkhwa Province by 2012.[274] The increase in domestic terrorism in Pakistan increased in step with these operations, conducted under U.S. pressure to "do more" to gain control over the "ungoverned spaces" in FATA. The resulting cycle of violence between terrorist groups and the military sunk Pakistan deeper into the terrorism trap. As a demonstration of this trend, figure 4.1 shows the annual number of terrorist attacks in Pakistan between 1996 and 2012.

While analysts often point to the Pakistani Taliban's religiously charged and internationalized rhetoric or its varying links with al-Qaeda core as explanations for its acts of terrorism, the above analysis demonstrates that revenge for the military's counterterrorism operations served as a key motivation for the TTP's attacks. Public statements by the TTP and other Taliban groups are replete with unambiguous references to revenge for the Pakistan's military actions in the periphery. In addition to direct attacks against military and government targets, Taliban groups further argued that attacks against the families of members of the Pakistani military, such as the Peshawar army school attack and the Rawalpindi mosque attack, were revenge for civilian deaths in FATA in a warped application of *Pashtunwali*.[275] A Pakistani scholar explained that people within the country's peripheral areas view their interests and government actions according to "tribal norms." The Pakistani government and its international backers have not fully appreciated this fact, which means that the application of force has been "counterproductive."[276]

There has been a failure to appreciate fully the local context of the violence within Pakistan and how best to approach the problem. With the tempo of domestic terrorism increasing, international pressure, summed up in the mantra of "do more," mounted on the Pakistan government to take decisive military action against terrorist groups operating within its borders, especially in the periphery. A former senior ISI official stated, "The pressure on partner states to take up the American fight is exactly the problem." The same official recognized that counterterrorism operations created a "reaction." Acknowledging Pakistan's culpability in partnering with the United States, he added, "We took a decision. We have sacrificed for this decision. It is not the U.S. that is suffering. We are suffering."[277] A Pakistani diplomat who served in the United States reiterated that Pakistani government officials are offended by the constant criticism from U.S. officials that Pakistan "has not done enough," citing the fact that over eighty thousand Pakistanis have been killed since 2001, including a number of soldiers "embracing martyrdom" in FATA as part of "America's war."[278] A former Pakistani Foreign Ministry official added that while Pakistan's "priority was [figuring out] how to cope with the implications of U.S. actions in Afghanistan" and the resulting "imposed war" on Pakistani territory, U.S. officials remained solely focused on "al-Qaeda and their decimation," and pressured their Pakistani counterparts to "keep pursuing relentlessly" this objective.[279] This served as a catalyst for domestic terrorism as the targeted groups committed increasingly deadly attacks in retaliation for Pakistani military operations and as a means of asserting their continued capabilities and power in the face of the government's counterterrorism efforts.

In looking back on the patterns of violence emanating out of FATA, General McChrystal argued there has been a "sense of naïveté" among senior U.S. officials in Washington concerning the Pakistani government's ability to control FATA and the resulting backlash against military operations in the region. "I never thought that the Pakistanis wouldn't have been happy to have al-Qaeda go away," he explained, "but the costs in terms of loss of stability and control—the threat of that was something I don't think Americans appreciated for a long, long time, and many still don't. Until you spend time there, it's hard to appreciate completely. I think we were slow to it, and I think people who hadn't been there or spent time there had a difficult time accepting that."[280] Ambassador Cameron Munter further recognized that U.S. priorities in Pakistan were "mainly military and intelligence driven," narrowing the scope of the bilateral relationship to security issues despite his and others' failed efforts to broaden it. "And their priority," he explained,

> was they wanted to kill the bad guys, understandably, and they wanted our troops not to be hit by people in the sanctuaries in Pakistan. And it was pretty well understood by the American intelligence and by the military guys, at least at the embassy, that there was a huge price to pay because of the tactics and the problems sending in the Pakistan military to clean out Pashtun territories, but the Americans didn't care. The Americans just said, "These guys, we have this evidence," and they'd give satellite photos. "Here's these guys coming across the border. Here's, you know, the people living here. They have safe haven, clean them out." And the Pakistanis would say, "It's not that easy," and the Americans would say, "Well then you're in bed with them." That was basically the line we heard for years and years between about 2008 and about 2012. So Pakistan in this sense was collateral damage to the American policy on Afghanistan.[281]

Former assistant secretary of state Richard Boucher, who served in that position from 2006 to 2009, recalled that during his visits to Rawalpindi, Pakistan's military leadership stressed that in FATA, "if we only use military force, they will band together against us." "And frankly," he observed,

> in the end that's what happened. We pressured them so hard to go after these guys that, starting in Khyber and the moving onto other areas, they would do their piece-by-piece military operations, and that's how you got the TTP, the Pakistani Taliban, which did not exist before. It was something that was created because U.S. military pressure and U.S. military tactics, which the Pakistanis told us wouldn't work, didn't work.[282]

# 5

## THE TERRORISM TRAP IN YEMEN, MALI, AND EGYPT

A s al-Qaeda's members fanned out from Afghanistan and Pakistan, the U.S. government tracked them to new safe havens around the world from which it was feared they could further threaten the United States and its national security interests. As a result, the countries presented in this chapter—Yemen, Mali, and Egypt—quickly became wrapped up in the U.S. quest to defeat al-Qaeda. These three states all possess "ungoverned spaces" on the periphery that U.S. officials feared al-Qaeda or al-Qaeda-linked groups could exploit as safe havens. While the tension between center and periphery in each case predated the war on terror, the use of military force for domestic counterterrorism operations served as a key catalyst for the spike in domestic terrorist attacks in these countries. This began a process in which the tactical responses of each government and the terrorist groups operating in their respective territories resulted in a deadly cycle of violence.

While all three cases demonstrate this backlash to U.S.-backed counterterrorism operations, each government's approach to security in the periphery varied prior to the use of concerted military force: Yemen's was characterized by duplicity in order to placate the U.S. government and ensure the continued flow of U.S. assistance; Mali failed to act against terrorist groups in its northern periphery given low government capacity in the region; and Egypt relied on traditional law enforcement given the legal restrictions placed on the deployment of its military in the Sinai

Peninsula under the Camp David Accords. In each state, the drastic rise in domestic terrorism only occurred after each government shifted to an offensive military approach. This hard-handed military approach destabilized the political environment within these respective peripheries, increased terrorist groups' recruiting efforts, and served as a motivation for increased attacks.

The structure of these case studies mirrors the approach used in the previous chapter and shows the sequence of steps connecting U.S. counterterrorism to the increase in domestic terrorism, with partner states' domestic counterterrorism actions serving as the key intervening step. The different sections provide a narrative description of relevant interactions within each step—between the United States and partner states' governments and between the central government and periphery. Following the opening "scene-setter" discussion laying out the historical and political context for the periphery's engagement with the center, the case studies focus on each state's counterterrorism cooperation with the United States as part of the war on terror, showing how the focus of partner states' counterterrorism efforts shifted toward the periphery as a safe haven for terrorist groups, with U.S. officials pressing partner states to confront these groups in the periphery (the first step). Next, they show how the use of the military for domestic counterterrorism operations provoked a violent backlash from targeted groups, leading to an increase in domestic terrorism (the second step). Finally, they discuss how the retaliatory attacks from terrorist groups and the response from the government escalated into the same cycle of violence that has plagued Pakistan (the third step).

## YEMEN: "DANCING ON THE HEADS OF SNAKES"

Yemen has been one of the key frontline states since the outset of the war on terror, with U.S. officials expressing concern about the known presence of al-Qaeda members in the country immediately after the 9/11 attacks. As U.S. officials increasingly pushed for cooperation from their Yemeni counterparts, Yemeni president Ali Abdullah Saleh's initial approach to counterterrorism was characterized by duplicity. He instituted a "revolving door" policy in which the authorities would arrest al-Qaeda suspects only to quietly release them later. Saleh wished to do enough to keep U.S. aid flowing into Yemeni coffers but not enough to upset the political status quo given the precarity of the government's position over Yemen's powerful tribal confederations. U.S. officials continued to press Saleh to do more against terrorists operating within Yemen's deserts and mountains, especially following the formation of al-Qaeda in the Arabian Peninsula.

In the wake of the attempted bombing of a U.S. airliner on Christmas Day 2009, which ultimately connected back to AQAP, Yemen was under mounting U.S. pressure to act strongly against the growing terrorist threat in the country, and it subsequently increased its military operations to target AQAP and its perceived supporters among the tribal groups in the South. Domestic terrorist attacks increased drastically in response to Yemeni military operations and the government's use of indiscriminate force against AQAP and the southern tribes. The vast majority of these attacks were directed against military and government targets, with AQAP's rhetoric filled with explicit references to revenge for military operations in the South. AQAP in turn garnered increased attention from U.S. officials, who saw in its rhetoric and behavior a threat to the United States and its interests. The U.S. government increased its support for the Yemeni government's counterterrorism operations, supplemented with U.S. cruise missiles and drones strikes. This, however, led to further increases in domestic terrorist attacks, a trend demonstrated in figure 5.1.

## NORTH AND SOUTH YEMEN: A SCENE SETTER

Yemen today is comprised of two separate states—North Yemen (the Yemen Arab Republic) and South Yemen (the People's Democratic Republic of Yemen)—that were joined together in 1990. North Yemen had been the seat of the Shia Zaidi Imamate dating back to the late ninth century CE. The imamate and its successive rulers, whose political legitimacy was derived from their religious authority, nominally ruled over a tribal confederation under varying governance arrangements and with brief intervals of Ottoman occupation for over a millennium, lasting until

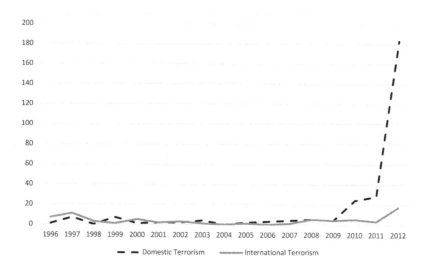

**FIGURE 5.1** Annual count of terrorist attacks in Yemen, 1996–2012.

*Source:* Enders, Sandler, and Gaibulloev, "Domestic Versus Transnational Terrorism"; Gaibulloev, Piazza, and Sandler, "Regime Types and Terrorism."

1962. That year, the government of the final Zaidi king, Muhammad al-Badr, was overthrown by Arab nationalists inspired by Egyptian president Gamal Abdel Nasser only one week after rising to power following his father's death. The country quickly fell into a deadly, eight-year-long civil war between republican forces backed by nearly seventy thousand troops of the Egyptian military and royalist forces loyal to al-Badr and supported by Saudi Arabia, along with covert assistance from the British government. After Saudi Arabia ceased its support and Egypt withdrew its troops, the civil war concluded in 1970 with international recognition of the republican government in Sana'a.

South Yemen, on the other hand, was the former Aden Protectorate, held by British colonial authorities from 1839 to 1967. First occupied by the East India Company in January 1839, Aden, whose port was a key way station on the route to British India, had been under the control of the Government of India until 1937, when it became a Crown Colony. British colonial authorities withdrew in 1967 after fighting a four-year, anticolonial insurgency spearheaded by the Marxist National Liberation Front, with the republican government in North Yemen providing the insurgents with safe haven and Egypt providing material support. Following the British withdrawal, Marxist forces, in opposition to the traditional, British-allied tribal chieftains, formed the Soviet-backed communist government of the People's Republic of Southern Yemen (renamed the People's Democratic Republic of Yemen in 1970). Many tribal leaders who worked with the British fled the country as the new government attempted to impose a uniform communist ideology and stamp out traditional tribal identities. This ultimately proved unsuccessful. Under communist rule, a Russian anthropologist noted, tribesmen in South Yemen were less concerned with promoting a particular political ideology and more focused on the "reinforcement of the overall position of the tribe," with factionalism defined by family and tribal ties continuing to shape the politics of the ruling elite.[1] During the 1980s, the South Yemen government faced a rapid period of decline precipitated by various liberalization policies and the loss of Soviet support.

On May 22, 1990, the two governments united into a single state after the dissolution of the communist government in the South. While the new government introduced various political reforms, including multiparty parliamentary elections, the political structures of North Yemen were maintained virtually unchanged in the now unified Republic of Yemen, with Saleh (selected as president by North Yemen's parliament in 1978) remaining the head of state and Sana'a continuing as the capital.[2] Many southerners saw the unification as a northern victory, especially with supply shortages plaguing the South, massive land seizures by northern officials, and an increase in the number of provincial officials who sought to more forcefully assert central government control. There also was a growing apprehension that Saleh was prioritizing his own patronage network and was not forthcoming with resources across the country as many regions lagged in all development measures, especially in the South; there was a saying that "Yemen is the Republic of the Sinhan [the president's tribe]."[3]

A brief civil war broke out in 1994 during which the Yemeni government found allies among southern tribal leaders now returning from exile, many of whom had fought in Afghanistan during the 1980s against Soviet forces, partly in revenge for the communist takeover of their native lands.[4] With Yemeni leaders seeking southern allies against supporters of the former communist government, the central government was caught in a dilemma. On the one hand, as Yemen scholar Sarah Phillips notes, Yemeni officials "worked to revitalise tribal leaders and certain tribal structures in the former South where they had been deliberately dismantled by the Marxist government." To this end, they co-opted key tribal leaders and intentionally relied on tribal customs and the tribal system of arbitration in place of the government's own judicial system to bolster their authority. Yet, on the other hand, Saleh's regime also claimed its rule was "continually threatened by the tribes" and that the central government needed "to shore up its coercive power against the threat that they constitute." Understanding that the "threat the tribes pose is real, and the number of weapons they possess dwarfs that of the state," Saleh sought to inculcate a "politics of permanent crisis" to undermine tribal leaders' authority and fragment any potential opposition to his rule.[5] The balance between the self-reliant and resilient Yemeni tribal groups, who frequently challenged state authority, and the writ of the central government, which favored a strong, centralized state, shifted over time.[6]

Yet, the unified Yemeni government never fully established effective control over the entirety of its territory, with large swaths of Yemeni territory still dominated by tribal groups and tribal customs.[7] In the 1980s, on the eve of unification, anthropologist Paul Dresch observed that "the tribes were often as little subject to direct government control as they had been in, say, the mid-nineteenth century."[8] Colonel Patrick Lang, the former U.S. defense attaché in Yemen, explained,

> There's a precarious balance all the time between the authority of the government and the authority of these massive tribal groups. The government normally only controls the land its forces sit on, or where it's providing some service that the tribal leaders and population wants, like medical service, or education. So you end up with a lot of defended towns, with a lot of checkpoints around them, and little punitive expeditions going on, all the time, by the government around the country, to punish people with whom they are quarreling over some issue.[9]

Edmund Hull, who served as U.S. ambassador to Yemen from 2001 to 2004, further argued that the tense relationship between the central government and its tribal periphery led to a perpetual cycle of bad governance and violence between the two. He stated that in Yemen's rural areas, where government control was limited, "You had bad governance which led to an alienated population, which led to continuing violence, which led to discouraging any kind of investment, which meant unemployment, which meant more violence and fed into the government ignoring the area and back to bad governance."[10] Given the strength of these tribal networks and the weak position of the central government, Saleh famously described governing Yemen as "dancing on the heads of snakes."[11]

As a result of this persistent political reality, successive governments were forced to use alliances and negotiations with tribal leadership to assert their influence. During the period of British rule, there was not a single government that exercised direct control over the entirety of the Aden Protectorate. At the heart of the protectorate was the British-administered Colony of Aden, an area of roughly seventy-four square miles consisting of the colony's strategic port and its surrounding areas and encapsulating the British Empire's primary interest in the region. Beyond this, the Aden Protectorate consisted of tribal territory presided over by various tribal chiefs who entered protective treaty relationships with the British government—the tribes selected their own chiefs but were subsequently required to be recognized by the British governor of Aden. In these areas, the tribal chiefs ruled largely through tribal custom (though some chiefs also maintained sharia courts), with colonial officials cognizant that not all chiefs had complete control over their subjects, and raiding and tribal vendettas were a frequent concern of British authorities.[12] A former colonial official referred to tribal fighting as a "curse" and "the major preoccupation of the political officers."[13]

Under these treaty relationships, the governor of Aden during the late 1930s, Sir Bernard Reilly, described British policy as "one of indirect rule through advice to the tribal chiefs and direct assistance in matters that the Arabs cannot cope with themselves."[14] British interests were represented by a British agent supported by a cadre of political officers who primarily offered their advice and worked through negotiation with local tribal leaders. A British political officer in the 1930s, Harold Ingrams, explained that negotiations for a three-year truce between two feuding tribes in the Hadhramaut region could only have been done through direct approach to each tribe. The final agreement was signed by between thirteen and fourteen hundred tribal leaders, with Ingrams noting, "Sultans were generally disregarded not only by the tribes but even by other local rulers and peace could not have been secured in any other way than personal intervention and the help of men of influence. There were in fact not two governments to deal with but nearly 2,000."[15]

Many colonial officials were aware that they ignored these tribal dynamics at their own peril, particularly regarding the use of force. When tribal clashes or other disturbances occurred, British forces conducted punitive expeditions but frequently restored order "with a show of force" and "no actual fighting," an approach that followed the British imperial tradition of "bombing, bribery, and bluff."[16] Stephen Day, a former British political officer who served in the Aden Protectorate during the 1960s, recalled,

> Knowing and living within the tribal system we political officers developed top-quality intelligence and went to extreme lengths to avoid human casualties, dropping leaflets calling for the miscreants to come down and submit to authority and only attacking physical targets as a last resort and after due warning. We worked within the tribal system and knew full well a feud … would develop if we killed tribal people— and we would personally be the targets.[17]

Officials from other foreign governments entangled in Yemeni politics also noted their governments' failures to learn how to operate within the country, the importance of understanding the local tribal structures, and the futility of military force. After departing from Sana'a, the last Ottoman pasha of Yemen explained, "In my opinion, this is what happened, from the day we conquered it to the time we left it we neither knew Yemen nor did we understand it nor learn [anything] about it, nor were we, for that matter, able to administer it."[18] Egyptian field marshal Abdel Hakim Amer similarly stated of Egypt's military campaign in North Yemen in the 1960s, dubbed Egypt's Vietnam, "We did not bother to study the local, Arab and international implications or the political or military questions involved. After years of experience we realized that it was a war between the tribes and that we entered it without knowing the nature of their land, their traditions and their ideas."[19] A British political officer surmised, "If they keep up their guerilla spirit, the tribes cannot really be beaten. The worst they have had to suffer has been Egyptian bombing. . . . Arab tribesmen, however, are not easily thus defeated."[20] In an October 2001 meeting with Donald Rumsfeld, even Egyptian president Hosni Mubarak cited lessons from the ineffectiveness of Egypt's past military campaigns in Yemen to advise the U.S. defense secretary against an overreliance on air power in Afghanistan. "Don't be in a hurry, take it easy," he stressed. "Put your money into buying allies on the ground."[21]

## YEMEN'S SOUTH AND THE WAR ON TERROR: THE FIRST STEP

Even before the 9/11 attacks, U.S. officials saw Yemen as a hub of international terrorist activity. It was the site of al-Qaeda's 2000 USS *Cole* bombing and the 1992 Aden hotel bombing targeting U.S. soldiers awaiting deployment to Somalia. U.S. officials also were aware that Yemenis played a key role in the al-Qaeda organization, comprising around 95 percent of its ranks and serving as its primary foot soldiers.[22] In fact, eighteen of the nineteen al-Qaeda hijackers on 9/11, all but the Egyptian Mohammad Atta, had Yemeni backgrounds—as did bin Laden himself—whether from Yemen proper or ethnic Yemenis from other regions of the Middle East, such as Saudi Arabia's southwestern periphery of Asir.[23]

With Saleh's method of governance (noninterference and cultivating a patronage network with autonomous tribes), al-Qaeda had room to operate in Yemen during the 1990s. In a 1996 interview, bin Laden observed that the country's tribal regions are those in which "the writ of the national government barely reaches, and whose people allow one to breathe the clear air unblemished by humiliation."[24] Saleh also tacitly welcomed former mujahedeen fighters, including Ayman al-Zawahiri's Egyptian Islamic Jihad and others who had worked with bin Laden in Afghanistan, to use Yemen as a base of operations. A number of Yemenis had joined the ranks of the mujahedeen due to Soviet support of the communist regime in South Yemen, with a former Afghan Arab fighter even arguing this was a motivation for bin Laden to participate in the anti-Soviet jihad in Afghanistan.[25] Following the Soviet withdrawal, Saleh took advantage of these fighters' presence to bolster his regime during the 1994 civil war against southern separatists and to target his political opponents. Following the USS *Cole* attack off Aden in October 2000, Saleh even bragged on Al Jazeera that he had stymied the resulting FBI investigation, stating, "We denied them access to Yemen with forces, planes, and ships. We put them under direct monitoring by our security forces. They respected our position and surrendered to what we did."[26] Despite growing U.S. concerns with international terrorists operating within Yemen's border, the country ultimately remained peripheral to broader U.S. interests in the Middle East prior to 2001. Former U.S. ambassador to Yemen Barbara Bodine, appointed in 1997, described the pre-9/11 U.S. relationship with Yemen as one of "benign neglect."[27]

With the declaration of the war on terror, the U.S. relationship with Yemen, as with so many other states in the region, was drastically altered, and it would come to focus predominately on security issues. The Yemeni government quickly shifted its domestic security position in line with U.S. priorities. After the U.S. invasion of Afghanistan, Saleh feared Yemen could be the United States' next military target, given the known presence of al-Qaeda forces within its borders.[28] Some U.S. officials did advocate for a similar approach to Yemen as had been taken in Afghanistan, an idea that went as far as U.S. Central Command beginning operational planning for the opening of a military front in Yemen.[29] In order to stymie any potential U.S. military action that would inevitably take him out of power, the Yemeni president arrived in Washington, DC, in November 2001 to discuss his country's cooperation with U.S. counterterrorism efforts. During the visit, CIA director George Tenet bluntly told Saleh that Yemen could either be a target or a partner of the United States. In a meeting with Bush in the White House, in which the U.S. president reinforced this message, Saleh strongly condemned al-Qaeda's attacks and expressed Yemen's denunciation of all forms of terrorism. He strategically added that Yemen would be "a principal partner in the coalition against terrorism."[30]

In particular, U.S. officials wanted Saleh's cooperation in targeting al-Qaeda members operating out of Yemen. Shortly after the 9/11 attacks, Ambassador Hull handed Saleh a list of al-Qaeda members suspected of operating in Yemen and asked the Yemeni head of state for his assistance in either "capturing or killing these specific individuals."[31] Bush reiterated this request during his November 2001 meeting with Saleh. Prior to the meeting, Hull briefed the president to be "very direct, very clear about what we wanted" regarding Yemen's cooperation. Hull recommended that U.S. objectives should focus on targeting specific al-Qaeda leaders and establishing a partnership with Saleh and the Yemeni government to jointly eliminate al-Qaeda's operations in Yemen. Saleh responded positively to these requests, promising Bush he would "butcher" the fighters he had previously supported.[32]

The following month, Saleh ordered raids by Yemeni special forces in the Marib and al-Jawf Governorates against suspected al-Qaeda hideouts in compliance with U.S. demands. The raids ended up angering local tribes as an unwelcome intrusion by the government, with local tribesmen attacking and killing several Yemeni soldiers and taking hostages. These unsuccessful operations were followed by the arrests of suspected al-Qaeda operatives in southern Yemen, with some U.S. officials fearing these actions were only meant to demonstrate cooperation with the United States rather than actually weakening al-Qaeda.[33] Despite the failure of these early operations, coupled with lingering fears over Yemen's duplicity, senior U.S. officials were encouraged by the fact that, according to Hull, "Yemenis had spilled their own blood in pursuit of these terrorist targets," which they saw as "a stronger argument for a potential partnership than any words that we could have had."[34] The failure of these operations also highlighted that Yemen's military forces needed increased U.S. training and support to be effective. In the following years, the Yemeni government continued sporadic and limited operations against individuals and groups with suspected links to al-Qaeda to satisfy U.S. requests for increased cooperation without taking any decisive actions, fearful of a potential backlash against the government. At this time, however, much of the U.S. government's attention remain fixed on military operations in Iraq, which consumed its available resources and attention in the Middle East.

Adroit at playing a given political situation to his own advantage and balancing between competing interests, Saleh saw counterterrorism cooperation with the United States as a means of gaining increased levels of U.S. assistance while strengthening his own domestic standing. He wanted to do enough against suspected terrorists within Yemen to keep U.S. officials satisfied, focusing on short-term tactical successes rather

than any long-term goals, but not enough to endanger his political position.[35] Understanding the need to balance international and domestic
politics, and aware of the potential for a violent backlash against the
state, Saleh initially had apprehensions about the domestic use of military
force. In 2004, a close advisor to Saleh stated, "Paying the tribal leaders to
co-operate was cheaper than any other way, like doing it in a forceful way.
It has been faster, cheaper and easier and has worked very well."[36] In relying on traditional approaches, Saleh assumed that the people U.S. officials
were referring to as terrorists were a known commodity. He expected
these men, many of whom he knew to be Afghan war veterans whom he
had relied on for domestic political support in the past, to behave like
traditional tribesmen and thus maintained a revolving-door policy of
arrest and release. Following these arrests, the government "rehabili-
tated" the suspected terrorists or made arrangements with their families
and tribal leaders to keep them out of trouble. This policy, as well as
Yemen's reticence to engage in intelligence sharing with the United States,
continually frustrated U.S. officials, who consistently urged Saleh to take
stronger action against suspected terrorists.[37]

During this period, Saleh also faced growing discontentment among
the southern tribes stemming from the increased government presence
in their territory in the form of counterterrorism operations and the
ongoing corruption of Saleh and his senior officials. In late 2005 and
early 2006, tribes in the Marib and Shabwa Governorates began kidnapping foreigners, a traditional method of bringing attention to tribal
grievances and pressuring the government to address them.[38] Local
tribes were particularly concerned with the arrest and imprisonment of
their fellow tribesmen in sweeps by the Political Security Organization
(PSO) against suspected terrorists or individuals thought to be attempting to travel to Iraq to fight against U.S. forces. The military-led PSO was
one of the primary organizations for domestic counterterrorism and
intelligence operations, reporting directly to the president outside normal bureaucratic and judicial control. The 150,000-member organization
also ran its own detention centers for holding suspected terrorists, where
it was accused of a range of human rights abuses against detainees.[39]
During 2007 and into 2008, clashes between the government and local
tribes increased, leading to a string of antigovernment attacks in the
South. The tension in the South was made worse by the security forces'

use of indiscriminate violence against protestors, further stoking antigovernment sentiment among the local tribes.[40] As this unrest grew, there was a mounting fear that al-Qaeda would use the chaos to regroup, necessitating increased U.S. support for Saleh and the Yemeni government to confront the terrorist threat.

## YEMEN AND DOMESTIC TERRORISM: THE SECOND STEP

The emergence of AQAP refocused U.S. attention on Yemen as a terrorist safe haven, with U.S. officials promising increased support and pushing for Yemeni authorities to increase counterterrorism operations in its vast "ungoverned spaces." They saw the limitations of the government's authority in tribal territory as a key factor allowing AQAP to operate and remain a terrorist threat. During his tenure in the White House and CIA, John Brennan (the Obama administration's point person on Yemen) made ten trips to Yemen to meet with Saleh and push for Yemeni action against AQAP.[41] As Yemen expanded its domestic counterterrorism operations under pressure from U.S. officials, AQAP increased its retaliatory attacks against Yemeni targets, helping to pull a number of southern tribal communities into direct conflict with the government.

The initial formation of AQAP was triggered by the 2006 escape from a PSO prison of twenty-three individuals detained as suspected terrorists, with suspicions that their escape was aided by sympathetic Yemeni officials.[42] The escaped prisoners included the future leader of AQAP, Nasir al-Wuhayshi, from Yemen's al-Bayda Governorate. Al-Wuhayshi had traveled to Afghanistan in the 1990s and served with al-Qaeda, including as a personal secretary to bin Laden. He left Afghanistan in 2001 but was arrested by Iranian authorities and handed over to the Yemeni government and was subsequently imprisoned without charge. Amid growing unrest in the South, AQAP was formed as a union of the local al-Qaeda in Yemen and al-Qaeda members from Saudi Arabia who fled to the safety of Yemen in the wake of the Saudi government's own counterterrorism crackdown. Following its formation, AQAP began ramping up its attacks, including a September 17, 2008, attack against the U.S. embassy compound in Sana'a. Following the attack against the embassy, the U.S. government sought to bolster Yemeni military efforts against the group as it exploited the government's inability to exert control in the tribal periphery. In July 2009, General David Petraeus traveled to Yemen to confirm the increase in military assistance to escalate Yemen's anti-AQAP operations. With the uptick in assistance, Petraeus also stressed that the United States expected increased cooperation from the Yemeni government.[43]

To demonstrate this cooperation, Saleh sent his nephew Ammar Muhammad Abdullah Saleh, a senior commander in the National Security Bureau, into Marib Governorate to lead an attack on an AQAP compound. In the ensuing operation, the Yemeni forces shelled the wrong compound, leading to a running gun battle with both AQAP members and local tribesmen from the struck compound.[44] Anwar al-Awlaki referred to these clashes as the "beginning of the greatest Jihad . . . to free the Arabian Peninsula from tyrants," with AQAP announcements urging fellow Yemenis to organize and fight against the "traitor, oppressive, corrupt rulers of the Arabian Peninsula."[45]

U.S. drone and cruise missile strikes also were restarted in December 2009 and were concentrated in the two southern governorates of Abyan and Shabwah. The drone campaign began by targeting a suspected AQAP camp in Abyan. The Yemeni Air Force took credit for the strike, claiming thirty-four al-Qaeda fighters had been killed. However, local video the following day showed several civilians, including children, had been killed instead. Shortly after, a U.S. cruise missile hit an Aulaq tribal village in Abyan Governorate suspected of being an al-Qaeda training camp and weapons store; the attack was reported at the time to be a Yemeni air strike. Saleh soon received congratulatory calls from foreign leaders as Yemeni officials claimed that thirty-four terrorists associated with AQAP were killed, along with fifty-one arrested in a coordinated series of raids by Yemeni security forces. The head of the Aulaq tribe, however, claimed that the victims were innocent civilians including women and children.[46]

In its messaging and recruitment, AQAP highlighted the civilian casualties and collateral damage sustained during Yemen's military operations and missile strikes, actions that instigated revenge attacks from the impacted tribes. They held these government attacks up as evidence of the brutality and illegitimacy of Saleh's regime and its

American backers. On February 20, 2009, al-Wuhayshi released a recording stating that

> This military campaign amassing in Ma'rib, Al-Jawf, Shabwah, Abyan, Sanaa, and Hadramawt . . . is just a step towards striking on the tribes and their sons with flimsy and false pretexts that are really aimed at breaking the dignity of the tribes, disarming them, controlling their land, and killing their sons in order to make it easy for mean agents and the Crusade to humiliate them. . . . Their compass went astray and they moved their armies, tanks, and aircraft to the tribes of Al-Ashraf, Abi-dah, Nihim, Jaham, Daham, Murad, Al-Awaliq, Ilah, Al-Awazil, Khaw-lan, Wa'ilah, Al-Mayasir, Bilharith, and other tribes. . . . This is your day, so fight against them before they control you tomorrow. Fight against them as one man, fight for your religion and your good qualities. . . . Get prepared with anti-tank mines, explosive charges, explosive belts, snip-ers, well-planned ambushes, and daring assaults.[47]

He also chastised the Yemeni soldiers involved in the counterterrorism operations. "As for you, O oppressive soldiers, who attack your own kin-folks, tribes, and own people," al-Wuhayshi declared, "where have your sense of reason and conscience gone? You kill your own people for the sake of the Jews and Christians."[48] An AQAP spokesperson further stated, "The mujahideen target criminals from America, Crusaders, and henchmen from security forces and intelligence officials responsible for shedding blood of women and children in Aden, Mu'ajalla [Abyan], al-Dal'a, Lahj, Lawdar, Marib, Ta'izz, and Shabwah."[49] In a statement to local tribes in Marib the following summer, AQAP exclaimed, "Who, by God, is it that destroys your mosques and kills your women and chil-dren? Is it the mujahideen or Ali Abdullah Salih? And who violates the sanctity of your homes and bombs your farms. . . . Is it the mujahideen or Ali Abdullah Salih?"[50] A December 27, 2009, AQAP statement further read, "Five American fighter jets carried out a savage raid against the innocent Muslims of Bal Kazim tribes in the al-Muajila village of the al-Mahfad region in the state of Abyan after dawn prayer on Thursday. Fol-lowing this savage bombing on the village of Bal Kazim almost 50 women, children, and men were killed. [This] occurred simultaneously with a military campaign against the tribes of Arhab, under the pretext of counterterrorism and elimination of the mujahid vanguard from the sons of the proud tribes of Yemen."[51]

As the group ramped up its attacks against Yemeni targets, AQAP's statements frequently referenced revenge against Saleh's government as one of its primary motivations. In spring 2009, following an AQAP bombing at the Sana'a airport, a statement released by the group explained, "The government of Al-Aswad al-'Ansi [an epithet comparing Saleh with a false Yemeni prophet of the seventh century] has already spilled the blood of many Muslims with air raids and the military advance with tanks in Sana'a, Amran, Marib, Jawf, Dhal'a, Abyan, and Shabwah."[52] Later that month, the AQAP announced that an attack on a prison run by the PSO in Aden had been carried out in revenge for "the brutal aggression imposed on our people in Marib in order to humiliate the tribes under the pretext of fighting terrorism."[53] An AQAP member stressed that attacks against government targets were "in self-defense."[54]

While many southern tribes fought against the government in line with AQAP's rhetoric, they held varying views of AQAP and its offshoot Ansar al-Sharia. Many Yemeni tribal leaders rejected the religious fundamentalism of AQAP and their attempts to replace customary law and the Yemeni government's rule with a governance system based on their interpretation of sharia.[55] Yet, the military actions of the government angered local communities and further turned them against Saleh's regime. The tribal communities were accustomed to the government working with tribal leadership rather than using brute force to extend the writ of the state or address matters of law and order. As a result of the use of military force in tribal territory, many tribal leaders were unwilling to cooperate with the government against AQAP. Ali Abdullah Abdulsalam, a southern tribal leader in Shabwah Governorate backed by thirty thousand fighters, explained his reticence to cooperate with the government in its counterterrorism efforts as follows: "Why should we fight [al-Qaeda]? Why? If my government built schools, hospitals and roads and met basic needs, I would be loyal to my government and protect it. So far, we don't have basic services such as electricity, water pumps. Why should we fight al-Qaeda?" He added that at least AQAP helped to "provide security and prevent looting. If your car is stolen, they will get it back for you." Under Saleh, he added, "there is looting and robbery. You can see the difference."[56] Saleh and other senior Yemeni officials also reportedly used counterterrorism as an excuse to target political opponents in the South.[57]

Rather than wholly embracing the ideology espoused by AQAP, many tribesmen saw the group as a vehicle for opposing the Yemeni government. AQAP rhetoric was able to tap into this growing antigovernment sentiment, a sentiment that only increased with the ongoing military operations. During interviews with various tribal leaders, tribal youth, and civil society activists, Yemeni researcher Nadwa al-Dawsari found that many tribesmen who joined AQAP's ranks did not subscribe to "al-Qaeda's radical ideology—some of them do not even observe Islamic religious duties such as praying and fasting. Instead, AQAP has more often been able to recruit tribal youth who are frustrated, without good economic prospects, isolated in their communities, and vulnerable to its propaganda. AQAP speaks directly to their grievances and offers a call to action—to fight the state and other enemies."[58]

The state's continued military operations increasingly pushed southern tribesmen to openly declare their support for AQAP and Ansar al-Sharia, such as former presidential advisor Tariq al-Fadhli, the son of the last British-backed sultan of the Fadhli Sultanate. During a 2010 interview with the *New York Times*, he discussed his previous experiences fighting with bin Laden in Afghanistan and argued that this put him in an ideal position to work with the U.S. government and mediate with al-Qaeda.[59] Al-Fadhli, however, couched his support of American objectives in terms that reflected his opposition to the Yemeni government. Saleh soon declared his former advisor an al-Qaeda-linked terrorist. Following a Yemeni military strike against his home, al-Fadhli stated in 2012, "As for my sons, they are youth and were present with me in Abyan when my house was attacked for several times. When my sons saw what happened to me and their country and the creation of Ansar Al-Sharia, they joined Ansar Al-Sharia and fought with them, and I'm proud of that. . . . And if I had one thousand sons I wouldn't chose [sic] for them any other but this path."[60] The Yemeni government quickly put al-Fadhli under house arrest in Aden. In 2014, he escaped and fled into the mountains of Maraqsha in Abyan, where he officially joined AQAP and its fight against the government.[61]

## YEMEN FALLS DEEPER INTO THE TERRORISM TRAP: THE THIRD STEP

The attempted bombing of a U.S. passenger plane on December 25, 2009, by the Nigerian Umar Farouk Abdulmutallab was connected back to AQAP and led to an increase in U.S. military support and an escalation of U.S.-backed Yemeni operations targeting the terrorist group. On January 19, 2010, Secretary Clinton officially designated AQAP a Foreign Terrorist Organization. U.S. officials were also growing increasingly concerned with AQAP ideologue Anwar al-Awlaki, a Yemeni American Islamic cleric whose international profile and jihadist message were growing in prominence since he was released from a Yemeni prison in December 2007. (Yemeni authorities arrested him in August 2006, reportedly for his involvement in a plot to kidnap a U.S. military attaché.) In July 2010, the U.S. government designated al-Awlaki a foreign terrorist due to his operational role in recruiting and training individuals for AQAP, including directing Abdulmutallab in his attempted bombing. U.S. officials were also concerned with his widely disseminated English-language speeches and articles over the Internet, which "focus[ed] specifically on the importance of providing funding to 'jihad,'" which the U.S. government assessed "likely inspired funding from many jurisdictions for [al-Awlaki], AQAP, and other terrorist and violent extremist causes."[62] In September of the following year, the U.S. government killed al-Awlaki, along with his sixteen-year-old son, in a drone strike in Yemen's al-Jawf Governorate, with a senior administration official explaining that he posed "a continuing and imminent threat to the United States as a chief of external operations for AQAP."[63]

During 2010, as U.S. pressure mounted, the State Department reported that the Yemeni government had launched "large-scale kinetic operations against suspected AQAP members in the south." This was an unprecedented effort on the part of the Yemeni government, though it was plagued by poor intelligence and succeeded only in putting local tribes on the defensive.[64] Moreover, this increase in Yemeni military operations was met with a corresponding increase in domestic terrorist attacks. In 2009, AQAP was responsible for only 3 terrorist attacks. In 2010, this number increased to 48. In the following year, AQAP attacks again rose to 75, and in 2012 spiked at 199 attacks. These were largely directed against Yemeni military and government targets as revenge for ongoing military operations.[65] On June 19, 2010, AQAP members, disguised in Yemeni military uniforms, attacked the headquarters of the Yemeni PSO in Aden during a morning flag-raising ceremony, killing ten officers. Following the attack, AQAP called on local tribes to "light up the ground with fire under the tyrants of infidelity in the regime" in revenge for government air strikes.[66] During Ramadan in the summer of 2010, AQAP targeted senior Yemeni military and intelligence officials directly involved in counterterrorism operations, killing sixty by September 2010. The increase in domestic terrorism, however, was not paired with an increase in international attacks. As one analyst noted, "In addition to systematically targeting senior and field-level security officials, AQAP militants repeatedly assaulted security officers, soldiers, and police with small arms fire and hand grenades throughout southern and central Yemen. There were no reported attacks executed against traditionally preferred targets such as western embassies or the country's oil infrastructure within Yemen."[67]

In response to the killing of senior Yemeni officials and under continued pressure from the U.S. government, Yemen launched a major military offensive against AQAP in the Lawdar District of Abyan Governorate in August 2010. The offensive lasted several days and led to the deaths of a dozen soldiers, nineteen people identified as al-Qaeda members, and at least three civilians. The fighting forced many local civilians to flee their homes. Yemen's deputy interior minister, General Saleh al-Zaweri, stated, "Security forces have taught the terrorists of Al-Qaeda a hard lesson and inflicted painful hits on them, forcing those terrorist elements that tried to hide, to flee after dozens were killed and wounded."[68] The following month Saleh launched another military offensive against AQAP, this time using forces armed and trained through U.S. assistance programs, in the city of Hawta in Shabwah Governorate. Yemeni troops besieged the city, relying on artillery shelling and strafing runs by attack helicopters. The operation coincided with a visit to Sana'a by John Brennan to discuss Yemeni counterterrorism efforts, allowing Saleh to present concrete evidence of Yemen's cooperation. U.S. officials viewed these operations as largely ineffective, particularly given the lack of solid intelligence, with U.S. cruise missiles and drone strikes helping fill the gap in Yemeni counterterrorism efforts.[69]

Yet, Yemeni officials frequently took public credit for various strikes, including those conducted by the United States, which created difficulties for the Yemeni government. A May 24, 2010, U.S. missile strike hit a convoy under the belief it was carrying local terrorists to a meeting with al-Qaeda operatives. Rather than al-Qaeda-linked terrorists, the strike killed Jabir al-Shabwani, the deputy governor of Marib Governorate, along with other members of a Yemeni mediation team. When the Yemeni government took responsibility for the air strike, the Shabwani tribe responded the following day by blowing up an oil pipeline running from Marib to the Ras Isa terminal on the Red Sea coast. Tribesmen also attacked the presidential palace in Marib but were repelled by Yemeni soldiers and tanks stationed around the palace's perimeter.[70]

In May 2011, the AQAP spin-off group Ansar al-Sharia targeted the southern city of Zinjibar and took control of it within two days. AQAP's top cleric stated, "The name Ansar al Sharia is what we use to introduce ourselves in areas where we work to tell people about our work and goals, and that we are on the path of Allah."[71] The group was now transitioning to controlling and governing territory and providing the local population with social services and security, complete with a harsh fundamentalist vision of law and order based on their interpretation of sharia. Their support of a sharia-based system of governance was seen to be the antithesis of the Saleh regime and a means of undermining state authority. An AQAP spokesperson pushed back against the corrupt political status quo in Yemen, stating, "People have become fed-up with socialism and democracy. . . . The Mujahideen are capable of being the only alternative, and in their hands is the solution for all these transgressions. If the [Yemeni] people stand with them, they will arrive [at the desired Yemeni state] by the shortest path."[72]

With the shift to controlling territory, Abdul Ghani al-Iryani, a Sana'a-based political analyst, stated, "As these group of militants took over the city, then AQAP came in and also tribes from areas that have been attacked in the past by the Yemeni government and by the U.S. government. They came because they have a feud against the regime and against the U.S. There is a nucleus of AQAP, but the vast majority are people who are aggrieved by attacks on their homes that forced them to go out and fight."[73]

The back-and-forth violence between militants and government forces continued unabated following Saleh's resignation in November 2011 in the wake of the Arab Spring protests and with the establishment of a new government in February 2012 under Saleh's successor, President Abdrabbuh Mansur Hadi, who had served as Saleh's vice president since 1994. In May 2012, AQAP targeted a military parade in Sana'a. The bombing killed ninety people, mostly soldiers. After the attack, an AQAP spokesperson made an announcement directed at Yemeni military leadership: "We will take revenge, God willing, and the flames of war will reach you everywhere, and what happened is but the start of a jihad project in defense of honor and sanctities."[74] The following month in Aden, an AQAP suicide bomber killed the senior Yemeni commander for southern operations, Major General Salim Ali Qatn, who had initiated a further crackdown on AQAP militants following his appointment by President Hadi.[75] In August 2012, AQAP fighters launched another attack against the government's intelligence headquarters in Aden, killing twenty intelligence officers and wounding another thirteen.

The pressure of fighting on two fronts—against AQAP in the South and the growing Houthi rebellion in the North—was too much for the Yemeni government to handle. In August 2014, Houthi forces advanced into Sana'a and pushed Hadi's government into exile in the southern port city of Aden. The Houthis' military successes and capture of the capital prompted a 2015 Saudi military intervention, backed by U.S. military assistance, in support of the Yemeni government, with the Saudi government accusing Iran of backing the Houthis across Saudi Arabia's southern border. This intervention has been heavily criticized for its targeting of Yemeni civilians and contributing to a humanitarian crisis in Yemen.[76] In the opportunities provided by the chaos of the civil war and the emergence of new terrorist groups, including an Islamic State affiliate, terrorist violence in Yemen continued to climb ever higher in the coming years.

## MALI: THE STRUGGLE FOR AZAWAD

In the early months of the war on terror, U.S. security officials saw the potential for al-Qaeda to exploit the vast Sahel region of western Africa, with Mali part of a broader conversation about al-Qaeda's movements outside of Afghanistan. At the time, this region was of secondary concern to more immediately troublesome areas such as Afghanistan, Iraq, Pakistan, and Yemen. U.S. attention was pulled to Mali's northern deserts with the increased activity of the Salafist Group for Preaching and Combat (GSPC), which, in an effort to bolster its perceived legitimacy, publicly claimed allegiance to al-Qaeda and renamed itself al-Qaeda in the Islamic Maghreb (AQIM) in 2007.[77] As it was using Mali's northern periphery as a safe haven, there were apprehensions that the group had ambitions beyond West Africa and could launch attacks against Europe or even the United States. In response, U.S. officials increasingly pushed the Malian government to confront GSPC/AQIM and provided military assistance to support these efforts.

Mali initially did little against the group due to limited state capacity and concerns that any military actions in the North would stir up further resistance from the region's Tuareg tribes, who had a history of rebellion, including a breakaway Tuareg rebellion in 2007. As GSPC/AQIM's activities increased, so, too, did U.S. pressure, with Mali finally deploying its military in the North in the fall of 2011 to target the group and establish control over the periphery through a stronger military presence. Local Tuareg saw the new military deployments as an external intrusion by the government, a sentiment amplified by civilian casualties and various human rights abuses during the operations. This helped lead to the formation of several antistate militant groups from the local population, most notably the religious group Ansar Dine, which the U.S. government argued had connections with al-Qaeda.

As Mali increased its military efforts in the northern Tuareg region against GSPC/AQIM, domestic terrorism increased in response. A 2021 Security Assistance Monitor report found that "the U.S. counterterrorism policy in the Sahel led to a substantial increase in military aid, equipment, training and operations over the past decade. It has, however, been followed (not preceded) by an actual increase in violent extremist activity in the region."[78] The escalating violence in northern Mali eventually spurred an international intervention to confront the terrorist threat. However, the initial spike in domestic terrorism can be traced to Mali's introduction of a military approach to counterterrorism, in line with the demands of U.S. officials, which negatively impacted the government's already troubled relationship with its Tuareg periphery. Figure 5.2 shows the overall trend of terrorism within Mali from 1996 to 2012.

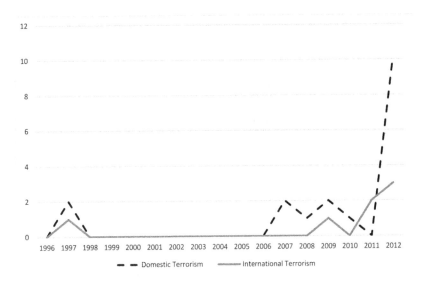

**FIGURE 5.2**  Annual count of terrorist attacks in Mali, 1996–2012.

*Source:* Enders, Sandler, and Gaibulloev, "Domestic Versus Transnational Terrorism";
Gaibulloev, Piazza, and Sandler, "Regime Types and Terrorism."

## THE TUAREG'S STRUGGLE FOR AZAWAD:
## A SCENE SETTER

Due to the difficult environment of the Sahel's deserts and their traditional nomadic lifestyle, the Berber Tuareg tribes had long lived outside
of direct government control and maintained their tribal customs, with
a reputation for banditry and raiding, fierce independence, and extraordinary survival skills in the harshest of desert climates. In the 1820s,
French explorer René Caillié observed that anyone "exposed to [the
Tuaregs'] attacks stand in such awe of them that the appearance of three
or four [Tuaregs] is sufficient to strike terror into five or six villages."[79]
The intrusion of French colonialism into the region in the latter half of
the nineteenth century quickly led to clashes with the Tuareg, with early
efforts to extend French influence stymied by Tuareg resistance. It was
not until the turn of the twentieth century that French forces restarted
efforts to extend French control within Tuareg territory, among the last
remaining spaces that European colonizing efforts had yet to reach in

Africa. The French resorted to military force backed by modern armaments to assert influence over the Tuareg, with French colonial administration in West Africa dominated by the military and its interests.[80]

French efforts to control the region at the turn of the twentieth century were frequently noted for their brutality. In 1898, the governor of French Sudan (as Mali was known under French rule) explained, "Considering that we will never succeed in making friends with these [Tuareg and Arab] tribes because of their religious and racial hatred towards us, and because we have deprived them of their only resource, namely plunder and theft, we have to eliminate them if we can. This is best done by starving them. . . . The tribes will either starve, or escape to other areas, or else they will feel powerless and will unconditionally surrender, and then we will be able to force them to adopt a way of life that will prevent them from doing any harm."[81] At this time, French officials kept tabs on the locations of the wells and markets where Tuareg tribesmen found provisions as means of exerting control over their behavior. As a result, the Tuareg could, as one traveler through the region noted, "be brought back to reason if they did not want to be starved to death or die of thirst."[82]

French policy toward the Tuareg initially aimed at "pacification" of the tribes, relocating and settling the traditionally nomadic communities, and dismantling customary Tuareg society and leadership as a means of asserting French control, with several Tuareg rebellions breaking out in the early twentieth century in response.[83] Yet, the French colonial government was unable to assert direct political control uniformly over the northern periphery. French policy eventually shifted to isolating the Tuareg, along with exempting them from forced labor and military conscription, which kept the Tuareg separated from the general population of the West African colony. French officials even increasingly romanticized the desert-dwelling Tuareg, with their indigo-dyed turbans (they were known as the "blue men of the Sahara"), and they would subsequently come to "occupy a privileged place in the French colonial imagination."[84] Despite these romanticized views, however, Tuareg areas in the northern deserts continued to suffer from a chronic lack of development and attention from colonial authorities.

As French West Africa began its transition to independence, many Tuareg hoped to form their own postcolonial state, free from the continued political domination of remote European capitals. These hopes were bolstered by the creation under French law of a Common Organization of the Saharan Regions in January 1957, which was presented as an economic initiative to exploit the Sahel's resources. Two years later, Tuareg leaders, with the encouragement of some officers from the French Army, petitioned to form an independent state known as Azawad, the traditional name for their territory. The following year, the first president of Niger, Hamani Diori, denounced such French interventions as the work of colonial officers "wishing to play the role of colonel Lawrence of Arabia toward the nomads."[85]

The effort to establish a unified Tuareg state was ultimately unsuccessful, and, following the French withdrawal, the Tuareg found themselves split largely between five states—Mali, Niger, Libya, Algeria, and Burkina Faso—as minorities with little access to the distant centers of power. In Mali, the independent government would be controlled by southern political leaders assimilated into French colonial power structures and culture and with little knowledge or contact with the northern Tuareg periphery.[86] When Mali gained independence from French colonial rule in 1960, the new president, Modibo Keita, established a centralized one-party state devoted to large-scale economic planning, including a policy of industrial and agricultural modernization for the new African nation. The government saw the Tuaregs' nomadic practices as antithetical to this new policy, which emphasized agriculture as the only proper use for land, and to Keita's vision for a modern Malian state, with the northern region labeled "the useless Mali."[87] The government, dominated by the Bambara and Malinke ethnic groups from the South, attempted to convert the northern tribes into "productive" and "taxed" citizens by encouraging them to settle into villages and become farmers, as well as conscripting young men for labor on infrastructure projects.

This settlement policy was accompanied by a ban on the Tuareg language, government interference into traditionally autonomous tribal governance, and the introduction of a military administration in the North to assert central government control. The tensions sparked by coerced settlement were made worse by widespread droughts during the 1960s and 1970s, when it was reported that the government was hoarding food in support of its effort to control the periphery. A 1973 cable from the U.S. embassy in Bamako stated, "There is evidence piling up that [the Government of Mali] is hoarding grain in government warehouses at distribution points. . . . [The government] is doing only small amounts of food and hoarding [the] rest to keep fiercely independent and sometimes hostile desert nomads, i.e. Touaregs, under government control in towns. There have been some missionary reports that [the state is] not supplying Touaregs with grain which may relate to historical struggle between black/non-black peoples of Sahel/desert region."[88] Scholar of the Sahel Delphine Perrin observed that the tension between the Tuareg periphery and the central government lay less with a "principled antagonism between a nomadic culture and the state logic" than a "persisting feeling of marginalization of a community whose members expect or grasp at rights and benefits that they associate with citizenship. Most Tuaregs have deplored the deprivation of their rights both as a community (loss of their resources, way of living, territory) and as citizens (discrimination in their access to various rights)."[89]

From independence, Mali faced "competing nationalisms," as described by historian Baz Lecocq, between the southern-dominated center of the country and the Tuareg-populated North.[90] Tuareg anger over their persistent marginalization, combined with the heavy-handed tactics of the Malian military, soon led to the first of four rebellions to take place over the next five decades. The leader of the first rebellion, in the 1960s, Elledi ag Alla of the Kel Adrar tribal confederation, whose father was beheaded by French authorities when he was seven years old, explained, "I became a rebel to avenge my father, killed by the French administration, and to personally avenge myself for what the security agents of the Malian security post at Bouressa kept repeating at me—that if I did not stay quiet I would be slain like my father had been."[91] In the coming years, the presence of Malian troops in the North remained a key point of conflict as they were perceived as an outside invading force. Following a further Tuareg rebellion in the early 1990s, the resulting peace agreement promised the demilitarization of the North with greater political and economic opportunities for the Tuareg.

Following the signing of this agreement, Tuareg leaders quickly began criticizing the government for failing to live up to its conditions, and they continued clamoring for greater political autonomy and increased development in the North. To resolve the situation, the political leadership of the Tuareg Alliance for Democracy and Change (ADC) and the Malian government signed an Algerian-mediated peace agreement in

2006, the Algiers Accords. The key components of the new agreement were promises for an increase in development in the North and the establishment of a northern security force consisting of local Tuareg instead of the regular military, which was largely comprised of southerners.[92] The following year, a small group of Tuareg under Ibrahim ag Bhanga of the Kidal region again rebelled against the government over anger at the continued presence of regular military forces in the North, which they saw as a violation of the Algiers Accords.

Many leading Tuareg from competing tribes opposed this new rebellion, including the leader of the ADC, Iyad ag Ghaly. Ag Ghaly was a prominent Tuareg leader who led the rebellion in the 1990s and, following reconciliation, became an intermediary and advisor for the central government in its relations with the North. Though Tuareg political leaders rejected the rebellion's use of violence, they still embraced the objectives ag Bhanga pursued, including greater political representation for northern Mali, increased funds for development projects, the removal of the southern-dominated Malian army from the North, and recruitment of Tuareg for a local security force. With Malian president Amadou Toumani Touré pushing for a negotiated settlement to the conflict, government efforts were marked by restraint and a seeming awareness of the broader backlash that military operations would provoke. The government's traditional approach to fighting the Tuareg, especially given the limited capacity of Mali's military, was to "fight the Tuaregs to the negotiating table."[93] The government ultimately relied on local Tuareg and Arab militias to drive ag Bhanga's forces into Algeria in February 2009. Despite the defeat of ag Bhanga's rebellion within Mali, the government made little effort to address the underlying causes behind the conflict, with broader tensions between the Tuareg periphery and the central government remaining in place.

## NORTHERN MALI AND THE WAR ON TERROR: THE FIRST STEP

As the war on terror expanded outside of Afghanistan and Iraq, U.S. officials viewed the empty deserts of the Sahel with concern. In particular, Mali's vast "ungovernable North," as described by President Touré, was recognized as a potential problem by both Malian and U.S. authorities.[94] Officials within the Bush administration feared that terrorist groups, especially GSPC/AQIM, could exploit the region as a safe haven. This group originally formed as a breakaway faction of the Armed Islamic Group (GIA) during the Algerian Civil War in the 1990s. It had connections with Tuareg tribes in northern Mali through its Algerian leader Mokhtar Belmokhtar, who fought with the mujahedeen in Afghanistan against the Soviet-backed government in the early 1990s and trained in al-Qaeda camps while there. He returned to Algeria in 1993 to fight in the civil war and eventually left GIA to join the splinter group. Belmokhtar eventually moved into northern Mali to exploit its smuggling networks and fund the group's activities, and he married the daughters of prominent Tuareg families.

To help build Mali's domestic counterterrorism capacity, the U.S. government included the West African state in its Pan-Sahel Initiative (PSI), announced in late 2002. The program was meant to "assist Mali, Niger, Chad, and Mauritania in detecting and responding to suspicious movement of people and goods across and within their borders through training, equipment and cooperation. Its goals support two U.S. national security interests in Africa: waging the war on terrorism and enhancing regional peace and security."[95] In October 2002, Robert Perry, the deputy assistant secretary of state for African affairs, along with Stephanie Kinney, the State Department's deputy counterterrorism coordinator, traveled with the PSI team to Mali and met with officials from Mali's Directorate-General for State Security (DGSE) to discuss the country's domestic counterterrorism efforts. Perry explained the importance of the PSI, especially for intelligence sharing, to the DGSE's director general, Colonel Sambo Ilo Diallo. During the meeting, Colonel Diallo stressed that counterterrorism was the DGSE's "top priority."[96] In 2005, the PSI was superseded by the more comprehensive Trans-Sahara Counterterrorism Partnership in 2005, which sought to build military capacity among participating states. While the U.S. government addressed the potential for terrorist activity in the Sahel through a regional approach under these programs, the bilateral relationship with Mali ultimately remained on the back burner in the early years of the war on terror, with U.S. officials aware of the potential problems but lacking the resources and the policy focus to adequately address them.

Senior Malian officials perceived the northern region's Tuareg tribes as one of its primary security challenges, and they understood the war on terror as an opportunity to gain U.S. support in extending the writ of the state into the periphery. During a June 2, 2003, meeting in Bamako with the deputy commander of U.S. European Command, General Charles Wald, and the U.S. ambassador to Mali, Vicki Huddleston, Touré expressed his desire "to deepen Mali's military relationship with the U.S. in order to better control the northern desert regions, which cover 60 percent of the country and are ripe for contraband and terrorist activity. . . . Mali's geographic location lends it to infiltration." He further added, "Mali does not have the means to continue its counter-terrorist activities without U.S. assistance . . . and welcomes the Pan-Sahel Initiative."[97] In the meeting, General Wald highlighted the importance of continuing and strengthening military cooperation between the United States and Mali for counterterrorism purposes, "since terrorist activity in the region will likely increase unless we work together to stop it . . . at a time when potential terrorists from Pakistan, Afghanistan, and the Middle East are moving through Africa searching for safe places to hide and train their followers."[98] In a meeting with Malian foreign minister Lassana Traoré that same day, General Wald further stated, "Africa is growing in strategic importance particularly in the Global War on Terror; and Mali, in the heart of Sahel, is strategically placed to play an important role in that war. The US is seeking good partners, and Mali, given its vision and location, can definitely be one." Traoré reiterated that while Mali "fully supports the Global War on Terror," the country "needs U.S. assistance to succeed in its goal of being a leader in peace and security in the region."[99]

U.S. officials increasingly became concerned that al-Qaeda operatives and other al-Qaeda-linked groups could exploit the historical tensions between the northern periphery and Mali's central government, a point stressed by several Malian officials in appeals for increased U.S. military support. The head of DGSE explained to visiting U.S. officials in October 2002 that Malian state security "is doing everything possible to wrest control of Mali's enormous northern desert land from bandits, traffickers and smugglers, but it needs a great deal of help in order to improve its capabilities. . . . Communication with and within the vast north is difficult due to a small existing network of poor-quality roads, great distances between population centers, a lack of means of transport, and limited means of communication."[100] In a March 2003 meeting with the Malian defense minister Mahamane Kalil Maiga, Ambassador Huddleston agreed that "the north of Mali is becoming a haven for suspicious activities," with the PSI created "to address northern instability." According to a 2003 cable from the U.S. embassy in Bamako, Minister Maiga told the U.S. ambassador, "US efforts in Iraq and the War on Terror will lead fleeing terrorists to new locations. Mali with its isolated desert north, will become a haven for terrorist activity."[101] With security and development in the North going "hand in hand," Huddleston further argued in an April 22, 2004, meeting with Touré that a major issue facing Mali's North was "youth susceptible to recruitment by religious fundamentalists and GSPC [AQIM] because of poverty, isolation, and joblessness," a problem made worse by "growing religious tensions," the "proliferation of arms," and "weak governance" in the region. Given these conditions, U.S. diplomats in Bamako recommended that the Malian government "establish an effective military presence throughout the North, including re-establishing small bases in isolated villages," in addition to increasing development and improving governance.[102]

Even with GSPC/AQIM increasing its presence and connections among the Tuareg tribes and U.S. officials pushing for offensive action, Touré was initially reluctant to engage the military in difficult counterterrorism operations in the North. He wanted to avoid pushing the Malian military into direct conflict with GSPC/AQIM, which was not targeting Mali at the time, and was wary of the impact military operations would have on the government's fragile relationship with the Tuareg periphery. In 2005, the State Department reported that the Malian government

has maintained a limited military presence in the north since the negotiated end of a rebellion by elements of the Tuareg population in 1996. The size of the country and the limited resources of the Malian government hamper the effectiveness of military patrols and border control measures. There have been no confrontation between the military and the GSPC [AQIM] in 2005, and the government has not taken any steps to modify its military force posture in the region or directly confront GSPC [AQIM] elements in the north because of the perceived potential to create unrest.[103]

U.S. officials' focus on GSPC/AQIM increased when the group swore allegiance to al-Qaeda in September 2006 and rebranded itself as AQIM in January 2007. With GSPC/AQIM seemingly able to operate with a free hand in the northern periphery due to the limited capacity of the Malian state, U.S. officials increased their pressure on their Malian counterparts to move against the rebranded group, with Malian leaders continuing to hesitate to commit their security forces to offensive military action over the potential internal backlash. In considering whether to confront GSPC/AQIM in the North, the Malian government, according to a former U.S. defense attaché, felt that "it was best not to poke the hornet's nest."[104] Yet, Ambassador Huddleston understood that U.S. support for the Malian military, and the resulting U.S. pressure to act, was necessary for the "termination" of GSPC/AQIM, and she urged her successor, Gillian Milovanic, to focus on creating units of elite Malian troops to target and destroy al-Qaeda in the North. Milovanic, for her part, highlighted the limitations of U.S. military aid at the time and thought such a plan was untenable given the poor condition of Mali's troops. She instead argued that Malian military forces should work to control desert roads in the North and hunt down al-Qaeda's weapons and fuel caches.[105]

As Bahanga's rebellion died down at the beginning of 2009 with the disarmament of the Tuareg rebels in Kidal, GSPC/AQIM increased its kidnapping of Westerners. Malian officials feared that any negotiations would simply strengthen the group's position and lead to further hostage taking. U.S. officials also reported that GSPC/AQIM was attempting to infiltrate Europe for operations against Western targets.[106] Under pressure from U.S. authorities, the Malian military launched an operation to confront GSPC/AQIM, leading to limited engagements with the group in the summer of 2009.[107] This operation was unsuccessful in limiting the group's activities given the Malian military's supply difficulties in the North, government troops' limited knowledge of the region, and the country's general lack of resources. Following the military's failed operation, Touré requested increased U.S. military support for military action against GSPC/AQIM. In October 2009, Milovanovic announced the U.S. government was increasing its military assistance to "help Mali fight militants in its northern desert."[108]

The following year, Mali began preparing its Special Program for Peace, Security, and Development as a means of establishing control over the security situation in the North. This initiative, launched in August 2011 with a drastic increase in U.S. military assistance, established Secure Development and Governance centers at eleven strategic locations in the northern deserts.[109] Malian military forces manned each location to provide security for development projects within the surrounding region. However, the military's presence undermined the legitimacy of the projects among the local tribal communities, who simply saw this as a further effort to militarize the North. Tuareg leaders complained that the government did not consult them before implementing this program and criticized the high proportion of the budget used for security. As construction on the centers began, the project quickly faced opposition from local tribes due to the strong military presence, with a series of attacks against the military barracks then in construction. While Malian government officials claimed GSPC/AQIM committed the attacks, the International Crisis Group reported that local Tuareg were responsible.[110]

## MALI AND DOMESTIC TERRORISM: THE SECOND STEP

As the Malian military increased its presence in the North, the National Movement for Azawad, founded the previous year to promote Tuareg rights, joined with other Tuareg groups and formed the National Movement for the Liberation of Azawad (MNLA) in October 2011 to advocate for an independent Tuareg state. The MNLA was comprised predominately of younger tribesmen who had previously pushed for equal representation of Tuareg in the army and universities, increased economic opportunities, infrastructure development, and a greater share of resource wealth from their territory. The movement initially declared its intention to find a political route to Tuareg independence, and it gained momentum with the arrest of its leadership after the founding meeting in Timbuktu and violent repression of its demonstrations. The group was also bolstered by the return of Tuareg serving in the Libyan Army, disbanded after Muammar Gaddafi's fall from power in 2011, along with the accompanying flood of weapons. There were serious concerns within the U.S. and Malian governments that these Tuareg and their fight for independence could be exploited by GSPC/AQIM.

With Mali signaling its commitment to a military approach in the North, violence broke out in January 2012 as the MNLA began targeting Mali's military forces in an effort to drive them out of the region. Emotions stemming from previous rebellions were never far from the surface. During the first Tuareg uprising in 1963, for example, the Malian army killed the father of the MNLA's military leader, Mohamed ag Najem. As the fighting intensified, the Tuareg group occupied several major towns across northern Mali, including Kidal, Gao, and Timbuktu. It then set up its own system of governance to contest the government's sovereignty over Tuareg territory. On April 5, 2012, the group declared independence for a Tuareg state of Azawad. Between 2011 and 2012, there was an accompanying increase in GSPC/AQIM attacks as it exploited the political instability and increased its activities in Mali.[111]

In fighting for an independent state, the MNLA leadership was opposed to working with Tuareg that had previously cooperated with the Malian government, most notably Iyad ag Ghaly. They were wary of ag Ghaly's past links with Touré and other central government officials. With the increasing military operations in the North, ag Ghaly, who had returned from a diplomatic posting in Saudi Arabia in November 2008 and had since been relegated to minor duties, switched his loyalties and founded Ansar Dine to join the Tuareg fight against the Malian government. Unlike MNLA's secular nationalism, Ansar Dine's goal was to replace Malian secular law with their interpretation of sharia, which ag Ghaly saw as an antidote to corruption within the government and the continued exploitation of the northern periphery. Many of his supporters were Tuareg from his Ifogha tribal group who saw Ansar Dine as a means of protecting Ifogha interests in the ensuing violence.[112] The group's first attack took place in March 2012, with Malian military officials quickly pointing to a connection between Ansar Dine and GSPC/AQIM.[113] The following year, the State Department designated Ansar Dine a Foreign Terrorist Organization. Despite the fact that the group was comprised of local Tuareg, U.S. officials saw it primarily as an al-Qaeda-linked terrorist organization given its religious-based goals.[114]

The fighting in the North soon led to the collapse of the Malian government. In March 2012, the military staged a coup in response to what it perceived as a lack of support for its counterterrorism operations. The coup leaders justified their actions by referencing "the government's failure to provide adequate equipment to the defense and security forces fulfilling their mission to defend the country's territorial integrity."[115] Following a negotiated settlement, power passed to the hands of the speaker of the National Assembly, Dioncounda Traoré, who promised to "wage a total and relentless war" against the Tuareg.[116] Despite the U.S. government suspending its military assistance to Mali following the coup, U.S. officials voiced support for Traore's efforts in the North. Speaking at the United Nations in September 2012, Secretary Clinton offered the following warning:

> We all know what is happening in Mali, and the incredible danger posed by violent extremists imposing their brutal ideology, committing human rights abuses, destroying irreplaceable cultural heritage. . . . We have to train the security forces in Mali, help them dislodge the extremists, protect human rights, and defend borders. . . . For some time, al-Qaida in the Islamic Maghreb and other groups have launched attacks and kidnappings from northern Mali into neighboring countries. Now, with a larger safe haven and increased freedom to maneuver, terrorists are seeking to extend their reach and their networks in multiple directions.[117]

As Ansar Dine and the MNLA competed with one another for resources and territory, they faced off in the Battles of Gao and Timbuktu in June 2012. Following an Ansar Dine victory, it replaced MNLA as the leading Tuareg group in the fight against the state. Oumar Ould Hamaha, Ansar Dine's chief of security in Gao, stated after the battle, "Our fighters control the perimeter. We control Timbuktu completely. We control Gao completely. It's Ansar Dine that commands the north of Mali. Now we have every opportunity to apply Shariah."[118] Spurred on by Ansar Dine's success, other religious groups soon followed in its steps and joined the conflict, including the GSPC/AQIM splinter group Movement for Oneness and Jihad in West Africa in March 2012 and the Islamic Movement of the Azawad in January 2013.

Al-Qaeda core's leadership opposed the increase in domestic-focused violence within Mali and pushed its affiliates to use the region's deserts as a safe haven from which to focus efforts against Western targets. They also instructed their followers to avoid antagonizing or fighting the local government, except in direct self-defense, and sign truces with the "near enemy."[119] The GSPC/AQIM leadership, based in Algeria's Kabylie region, similarly opposed Ansar Dine's activities, wishing to retain northern Mali as its rear base. They condemned its battles with the MNLA to assert political control over the northern territory, viewing it as a major mistake. In a 2012 letter to Ansar Dine's ag Ghaly, Mokhtar Belmokhtar, and other groups operating in northern Mali, the head of GSPC/AQIM, Abdelmalek Droukdel, wrote that the goal in northern Mali should be to outlast the U.S.-backed military intervention to "gain a region under control and a people fighting for us and a refuge for our members that allows us to move forward with our program." Moreover, he considered the declaration of an "Islamic State of Azawad" premature because "establishing a just Islamic regime ruling people by the Shari'a of the People's Lord is [a] very big duty that exceeds the capabilities of any organization or movement [now operating in Azawad]." He warned that the "extreme speed with which you applied Shari'a Law . . . in an environment ignorant of religion" was wrong as "our previous experience proved that applying Shari'a this way, without taking into account the environment into consideration will lead to people rejecting religion and engender hatred toward the mujahiden." The letter also chastised Ansar Dine for its use of violence against civilians and "the destruction of shrines," which could bring "negative repercussions."[120] Above all, Droukdel pushed for the groups in northern Mali to show restraint and "not to monopolize the political and military stage."[121]

In a September 2012 letter back to GSPC/AQIM leadership, Belmokhtar questioned their ability to direct the local fight in Mali and responded, "Your board gives orders whereas there is no single leader in it who knows this area [the Sahel] or lived here."[122] In response, GSPC/AQIM leadership stated that Belmokhtar had "too much independence, having no link other than in name with the organization's command, showing no interest, no consideration, no respect to the guidance and to the orders issued by the Emirate [AQIM]."[123] After this dispute, Belmokhtar disassociated himself from GSPC/AQIM and formed the splinter group known as the Signed-in-Blood Battalion. This new group began to conduct attacks within both Mali and neighboring Algeria. Belmokhtar warned the

Malian government of the consequences of further military action: "We will respond forcefully [to all attackers]; we promise we will follow you to your homes and you will feel pain and we will attack your interests."[124] Ansar Dine also ignored the GSPC/AQIM orders not to launch attacks against government targets and provoke a retaliatory response. In January 2013, the group entered southern Mali and captured the town of Konna. The group announced to the town's residents in a mosque, "Your town was long terrorized by the Malian government, and now we have taken it. There is no mayor, no police, and no army. There is only us."[125]

As a new national unity government was being formed in August 2012, there were increasing reports that the Malian army was committing extrajudicial killings and human rights abuses against Tuareg civilians, including indiscriminate shelling of Tuareg camps, as reprisals against terrorist attacks.[126] In one incident in Diabaly in late 2012, for example, the military executed sixteen Muslim religious figures after suspecting them of being militants. Shortly after, Ansar Dine fighters attacked the military units positioned in Diabaly and occupied the town in revenge for the incident.[127] Mali's minister of justice, Malick Coulibaly, attempted to explain away the incident, stating, "No army in the world is perfect. The US army is one of the most professional in the world, yet they have been found to have committed acts of torture and unlawful killings. That exists in all armies."[128] These abuses, he was quick to add, were matched by the militant groups' own atrocities against civilians. Nevertheless, Ansar Dine continued its southern march at this time and would soon attack the town of Mopti, only 460 kilometers from the capital city of Bamako.

## MALI AND THE TERRORISM TRAP: THE THIRD STEP

With the rising levels of violence and the looming threat to the capital city, the international community saw the need to increase its support for Mali's military efforts in the North. In December 2012, the U.S. Africa Command head General Carter Ham stated, "As each day goes by, al-Qaeda and other organizations are strengthening their hold in northern Mali."[129] That same month, UN secretary-general Ban Ki-moon supported a plan for the deployment of regional troops to assist in taking back control of the North. He wrote, "Northern Mali is at risk of becoming a permanent haven for terrorists and organized criminal networks where people are subjected to a very strict interpretation of Shariah law and human rights are abused on a systematic basis."[130] GSPC/AQIM was defiant in the face of such international condemnation, responding, "We warn all the countries that are planning aggression against us, [we will mete out] merciless punishment."[131]

Following the January 2013 attack on Konna, France launched Operation Serval, a military intervention into northern Mali involving twenty-five hundred troops and extensive air support at the invitation of Mali's transitional government.[132] This operation was supported by Malian and Economic Community of West African States troops as part of the African-led International Support Mission to Mali, and, beginning in April 2013, the UN Multidimensional Integrated Stabilization Mission in Mali, with U.S. logistical and intelligence assistance. The French motivation for intervening was partially tied to France's economic interests in the region, especially the two uranium mines run by the French nuclear energy company Areva across the border in Niger, from which France derived 18 percent of the fuel needed for its fifty-eight nuclear reactors. There were concerns that unrest in Mali could spill across the border and negatively impact the mining operations. Simultaneous to the deployment of French troops into Mali, France deployed special forces to guard the two uranium mines.[133]

As the international military operations pushed back the militants and reclaimed territory, terrorist attacks increased against French, UN, and other international targets; this included the November 2013 kidnapping and killing of two French journalists by GSPC/AQIM and a December 2013 attack against a UN camp in Kidal. In April 2014, protests were held against the presence of foreign troops in the country, with protestors arguing that they only served to provoke further violence. As France decreased its focus on Mali itself and embraced a regional approach to counterterrorism in West Africa, protestors asked why, "despite their large numbers, these [UN and Serval forces] fail to provide the necessary support for the Malian army in its fierce fight against terrorists."[134] The international intervention also helped to trigger an increase in locally oriented violence by creating opportunities for terrorist groups to launch a series of domestic terrorist attacks.[135] The Malian military also continued its own operations, which in turn further motivated a spike in anti-state attacks by local Tuareg groups.

With the increase in violence in the North, the Malian government moved to broker peace negotiations with the MNLA. President Traoré, however, refused to negotiate with Ansar Dine, arguing that the group was disqualified from the talks due to its brutality against civilians and terrorist attacks against the government.[136] A peace agreement between the government and a coalition of various Tuareg factions was signed in June 2015, promising greater political autonomy for the North and the establishment of a new northern security force consisting of local Tuareg—the same promises made in previous peace agreements. With this agreement in place, the government hoped it would allow Mali's military, again receiving U.S. military assistance, to focus attention on the threat from GSPC/AQIM and Ansar Dine. These two groups, which were left out of the peace negotiations, continued attacking domestic targets as well as the UN peacekeepers who remained in the North. By 2016, the UN mission in northern Mali had become the deadliest ongoing mission by UN peacekeepers anywhere in the world.[137]

## EGYPT: THE MIDDLE EAST'S "BULWARK AGAINST TERRORISM"

Following the signing of the U.S.-mediated Camp David Accords between the Egyptian and Israeli governments in 1978, Egypt, alongside Israel, has consistently received some of the highest levels of U.S. military assistance of any country in the world. The war on terror was an opportunity to further strengthen this military relationship. Terrorism was already a key focus of the Egyptian government as it maintained a zero-tolerance position given past security threats from domestic religious groups such as Egyptian Islamic Jihad and al-Jama'a al-Islamiyya.[138] These groups opposed the peace treaty with Israel, with members of Egyptian Islamic Jihad assassinating Egyptian president Anwar Sadat in 1981 as a result. Throughout the 1980s and 1990s, they sought to replace

Egypt's secular authoritarian government under Sadat's successor, Hosni Mubarak, with an Islamic state. During this period, they were active in committing a number of domestic terrorist attacks in the country's urban areas.

After the 9/11 attacks, the Sinai Peninsula, straddling the Israeli and Egyptian border, became a key security concern for both the Egyptian and U.S. governments, with U.S. officials pointing to the possibility that al-Qaeda could take advantage of the region's mountainous interior as well as Palestinians' cross-border movement between Sinai and the Gaza Strip. International terrorism first arrived in Sinai in 2004 as a spillover from the Israeli-Palestinian conflict. In its response to these attacks, largely directed against Israeli tourists in Sinai's coastal resort areas, the Egyptian government was restricted to using traditional law enforcement due to the conditions of the Camp David Accords, which limited Egypt's ability to unilaterally deploy its military forces along the border with Israel. Yet, during the resulting police operations in Sinai, human rights organizations criticized the police for mass arrests of Sinai Bedouin. Domestic terrorism, however, remained low, with many Bedouin resorting to protests to express their anger at government actions. Following Israel's decision in August 2011 to allow the deployment of Egyptian military forces to Sinai, Egypt launched U.S.-backed military operations in the region, which resulted in civilian casualties among the local Bedouin tribes due to the use of indiscriminate violence. This served as a catalyst for an increase in domestic terrorism as local groups, especially Ansar Bayt al-Maqdis, committed retaliatory attacks against the Egyptian government both inside and outside of Sinai. This increase in terrorism resulted in a series of counterattacks by the military, leading to even higher levels of terrorist activity. Figure 5.3 shows the trend in international and domestic terrorist attacks in Egypt from 1996 to 2012.

## THE BEDOUIN OF SINAI: A SCENE SETTER

Historically, the sparsely populated Sinai Peninsula was little more than a buffer zone between Egypt and Palestine. Prior to being brought into the fold of British administration in Egypt, Sinai was loosely

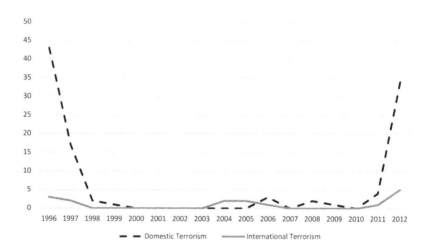

**FIGURE 5.3** Annual count of terrorist attacks in Egypt, 1996–2012.

*Source:* Enders, Sandler, and Gaibulloev, "Domestic Versus Transnational Terrorism";
Gaibulloev, Piazza, and Sandler, "Regime Types and Terrorism."

administered by a regional Ottoman governor at al-Arish on the Mediterranean coast. His only responsibility was to ensure the safe passage of
caravans and pilgrimages through the region, largely leaving the Bedouin to manage their internal affairs so long as any problems remained
within the tribe.[139] In 1884, the British closed the hajj route through Sinai,
which was constantly harassed by Bedouin raiding parties as pilgrims'
caravans served as a key source of local income. Pilgrims were instead
required to pass by steamship through the Suez Canal, which had been
completed in 1869 to provide a more direct sea route to British India. This
diminished the need for a government presence in the region, leaving
Bedouin tribal customs as the primary means of maintaining law and
order in this periphery. With the absence of any significant government
presence, as scholar Clinton Bailey has written, "Security is thus the focal,
obsessive concern of every Bedouin man, and he has a strategy for maintaining it. It begins with the understanding that he must, first and foremost, deter others from violating him and that his first line of defense in
deterring violations is to project an image of strength and sustain a reputation for being resolute in rectifying each and every infraction of his
right."[140]

In the early twentieth century, Egypt recognized Ottoman sovereignty over Sinai, with Ottoman authorities in turn granting Egypt the right to administer the peninsula under British guidance. The first British agent in Sinai, W. E. Jennings-Bramley, was appointed in 1904, and, upon his arrival in the region, he noted seeing only one manned garrison, which housed the regional governor and ten soldiers. A decade later, a British intelligence agent observed that the number of garrisons had expanded to nine but the total number of troops occupying them amounted to a mere 126.[141] While many travelers were able to bypass Sinai through the Suez Canal, traffic decreased even further when the British built a railroad during World War I from Qantara in the northwest corner of Sinai across the coast to Rafah in the present-day Gaza Strip.[142] At the time, Sinai remained outside of Egypt's customs borders and entry into the region was controlled by the Frontiers Administration in Cairo.[143] With the government's limited administrative reach into the peninsula, a British scholar observed in 1927 that the Sinai Bedouin "retain almost unchanged the habits and characteristics of the untamed denizens of the Arabian deserts."[144]

The period following the tumultuous years of World War I, the interwar period, and World War II saw rapid changes for the Sinai Bedouin. Beginning in 1953, when the Republic of Egypt was established following the previous year's military coup, the Sinai Peninsula fell under a military administration to increase government control in the region. The encroachment of the Egyptian government altered the economic and cultural life of the Bedouin tribes, as distinct from the approach of the British authorities, who were content to neglect the region and work through tribal structures when necessary. Bedouin were conscripted as unskilled laborers in numerous government projects in such areas as mining and roadbuilding. The government during this period also began the process of settling the tribes into villages to increase its ability to tax the Bedouin.[145]

During the Six Day War with Israel in 1967, Egypt lost the Sinai Peninsula to Israeli forces. The control of the peninsula quickly became a key political symbol for both countries. As part of the 1978 Camp David Accords and the 1979 peace treaty between Egypt and Israel, Israel committed to a staged withdrawal from Sinai and the return of political control to Egypt. Both nations also agreed to limitations on military deployments on either side of the international border along with the creation of the Multinational Force and Observers (MFO), a peacekeeping force to monitor compliance with the peace treaty.[146] In 1982, Israel withdrew the last of its troops and handed full control of Sinai back to the Egyptian government. Under the peace treaty, the Sinai Peninsula was established as an essentially demilitarized zone, with the Egyptian government only permitted to deploy civilian police in Sinai for security, often working with local Bedouin tribes to increase their effectiveness. Small numbers of military units were deployed at the border to support the police in apprehending (using minimal force) Palestinians who illegally crossed into Egypt. For Egypt to increase these border forces, the Israeli government had to agree to any new deployments, agreement that was rarely forthcoming given Israeli concerns that Egypt would attempt to alter the political status quo of the region.

Due to the period of Israeli rule and the tribal connections between the Sinai and the Negev Bedouin in southern Israel, the Egyptian government saw the Bedouin as potential fifth columnists for Israel and denied some Bedouin tribes Egyptian citizenship.[147] Even when their status as citizens was recognized, the Sinai Bedouin were politically and economically marginalized. The Egyptian government declared the peninsula as state-owned land and refused to recognize communal or tribal ownership; the Egyptian Army controlled any land of strategic military importance within the country, as designated by the defense minister under Law 143 of 1981, such as in the Sinai Peninsula.[148] Many Bedouin also were denied the right to own land for fear they would sell it to Israelis, and they were excluded from serving in the Egyptian military and police forces and blocked from holding key positions in Sinai's two governorates—North Sinai and South Sinai—all of which worsened their already marginalized status.[149]

After Egypt regained control of Sinai, the government focused on developing the Sinai region, particularly its tourist industry. Beginning in the 1990s, Egypt's Tourism Development Authority opened the sparsely populated region to land developers to build large hotels, resorts, and other tourist amenities on Sinai's coasts in a bid to attract private and foreign investment in these areas, while largely ignoring the interior of the peninsula. These new developments were promoted primarily to international tourists, as was the case with Sharm el-Sheikh's high-priced resorts like the Four Seasons, opened in 2002. The tourist industry in Sinai quickly expanded with the number of tourist establishments rising from just 17 in 1994 to 274 in 2003. By the early 2000s, hotel rooms in South Sinai comprised nearly one-quarter of all hotel rooms in Egypt.[150] Most of this growth occurred in four- and five-star resorts aimed at attracting foreign tourists.[151]

Yet, local Bedouin have derived relatively little benefit from Sinai's rapid economic development over the previous three decades. Egyptian workers migrated into Sinai in large numbers to fill newly created tourism jobs, part of the government's efforts to increase the settlement of urban Egyptians in Sinai to help relieve population pressures in the Nile Valley. Local Bedouin, on the other hand, were largely hired for low-paying and seasonal odd jobs or as outdoor guards with little benefits derived from the economic development surrounding the resorts. Urban development scholar Dona Stewart observed, "Employers do not generally hire Bedouin, preferring to bring in Egyptians from the Nile Valley who have a better knowledge of the tourist industry and foreign languages."[152] Many younger Bedouin were forced to rely instead on illegal smuggling and trafficking through Sinai's empty deserts and mountains.[153] The expansion of Sinai's tourist facilities also necessitated a reallocation of the scant resources of the desert, primarily water. With the drain from the local water table due to the expanded use by resorts located on the coast, Bedouin communities have suffered from constant water shortages. The growth of the tourist industry was paired with efforts to "settle the Bedouins into developed areas" to "help end the smuggling of goods, such as food and petrol, through tunnels to Gaza and the smuggling of migrants across the border," according to the governor of North Sinai.[154] With development projects further marginalizing communities in the periphery, government officials in Sinai were often viewed as outsiders by local Bedouin, with a distinct Bedouin identity frequently articulated "in direct opposition to an 'Egyptian' identity."[155] One resident of North Sinai remarked, "We have known four periods of occupation [ihtilal]: British, Egyptian, Israeli and, for the last 30 years, Egyptian again. Look, there they are, the colonialists of today."[156]

## THE SINAI PENINSULA AND THE WAR ON TERROR:
## THE FIRST STEP

With Egypt's past experiences with terrorism during the 1980s and 1990s, and understanding the importance of maintaining its military relationship with the United States, the Egyptian government was swift in offering its cooperation following the 9/11 attacks. On September 11, 2001, President Mubarak called a press conference to condemn publicly al-Qaeda's attacks and to express his sorrow and sadness over the day's events. Within days, the Egyptian government increased its domestic security efforts and began arresting terrorist suspects within the Cairo area. The Egyptian foreign minister proclaimed, "There is war between bin Laden and the whole world."[157] The U.S. intelligence community also worked closely with the Egyptian intelligence services, which shared information on terrorist suspects within the country, including biometric data.

U.S. and Egyptian focus soon shifted to the Sinai Peninsula. Despite the Egyptian government's "well-known opposition to Islamist terrorism and its effective intelligence and security services," the State Department pointed to "rugged northern Sinai" as a potential safe haven for terrorists, abetted by its smuggling networks and the fact that it served as "a transit point for Gazan Palestinians trying to infiltrate Israel."[158] The region would soon experience a series of international terrorist attacks that initially targeted Israeli tourists. The first attack occurred on October 7, 2004, with the bombing of the Hilton Hotel in Taba, on the Gulf of Aqaba near the Israeli border. A car bomb was detonated in front of the hotel killing 34 and injuring 105, many of whom were Israeli.[159] There were additional bombings at two campsites in Ras Shitan thirty-five miles south of Taba, similarly a destination point for Israeli tourists. The Egyptian Ministry of Interior soon produced nine suspects and identified the main perpetrator as Iyad Salah, a minibus driver of Palestinian origin from al-Arish in northern Sinai who died in the explosion. It was reported that he had ties to an unidentified Palestinian group in Gaza and, according to a government statement, "the bombings were a reaction to the deterioration of the situation in the occupied territories, and targeted Israelis staying in the hotel and at the camping ground."[160] U.S. and Israeli officials also argued that al-Qaeda was involved in the bombing. U.S. counterterrorism officials suspected that "Osama bin Laden's network played a role because the bombings showed a level of sophistication fitting al-Qaeda's usual operational style."[161]

Despite naming nine suspects, Egyptian police began making mass arrests throughout North Sinai, especially Bedouin who had regular access to explosives such as workers in mines. Human rights organizations reported that nearly three thousand people were arrested and held without charge. The security forces were also arresting women and children "as pawns to force men to turn themselves in."[162] One local resident near al-Arish stated that the police were initially confused. "They'd arrest whole villages and release them the same day, day after day, village after village," he explained. "The shaikhs said, 'You can't do this: tell us who you want, and we will bring them to you. Don't violate our homes and our women.'" Soon, the police began to target specific types of individuals, including men named Mustafa, those who drove red pickups, or individuals who had beards and therefore were "presumed adherents of Islamist congregations."[163]

In January 2005, the Egyptian government instituted a formal agreement with Bedouin leadership to work closely with local tribes on security issues. Bedouin leaders agreed to notify government authorities of criminal activity within their territory, instead of simply dealing with matters internally as the tribes had done in the past. Some Bedouin disapproved of this new arrangement, seeing it as a violation of the customary tribal system, and were especially concerned with the government's efforts to play a larger role in the selection of tribal leaders, traditionally picked by consensus within the tribe, so as to ensure the Bedouin's loyalty to the government. Under this new arrangement, local police worked with the tribes in early February 2005 to corner and kill a suspect involved with the October bombing in Taba. In the next month, the Egyptian government brought to trial two additional suspects arrested for their connection with the bombing, with other suspects released for lack of evidence.[164]

The following year, early on the morning of July 23—the height of tourist season—three bombs ripped through the resort city of Sharm el-Sheikh in Sinai's southern tip. The first was a car bomb in the Old Market bazaar, the second detonated outside the Movenpick Hotel, and the third was a truck bomb driven into the lobby of the Ghazala Garden

Hotel. Eighty-eight people were killed and more than two hundred injured, with the victims consisting of both foreign tourists and local Egyptians.[165] Following the Sharm el-Sheikh bombing, Egyptian police again took the lead in sweeping the region of al-Arish in North Sinai for suspects and continued to conduct regular patrols in the region over the coming months, along with heightened security at tourist facilities. Despite the Lebanese group known as the Abdallah Azzam Brigades, with suspected links to al-Qaeda, taking responsibility for the bombing, Egyptian government officials maintained that the bombings were perpetrated by local Bedouin rather than an international terrorist group.[166]

In late April 2006, two more terrorist attacks struck Sinai—one in the resort city of Dahab targeting tourists in a market, killing 24 and injuring 100, including 4 American citizens; and a suicide attack against MFO troops (2 Egyptians, 1 Norwegian, and 1 New Zealander) traveling in an SUV in northeastern Sinai near their camp, with the targeted soldiers only sustaining minor injuries. Egyptian police announced that Al-Tawhid wa al-Jihad, an "indigenous group comprised mostly of radicalized Bedouin extremists" that "espouses a pro al-Qaida, Salafist ideology," was responsible for the bombings.[167] Soon after, the government announced that it had arrested or killed the group's leadership in police raids. At this time, the State Department reported that the radicalization of some Bedouin in Sinai could be linked to "heavy-handed Egyptian efforts" to dismantle smuggling networks in the region and "to the Bedouin's long-standing distrust of the central government."[168]

Throughout this period, tensions remained high between the Egyptian government and the Sinai Bedouin, with two thousand local tribesmen holding a multiday sit-in at the Israeli border in late April 2007.[169] The protestors advocated for greater economic opportunities and claimed that police actions in the region discriminated against the Bedouin. They highlighted cultural insensitivities and brutality by the police and sought the release of fellow Bedouin imprisoned during security sweeps. In 2009 and 2010, Bedouin protests continued to erupt with the goal of bringing attention to these issues. With the continued unrest and lingering terrorist threats in Sinai, the U.S. government hoped to expand its military cooperation with Egypt beyond the conventional U.S. military support provided under the auspices of the peace agreement with Israel and focus more on asymmetric threats emanating from Sinai.

## EGYPT AND DOMESTIC TERRORISM:
## THE SECOND STEP

The Arab Spring protests in spring 2011, which led to Mubarak's resignation, and resulting political transitions resulted in a political and security vacuum in Sinai. Criminals, smugglers, and militants used the instability in the region as an opportunity to organize and operate, including conducting attacks against natural gas pipelines as a symbol of the government's exploitation of the region.[170] In this environment, the terrorist group Ansar Bayt al-Maqdis (Supporters of Jerusalem) formed in July 2011 in North Sinai. It was suspected of collaborating with Palestinian groups in cross-border attacks against Israel. The leadership and ranks of Ansar Bayt al-Maqdis (ABM) emerged from local Bedouin tribes, especially among marginalized tribal youth, with the group appealing to local grievances and tribal connections for recruitment.[171] However, there were concerns that the group also had connections with al-Qaeda.[172] In August 2011, a general in Egyptian intelligence stated, "Al-Qaeda is present in Sinai mainly in the area of Sakaska close to Rafah [in the Gaza Strip]. They have been training there for [a] month, but we have not identified their nationalities yet."[173] Analysts later noted that the group's "appropriation of the themes of global jihad should be understood in primarily strategic terms" as "ABM is an entirely Egyptian phenomenon."[174]

With the emergence of ABM and suspicions over its potential connections to al-Qaeda, Egyptian officials argued that Israel's unwillingness to permit the deployment of the Egyptian military into Sinai was an impediment to dealing decisively with the group, with unrest among the Bedouin exploited by ABM for recruitment purposes. Major General Safwat al-Zayyat, an official within Egypt's General Intelligence Service, stated,

> There are also sympathisers among the Bedouin tribes, because no one has paid attention to them. We must realise that the farther away you get from the centre towards the periphery the more tenuous are ties based on national loyalty and patriotism. This is happening in Sinai, which was marginalized before and after liberation. Unfortunately, the peace agreement limits our control over our own territories, at a time when we are dealing with the border as a security issue, forgetting that

> Camp David restricts our ability to exercise sovereignty while it places no restrains on Israel.[175]

Israeli officials' perception of the security situation in Sinai changed in August 2011. On August 8, Palestinian militants attacked a bus in southern Israel, killing eight people. The Israeli government reported that the militants had crossed into Sinai from Gaza and then reentered Israeli territory to commit the attack. Israeli defense minister Ehud Barak stated, "The incident underscores the weak Egyptian hold on Sinai and the broadening of the activities of terrorists."[176] He added, "The real source of terror is in Gaza and we will act against them with full force." And indeed, the Israeli military soon launched air strikes into the Gaza Strip. In the days following the attack, the Israeli government shifted its position on military deployments in Sinai and granted permission to Egypt to strengthen its military presence in the region, including the use of helicopter gunships and armored vehicles. As one Israeli intelligence officer explained, "Following recent violence at the border, Israel has become more understanding of the security situation we are dealing with in Sinai."[177]

The Egyptian military initially deployed two thousand troops into North Sinai as part of Operation Eagle, hoping to serve as a deterrence to terrorist groups operating in the periphery.[178] The U.S. government supported the operation with Apache gunships and M-60 tanks. A statement by the Egyptian Defense Ministry said, "The armed forces will continue Operation Eagle to pursue the terrorists and will . . . start to redeploy its forces to complete its pursuit of the fugitive terrorists and finish off all terrorist cells in the Sinai."[179] Many Bedouin saw the presence of the military as an unwelcome intrusion into their territory, with the deployment provoking retaliatory attacks from local tribes. One village brandished their weapons and chased troops out of their territory during a raid by military forces that "ravaged Bedouin houses" and was seen "as a violation on the conservative customs and traditions of their community."[180]

With the election of the new Muslim Brotherhood government in June 2012, the new Egyptian president, Mohamed Morsi, tried to shift to a development approach to handle unrest in Sinai and began to negotiate directly with militants, withdrawing a portion of the military in the process.[181] U.S. officials unsuccessfully pressed for the government to continue operations against terrorist groups in Sinai.[182] When ABM targeted Morsi directly, the Egyptian government began to reengage with the United States on domestic counterterrorism, with the U.S. continuing to support Egypt's military efforts in Sinai.[183] Morsi and the Egyptian military leadership also saw the importance of working with Israel on the security situation in Sinai and reportedly wanted to modify the peace treaty with Israel to allow the Egyptian Army to station permanently its forces and helicopters in the peninsula.[184] However, Morsi's critics, especially among the military's leadership, argued that the government's fundamental approach gave militants a free hand to operate in Sinai, a contributing factor to the July 2013 military coup led by General Abdul Fattah al-Sisi that overthrew Morsi and the Muslim Brotherhood.[185] After Morsi's removal, the military government redeployed large numbers of additional troops into Sinai. This quickly led to increased attacks against military positions, such as the August 2013 attack on two military buses transporting military units into the peninsula, which killed twenty-five soldiers.

## DESCENDING INTO THE TERRORISM TRAP IN SINAI: THE THIRD STEP

In 2013, domestic terrorist attacks within Sinai saw a dramatic increase as the Egyptian military continued "an aggressive military campaign in northern Sinai in an effort to disrupt the smuggling of arms and explosives between Gaza and Egypt, as well as to kill suspected militants and deny extremist groups a place from which to plan attacks," according to the State Department.[186] The counterterrorism operations relied on an indiscriminate "scorched-earth policy," including torching entire villages due to suspected terrorist activity.[187] ABM exploited the resulting civilian casualties for recruitment purposes and as motivation for its attacks against military and government targets.

In early September 2013, two days after an attempted assassination of Interior Minister Mohamed Ibrahim by ABM, the Egyptian military launched retaliatory operations against a group of villages in North Sinai described as "the biggest of its kind in recent years in Sinai."[188] An

Egyptian security official stated that the operations intended to "clean all the villages in Rafah and Sheikh Zuweid area from dangerous terrorists." Eyewitnesses reported seeing ten military helicopters hovering above as "clouds of smoke could be seen rising from the villages."[189] Following the operation, ABM released photos showing that innocent people were killed by the army and stated that the targeted homes "belonged to families that have no religious leaning and belong to no organization." Its statement further accused the army of knowing the villages were empty of militants and of instigating a "terror campaign for the families of the area in general." ABM announced that they had launched three attacks as a "fast, painful response" for these "crimes."[190] The group also stated it would continue attacking economic targets in retaliation for ongoing military operations in Sinai.[191] After another 2013 military raid in which seven civilians (including four children) were killed, ABM announced that "it is obligatory to repulse [the Egyptian Army] and fight until the command of Allah is fulfilled. . . . We in Ansar Jerusalem and all the mujahideen in Sinai in Egypt as a whole stress that the blood of innocent Muslims will not go in vain."[192] As a result of military operations targeting "innocent Muslims," ABM declared members of the Egyptian military and police apostates who could be killed.[193]

On the other hand, the director of North Sinai security, Major General Sameh Bashady, argued that military forces have only assaulted "very specific targets and that is why it is very difficult, because everything is very close to one another. We only assault specific targets without harming any innocent, and it is based on very accurate information."[194] Two journalists reporting from the area, however, observed that in the "tit-for-tat" violence, "The military not only attacks suspected insurgents, but it's also taking out its wrath on everyone related to an alleged insurgent. Here in this Bedouin community that means everyone, as kin is never more than a house away. The tribesmen promise more attacks and warn that every army response earns more support for radical groups with links to al Qaida."[195] Local Bedouin argued that the indiscriminate actions of the military against anyone suspected of being a terrorist, such as Salafists "who happen to look devout," breeds further anger against the government. An Islamic judge in North Sinai stated, "Those who renounced violence and made ideological recantations will once again carry arms to defend themselves against the unjust and humiliating security measures."[196]

By fall 2013, ABM increasingly expanded their retaliatory attacks outside of Sinai with an assassination attempt against the interior minister and the bombing of a military intelligence building in the city of Ismailia on the west bank of the Suez Canal. The group claimed the bombing in Ismailia was a response to the "repressive practices carried out by the Egyptian army against our people." This bombing came in the wake of a string of attacks against Egyptian military forces in Sinai, including an October 7, 2013, suicide bombing of the South Sinai Security Directorate. The group warned, "We reiterate our advice to our people in Egypt to stay away from all military and police headquarters, for they are legitimate targets for the mujahideen."[197] During 2013, the State Department reported that "The majority of attacks were concentrated in northern Sinai. . . . This violence was primarily directed against Egyptian government security forces and rarely targeted Egyptian civilians, foreigners, or foreign economic interests, although there were several bombings or attempted bombings of public buses in Cairo in late December. The Sinai-based terrorist organization Ansar Bayt al-Maqdis (ABM) claimed responsibility for most of the more complex attacks on the security services."[198] In April 2014, the State Department designated ABM a Foreign Terrorist Organization, stating in its announcement that the group shared some aspects of al-Qaeda's ideology, but "is not a formal AQ affiliate and generally maintains a local focus."[199]

In October 2013, the Obama administration put a hold on a portion of U.S. military assistance to Egypt due to the army's role in a crackdown on protestors in Cairo that resulted in the deaths of eight hundred civilians. This stopped the transfer of large-scale military equipment such as Apache helicopters, F-16 fighter jets, Harpoon missiles, and M1A1 tanks. In a State Department press release, however, the U.S. government pledged, "We will continue assistance to help secure Egypt's borders, counter terrorism and proliferation, and ensure security in the Sinai. We will continue to provide parts for U.S.-origin military equipment as well as military training and education."[200] Following an October 2014 suicide bombing by ABM in central Sinai that killed thirty soldiers, the Egyptian government declared a three-month state of emergency and increased its military efforts to target terrorism in the region.[201] The U.S. government responded to this state of emergency by lifting part of the freeze on military assistance, delivering ten Apache helicopters to the Egyptian military in December 2014 specifically for use in counterterrorism operations in Sinai.[202] The remainder of the military hardware was released by late March 2015. In meetings with senior U.S. officials, who continued to express "steadfast support for Egypt in its fight against terrorism in the Sinai," President Sisi presented himself and the Egyptian military as a "bulwark against terrorism" in the region.[203]

Like Pakistan, and in line with the expectations of the terrorism trap theory, the Yemen, Mali, and Egypt case studies demonstrate the connection between domestic terrorism and the use of military force for counterterrorism within the periphery. In all three cases, the war on terror helped to bring focus to the "ungoverned" periphery as a potential safe haven for al-Qaeda-linked terrorist groups. With the United States' inability to pursue unilateral military action in these states, U.S. officials pressured their counterparts to target al-Qaeda and al-Qaeda-linked terrorist groups within their borders and to assert state control over the periphery. The resulting U.S.-supported military operations led to a violent backlash from the periphery, with local terrorist groups' rhetoric stressing revenge against the military as one of their key motivations.

Despite the affiliate groups' international links and influence, the rhetoric and patterns of attacks by groups emerging from these targeted peripheries highlight the importance of understanding local political dynamics to explain the resulting patterns of violence. As al-Qaeda core's leadership pushed its affiliates to ignore the "near enemy" and devote their energy and resources to attacking U.S. targets, the terrorist groups operating in the periphery of these three states primarily focused their efforts on campaigns of domestic terrorism against the state. As the Yemeni, Malian, and Egyptian governments pursued expanded military operations in response to the rising levels of domestic terrorism, with Mali's efforts eventually being backed by an international intervention, each country fell deeper into a cycle of violence with targeted terrorist groups in the periphery. As demonstrated in the above analysis, the use of military force only exacerbated the underlying problems between center and periphery, leading to increased levels of intra-state violence.

This outcome is evident in other states where governments have confronted terrorist threats in their peripheries, including the Philippines' struggles against Moro groups in the South; Turkey's ongoing fight with the PKK in its Kurdish-populated southeastern periphery; the emergence of Boko Haram in northeastern Nigeria; and Kenya's military interdiction and counterterrorism efforts in its northeastern periphery. Some of these states, however, were already engaged in ongoing conflicts in the periphery by 2001, conflicts that were soon co-opted by the narrative of the war on terror. After 2001, the U.S. government provided military support to increase partner states' capacity to continue and expand these military operations in the periphery. Due to this co-optation, the underlying problems involved in these conflicts were intensified.

The Philippines, for example, increased the scope of its military operations in its Muslim-majority southern periphery under pressure from U.S. officials.[204] They feared connections between al-Qaeda and local Moro groups, in particular Abu Sayyaf, in this "ungoverned" island region with porous borders, limited administrative presence, long-standing grievances among local communities centered around high poverty and corruption, and active insurgencies—the struggles between the Moro in the South and the central government date back to Spanish colonial rule. The commander of the U.S. Pacific Command, Admiral Dennis Blair, stated that "we're seeing increasing evidence that there are potential current links" between Abu Sayyaf and al-Qaeda.[205] In January 2002, Operation Enduring Freedom was expanded to include the Philippines "to support the comprehensive approach of the Armed Forces of the Philippines (AFP) in their fight against terrorism in the southern Philippines," and, the following year the United States designated the Philippines a major non-NATO ally to aid these efforts.[206] The U.S. government subsequently increased its support for the Philippine government to expand military action against the various Moro groups operating in the South, including plans for the U.S. military to train the Philippine Army for counterterrorism operations.[207] These operations, such as the U.S.-supported Operation Ultimatum, launched in 2006 against Abu Sayyaf on the southern Jolo Island, resulted in a steady increase in domestic terrorism from the targeted groups. After the bombing of a ferry in Manila

Bay, which killed 116 people and wounded another 300, for instance, Abu Sayyaf declared the attack as "just revenge" for the killing of Muslim civilians by military forces on the southern island of Mindanao.[208] Figure 5.4 demonstrates the trends in domestic and international terrorism for the Philippines from 1996 to 2012.

Given these findings, the absence of military force for counterterrorism—the key intervening step connecting U.S. counterterrorism policy to the increase in domestic terrorism—is expected to avoid this violent internal backlash, disrupting the causal process leading to the terrorism trap. As a counterfactual example, Saudi Arabia, a key U.S. partner in the war on terror, has relied on discriminate counterterrorism operations by its security forces instead of indiscriminate violence as part of expansive military operations.[209] While Saudi counterterrorism cooperation with the U.S. government improved after 2001, especially in the area of intelligence sharing, U.S. officials were still frustrated in the early years of the war on terror with the "lack of Saudi initiative," according to then U.S. ambassador to Saudi Arabia Bob Jordan.[210] In May 2003, the Saudi government became more proactive in its counterterrorism efforts following an al-Qaeda attack in Riyadh on three residential

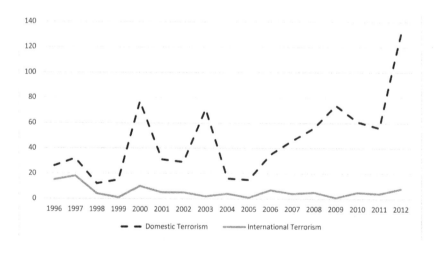

FIGURE 5.4 Annual count of terrorist attacks in the Philippines, 1996–2012.

*Source:* Enders, Sandler, and Gaibulloev, "Domestic Versus Transnational Terrorism"; Gaibulloev, Piazza, and Sandler, "Regime Types and Terrorism."

compounds for Westerners and other non-Saudi residents that killed 35 people and injured over 160.

In the wake of this attack, the Saudi government targeted suspected fundraising activities, for example, by removing collection boxes in mosques, "viewed as a cataclysmic event in Saudi Arabia" according to Ambassador Jordan, and suspending funds for foreign Saudi charities.[211] It also arrested over 600 suspected al-Qaeda-linked terrorists, with some suspects hunted down and killed in raids by the security forces.[212] By September 2003, the White House announced, "Our counterterrorism cooperation with Saudi Arabia has significantly increased. Joint counter-terrorist operations have been established, information is being shared more broadly than before, and Saudi security forces have put several al-Qaida ring leaders and facilitators out of action, many of whom were involved in the May attacks in Riyadh, and arrested scores of other terrorists."[213] In the coming years, the Saudi government continued its cooperation with U.S. counterterrorism, focusing its efforts on the capturing and killing of suspected al-Qaeda-linked terrorists, challenging extremist ideologies, strengthening its borders, and combating terrorist financing. In 2009, the State Department reported that 900 trials for terrorist suspects arrested over the previous eight years were ongoing, with 270 convictions resulting in sentences ranging from a few months in jail to the death penalty.[214]

While Saudi cooperation improved, the Saudi government avoided the use of offensive military force for domestic counterterrorism operations. With its vast oil wealth and resulting strategic importance, the Saudi government had well-funded security forces and remained largely free from U.S. influence in this regard.[215] Rather than adopting the war framing of the United States, the Saudi government's approach to terrorism, under direction from its Interior Ministry, focused on undermining pull factors that aided terrorist groups' recruitment and treating those arrested as essentially misguided in their views of religion.[216] Within the five high-security prisons the Saudi government constructed to house individuals arrested during counterterrorism operations, the jailers instituted an educational and religious study program "designed to try to alter [prisoners'] thinking and behavior."[217] The government also implemented a rehabilitation program that focused on monitoring and supporting individuals released from prison, including providing counseling, dowries to promote a stable marital life, and job support. Saudi officials hoped to rehabilitate arrested terrorists and avoided actions that could further radicalize them or serve as a tool for terrorist groups' recruitment efforts, such as the domestic use of military force.

When force was applied for counterterrorism purposes, the Saudi government relied instead on police action against specific terrorist cells or individual terrorists with suspected links with al-Qaeda, which at times resulted in the killing of the targeted individuals but did not result in widespread and indiscriminate civilian casualties. As a result of these efforts, and despite the presence of highly repressive government policies and actions—including continued tensions between the Saudi central government and the peripheries of the Eastern and Asir Provinces[218]— groups operating in Saudi Arabia were never able to generate public support for a domestic-oriented "jihad" against the Saudi government.[219] Domestic terrorist attacks, therefore, remained low during the period under study, as shown in figure 5.5.

In Yemen, Mali, Egypt, and Pakistan, on the other hand, the focus on the use of the military for counterterrorism operations in the periphery exacerbated the conditions that led to the dramatic uptick in antistate

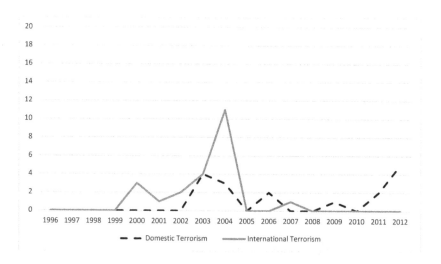

FIGURE 5.5 Annual count of terrorist attacks in Saudi Arabia, 1996–2012.

Source: Enders, Sandler, and Gaibulloev, "Domestic Versus Transnational Terrorism"; Gaibulloev, Piazza, and Sandler, "Regime Types and Terrorism."

violence. The selection of these cases, along with the variation in counterterrorism approaches prior to the deployment of the military in the periphery, provides evidence for the relationship between the use of military force for counterterrorism operations, in line with U.S. counterterrorism priorities, and the increase in domestic terrorist attacks. While the war on terror did not create the problems between center and periphery, the military actions of partner states helped to serve as a catalyst for the rapid increase in domestic terrorism, an unintended impact of often short-sighted policies.

# CONCLUSION

I n December 2018, more than fourteen years after releasing their semi-
nal report, Lee Hamilton and Tom Kean, the cochairs of the 9/11
Commission, looked back on the war on terror and observed,

> Our nation has devoted trillions of dollars to protecting the homeland
> and confronting insurgencies since 9/11, yet the threat of violent extrem-
> ism to the U.S. is greater than ever before. Violence has increased, and
> new generations of terrorists have emerged in fragile states across the
> Middle East, the Horn of Africa and the Sahel. In these fragile states—
> many of which lack adequate governance, effective and responsible secu-
> rity forces, and other basic services—extremist groups are easily able to
> recruit fighters, hide out and, worse still, capture and hold territory.[1]

The following year, the U.S. intelligence community also continued to
see a lingering threat from the al-Qaeda network. The director of national
intelligence's 2019 *Worldwide Threat Assessment* stated, "Al Qa'ida senior
leaders are strengthening the network's global command structure and
continuing to encourage attacks against the West, including the United
States, although most al-Qa'ida affiliates' attacks to date have been small
scale and limited to their regional areas. We expected that al-Qa'ida's
global network will remain a CT challenge for the United States and
its allies during the next year."[2] In August 2019, the State Department's

coordinator for counterterrorism, Nathan Sales, likewise interpreted the affiliates' ongoing attacks as a persistent threat to the United States and warned, "What we see today is an al-Qaida that is as strong as it has ever been."[3]

During an April 28, 2021, speech before a joint session of Congress, President Biden maintained this perspective on the terrorist threat to the United States. While announcing the withdrawal of American troops from Afghanistan, he affirmed that the United States will "maintain an over the horizon capacity to suppress future threats to the homeland. Make no mistake, in 20 years, terrorists—the terrorism threat has been metastasized. The threat evolved way beyond Afghanistan. . . . We have to remain vigilant against the threats to the United States wherever they come from. Al-Qaeda and ISIS are in Yemen, Syria, Somalia, and other places in Africa and the Middle East and beyond."[4] Three months later, Biden announced the end of U.S. combat operations in Iraq but stressed, "Our role in Iraq will be . . . just to be available to continue to train, to assist and to help, and to deal with ISIS as it arrives." While many commentators in the media repeated ad nauseum that Biden was bringing the "forever war" to an end with the withdrawal from Afghanistan and pushing U.S. diplomacy "past a post-9/11 worldview," they failed to engage with the implications for the broader war on terror. On September 28, 2021, General Kenneth McKenzie Jr., head of U.S. Central Command, asserted in front of the Senate Armed Services Committee that the war on terror was not over.[5] Under the Biden administration, as has been the case under its predecessors, it has been clear that U.S. counterterrorism efforts would remain fixated on confronting various terrorist groups operating from the "ungoverned spaces" that have long been the target of the United States and would continue to rely on cooperation with America's partner states to protect U.S. national security interests.

Even with over two decades of experience in conducting the war on terror, it seems that the broader understanding of terrorism and the nature of the terrorist threat within policy circles has failed to evolve. While many in Washington, DC, have pointed to either a grand historical narrative of Islam versus the West or the global jihad of terrorist groups like al-Qaeda or the Islamic State, the driving forces for much of the continued violence around the world are decidedly more local, with many senior U.S. officials failing to appreciate fully the long-standing tensions between center and periphery and the implications for U.S. counterterrorism efforts. The case studies of Pakistan, Yemen, Mali, and Egypt demonstrate that the increase in domestic terrorism in key partner states—a large part of the perceived threat from al-Qaeda's global network—has been in part a consequence of the United States' own counterterrorism policies and the resulting actions of U.S.-supported domestic military operations within terrorist groups' areas of activity. Understanding the limitations and difficulties of U.S. military action in these regions, U.S. officials hoped that partner states' militaries would be more effective in targeting terrorist groups operating within their borders, but these states' efforts have had the unintended impact of destabilizing conditions in the periphery and increasing the levels of domestic terrorism. In pushing this approach, U.S. officials did not fully consider or understand the limitations of the partner states' reach into these border areas and the inevitable backlash that offensive actions would create.

As the levels of domestic terrorism and political instability spiked, U.S. officials interpreted these attacks through the frame of U.S. strategic interests and expressed concern that al-Qaeda or al-Qaeda-linked groups would exploit the violence in the periphery to continue planning and executing attacks against the United States and its interests. U.S. officials, therefore, increased funding and pressure on their counterparts in key partner states to expand their counterterrorism efforts and establish control over the periphery. States with U.S.-designated safe havens have been four and a half times more likely to deploy their militaries for domestic counterterrorism operations than states that lack an identified safe haven, as statistical analysis shows (see the appendix for further details of the quantitative models on which this book is based). Mounting international pressure, along with pressure from domestic audiences, led to expanded domestic counterterrorism operations by partner states' militaries, exacerbating the underlying conditions that led to the initial outbreak of domestic terrorism. This sunk the partner states further into the terrorism trap, as their militaries and local terrorist groups became locked in an escalating tit-for-tat cycle of violence. According to statistical analysis, states that relied on military force for domestic counterterrorism experienced, on average, four times as many domestic terrorist attacks due to their military operations as compared to states that relied on nonmilitary approaches, while controlling for other relevant factors. To prevent a potentially catastrophic act of international terrorism, the U.S. government ended up setting dozens of smaller fires across the Muslim world, many of which continue to burn today.

Writing in 2016, David Kilcullen, one of the architects of the disaggregation strategy, recognized its failure with the emergence of new terrorist groups like the Islamic State in Iraq and Syria, which has mimicked al-Qaeda's global ambitions.[6] He argued that Obama's policy of "strategic divestment" from Iraq contributed to this outcome. In advocating for an improved U.S. counterterrorism strategy, Kilcullen recommended an increase in better-funded military operations, though he stresses that these should be paired with a broader approach aimed at protecting local communities and should not only focus on killing terrorists. In these efforts, Kilcullen stated that the U.S. government should establish a counterterrorism policy "always—*always*—preferring operations by, with and through local partners, conducted in their own way and in accord with their own priorities."[7] While Kilcullen's critique points specifically to the emergence of the Islamic State and its growing network of affiliates, which remains problematic, he does not grapple directly with the increasing levels of domestic terrorism outside of the Middle East and the patterns of retaliatory violence bound with partner states' use of offensive military force.

This book demonstrates that if we are to understand the dramatic rise in domestic terrorism it is necessary to understand how the actions of America's partner states changed local conflict environments and thereby shaped the motivations, decisions, and actions of various terrorist groups.[8] While a number of explanations for domestic terrorism have largely examined relatively static features of the state such as economic conditions, political systems, and the marginalization of various social groups, it is vital to consider the role of international politics and the resulting domestic actions of governments in the rise in domestic terrorist attacks. Within policy discussions and popular media, there has been an overreliance on al-Qaeda's own narrative and the global goals that the group espouses, even after U.S. counterterrorism shifted to a "disaggregation" approach intending to localize the violence. This has been paired with a fundamental misunderstanding of the nature of the al-Qaeda network and the relationship between al-Qaeda core and its affiliate groups. The promotion of an international al-Qaeda narrative by politicians and media alike too often overshadows the influences of the local political context for many of al-Qaeda's affiliates. By favoring an international explanation for the continued violence without disaggregating the differing trends between international and domestic terrorism, there has been a failure to appreciate the impact of U.S. counterterrorism policy on the levels of terrorist violence within America's partner states. This book's findings have several implications in terms of understanding the causes and the context of ongoing terrorist activity and U.S. counterterrorism efforts.

## UNDERSTANDING THE CAUSES OF TERRORISM

As practically every single study of terrorism rightly concludes, it is imperative to recognize the underlying causes of terrorism so as to construct more effective counterterrorism policies. Theories of terrorism have connected the outbreak of violence with minority discrimination, political repression, and poor economic conditions. Therefore, many scholars have argued that to combat terrorism governments need to promote greater political and economic equality, increase access to development and various social services such as education and health care, strengthen democratic institutions, and respect human and civil rights for both majority and minority communities.[9]

These ideas have been mirrored in policy discussions as government officials have pushed for a "whole of government" approach to counterterrorism, understanding that an offensive military approach alone leaves the root political and economic causes in place to feed future terrorism. A January 2010 Senate Foreign Relations Committee report argued that "a viable counter-terrorism strategy must consider the fact that terrorism is not created in a vacuum, and its causes must be addressed. The U.S. government must engage foreign partners on issues such as literacy, high birth rates, economic development, and human rights. All countries concerned must understand the dangers of attempting to solve the complex problem of terrorism through a one-dimensional military approach."[10] To proactively and preemptively address the problem of terrorism in the long run, governments have also implemented policies under the umbrella of

countering violent extremism focused on "preventing all forms of ideo-
logically based extremist violence, to include prevention of successful
recruitment into terrorist groups," as distinct from "disruptive actions"
aimed at stopping terrorist acts by those already committed to violence.[11]
For many governments, however, long-term political or economic strategies are often pursued parallel with military-centric approaches to challenge terrorist groups in the short term.

The real challenge for policy makers is to understand how the impact
of short-term counterterrorism efforts by the military, whether conducted by the United States or by partner states' security forces, can
undermine the potential success of long-term political and economic
efforts. These two approaches do not exist independently and must be
understood as intertwined with one another. As evident from the case
studies, the use of military force to challenge terrorism in the short term
has actively contributed to the outbreak of domestic terrorism, potentially negating any positive impact from various political or economic
reforms or initiatives pursued alongside these efforts. This is especially
the case within the periphery, where counterterrorism operations have
frequently exacerbated long-standing points of contention with the central government. An overreliance on military force is particularly troublesome when it uses indiscriminate violence and results in civilian casualties, as so often has been the case in both the United States' and partner
states' military operations. In March 2010, Admiral Michael Mullen
stated, "Each time an errant bomb or a bomb accurately aimed but against
the wrong target kills or hurts civilians, we risk setting our strategy back
months, if not years. Despite the fact that the Taliban kill and maim far
more than we do, civilian casualty incidents such as those we've recently
seen in Afghanistan will hurt us more in the long run than any tactical
success we may achieve against the enemy."[12]

Civilian casualties were a constant concern for General McChrystal
during his operational commands during the war on terror. McChrystal
reiterated that, while there are valid moral and humanitarian arguments
to be made for avoiding civilian casualties, his focus on this problem was
strategic in nature. While he was serving as ISAF commander in Afghanistan, U.S. military leadership brought in a research team to conduct a
study on the connection between Taliban attacks and civilian casualties. The team found that if civilian casualties in a region increased,

regardless of whether the Taliban or military were responsible, antigovernment and anti-U.S. violence likewise increased. McChrystal explained, "So it kind of didn't matter who killed the civilians, we became the loser. And so the only thing that really helped you was to get the level of civilian casualties down." He saw this same challenge existing for partner states conducting domestic military operations. Civilian casualties lead the military to "lose their own credibility. They lose their own legitimacy with the people." This problem is exacerbated when operations are conducted in the periphery, where the military is viewed by the local population as an outside, invading force. "There's just a spring-loaded resentment," he observed, "and so that's where discipline of security forces is so damn important, where focus, where an understanding of what they're trying to do in the long term is critical because you can focus on these short-term things, winning the firefight, but you lose the war."[13]

The worsening security conditions created by domestic military operations can make long-term counterterrorism objectives difficult to achieve. A 2008 study by conflict scholars Seth Jones and Martin Libicki found that military force rarely leads to victory over terrorist groups, accounting for the defeat of only 7 percent of terrorist groups between 1968 and 2006.[14] Their analysis shows two primary reasons for groups giving up their violent struggle: their leadership deciding to enter the political process (43 percent), and law enforcement arresting or killing key group members (40 percent). Among religious-oriented groups, law enforcement proved to be even more successful, with police action resulting in the termination of 73 percent of terrorist groups' operations. A military approach is particularly problematic when attempts to target one terrorist group in fact help to spur the formation of other groups, as has occurred in Pakistan and Mali. Akbar Ahmed argued that in his experience administering large swaths of Pakistan's border regions, "Force can only take you so far and beyond that it's not effective." He especially stressed how counterproductive military action can be as it breeds further resentment of the government within the periphery. Falling back on military force is "no way to solve a local problem. When you use a crude military strategy resulting in civilian deaths, you will not be successful."[15] Ahmed further argued, "If force is to be used, then it should be in the form of local police in place of external troops. The imposition of military rule should be avoided at all costs: it sends the message that the periphery is not part of the nation but rather a fringe of troublemakers and outsiders that the government needs to 'defeat' or 'punish.'"[16]

Research suggests that conflicts between center and the periphery can be resolved by successfully negotiating political autonomy agreements for the periphery, thereby reducing local grievances, and providing alternative, nonviolent paths to pursue political and economic opportunities and change.[17] The decentralization of political authority can also limit the reach of historically repressive central governments. Local, democratically elected governments help to provide a layer of institutional and political protection for communities in the periphery. This can discourage local communities from supporting antigovernment militant groups and provide mechanisms to keep armed actors, as well as a potentially predatory state, at bay.[18] Moreover, the emphasis on local governance can strengthen ex-combatants' peaceful participation in a political process that has lower stakes than challenging political leaders at the national level under a highly centralized state.[19]

Yet, a broad reliance on the war framework by the military against an ill-defined terrorist threat is not conducive to connecting short-term tactical successes with such long-term political goals. Despite a lack of clear success and the worsening violence over the past two decades in many societies wrapped up in the war on terror, the view that military force focused on killing the enemy is a vital part of any counterterrorism strategy has persisted.[20] Many policy makers and analysts have argued that it is necessary to use the military to fight terrorists "over there" so that the United States does not have to fight them at home. They further argue that the low level of terrorist incidents and fatalities within the United States is evidence that U.S. counterterrorism policies have been successful in pushing the fight to the "frontline wars of the War on Terror."[21]

In a point-by-point analysis, scholars John Mueller and Mark Stewart find such arguments about the effectiveness of U.S. counterterrorism policy "wanting." They conclude that "terrorism is rare outside war zones because, to a substantial degree, terrorists don't exist there," reporting an annual fatality risk from an act of terrorism in the United States as only 1 in 39,000,000.[22] The argument that U.S. counterterrorism has been successful in reducing terrorism is premised on an assumption that the terrorist threat against the United States has remained relatively static since September 11, 2001, and that al-Qaeda's affiliate groups, responsible for the overwhelming majority of the al-Qaeda network's terrorist activity since 2001, have prioritized the same internationally focused goals as al-Qaeda core. It does not consider the local impact of partner states' counterterrorism actions within dynamic conflict environments and how these operations serve as a catalyst for locally oriented terrorist violence. As this study demonstrates, military force can be a counterproductive means of challenging terrorism, especially in the periphery, where the deployment of the military inevitably leads to a violent backlash. The increase in domestic terrorism within partner states, therefore, should not be viewed as a sign of counterterrorism success, but rather as a potential indication of a policy failure, with partner states suffering the consequences.

## THE WAR ON TERROR'S OVERLY AMBIGUOUS GOALS

The broad scope of the war on terror has made victory an impossible concept to define. While successive U.S. administrations sought to destroy al-Qaeda militarily, their prevailing view of the al-Qaeda network made such a task nearly impossible, a metric for victory that can never be attained as the brand can survive even if the group does not.[23] Former U.S. Central Command head General John Abizaid warned, "You can destroy the people of al-Qaeda, but you can't destroy the idea of al-Qaeda."[24] The al-Qaeda brand was one that affiliates increasingly embraced for their own locally oriented political ends distinct from al-Qaeda's international focus on challenging the United States and American global hegemony.

Making this task all the more difficult, senior officials in the Bush administration, when crafting the initial policy framework for the war on terror, understood their fight to be against an enemy broader than al-Qaeda alone.[25] In recognition of this fact, and sensitive to the great uncertainty of future events, they formulated the goal of U.S. counterterrorism efforts to defeat terrorism "as a threat to our way of life." However, the ambiguity of this objective did not lend itself to concrete political goals and resulted in the scope of the war on terror drifting to encompass a wide range of emerging conflicts. The top-down narrative of the war allowed for different groups to be subsumed into a global conflict, despite the drivers of the violence often being decidedly more local in nature.

Scholars examining other policy areas have recognized that overly broad "wars" against concepts, like the wars on drugs or poverty, simply do not work, despite their rhetorical popularity and policy makers' preference for large-scale planning. In his book *The White Man's Burden: Why the West's Efforts to Aid the Rest Have Done So Much Ill and So Little Good*, development economist William Easterly argues that the global war on poverty, with its long-term utopian goals, is an impossible undertaking that has, in fact, harmed the developing world more than it has helped. Under its current framework, the war on poverty is based on international donors' provision of aid through large-scale, top-down central planning and is often dismissive of local conditions and local practitioners in its efforts to eradicate global poverty. The advocates of this approach—Easterly's "planners"—envision poverty as "a technical engineering problem" that their answers will solve. By ignoring local conditions, Easterly argues, "Planners' global social engineering has failed to help the poor, and it will always fail."[26] He instead pushes for more moderate, piecemeal objectives premised on knowledgeable "searchers" attempting to find and build local solutions to poverty and development while working with local communities. This leverages a short-term, ground-up strategy, rather than implementing preformed, long-term ideas from "planners" without considering or adapting them to varying local conditions. In an analysis of governance arrangements for socio-ecological systems, Nobel Prize–winning political scientist Elinor Ostrom similarly warned of an overreliance on transplanting "simple panaceas" to answer increasingly complex political and policy questions. She recommended, instead, a diagnostic approach to varying policy problems.[27]

While understanding that many politicians push the rhetoric of a global war against al-Qaeda and Islamic extremism for political gains, the dangers of the global war narrative for counterterrorism should be no different than for other policy areas. This study has highlighted the perils of relying on "simple panaceas" and "planners" seeking a top-down approach to counterterrorism, an approach that often blinds them to the local drivers of violence. Governments should reject a conception of the al-Qaeda network as a monolith and an overly simplistic under-standing of the causes of terrorism, which underpins a one-size-fits-all approach to counterterrorism. Instead, governments should rely on a diagnostic approach to fighting terrorism and find more moderate, piece-meal, and attainable objectives. These should be grounded in local politi-cal, social, or economic contexts and adapted to the evolving conflict dynamics that motivate and influence terrorist groups' behavior.

To this end, the U.S. government should discard the global war narra-tive; not simply the rhetoric of the global war on terror that Obama had already moved away from, but the policy framework positing that the United States is engaged in a global war with a single enemy. In particu-lar, this approach should include repealing the 2001 Authorization for the Use of Military Force. In July 2020, following intense political debates in the preceding years over the status of the AUMF, a bipartisan group of legislators introduced a bill known as the Limit on the Expansion of the Authorization for Use of Military Force Act. Its purpose was to limit the AUMF's use to countries in which the U.S. military was already engaged in counterterrorism operations and to block the administration from using the AUMF as legal justification for expanding operations to other countries.[28] Even with such limitations, this bill would still maintain the current legal framework for the use of military forces in a number of states around the world with which the United States is already engaged. Furthermore, the bill would still allow the government to use the AUMF as legal authorization for expanding operations against emerging terror-ist groups, so long as the U.S. military has a presence within the country under the framework of the AUMF. Such a bill is, at best, a first step toward reforming the law.

Congress needs to move away from a single, overarching, and decon-textualized legal authorization for U.S. counterterrorism operations and repeal the AUMF.[29] When introducing replacement legislation, Congress should limit new authorizations to the actual scope and region of the targeted groups' behavior, with specific objectives outlined that are suited to the context of any operations and mechanisms for regular oversight of the government's counterterrorism actions. Wars are discrete events with identified combatants in which victory is claimed over an enemy and political goals achieved. Framing the struggle against terrorism, with an amorphous and ill-defined enemy, as a war to be won leads to a costly status quo of perpetual conflict. By limiting and clarifying the strategic purposes of counterterrorism actions according to the local context in which they occur, the U.S. government can more effectively achieve concrete progress toward achievable goals and move away from its reliance on "planners" who formulate overly broad counterterrorism policies susceptible to mission creep. While the threat from terrorism can perhaps never be definitively defeated, much like poverty or drugs, it can be drastically reduced and managed on an appropriate scale.

## CONTEXT MATTERS

With many policy makers failing to grasp fully the local dynamics shaping terrorist groups' beliefs, motivations, and behavior, they frequently attribute blame to a singular cause, leading to ill-informed policies. Political scientist Stephen Walt argued, "One of the things that gets in the way of conducting good national security policy is a reluctance to call things by their right names and state plainly what is really happening. If you keep describing difficult situations in misleading or inaccurate ways, plenty of people will draw the wrong conclusions about them and will continue to support policies that don't make a lot of sense."[30] U.S. officials have been quick to blame the long arm of al-Qaeda and its internationally oriented goals as the primary driving forces of much of the terrorist violence that has occurred since 2001, a perspective that often blinds them to the local drivers of violence, as seen in the case studies of Pakistan, Yemen, Mali, and Egypt. Moreover, shallow and often ill-informed arguments pointing to varying attributes of the Islamic faith, or punditry describing ancient hatreds and other crude stereotypes of Muslim societies, which have proliferated in the public sphere since 9/11, cannot explain the variation between Muslim-majority states that experience high levels of terrorism and those that do not. As Aaron Zelin argues in his study of the jihadist movement in Tunisia, "Indeed, any commentator who boils jihadist mobilization down to one particular cause should not be taken seriously."[31]

It is important to recognize that the Salafist ideology embraced and disseminated by al-Qaeda has played a key role in mobilizing terrorist groups or inspiring terrorist attacks around the world. As several scholars have argued, religious ideologies are often strategic or instrumental tools used to further political or material agendas within dynamic conflict environments. Appeals to religion and the use of religious ideologies in varying ways can help manage and overcome the collective action problem that plagues nonstate actors by providing a common bond for diverse populations, can serve as a justification for violence sparked by other underlying political or economic factors, or can differentiate groups from rivals to gain adherents and supporters.[32]

Yet, a Salafist or jihadist ideology alone cannot explain the variation in individuals who become terrorists and those who do not, especially with such a miniscule minority of Muslims ever committing an act of terrorism.[33] In referencing the influence of Anwar al-Awlaki, whom scholar Thomas Hegghammer calls "one of the most influential jihadi ideologues of all time,"[34] former DIA analyst Joshua Foust argued, "I would say that 99.99 percent of all the people who either listen to, or believe in Awlaki's ideology, never act on it. So if you're going to argue that ideology is what caused someone to do something, you need to actually—to me at least—to be intellectually honest and analytically rigorous. You need to explain why that ideology compelled that person to act, but it didn't compel everyone who didn't act to not act."[35] In their book *Friction: How Conflict Radicalizes Them and Us*, social psychologists Clark McCauley and Sophia Moskalenko identify thirteen distinct mechanisms that can radicalize individuals to commit acts of violence. Ideology is not found among them. "As explanation of action," they similarly argue,

> ideology is too general and too indefinite; it cannot prescribe action under changing circumstances. Ideology requires interpretation in order to connect with current action. But every major ideology, from Christianity to Marxism, offers some textual foundation for use of violence. When we move to violence, we seek out the interpretations of our ideology that can support use of violence. There is always such an interpretation available, always someone who can claim authenticity for the interpretation.[36]

In seeking to understand ideology's influence over conflict, context matters. Political theorist Jonathan Leader Maynard examined the micro-foundations of ideology's impact on individuals' behavior in conflict situations. He pointed to the "dual causality" of ideology for individuals, stressing that "ideologies provide conflict actors with sincerely internalized worldviews *and* are constitutive of the social structures and environments in which those actors operate."[37] Political scientist Sarah Parkinson further distinguishes between formal and practical ideologies. Practical ideologies emerge organically and informally among militants as products of daily social interactions to create and reinforce collective norms. Such ideologies become key influences on militant beliefs and behavior, often more so than any formal ideology, but "potentially contain little or no explicit doctrinal content" and "may or may not reinforce an organization's official policies."[38]

While it has been demonstrated that religion can influence terrorist groups' behavior in a number of ways, such as their target selection and tactics,[39] the intensity of attacks,[40] and extending the length of a conflict,[41] ideology—including the embrace of a Salafist or jihadist ideology—can be understood as endogenous and adaptive to the conflict environment, and not an independent, predetermined, or static influence on individuals' or groups' behavior that can be divorced from local political or social contexts. Counterterrorism expert Stephen Tankel notes that terrorist groups' use of ideology is not uniform, and they frequently "adopt, develop, or adapt a certain ideology and make various strategic choices in response to their circumstances."[42] Local political and conflict dynamics can also influence the appeal exerted by terrorist groups espousing a religious-based ideology, with evidence from the case studies of Pakistan, Yemen, Mali, and Egypt pointing to some individuals using these groups as a vehicle for engaging in antistate violence. A survey conducted in Pakistan's North Waziristan Agency between 2016 and 2018, for instance, found that the TTP "exploited the grievances of the local communities and used religion as a tool to address those grievances. Initially, they addressed the injustices done with the local communities, whether by criminal gangs or by the government. While executing these activities, they use religious narratives to attract the common people and succeeded eventually by getting immense support."[43]

It is, perhaps, more useful to consider the interaction of ideology (as a pull factor) and the catalyst of various grievances (as a push factor) as mutually reinforcing phenomena to explain individual or group engagement in terrorist violence. Moreover, the embrace of a jihadist ideology or a fundamentalist interpretation of a religion can be bound up with similar underlying factors in a conflict environment that lead to individuals' engagement in acts of terrorism.[44] Shocks at the individual level associated with state violence or broader insecurity, such as witnessing friends and loved ones being injured or killed, can serve as a push factor for an individual to both embrace extremist ideologies and engage in violence.[45] In this way, a group's or individual's political or social context can amplify an ideology's influence.[46]

Within the societies examined in this study, the importance of understanding the local context in explaining terrorist groups' embrace of a jihadist ideology and religious-based goals is clear. They frequently used their religious messaging and stated commitment to a sharia-based system of governance not only to justify their acts of violence but to generate support from disadvantaged and marginalized individuals in the periphery and to counter the narratives espoused by existing political actors or local systems of government noted for their corruption, ineffectiveness, or oppression.[47] Many terrorist groups, including Pakistan's TTP, AQAP in southern Yemen, Ansar Dine in northern Mali, and Ansar Bayt al-Maqdis from Egypt's Sinai Peninsula, hoped to tap into this social and political sentiment to serve as a vehicle for individuals to challenge the government and consolidate their political control.

In regions with an absence of centralized state authority, such as Afghanistan and Somalia in the 1990s and 2000s, the emergence of religious-based militant groups like the Taliban and Islamic Courts Union (and later al-Shabaab) has also been a means of filling the political vacuum left by the collapse of the Afghan and Somali governments and establishing a local system of governance based in their interpretation of sharia, often in opposition to customary tribal authority or the violence and oppression associated with the prevalence of warlords and their supporting militias.[48] As international security scholar Aisha Ahmad argues, local business communities also strategically supported these militant groups and helped build up their religious-based authority to promote local security and, as a result, their own economic interests.[49] By appealing to a common Muslim identity and using Islamic rhetoric as a source of common interests, these groups hoped to bypass customary tribal leadership or other political actors and unite local populations across tribal or clan divisions for the purpose of establishing law and order, supporting their own authority, and challenging rivals or other external actors. This use of religion as a means of unifying highly egalitarian tribal populations has been a recurrent tactic throughout history as persistent tribal or ethnic divisions have limited widespread mobilization in these societies.[50]

Scholars of political violence have recognized how variations in local conditions alter the strategy of militant groups and the opportunities or incentives to commit terrorist attacks or pursue other types of political violence.[51] Yet, within the broad scope of the war on terror, many groups' adoption of extremist ideologies has frequently overshadowed local conditions that serve as key influences on their patterns of violence. "Countries are different," Lawrence Wilkerson explained. "Peoples are different. And so your approaches to them have to be different and hopefully adapted to the actual differences in the country."[52]

## THE RISE OF THE ISLAMIC STATE

In recent years, the perceived threat from the al-Qaeda network has been equaled, if not eclipsed, by the emergence of the Islamic State (variably abbreviated as ISIL or ISIS) as a global terrorist brand.[53] In September 2014, Obama announced that the U.S. military had conducted over 150 air strikes against Islamic State forces in Syria and was working on putting together a global coalition to fight the group. He stated, "If left unchecked, these terrorists could pose a growing threat beyond that region, including to the United States. While we have not yet detected specific plotting against our homeland, ISIL leaders have threatened America and our allies. . . . We will degrade, and ultimately destroy, ISIL through a comprehensive and sustained counterterrorism strategy." This strategy would similarly be based on the use of U.S. military strikes and military assistance to partner states. Obama pledged,

> This counterterrorism campaign will be waged through a steady, relentless effort to take out ISIL wherever they exist, using our air power and our support for partner forces on the ground. This strategy of taking out

terrorists who threaten us, while supporting partners on the front lines, is one that we have successfully pursued in Yemen and Somalia for years. And it is consistent with the approach I outlined earlier this year: to use force against anyone who threatens America's core interests, but to mobilize partners wherever possible to address broader challenges to international order.[54]

In the following year, the State Department's Bureau of Counterterrorism also expressed concern that foreign fighters in Syria and Iraq could return to their home countries across the Muslim world and further expand the Islamic State franchise—the same fear from a decade prior that foreign fighters leaving Iraq could spread the al-Qaeda brand back to their home countries.[55]

After establishing itself on the world stage with its brutality in the Middle East, Islamic State affiliates, as well as individual attacks "inspired" by the Islamic State, began to appear in a number of different regions, with one 2018 CNN headline warning, "ISIS Goes Global."[56] The director of national intelligence warned in the 2019 *Worldwide Threat Assessment* that

> ISIS still commands thousands of fighters in Iraq and Syria, and it maintains eight branches, more than a dozen networks, and thousands of dispersed supporters around the world, despite significant leadership and territorial losses. The group will exploit any reduction in CT pressure to strengthen its clandestine presence and accelerate rebuilding key capabilities, such as media production and external operations. ISIS very likely will continue to pursue external attacks from Iraq and Syria against regional and Western adversaries, including the United States.[57]

Analysts have argued that the Islamic State's approach was based in al-Qaeda's model of a "leaderless resistance movement."[58] The group's core leadership relied upon the tools of globalization, such as the Internet and social media, to broadcast a broad and ambiguous message of resistance. It encouraged self-starters to use whatever means and resources were at hand to commit attacks against Western targets, but often with little coordination or operational control from Islamic State core. In May 2017, Islamic State leaders broadly called for their supporters around the world to wage "all-out war" against the West, even providing instructions for stabbing attacks and driving cars into crowds.[59]

With international attention fixated on the Islamic State, terrorist groups increasingly embraced its global brand, just as they had earlier pledged themselves to al-Qaeda. For instance, Ehsanullah Ehsan, the cofounder of Pakistan's Jamaat-ul-Ahrar (a breakaway faction of the TTP formed in 2014), explained in an April 2020 interview with Al Jazeera that his group sought to align itself with the Islamic State due to its global PR efforts. Ehsan, who hailed from Mohmand Agency in Pakistan's FATA, stated, "The way that Daesh [the Arabic-language acronym for the Islamic State] was handling the media and its propaganda, there was definitely a race within the groups to join them. . . . It seemed a solid and attractive organization."[60] By May 2018, the State Department had designated seven Islamic State affiliates as Foreign Terrorist Organizations: ISIS-Sinai, ISIL-Khorasan, ISIL-Libya, ISIS-Bangladesh, ISIS-Philippines, ISIS–West Africa, and ISIS–Greater Sahara.[61] In July 2019, Russ Travers, the deputy director of the National Counterterrorism Center, stated, "The global nature of this can't be overestimated" as terrorist groups have "wrapped themselves in the ISIS flag."[62]

Despite this rebranding, the Islamic State's affiliate groups continued to be motivated by the political context within which they operated and focused their efforts locally. Ansar Bayt al-Maqdis, which emerged in Egypt's Sinai Peninsula in 2011, changed its name to ISIS-Sinai in 2014 after pledging allegiance to the Islamic State. The newly branded Islamic State affiliate, however, continued to focus its attacks against the Egyptian military and other government targets as counterterrorism operations in Sinai expanded. In March 2015, Boko Haram, which had pledged allegiance to al-Qaeda in 2012, similarly switched its loyalty and pledged allegiance to the Islamic State. This rebranding came at a time when the group had suffered territorial losses to the Nigerian military; it hoped that by "hitching its wagon to the rising star of the Islamic State," it could build its legitimacy and international profile and reinvigorate its followers.[63] Boko Haram's embrace of the Islamic State brand, much like its earlier embrace of the al-Qaeda brand, resulted in little substantive change to its operations or behavior. The group's activities remained domestically oriented and responsive to local political developments. The majority of its terrorist attacks, even after becoming an Islamic State affiliate, continued to be directed against Nigerian targets, with some spillover into neighboring countries such as Cameroon and Chad.

Other Islamic State affiliates emerged as splinter groups of existing al-Qaeda affiliates, such as Jamaat-ul-Ahrar, and used this new brand to challenge the leadership within their original organizations, as well as serving as spoilers in peace negotiations with local governments. ISIS-Somalia emerged as a competing faction within al-Shabaab, switching allegiance to challenge the group's existing leadership.[64] Al-Shabaab leaders soon ordered their supporters to target and eliminate Islamic State fighters, leading to violence between the two factions.[65] Like ISIS-Somalia, the Maute Group, also known as ISIS-Philippines, was formed in the southern Philippines by the brothers Omar and Abdullah Maute as a splinter group from the Moro Islamic Liberation Front. They pledged allegiance to the Islamic State in opposition to the 2014 peace agreement between the group's original leadership and the Philippine government. The newly minted Islamic State affiliate continued its campaign of violence against the Philippine Army as a spoiler for peace negotiations.[66] In Pakistan, similarly, with the appointment of Maulana Fazlullah as head of the TTP in 2014, the organization was riven with internal disputes as Fazlullah, the first TTP leader not from the Mehsud tribe, was unable to maintain the fragile tribal coalition.[67] The Islamic State affiliate in Pakistan first emerged in 2015 and largely consisted of former TTP members from FATA who defected to the new organization. After 2017, it was led by Daud Mehsud, a member of the Mehsud tribe and a former TTP commander in Karachi, where many Pashtuns from FATA found themselves after being displaced by the military's operations in the northwestern periphery. With the TTP organization in Karachi riven by factional fighting, Daud and his supporters switched their loyalties and swore allegiance to the Islamic State.[68]

Regarding the Islamic State affiliate in Afghanistan, Islamic State–Khorasan Province (ISKP) emerged in late 2014. Journalist Anand Gopal attributed its rise over the following year largely to disaffected members of the Taliban and other militant groups operating within the country. "It's important to look at what we mean when we say ISIS," he wrote,

> because these were groups that were disgruntled and they essentially
> rebranded themselves as a way of reinvigorating their group or faction,

and attracting funding. There's been increased dissatisfaction among certain elements of the Taliban, and with the media talking about ISIS all the time and the Afghan government playing up the idea of ISIS as a way of keeping the United States interested, all of that sort of set the ground for the groups to rebrand themselves.[69]

A 2020 report by the U.S. Institute of Peace on ISKP recruits' motivations for joining the group further argued, "The military approach to ISKP as an alien problem overlooks the local appeal that drives a constant stream of young Afghan men and women into its ranks and accounts for its resilience. If the arrests by Afghan security forces are indicative, ISKP's Kabul cell is an almost entirely Afghan phenomenon, with the overwhelming majority of detained ISKP members and recruiters having grown up in Kabul and surrounding cities."[70] The sectarian-oriented group would come to serve as a potential spoiler to the Afghan peace process, such as with its deadly attack on a Jalalabad prison in early August 2020 amid the Eid al-Adha ceasefire with the Taliban.[71] Following the August 2021 collapse of the Afghan government and the Taliban takeover, ISKP continued its campaign of terrorist attacks against the Taliban-controlled government, including the August 26 suicide bombing at the Kabul airport amid the U.S. evacuation, in which 13 U.S. service members and around 170 Afghan civilians were killed, as well as continuing to target vulnerable populations, such as Hazara Shia Muslims in the country, to demonstrate the Taliban's inability to provide security.[72] Looking at Indonesia and Malaysia, conflict scholars Kirsten Schulze and Joseph Chinyong Liow likewise demonstrate how the appeal of the Islamic State brand among militant organizations was a byproduct of local political dynamics.[73] Even the Islamic State–inspired attacks in Europe have for the most part been conducted by European nationals largely motivated by the marginalization of the continent's Muslim population.[74]

This is not to say that these terrorist groups do not pose a very serious and deadly threat that must be strongly confronted. Many governments, however, have fallen back on the same military approaches used in the past, with backing from the United States. In September 2015, the Egyptian military launched Operation Right of the Martyr in the Sinai Peninsula against the rebranded ISIS-Sinai. By the following year, the Egyptian government claimed it had killed thousands of terrorists, with human rights groups criticizing the military's continued reliance on indiscriminate violence against civilians in the region.[75] In the Philippines, President Rodrigo Duterte declared martial law in the southern island of Mindanao in May 2017, promising that he would be "harsh" in dealing with the Islamic State affiliate in the region.[76] Following this announcement, the Philippine military launched a counterterrorism operation against the areas where the Maute Group was active, focusing on the southern city of Marawi. In fighting that lasted for months, the military relied on extensive and indiscriminate bombings and committed human rights abuses against civilians, alongside similar human rights abuses committed by the terrorists.[77] With a growing sense of urgency about how to deal with the Islamic State and its growing network of affiliates, one matched by past fears of the spread of al-Qaeda and its own global network, the United States and other governments appeared to be settling into familiar but counterproductive patterns in their continued counterterrorism efforts.

Sir Evelyn Howell, a British political officer who served in Waziristan in the early twentieth century, once remarked of the colonial government's frontier policy in India and its impact, "Let it be reflected how great a diversion of the ship follows from a slight deflection of the rudder."[78] Looking back on the conduct and global impact of the war on terror, it is remarkable to consider the wide-ranging repercussions of the fateful decisions made by a handful of individuals huddled around conference tables at the White House and Camp David in the days and weeks following the 9/11 attacks. The early policies and actions taken by the U.S. government spread like a ripple and helped to push its partner states on a path that trapped them in a deadly cycle of violence characterized by increasingly devastating acts of terrorism that, for many, continue to this very day.

The United States has relied on a broad spectrum of counterterrorism activities, including strengthening U.S. defenses, intelligence gathering, and targeting terrorist financing. However, at the heart of the U.S. counterterrorism strategy has been a reliance on military force, whether by direct U.S. action or through partnered operations, to proactively target terrorist groups abroad. As this study has demonstrated, the use of the military has done little to diminish the threat of terrorism; in fact, it has actively exacerbated it. This analysis exposes the unintended impact of counterterrorism policies implemented by the United States and its partners. Actions meant to target the terrorist threat only served as a catalyst for increased terrorism, shifting the violence onto domestic targets within partner states.

This helps to explain why, despite the trillions of dollars spent and seemingly endless government resources and attention dedicated to counterterrorism over the past two decades, many countries around the world continue to be plagued by excessive levels of violence. Government officials must recognize the fallacy of continuing to pursue a primarily military approach to a problem that does not have a military solution. The United States and other governments around the world need to change the way they think about and address terrorism. However, larger questions loom over this potential strategic shift—having to do, namely, with finding the political will to bring about such a change and the continued ability of the United States to project its influence abroad. The difficulty of pursuing significant changes in U.S. and global counterterrorism policy due to these intervening factors, however, makes such a reformulation no less urgent or necessary.

ACKNOWLEDGMENTS

While only my name appears on the cover, this book would not have been possible without the guidance and support of numerous individuals over the years. First and foremost, I wish to express my sincere gratitude to two people: Ambassador Akbar Ahmed and Professor Krista Wiegand. The seeds for this project date back over a decade ago when I was working as a researcher for Ambassador Ahmed at American University's School of International Service. While conducting research for his book *The Thistle and the Drone*, Ambassador Ahmed was a treasure trove of fascinating stories, unique insights, and unmatched expertise based on his decades of experience both as an administrator in Pakistan's frontier areas and as an anthropologist studying Pakistan's tribal societies, which served as a key foundation for my own research. Ever since working with him, Ambassador Ahmed has been an ever-present and enthusiastic supporter of my work, not only providing key guidance as I fleshed out the early ideas for this book but also throughout the process of researching and writing it.

I further developed the ideas that informed this project as I pursued my PhD in political science at the University of Tennessee, Knoxville, under the supervision of Professor Krista Wiegand. Professor Wiegand helped me to expand and refine the core arguments of *The Terrorism Trap* and its contributions to the broader field of terrorism studies. Throughout my time in Knoxville, she consistently provided valuable feedback on various drafts and was a tireless advocate for me and my research. I next would like to thank the other members of my dissertation committee—Brandon Prins, Gary Uzonyi, and Candace White—whose feedback and comments proved to be valuable as I eventually turned to the drafting and preparation of *The Terrorism Trap*. I also would like to thank other professors and colleagues from the University of Tennessee's Department of Political Science who contributed to the completion of this study in varying ways: Ian Down, Aaron Gold, David Houston, Nathan Kelly, Jana Morgan, and Richard Pacelle.

For her support throughout the research and writing of the book, I owe an immense amount of gratitude to my spouse, Dr. Marina Kozak. She has not only been an unfailing source of support during a consuming and arduous process but read through several drafts of the manuscript. Her keen scientific insights were an immense help in constructing and strengthening the arguments of the book and marshaling the evidence to support them. I have dedicated this book to her. Frankie Martin and James Smrikarov, both anthropologists, also kindly read and commented on several drafts of the manuscript, which greatly improved the overall state of the book and proved especially helpful in allowing me to incorporate discussions of anthropological literature. I am grateful not only for their feedback on the manuscript but for their unwavering friendship as I developed the ideas for this book through countless conversations with them over the past ten years. Marina, Frankie, and James never failed to help me get past the inevitable lows of working on a book while also making sure I paused to celebrate the highs as well.

I also want to thank the leadership and research staff of the Islamabad Policy Research Institute. During the research for this book, they kindly organized and participated in a December 2018 seminar in Islamabad, Pakistan, during which I was able to present the main ideas of this book and receive valuable feedback from participants. The research for this book was supported financially by awards and fellowships from the Office of the Dean of the University of Tennessee's College of Arts and Sciences and the University of Tennessee's Department of Political Science, and I am grateful for this support. I also would like to thank all of the interviewees who provided their time and valuable insights.

At Columbia University Press, I would like to thank Professor Bruce Hoffman, the series editor, for his support in including *The Terrorism*

*Trap* in the Studies in Terrorism and Irregular Warfare book series, as well as the two peer reviewers whose comments helped to improve the final manuscript. In particular, I would like to thank Columbia's global history and politics editor, Caelyn Cobb, who took on the project and guided the manuscript through the review process. I would also like to extend my gratitude to the others at Columbia University Press who worked on the production of this book: associate editor Monique Laban, production editor Marisa Lastres, and copy editor Ryan Perks.

I also would like to thank my parents, Darrell and Deborah Akins, for their constant support for my academic endeavors over the years, which did not always follow a clear and direct path.

Finally, I would be remiss if I did not recognize that scholarship is inherently a cumulative exercise, with my work building on and in conversation with the hard work of the many researchers before me who have dedicated their tireless efforts to providing a clearer and more nuanced understanding of the topics covered in this book. So, I would like to express my gratitude to the countless scholars who have unknowingly inspired me with their own research and writing. That said, all views expressed and any errors in this book are mine alone.

# APPENDIX

## STATISTICAL ANALYSIS

F or the large-N quantitative analysis, I used cross-sectional, time series models covering the years 1996–2012 for 173 states, with state-year as the unit of analysis.[1] The main dependent variable is an annual count of domestic terrorist attacks within each state.[2] This variable is based on the data set of conflict scholars Walter Enders, Todd Sandler, and Khusrav Gaibulloev that divides the Global Terrorism Database (GTD)—maintained by the START Center at the University of Maryland—between international and domestic terrorism for the years 1970–2007.[3] This data set was updated through 2012 by Khusrav Gaibulloev, James Piazza, and Todd Sandler relying on the same coding protocol.[4] In building their data set of terrorist attacks, Enders, Sandler, and Gaibulloev first excluded attacks that do not meet all three inclusion criteria outlined in the GTD, a stricter level than the GTD itself, which requires only two of the three criteria for inclusion. These are: "1) the attack is perpetrated for a political, socioeconomic, or religious motive; 2) the attack is intended to coerce, intimidate, or send a message to a wider audience than the immediate victim(s); and 3) the attack is beyond the boundaries set by international humanitarian law."[5] They excluded any attack identified as "Doubt Terrorism Proper," which includes incidents of guerilla warfare or criminal acts. They then coded attacks as either international or domestic by examining the nationalities of the target. If the nationality of the target is different than the state within which the attack occurred, the attack is coded as international terrorism. The remainder of the terrorist attacks fulfilling the outlined criteria are coded as domestic terrorism, which means that "the venue country matches the nationality of the identified victims, and that there are no diplomatic or multilateral entities involved."[6] Because the dependent variable is an event count with both over-dispersion and excess zeros, I use a zero-inflated negative binomial regression.[7] To account for issues of heteroscedasticity (unequal and nonconstant variance within the data leading to inconsistent and biased standard errors), I use robust standard errors clustered on state. I also include a dependent variable lagged by one year in all the estimated models to account for potential autocorrelation, as past incidents of terrorism increase the likelihood of future terrorist attacks.[8]

The key explanatory variable is a binary measure for domestic counterterrorism operations by the military. If the government used the military for domestic counterterrorism operations in a given year, I code that year as 1. Years in which the military was not used for counterterrorism are coded as 0. To code this variable, I relied on information from the State Department's *Patterns of Global Terrorism* reports from 1996 to 2003[9] and *Country Reports on Terrorism* from 2004 to 2012.[10] The State Department is required by law to submit to Congress an annual report providing "detailed assessments with respect to each foreign country in which acts of international terrorism occurred which were, in the opinion of the Secretary [of State], of major significance." These reports also provide an overview of the range of counterterrorism activities undertaken by partner states deemed to be of significance to the U.S. government in the fight against terrorism. Each annual report outlines,

with respect to each foreign country from which the United States Government has sought cooperation during the previous five years in the investigation or prosecution of an act of international terrorism against United States citizens or interests, information on: (A) the extent to which the government of the foreign country is cooperating with the United States Government in apprehending, convicting, and punishing the individual or individuals responsible for the act; and (B) the extent to which the government of the foreign country is cooperating in preventing further acts of terrorism against United States citizens in the foreign country.[11]

The activities the reports cover include the passage of new and stricter antiterrorism laws, key arrests of terrorist suspects, targeting terrorist financing, various political, economic, or education reforms, relevant police activities, intelligence sharing, cooperation with U.S. military operations in Afghanistan and Iraq, and domestic military operations.

The use of these reports in coding the explanatory variable has two empirical advantages. First, the information for each state within the reports only includes domestic military operations that the State Department considers to be part of the government's counterterrorism efforts and are targeting terrorist groups of interest to the U.S. government. This distinguishes counterterrorism operations from other domestic military operations that are against traditional insurgencies or rebellions and which the U.S. government does not consider to be part of the war on terror. Second, the reports discuss activities that the State Department deems to be evidence of a partner state cooperating with the U.S. government to target existing terrorist groups and "cooperating in preventing further acts of terrorism." Therefore, the domestic military operations included in the coding of this variable are those that are in line with U.S. counterterrorism priorities and that provide evidence of their cooperation with the United States.

There are concerns related to the simultaneity of ongoing domestic counterterrorism operations by the military and domestic terrorism. This can make it more difficult to parse out empirically the causal direction of this relationship, whether military operations cause domestic terrorism or the operations are in response to domestic terrorist attacks. To help address this issue, the explanatory variables are lagged by one year, meaning that counterterrorism operations are correlated with the count of domestic terrorist attacks in the following year. I also estimate models with an explanatory variable for the *introduction* of domestic counterterrorism operations by the military, which is therefore independent of this simultaneity dynamic. For this variable, the year in which a major military operation begins is coded as 1 while all other years of the same operation are coded 0, testing its relationship with domestic terrorism absent the tit-for-tat violence between terrorist groups and the military. When there are temporal breaks between counterterrorism operations, I code the reintroduction of military force as 1 and the remaining years of the operation as a 0. I similarly lagged this variable by one year to capture the causal direction. I also estimate a model limiting the dependent variable to domestic terrorist attacks against military targets to more closely connect the motivation for these attacks with the government's military actions. Given data restrictions, the variable for terrorist attacks against military targets only covers the years 1996–2007.[12]

Figure A.1 shows the annual count of states using their militaries for domestic counterterrorism operations each year from 1996 to 2012. The data shows an overall increase in such operations beginning in 2004, reflective of the changing priorities of U.S. counterterrorism policy toward cooperation with key partner states to target suspected al-Qaeda safe havens. Figure A.2 contains the pattern of domestic terrorism within states that relied on traditional law enforcement for counterterrorism

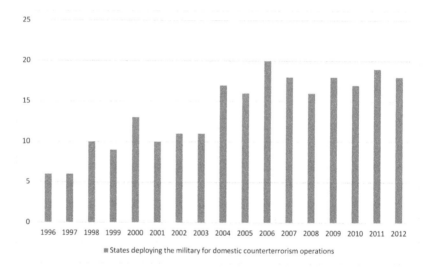

■ States deploying the military for domestic counterterrorism operations

FIGURE A.1 Annual count of domestic terrorist attacks in states that use their militaries for domestic counterterrorism, 1996–2012.

Source: Patterns of Global Terrorism, Office of the Coordinator for Counterterrorism, U.S. Department of State, 1996–2003, https://1997-2001.state.gov/global/terrorism/annual_reports .html, https://2009-2017.state.gov/j/ct/rls/crt/index.htm; Country Reports on Terrorism, Office of the Coordinator for Counterterrorism, U.S. Department of State, 2004–2012, https://2009 -2017.state.gov/j/ct/rls/crt/index.htm.

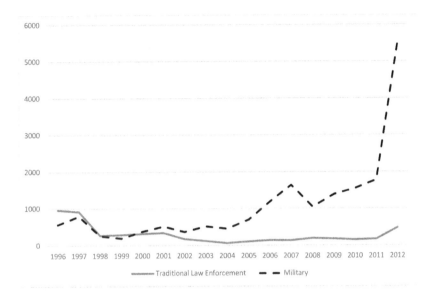

FIGURE A.2 Comparison between number of domestic terrorist attacks per year in states that use traditional law enforcement for domestic counterterrorism vs. states that use their militaries for domestic counterterrorism, 1996–2012.

*Source: Patterns of Global Terrorism*, Office of the Coordinator for Counterterrorism, U.S. Department of State, 1996–2003, https://1997-2001.state.gov/global/terrorism/annual_reports .html, https://2009-2017.state.gov/j/ct/rls/crt/index.htm; *Country Reports on Terrorism*, Office of the Coordinator for Counterterrorism, U.S. Department of State, 2004–2012, https://2009 -2017.state.gov/j/ct/rls/crt/index.htm; Enders, Sandler, and Gaibulloev, "Domestic Versus Transnational Terrorism"; Gaibulloev, Piazza, and Sandler, "Regime Types and Terrorism."

overlaid by the pattern for states that relied on the military from 1996 to 2012. Prior to 2001, these two approaches resulted in similar levels of domestic terrorism. After the beginning of the war on terror, there was a decrease in domestic terrorism within states relying on traditional law enforcement, as states began to take counterterrorism more seriously and undertake greater measures to challenge terrorist groups. However, for states that relied upon their militaries for counterterrorism, the level of domestic terrorism increased, especially after the U.S. government shifted its counterterrorism policy toward supporting the military capacity of partner states to offensively target terrorist groups within their borders.

The estimated models include several control variables that account for alternative explanations for domestic terrorism. I control for politically excluded ethnic groups as a proportion of the total state population, derived from the Ethnic Power Relations data set.[13] I also estimated models using an alternative measure for minority discrimination using data from the Minorities at Risk data set, which did not substantively change the output.[14] To control for regime type, I include a state's Polity IV score.[15] The Polity IV score is a ranking from -10 (hereditary monarchy) to +10 (full democracy). Regime type controls for a state's propensity to suppress political and human rights against its civilian population, which can stimulate terrorism through increased grievances.[16] The Polity IV score also controls for levels of democracy, which political scientists argue can increase the opportunity to commit terrorist attacks.[17] Using data from the World Bank, I include logged control variables for a state's GDP, total state population, and total land area.[18] I also include a logged variable controlling for the level of military expenditures by the government.[19] To control for U.S. influence, I include a dummy variable for a war on terror year, beginning in 2002, and a logged variable for total U.S. military aid lagged by one year, which can increase a state's military capacity and propensity to use its military. With military assistance a key point of leverage in gaining cooperation from states of strategic interest, this also helps to serve as a proxy for the importance of a partner state to U.S. security interests and the likelihood that it will experience pressure to conduct domestic counterterrorism operations. For this variable, I use data from the U.S. Agency for International Development's Green Book, which catalogues all U.S. foreign assistance since 1945.[20] To account for regional influences, I include regional controls for geographic regions most directly impacted by the war on terror: the Middle East and North Africa, sub-Saharan Africa, Central Asia, South Asia, and Southeast Asia.

## RESULTS: DOMESTIC TERRORISM

Figure A.3 displays the coefficient plot for the model testing the relationship between domestic counterterrorism operations by the military (the explanatory variable) and the annual count of domestic terrorist attacks (the dependent variable). A coefficient plot shows the coefficient value and the 95 percent confidence interval (represented by the lines on either side of the point defining the coefficient value) for each independent variable.

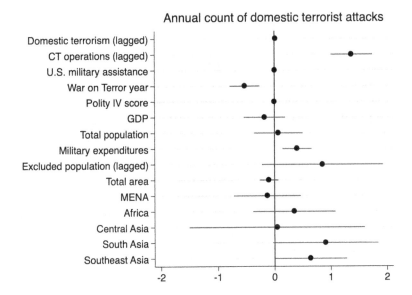

FIGURE A.3 Coefficient plot of the relationship between military handling of domestic counterterrorism (the explanatory variable) and number of domestic terrorist attacks (the dependent variable).

The independent variables have a statistically significant relationship with the dependent variable if the confidence interval does not cross the 0 line in the plot. If the coefficient value is to the right of the 0 line, it has a positive relationship with the dependent variable, meaning a positive change in the independent variable correlates with an increase in the annual count of terrorist attacks. If the coefficient value is to the left of the 0 line, it has a negative relationship—a positive change in the independent variable results in a decrease in terrorist attacks. The variable for domestic counterterrorism operations by the military has a positive and statistically significant relationship with the annual count of domestic terrorist attacks, at the 99.9 percent confidence level. The use of military force for counterterrorism, controlling for other relevant factors, leads to a higher level of domestic terrorism. This finding provides empirical support for the third step of the sequence of events underlying the terrorism trap theory—the tit-for-tat violence between the military and terrorist groups.

Among the control variables, the lagged measure of U.S. military assistance, however, is not statistically significant. This helps to demonstrate that the impact of U.S. policy on domestic terrorism is mediated through the actions of partner states, rather than perceived support from the United States. The logged measure of a state's military expenditures is positive and statistically significant. As military expenditures increase, consistent with domestic military deployments, domestic terrorism increases. This corresponds with the findings of political scientists Cullen Hendrix and Joseph Young, who observed that terrorist attacks occur more frequently against states with higher military capacity, as opposed to states with high bureaucratic capacity.[21] The war on terror dummy variable is also statistically significant but has a negative relationship with the dependent variable. During the war on terror, controlling for other relevant factors, there has in fact been on average an overall decrease in global levels of domestic terrorism, providing further evidence that the increase in domestic terrorism relates to partner states' actions.

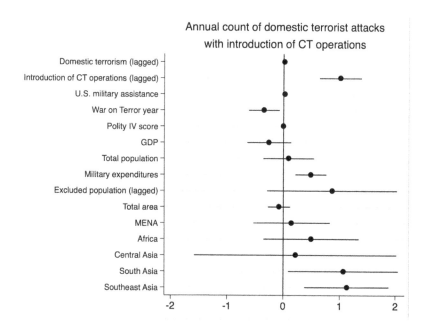

FIGURE A.4 Coefficient plot of the relationship between the introduction of the use of military force for counterterrorism (the explanatory variable) and number of domestic terrorist attacks (the dependent variable).

Figure A.4 shows the coefficient plot of the models estimated with the *introduction* of military force for counterterrorism operations as the explanatory variable. This also has a positive and statistically significant relationship with the annual count of domestic terrorist attacks at the 99.9 percent confidence level. This finding provides empirical support for the second step in the causal process of the terrorism trap theory—the introduction of military force for counterterrorism operations leads to a spike in domestic terrorism. The relevant control variables—war on terror year, U.S. military assistance, and military expenditures—had similar results as the model estimated in figure A.3. In the coefficient plot in figure A.5, counterterrorism operations by the military have a positive and statistically significant relationship with domestic terrorist attacks against military targets at the 99.9 percent confidence level, connecting the attacks to a backlash against military operations.

To understand the substantive impact of these relationships, figures A.6 and A.7 show the marginal effects on domestic terrorist attacks.

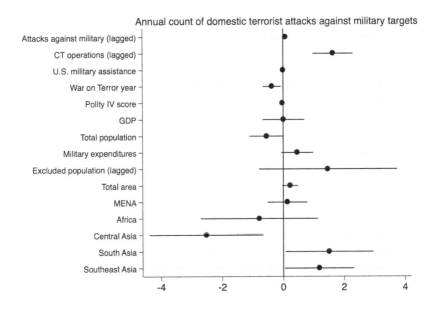

FIGURE A.5 Coefficient plot of the relationship between military handling of counterterrorism (the explanatory variable) and number of domestic terrorist attacks against military targets (the dependent variable).

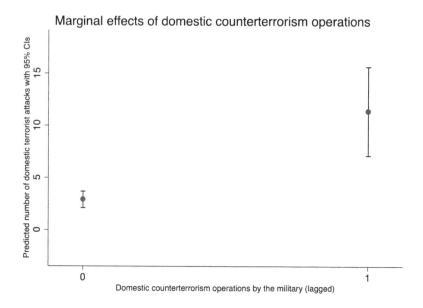

FIGURE A.6 Marginal effects of military handling of domestic counterterrorism on the number of domestic terrorist attacks.

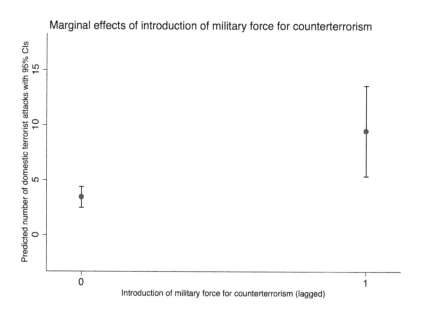

FIGURE A.7 Marginal effects of introduction of military force for counterterrorism on the number of domestic terrorist attacks.

Marginal effects measure the change in the predicted count of the dependent variable resulting from a change in the key explanatory variable from a 0 to a 1. In this way, marginal effects show the substantive relationship between the domestic use of military force and domestic terrorism by calculating the predicted number of attacks for states that rely on the military for counterterrorism against those that do not. If the 95 percent confidence intervals between the two measures do not overlap, then a change in the independent variable has a substantively significant impact on the annual count of the domestic terrorist attacks.

Figure A.6 shows that states that rely on domestic counterterrorism operations by the military are expected to experience 11.4 domestic terrorist attacks in the following year, holding other independent variables at their mean. States that do not use their militaries for counterterrorism, on the other hand, are expected to experience only 2.9 domestic terrorist attacks. In figure A.7, the introduction of military force for counterterrorism operations, holding other independent variables at their means, is expected to lead to 9.5 domestic terrorist attacks in the following year. Its absence is expected to produce 3.4 attacks. This provides empirical support for the claim that domestic counterterrorism operations by the military in line with U.S. counterterrorism priorities resulted in an increase in domestic terrorism, controlling for alternative explanations, as they lead to a backlash from the targeted groups.

## RESULTS: THE USE OF THE MILITARY FOR DOMESTIC COUNTERTERRORISM OPERATIONS

To demonstrate the factors that contribute to a state relying on its military for counterterrorism, I estimate models with domestic counterterrorism operations by the military and the introduction of counterterrorism operations as dependent variables. Because the dependent variables are binary variables, I use a logistic regression. I include as the key explanatory variable a dummy variable for a state possessing a safe haven identified by the 9/11 Commission as a potential al-Qaeda safe

haven. There are other regions in the world that could similarly be classified as terrorist safe havens not identified by the 9/11 Commission. However, by limiting this variable to only those safe havens listed in the
report of the 9/11 Commission I more clearly connect the classification of
a periphery as a terrorist safe haven with U.S. counterterrorism policy.
This coding excludes European cities. I also include as control variables
the annual counts of both domestic and international terrorist attacks
and the dependent variable lagged by one year. I replace the U.S. military
assistance variable with a dummy variable controlling for whether a state
receives any level of U.S. military assistance, independent of the actual
amount, which can serve as a signal to the partner state to use military
force in its counterterrorism efforts.

Figures A.8 and A.9 display the coefficient plots of the models estimated with domestic counterterrorism operations by the military and the
introduction of counterterrorism operations by the military as dependent

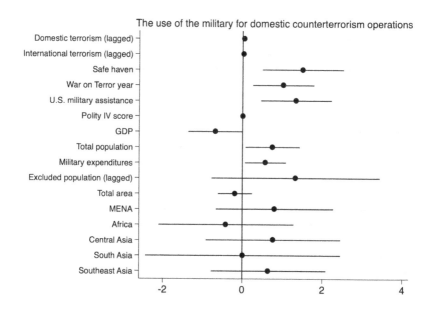

FIGURE A.8 Coefficient plot of the relationship between U.S. designation of a given
state as a safe haven for al-Qaeda (the explanatory variable) and that state's use of its
military for domestic counterterrorism operations (the dependent variable).

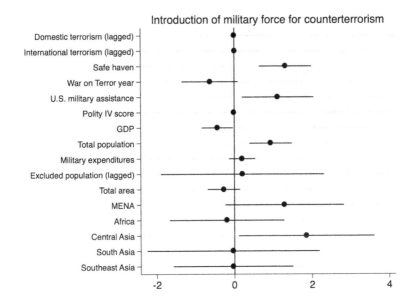

FIGURE A.9 Coefficient plot of the relationship between U.S. designation of a given state as a safe haven for al-Qaeda (the explanatory variable) and that state's introduction of military force for counterterrorism (the dependent variable).

variables, respectively. States possessing a safe haven identified by the 9/11 Commission have a positive and statistically significant relationship with both the use of the military for counterterrorism operations and the introduction of such operations, at the 99.9 percent confidence level. This provides empirical support to the first step in the causal process in the terrorism trap theory—partner states have a higher likelihood of deploying their militaries for domestic counterterrorism actions if the U.S. government suspects their periphery could serve as a safe haven for al-Qaeda or al-Qaeda-linked groups. By calculating the odds ratios for the logit model in figure A.8, states with a U.S.-designated safe haven are 4.5 times more likely to use the military for counterterrorism. This provides support for the argument that states with a U.S.-identified safe haven, and therefore under pressure from the U.S. government to target it, are more likely to deploy the military for domestic counterterrorism operations.

Moreover, a lagged annual count of domestic terrorist attacks has a statistically significant relationship with ongoing counterterrorism operations. However, it does not have a statistically significant relationship with the dependent variable for the introduction of military force for counterterrorism operations. International terrorism, on the other hand, does have a statistically significant relationship with the introduction of military force. This helps to demonstrate the influence of U.S. counterterrorism policy, focused as it is on international terrorism, in the domestic deployment of partner states' militaries, providing further empirical support to the first step of the causal process. The relationship between ongoing counterterrorism operations and domestic terrorism, on the other hand, is emblematic of the tit-for-tat violence that leads to the increase in domestic terrorist attacks within partner states.

## RESULTS: ROBUSTNESS CHECKS

I conducted several robustness checks on the models' results.[22] I first estimated models including a variable based on political scientist Peter Henne's Counterterrorism Cooperation Scale (CTCS), a quantitative measure of a state's level of counterterrorism cooperation with the United States.[23] The CTCS runs from -10 (completely uncooperative) to 10 (completely cooperative) for forty-seven Muslim-majority states from 1996 to 2009. To construct the CTCS, Henne similarly relied on the State Department's *Patterns of Global Terrorism* and *Country Reports on Terrorism* to count every action signifying a state's cooperation or noncooperation with the United States on counterterrorism. His coding aggregates the entire range of counterterrorism actions into a single measure, without distinguishing between offensive and defensive behaviors, military and police operations, or political and legal reforms and kinetic approaches. He then calculated the percentage of cooperative and uncooperative behavior for each state and took the difference between the two percentages to establish an annual measure.

The inclusion of the CTCS controls for a state's alternative counterterrorism actions used alongside military force, which can also have an impact on the levels of both domestic and international terrorism. I run separate models with the CTCS because of the data loss stemming from its inclusion.[24] The CTCS is limited in both years covered (ending in 2009) and the states included in its coding. Henne only includes Muslim-majority states in his coding and, therefore, key partner states in the war on terror that are not Muslim-majority but possess a Muslim periphery, such as the Philippines and Ethiopia, are not included. (Both countries were part of Operation Enduring Freedom.) Figure A.10 shows the coefficient plot of the models estimated with the CTCS variable included as an independent variable. Controlling for a partner state's overall level of counterterrorism cooperation with the United States, the variable for domestic counterterrorism operations by the military remains positive and statistically significant at the 99.9 percent confidence level.

I then excluded Iraq and Afghanistan from the data and reestimated the models. Iraq and Afghanistan are both outliers given the U.S. military invasions, U.S. military presence, and high levels of U.S. military assistance to both countries. Even with operations organized and conducted by Iraqi and Afghan security forces, the anti-Americanism

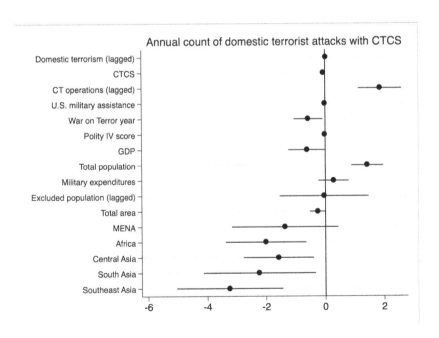

FIGURE A.10 Coefficient plot of the relationship between the counterterrorism cooperation scale (the explanatory variable) and domestic terrorist attacks (the dependent variable).

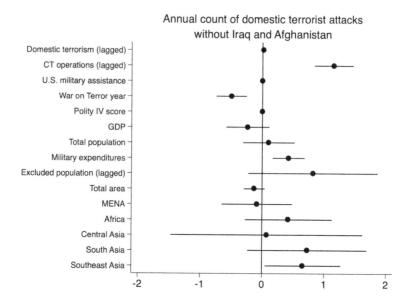

FIGURE A.11 Coefficient plot of the relationship between counterterrorism operations by the military (the explanatory variable) and domestic terrorist attacks (the dependent variable), *without* Iraq and Afghanistan.

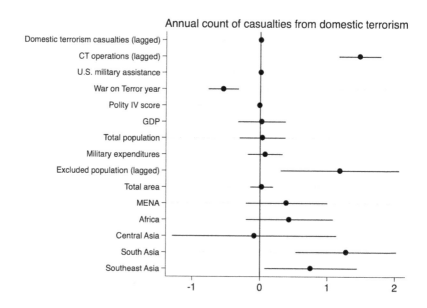

FIGURE A.12 Coefficient plot of the relationship between counterterrorism operations by the military (the explanatory variable) and the annual count of casualties from domestic terrorist attacks (the dependent variable).

generated by the U.S. military invasions, combined with strong U.S. support of the two governments, helped to undermine their legitimacy and generate an increased backlash to these military actions and potentially lead to higher levels of terrorism. The model's output, displayed in the coefficient plot in figure A.11, are consistent with the earlier results, providing further evidence for the terrorism trap theory.

Using an alternative measure of terrorist activity, I estimated a model with the total annual count of casualties from domestic terrorist attacks as the dependent variable.[25] As shown in figure A.12, the variable for counterterrorism operations by the military has a positive and statistically significant relationship with the annual count of casualties from domestic terrorism at the 99.9 percent confidence level. U.S. counterterrorism policy has not only led to an increase in domestic terrorist attacks within partner states but has increased the deadliness of these attacks as well.

# NOTES

## 1. THE TERRORISM TRAP

1. Donald Rumsfeld, "Memorandum for Paul Wolfowitz, Doug Feith, Torie Clarke, and Powell Moore," September 19, 2001, U15566/01, National Security Archive.

2. National Commission on Terrorist Attacks Upon the United States, *The 9/11 Commission Report: Final Report of the National Commission on Terrorist Attacks upon the United States* (New York: Norton, 2004), 379.

3. Author interview with Douglas Feith, former undersecretary of defense for policy, Washington, DC, October 31, 2018.

4. In this analysis, the term "partner states" refers to states that cooperated with the United States on counterterrorism efforts within their own borders. This does not refer to treaty allies and coalition partners, such as NATO members, that supported the U.S. military invasions of Afghanistan and Iraq or supported other counterterrorism activities outside of their borders. The terms "partner state" and "ally" are often used interchangeably. Yet, within international politics, it is important to recognize that these are two distinct concepts. As the Department of Defense's *National Defense Strategy* explains, "Our allies are countries with which we have formal, long-term relationships. For example, NATO was formally established by the North Atlantic Treaty in 1949, and its 29 members are allies." Partnerships, on the other hand, "usually focus on something mutually beneficial during a specific amount of time or for specific circumstances. The U.S. relationship with its Caribbean and Latin American partners, for instance, helps to stem the tide of illegal drug activity." See Katie Lange, "National Defense Strategy: Alliances and Partnerships," U.S. Department of Defense, October 8, 2018, https://www.defense.gov/Explore/Features/story/Article/1656016/national-defense-strategy-alliances-and-partnerships/.

5.   Author interview with former senior State Department official, Washington, DC, January 2019; Robert M. Hathaway, *The Leverage Paradox: Pakistan and the United States* (Washington, DC: Woodrow Wilson International Center for Scholars, 2017); Walter C. Ladwig, *The Forgotten Front: Patron-Client Relationships in Counterinsurgency* (Cambridge: Cambridge University Press, 2017); William M. LeoGrande, "A Splendid Little War: Drawing the Line in El Salvador," *International Security* 6, no. 1 (1981): 27–52.

6.   Peter S. Henne, *Islamic Politics, Muslim States, and Counterterrorism Tensions* (Cambridge: Cambridge University Press, 2016); Barak Mendelsohn, *Combating Jihadism: American Hegemony and Interstate Cooperation in the War on Terrorism* (Chicago: University of Chicago Press, 2009); Stephen Tankel, *With Us and Against Us: How America's Partners Help and Hinder the War on Terror* (New York: Columbia University Press, 2018).

7.   Neta C. Crawford, "The U.S. Budgetary Costs of the Post-9/11 Wars," Costs of War Project, Brown University, September 1, 2021, https://watson.brown.edu/costsofwar/files/cow/imce/papers/2021/Costs%20of%20War_U.S.%20Budgetary%20Costs%20of%20Post-9%2011%20Wars_9.1.21.pdf. This figure (current as of fiscal year 2022) includes War/Overseas Contingency Operations (OCO) appropriations, Department of Defense (DOD) spending, State Department/USAID spending, interest on borrowing for DOD and State Department OCO spending, increases in DOD's base budget as a result of post-9/11 wars, post-9/11 veterans' medical and disability spending, and homeland security prevention and response to terrorism spending. These accounts add up to $5.843 trillion. Crawford also includes in her accounting the estimated future obligations for veterans' medical and disability through fiscal year 2050, adding another $2.2 trillion to the total amount. This brings her reported total to $8.043 trillion.

8.   Walter Enders, Todd Sandler, and Khusrav Gaibulloev, "Domestic Versus Transnational Terrorism: Data, Decomposition, and Dynamics," *Journal of Peace Research* 48, no. 3 (2011): 319–337; Khusrav Gaibulloev, James A. Piazza, and Todd Sandler, "Regime Types and Terrorism," *International Organization* 71, no. 3 (2017): 491–522.

9.   Alex Braithwaite, "Transnational Terrorism as an Unintended Consequence of a Military Footprint," *Security Studies* 24, no. 2 (2015): 349–375; Seung-Whan Choi and James A. Piazza, "Foreign Military Interventions and Suicide Attacks," *Journal of Conflict Resolution* 61, no. 2 (2017): 271–297; Eric Neumayer and Thomas Plumper, "Foreign Terror on Americans," *Journal of Peace Research* 48, no. 1 (2011): 3–17; James A. Piazza and Seung-Whan Choi, "International Military Interventions and Transnational Terrorist Backlash," *International Studies Quarterly* 62, no. 3 (2018): 686–695; Burcu Savun and Brian J. Phillips, "Democracy, Foreign Policy, and Terrorism," *Journal of Conflict Resolution* 53, no. 6 (2009): 878–904.

10.   Ignacio Sanchez-Cuenca and Luis de la Calle, "Domestic Terrorism: The Hidden Side of Political Violence," *Annual Review of Political Science* 12 (2009): 31–49.

11.   Konstantin Ash, "Representative Democracy and Fighting Domestic Terrorism," *Terrorism and Political Violence* 28, no. 1 (2016): 114–134; Casey Crisman-Cox,

"Enemies Within: Interactions Between Terrorists and Democracies," *Journal of Conflict Resolution* 62, no. 8 (2018): 1661–1685; Alex Dreher and Justina A. V. Fischer, "Does Government Decentralization Reduce Domestic Terrorism? An Empirical Test," *Economics Letters* 111 (2011): 223–225; Krisztina Kis-Katos, Helge Liebert, and Gunther G. Schulze, "On the Origin of Domestic and International Terrorism," *European Journal of Political Economy* 27 (2011): 517–536; Patrick F. Larue and Orlandrew E. Danzell, "Rethinking State Capacity: Conceptual Effects on the Incidence of Terrorism," *Terrorism and Political Violence* 34, no. 6 (2022): 1241–1258; James A. Piazza, "Terrorism and Party Systems in the States of India," *Security Studies* 19, no. 1 (2010): 99–123; Joshua Tschantret, "Democratic Breakdown and Terrorism," *Conflict Management and Peace Science* 38, no. 4 (2021): 369–390; James I. Walsh and James A. Piazza, "Autocracies and Terrorism: Conditioning Effects of Authoritarian Regime Types on Terrorist Attacks," *American Journal of Political Science* 57, no. 4 (2013): 941–955.

12. Orlandrew E. Danzell, Yao-Yuan Yeh, and Melia Pfannenstiel, "Determinants of Domestic Terrorism: An Examination of Ethnic Polarization and Economic Development," *Terrorism and Political Violence* 31, no. 3 (2019): 536–558; Walter Enders, Gary A. Hoover, and Todd Sandler, "The Changing Nonlinear Relationship Between Income and Terrorism," *Journal of Conflict Resolution* 60, no. 2 (2016): 195–225.

13. Peter S. Henne, "Government Interference in Religious Institutions and Terrorism," *Religion, State and Society* 47, no. 1 (2019): 67–86; Peter S. Henne, Nilay Saiya, and Ashlyn W. Hand, "Weapon of the Strong? Government Support for Religion and Majoritarianism Terrorism," *Journal of Conflict Resolution* 64, no. 10 (2020): 1943–1967.

14. Roberto Ezcurra, "Group Concentration and Violence: Does Ethnic Segregation Affect Domestic Terrorism?," *Defence and Peace Economics* 30, no. 1 (2019): 46–71; James A. Piazza, "Politician Hate Speech and Domestic Terrorism," *International Interactions* 46, no. 3 (2020): 431–453.

15. Javed Younas and Todd Sandler, "Gender Imbalance and Terrorism in Developing Countries," *Journal of Conflict Resolution* 61, no. 3 (2017): 483–510.

16. Seung-Whan Choi and James A. Piazza, "Ethnic Groups, Political Exclusion and Domestic Terrorism," *Defence and Peace Economics* 27, no. 1 (2016): 37–63; Sambuddha Ghatak and Aaron Gold, "Development, Discrimination, and Domestic Terrorism: Looking Beyond a Linear Relationship," *Conflict Management and Peace Science* 34, no. 6 (2017): 618–639; Sambuddha Ghatak, Aaron Gold, and Brandon C. Prins, "Domestic Terrorism in Democratic States: Understanding and Addressing Minority Grievances," *Journal of Conflict Resolution* 63, no. 2 (2019): 439–467; Holly E. Hansen, Stephen C. Nemeth, and Jacob A. Mauslein, "Ethnic Political Exclusion and Terrorism: Analyzing the Local Conditions for Violence," *Conflict Management and Peace Science* 37, no. 3 (2020): 280–300; James A. Piazza, "Poverty, Minority Economic Discrimination, and Domestic Terrorism," *Journal of Peace Research* 48, no. 3 (2011): 339–353; James A. Piazza, "Types of Minority Discrimination and Terrorism," *Conflict Management and Peace Science* 29, no. 5 (2012): 521–546.

17. Background Briefing by Senior Administration Officials on the President's Speech on Counterterrorism, White House Office of the Press Secretary, May 23, 2013, C06594688, State Department Reading Room.

18. The term "ungoverned spaces," frequently employed by U.S. policy makers and found throughout this book, is something of a misnomer. The absence of effective state control at the periphery does not necessarily mean a total absence of governing institutions or completely anarchic conditions, and there are debates about what the meaning of "government control" actually means. Many of these regions did have some legal and political institutions that permitted partial government administration and influence, such as the 1901 Frontier Crimes Regulation in Pakistan's FATA, as well as local communities relying on informal, nonstate institutions and local customs for self-governance. Such customary governance has persisted parallel, and often in complement, to the development of the modern state with its various legal and political institutions at the center. As scholars have argued, the emphasis on maintaining complete state control over the entirety of a state's sovereign territory is a relatively recent phenomenon within the international system. This analysis uses the term "ungoverned spaces" only to reference how these peripheral regions were perceived and referred to within U.S. counterterrorism policy as potential al-Qaeda safe havens, and it therefore always appears in quotation marks. See Kate Baldwin and Katharina Holzinger, "Traditional Political Institutions and Democracy: Reassessing Their Compatibility and Accountability," *Comparative Political Studies* 52, no. 12 (2019): 1747–1774; Anne L. Clunan and Harold A. Trinkunas, eds., *Ungoverned Spaces: Alternatives to State Authority in an Era of Softened Sovereignty* (Palo Alto, CA: Stanford University Press, 2010); Jennifer Brick Murtazashvili, *Informal Order and the State in Afghanistan* (Cambridge: Cambridge University Press, 2016); Jennifer Murtazashvili, "A Tired Cliché: Why We Should Stop Worrying About Ungoverned Spaces and Embrace Self-Governance," *Journal of International Affairs* 71, no. 2 (2018): 11–29; Nicole Stremlau, "Governance Without Government in the Somali Territories," *Journal of International Affairs* 71, no. 2 (2018): 73–89; Andrew J. Taylor, "Thoughts on the Nature and Consequence of Ungoverned Spaces," *SAIS Review of International Affairs* 36, no. 1 (2016): 5–15; Shu De Teo, "Evaluating the Concept of Ungoverned Spaces: The Limitations of a Two Dimensional Worldview," *Journal of International Affairs* 71, no. 2 (2018): 125–133.

19. Marc Bloch, *The Historian's Craft* (Manchester, UK: Manchester University Press, 1954), 119.

20. Tony Addison and S. Mansoob Murshed, "Transnational Terrorism as a Spillover of Domestic Disputes in Other Countries," *Defence and Peace Economics* 16, no. 2 (2005): 69–82; Navin Bapat, "The Internationalization of Terrorist Campaigns," *Conflict Management and Peace Science* 24, no. 4 (2007): 265–280; Enders, Sandler, and Gaibulloev, "Domestic Versus Transnational Terrorism"; Neumayer and Plumper, "Foreign Terror on Americans"; Cameron Napps and Walter Enders, "A Regional Investigation of the Interrelationships Between Domestic and Transnational Terrorism: A Time Series Analysis," *Defence and Peace Economics* 26, no. 2 (2015): 133–151.

21. Bruce Bueno de Mesquita and Randolph M. Siverson, "War and the Survival of Political Leaders: A Comparative Study of Regime Types and Political Accountability," *American Political Science Review* 89, no. 4 (1995): 841–855; James D. Fearon, "Domestic Political Audiences and the Escalation of International Disputes," *American Political Science Review* 88, no. 3 (1994): 577–592; Robert D. Putnam, "Diplomacy and Domestic Politics: The Logic of Two-Level Games," *International Organizations* 42, no. 3 (1988): 427–460.

22. Peter Gourevitch, "The Second Image Reversed: The International Sources of Domestic Politics," *International Organization* 32, no. 4 (1978): 881–912; Kenneth N. Waltz, *Man, State, and War: A Theoretical Analysis* (New York: Columbia University Press, 1954).

23. Harrison Akins, "Violence on the Home Front: Interstate Rivalry and Pro-Government Militias," *Terrorism and Political Violence* 33, no. 3 (2021) 466–488; Sabine C. Carey, Michael P. Colaresi, and Neil J. Mitchell, "Governments, Informal Links to Militias, and Accountability," *Journal of Conflict Resolution* 59, no. 5 (2015): 850–876; Mark Toukan, "International Politics by Other Means: External Sources of Civil War," *Journal of Peace Research* 56, no. 6 (2019): 812–826; Gary Uzonyi, "Interstate Rivalry, Genocide, and Politicide," *Journal of Peace Research* 55, no. 4 (2018): 476–490.

24. Anthropologists have classified these tribal societies as "segmentary lineage systems" in which individuals are organized into different social groupings based on shared lineage, or "segments," that helped to define the limits of shared interests and obligations within a tribal community. The structure of this system has been portrayed in numerous classic works of anthropology, with the pyramid-like genealogical charters of clans and subclans showing smaller tribal groupings nested within larger segments defined by descent from a common ancestor. Akbar Ahmed identifies four primary characteristics of the "closed world" of the segmentary lineage system: "(a) highly egalitarian segments of a genealogical charter, and within them smaller and smaller segments, all claiming descent from a common, often eponymous ancestor; (b) male cousin rivalry and a council of elders to mediate conflict; (c) recognition of rights to territory corresponding to segments, as acknowledged by tradition; and (d) a normatively acknowledged set of customs that includes a code of honor and a distinctive language." See Ahmed, *The Thistle and the Drone: How America's War on Terror Became a Global War on Tribal Islam* (Washington, DC: Brookings Institution Press, 2013), 18–21; E. E. Evans-Pritchard, *The Nuer: A Description of the Modes of Livelihood and Political Institutions of a Nilotic People* (New York: Oxford University Press, 1940), 192–248; I. M. Lewis, *A Pastoral Democracy: A Study of Pastoralism and Politics Among the Northern Somali of the Horn of Africa* (London: Oxford University Press, 1961), 5, 12.

25. Among the sixty-nine groups (as of November 2020) designated by the State Department as "Foreign Terrorist Organizations," thirty-nine emerged from conflicts between center and periphery. See "Foreign Terrorist Organizations," Bureau of Counterterrorism, U.S. Department of State, accessed November 8, 2020, http://state.gov/foreign-terrorist-organizations.

26. Ahmed, *The Thistle and the Drone*, 97.
27. Ahmed, 15.
28. The use of the term "tribe" in the context of center-periphery relations has provoked strong scholarly debate and is not without controversy, evoking as it does the Orientalism and racism of much colonial-era scholarship. Discussions and debates around "tribes" and their accompanying characteristics in decades past were often based on romanticized stereotypes or harmful clichés about these populations, ignoring the complexities of their social realities and lived experiences. While understanding this background, I use this and other similar terms, such as "clan," in this study merely to reference the social identities and organizational structures of lineage-based societies. It is also worth noting that the regions' inhabitants themselves use these terms to describe the social features influencing their interactions with state structures.
29. Olaf Caroe, *The Pathans: 550 B.C.–A.D. 1957* (New York: St. Martin's Press, 1958), 391.
30. Lord Rennell of Rodd, *People of the Veil: Being an Account of the Habits, Organisation and History of the Wandering Tuareg Tribes which Inhabit the Mountains of Air or Asben in the Central Sahara* (Oosterhout, NL: Anthropological Publications, 1966), 189.
31. James C. Scott, *The Art of Not Being Governed: An Anarchist History of Southeast Asia* (New Haven, CT: Yale University Press, 2009), 26–32.
32. James C. Scott, *Against the Grain: A Deep History of the Earliest States* (New Haven, CT: Yale University Press, 2017), 33.
33. Clifford Geertz, *The Interpretation of Cultures* (New York: Basic Books, 1973), 297.
34. Alfred Lyall, "Frontiers and Protectorates," *Nineteenth Century: A Monthly Review* 30, no. 174 (1891): 315.
35. Lord Curzon of Kedleston, *The Romanes Lecture 1907: Frontiers* (Oxford: Clarendon Press, 1907), 7.
36. Evelyn Howell, *Mizh: A Monograph on Government's Relations with the Mahsud Tribe* (Karachi: Oxford University Press, 1979), 35–36.
37. Benjamin Claude Brower, *A Desert Named Peace: The Violence of France's Empire in the Algerian Sahara, 1844–1902* (New York: Columbia University Press, 2009), 23.
38. Walker Connor, *Ethnonationalism: The Quest for Understanding* (Princeton, NJ: Princeton University Press, 1994), 134.
39. Derick W. Brinkerhoff, "State Fragility and Governance: Conflict Mitigation and Subnational Perspectives," *Development Policy Review* 29, no. 2 (2011): 131–153; Daniel Bromley and Glen Anderson, *Vulnerable People, Vulnerable States: Redefining the Development Challenge* (Abingdon, UK: Routledge, 2012); John R. Heilbrunn, "Paying the Price of Failure: Reconstructing Failed and Collapsed States in Africa and Central Asia," *Perspectives on Politics* 4, no. 1 (2006): 135–150; Nicolas van de Walle, *African Economies and the Politics of Permanent Crisis, 1979–1999* (Cambridge: Cambridge University Press, 2001).
40. Robert H. Jackson, *Quasi-states: Sovereignty, International Relations and the Third World* (Cambridge: Cambridge University Press, 1990).

41. Berenice Guyot-Rechard, *Shadow States: India, China and the Himalayas, 1910–1962* (Cambridge: Cambridge University Press, 2017), 20.

42. Guyot-Rechard, 20–24; Harrison Akins, "The Assam Rifles and India's North-East frontier policy," *Small Wars & Insurgencies* 31, no. 6 (2020): 1373–1394.

43. Ahmed, *The Thistle and the Drone*; Donald L. Horowitz, *Ethnic Groups in Conflict* (Berkeley: University of California Press, 1985), 185–228.

44. Will Kymlicka, *Multicultural Citizenship: A Liberal Theory of Minority Rights* (Oxford: Clarendon Press, 1995), 11.

45. Dominik Balthasar, "State-Making at Gunpoint: The Role of Violent Conflict in Somaliland's March to Statehood," *Civil Wars* 19, no. 1 (2017): 65–86; David McDowall, *A Modern History of the Kurds* (London: I. B. Tauris, 2004).

46. Benedict Anderson, *Imagined Communities: Reflections on the Origin and Spread of Nationalism* (London: Verso, 1983).

47. Michael Hechter, *Internal Colonialism: The Celtic Fringe in British National Development* (Berkeley: University of California Press, 1975), 8–9, 119.

48. Horowitz, *Ethnic Groups in Conflict*, 5.

49. Ahmed, *The Thistle and the Drone*, 14; Julian Wucherpfennig, Philipp Hunziker, and Lars-Erik Cederman, "Who Inherits the State? Colonial Rule and Postcolonial Conflict," *American Journal of Political Science* 60, no. 4 (2016): 882–898.

50. Akbar S. Ahmed, *Mataloona: Pukhto Proverbs* (Karachi: Oxford University Press, 1975), 57.

51. Mark Mazzetti, *The Way of the Knife: The CIA, a Secret Army, and a War at the Ends of the Earth* (New York: Penguin Books, 2013), 137.

52. Mazzetti, xvi–xvii.

53. Unreported Speech of Baluchistan Governor Mohammad Akbar Khan Bugti, Political Situation in Baluchistan, Province of Pakistan, 1973, FCO/37/1336, National Archives (UK).

54. Anthropologist Lawrence Rosen observed this reality within tribally organized Muslim societies in his study *Bargaining for Reality: The Construction of Social Relations in a Muslim Community* (Chicago: University of Chicago Press, 1984).

55. Akbar S. Ahmed, *Pukhtun Economy and Society: Traditional Structure and Economic Development in a Tribal Society* (Abingdon, UK: Routledge, 1980); Akbar S. Ahmed, *Resistance and Control in Pakistan*, rev. ed. (Abingdon, UK: Routledge, 2004); Christopher Boehm, *Blood Revenge: The Enactment and Management of Conflict in Montenegro and Other Tribal Societies* (Philadelphia: University of Pennsylvania Press, 1986); Judith Matloff, *No Friends but the Mountains: Dispatches from the World's Violent Highlands* (New York: Basic Books, 2017); Shahmahmood Miakhel, "Understanding Afghanistan: The Importance of Tribal Culture and Structure in Security and Governance," *Asian Survey* 35, no. 7 (1995): 1–22.

56. Rod Nordland, Alissa J. Rubin, and Matthew Rosenberg, "Gulf Widens Between U.S. and a More Volatile Karzai," *New York Times*, March 17, 2012.

57. Anne Speckhard and Khapta Ahkmedova, "The Making of a Martyr: Chechen Suicide Terrorism," *Studies in Conflict & Terrorism* 29, no. 5 (2006): 467.

58.  Ahmed, *The Thistle and the Drone*; Virginie Collombier and Olivier Roy, eds., *Tribes and Global Jihadism* (London: C. Hurst and Co., 2017); Phillip M. Zeman, "Tribalism and Terror: Report from the Field," *Small Wars & Insurgencies* 20, nos. 3–4 (2009): 681–709.

59.  Abu Masab al-Zarqawi, "Leader of Al-Qaeda in Iraq Al-Zarqawi Declares 'Total War' on Shi'ites, States that the Sunni Women of Tel'afar Had 'Their Wombs Filled with the Sperm of the Crusaders,' " September 16, 2005, Global Terrorism Research Project, Haverford College, https://scholarship.tricolib.brynmawr.edu/bitstream/handle /10066/4810/ZAR20050914P.pdf?sequence=3&isAllowed=y.

60.  Gabriel Koehler-Derrick, *A False Foundation? AQAP, Tribes, and Ungoverned Spaces* (West Point, NY: Combating Terrorism Center at West Point, 2011), 97.

61.  Ahmed, *Resistance and Control in Pakistan*; Robert L. Hess, "The 'Mad Mullah' and Northern Somalia," *Journal of African History* 5, no. 3 (1964): 415–433; Jonathan Krause, "Islam and Anti-colonial Rebellions in North and West Africa, 1914–1918," *Historical Journal* 64, no. 3 (2021): 674–695; Lewis, *A Pastoral Democracy*, 225–228; E. E. Evans-Pritchard, *The Sanusi of Cyrenaica* (Oxford: Clarendon Press, 1949).

62.  Ahmed, *The Thistle and the Drone*, 18–34; Akbar S. Ahmed and David M. Hart, eds., *Islam in Tribal Societies: From the Atlas to the Indus* (Abingdon, UK: Routledge, 1984); Clinton Bailey, "Bedouin Religious Practices in Sinai and the Negev," *Anthropos* 77, nos. 1–2 (1982): 65–88; Ernest Gellner, *Muslim Society* (Cambridge: Cambridge University Press, 1981).

63.  A. Henry Savage Landor, *Across Widest Africa: An Account of the Country and People of Eastern, Central and Western Africa as Seen During a Twelve Month Journey from Djibuti to Cape Verde* (London: Hurst and Blackett, 1907), 346.

64.  Hassan Abbas, *The Taliban Revival: Violence and Extremism on the Pakistan-Afghanistan Frontier* (New Haven, CT: Yale University Press, 2014), 13–14.

65.  Author interview with Abdul Basit Mujahid, chairman of the Balochistan Intellectual Forum, Islamabad, Pakistan, December 14, 2018.

66.  Jean-Francois Ratelle and Emil Aslan Souleimanov, "Retaliation in Rebellion: The Missing Link to Explaining Insurgent Violence in Dagestan," *Terrorism and Political Violence* 29, no. 4 (2017): 573–592.

67.  Ratelle and Souleimanov, 581.

68.  Matloff, *No Friends but the Mountains*, 140.

69.  Emil Aslan Souleimanov and Huseyn Aliyev, "Blood Revenge and Violent Mobilization: Evidence from the Chechen Wars," *International Security* 40, no. 2 (2015): 174.

70.  Emil Aslan Souleimanov and Huseyn Aliyev, *How Socio-Cultural Codes Shaped Violent Mobilization and Pro-Insurgent Support in the Chechen Wars* (Basingstoke, UK: Palgrave Macmillan, 2017), 46.

71.  Theodore P. Gerber and Sarah E. Mendelson, "Security Through Sociology: The North Caucasus and the Global Counterinsurgency Paradigm," *Studies in Conflict & Terrorism* 32, no. 9 (2009): 831–851.

72. Souleimanov and Aliyev, "Blood Revenge and Violent Mobilization"; Matthew Janec-zko, "'Faced with Death, Even a Mouse Bites': Social and Religious Motivations Behind Terrorism in Chechnya," *Small Wars & Insurgencies* 25, no. 2 (2013): 428–456.

73. Speckhard and Ahkmedova, "The Making of a Martyr."

74. Paul J. Murphy, *Allah's Angels: Chechen Women in War* (Annapolis, MD: Naval Insti-tute Press, 2011), 140.

75. David Kilcullen, *The Accidental Guerilla: Fighting Small Wars in the Midst of a Big One* (New York: Oxford University Press, 2009), 34–35.

76. Kilcullen, 34.

77. Kilcullen, 210–244.

78. Allan Dafoe, Sophia Hatz, and Baobao Zhang, "Coercion and Provocation," *Journal of Conflict Resolution* 65, nos. 2–3 (2021): 372–402; Joao Ricardo Faria and Daniel Arce, "Counterterrorism and Its Impact on Terror Support and Recruitment: Accounting for Backlash," *Defence and Peace Economics* 23, no. 5 (2012): 431–445; John Stone, "Escalation and the War on Terror," *Journal of Strategic Studies* 35, no. 5 (2012): 639–661.

79. *Terrorism in the United States*, FBI Counterterrorism Division, 1999, https://www.fbi.gov/file-repository/stats-services-publications-terror_99.pdf/view; *Public Report of the Vice President's Task Force on Combatting Terrorism*, Office of the Vice President, the White House, February 1986, http://insidethecoldwar.org/sites/default/files/documents/Public%20Report%20of%20the%20Vice%20President's%20Task%20Force%20on%20Combating%20Terrorism.pdf; *Terrorism Counteraction Field Manual*, U.S. Army Field Manual No. 100-37, July 1987.

80. Daniel L. Byman, "Friends Like These: Counterinsurgency and the War on Terror-ism," *International Security* 31, no. 2 (2006): 88.

81. Seung-Whan Choi and Patrick James, "Why Does the United States Intervene Abroad? Democracy, Human Rights Violations, and Terrorism," *Journal of Conflict Resolution* 60, no. 5 (2014): 899–926. Choi and James interpret this empirical finding to mean that protection of human rights and preservation of liberal norms remain central to U.S. foreign policy, as opposed to only protecting U.S. national security interests. Yet, their analysis does not include U.S. military and counterterrorism foreign assistance or the U.S. government's growing reliance on partner state militaries to pursue counter-terrorism operations in place of direct U.S. military interventions abroad. By examining direct U.S. military interventions alone to shed light on U.S. foreign policy priorities, they omit a key aspect of U.S. foreign policy during the war on terror, as my own analysis demonstrates.

82. Shuja Nawaz, *The Battle for Pakistan: The Bitter US Friendship and a Tough Neigh-bourhood* (Delhi, IN: Penguin Random House, 2019), 248; Zafarullah Khan, "Federal-izing the Armed Forces," *Friday Times* (Pakistan), September 19, 2014.

83. Kilcullen, *The Accidental Guerilla*, 242–243.

84. Ahmed, *The Thistle and the Drone*; James A. Piazza, "Repression and Terrorism: A Cross-National Empirical Analysis of Types of Repression and Domestic Terrorism,"

*Terrorism and Political Violence* 29, no. 1 (2017): 102–118; Ratelle and Souleimanov, "Retaliation in Rebellion."

85. Seung-Whan Choi and James A. Piazza, "Internally Displaced Populations and Suicide Terrorism," *Journal of Conflict Resolution* 60, no. 6 (2016): 1008–1040.

86. B. Peter Rosendorff and Todd Sandler, "Too Much of a Good Thing? The Proactive Response Dilemma," *Journal of Conflict Resolution* 48, no. 5 (2004): 657–671.

87. Julie Chernov Hwang and Kirsten E. Schulze, "Why They Join: Pathways Into Indonesian Jihadist Organizations," *Terrorism and Political Violence* 30, no. 6 (2018): 911–932; Sidney Jones, "Radicalisation in the Philippines: The Cotabato Cell of the 'East Asia Wilayah,'" *Terrorism and Political Violence* 30, no. 6 (2018): 933–943; Eduardo F. Ugarte, "The Alliance System of the Abu Sayyaf, 1993–2000," *Studies in Conflict & Terrorism* 31, no. 2 (2008): 125–144.

88. Author interview with General Abdullah Dogar, former Pakistani brigade commander in Waziristan, Washington, DC, April 23, 2012.

89. Addison and Murshed, "Transnational Terrorism as a Spillover of Domestic Disputes in Other Countries"; Bapat, "The Internationalization of Terrorist Campaigns"; Napps and Enders, "A Regional Investigation of the Interrelationships Between Domestic and Transnational Terrorism."

90. Sambuddha Ghatak, "The Role of Political Exclusion and State Capacity in Civil Conflict in South Asia," *Terrorism and Political Violence* 30, no. 1 (2018): 74–96; Lisa Hultman, "Battle Losses and Rebel Violence: Raising the Costs for Fighting," *Terrorism and Political Violence* 19, no. 2 (2007): 205–222; Jessica A. Stanton, "Terrorism in the Context of Civil War," *Journal of Politics* 75, no. 4 (2013): 1009–1022.

91. Author interview with former senior Inter-Services Intelligence official, Islamabad, Pakistan, December 2018.

92. Ethan Bueno de Mesquita, "The Quality of Terror," *American Journal of Political Science* 49, no. 3 (2005): 515–530; Michael G. Findley and Joseph K. Young, "Fighting Fire with Fire? How (Not) to Neutralize an Insurgency," *Civil Wars* 9, no. 4 (2007): 378–401.

93. Al-Qaeda, "Letter Regarding Al-Qa'ida Strategy," 2012, SOCOM-2012-0000015, Harmony Program, Combating Terrorism Center at West Point.

94. Al-Qaeda, "Letter to Abu Basir," January 19, 2017 (Date of Declassification), Bin Laden's Bookshelf, Office of the Director of National Intelligence.

95. Al-Qaeda, "Letter to Nasir al-Wuhayshi," 2012, SOCOM-2012-0000016, Harmony Program, Combating Terrorism Center at West Point.

96. Al-Qaeda, "Letter to Abu Basir."

97. Monica Duffy Toft and Yuri M. Zhukov, "Denial and Punishment in the North Caucasus: Evaluating the Effectiveness of Coercive Counter-Insurgency," *Journal of Peace Research* 49, no. 6 (2012): 786.

98. Mustafa Cosar Unal and Petra Cafnik Uludag, "Eradicating Terrorism in Asymmetric Conflict: The Role and Essence of Military Deterrence," *Terrorism and Political Violence* 34, no. 4 (2022): 772–816.

99. Unal and Uludag, 773.

100. Victor Asal et al., "Carrots, Sticks, and Insurgent Targeting of Civilians," *Journal of Conflict Resolution* 63, no. 7 (2019): 1710–1735; Nazli Avdan and Gary Uzonyi, "V for Vendetta: Government Mass Killing and Domestic Terrorism," *Studies in Conflict & Terrorism* 40, no. 11 (2017): 934–965; Mustafa Kirisci, "Militarized Law Enforcement Forces, State Capacity and Terrorism," *Terrorism and Political Violence* 34, no. 1 (2022): 93–112.

101. Paul Gill, James A. Piazza, and John Horgan, "Counterterrorism Killings and Provisional IRA Bombings, 1970–1998," *Terrorism and Political Violence* 28, no. 3 (2016): 473–496.

102. Henda Y. Hsu and David McDowall, "Examining the State Repression-Terrorism Nexus: Dynamic Relationships Among Repressive Counterterrorism Actions, Terrorist Targets, and Deadly Terrorist Violence in Israel," *Criminology & Public Policy* 19 (2020): 483–514.

103. Piazza, "Repression and Terrorism"; Sara M. T. Polo and Kristian Skrede Gleditsch, "Twisting Arms and Sending Messages: Terrorist Tactics in Civil War," *Journal of Peace Research* 53, no. 6 (2016): 815–829; James I. Walsh and James A. Piazza, "Why Respecting Physical Integrity Rights Reduces Terrorism," *Comparative Political Studies* 43, no. 5 (2010): 551–577.

104. Emma Grace, "Lex Talionis in the Twenty-First Century: Revenge Ideation and Terrorism," *Behavioral Sciences of Terrorism and Political Aggression* 10, no. 3 (2018): 249–263.

105. Mendelsohn, *Combating Jihadism*.

106. Byman, "Friends Like These"; Daniel Byman, "US Counterterrorism Intelligence Cooperation with the Developing World and Its Limits," *Intelligence and National Security* 32, no. 2 (2017): 145–160; Henne, *Islamic Politics, Muslim States, and Counterterrorism Tensions*.

107. Navin Bapat, "Transnational Terrorism, US Military Aid, and the Incentive to Misrepresent," *Journal of Peace Research* 48, no. 3 (2011): 303–318; Andrew Boutton, "US Foreign Aid, Interstate Rivalry, and Incentives for Counterterrorism Cooperation," *Journal of Peace Research* 51, no. 6 (2014): 741–754; Tankel, *With Us and Against Us*.

108. Jesse Paul Lehrke and Rahel Schomaker, "Kill, Capture, or Defend? The Effectiveness of Specific and General Counterterrorism Tactics Against the Global Threats of the Post-9/11 Era," *Security Studies* 25, no. 4 (2016): 729–762.

109. The phrase "al-Qaeda core" refers to the individuals that served directly under Osama bin Laden and al-Qaeda's senior leadership in Afghanistan and Pakistan, representing a discrete and formal organization distinct from affiliate organizations or lone-wolf attackers.

110. Kyle T. Kattelman, "Assessing Success of the Global War on Terror: Terrorist Attack Frequency and the Backlash Effect," *Dynamics of Asymmetric Conflict* 13, no. 1 (2020): 67–86.

111. Peter S. Henne, "Assessing the Impact of the Global War on Terrorism on Terrorism Threats in Muslim Countries," *Terrorism and Political Violence* 33, no. 7 (2021): 1511–1529.

112. Andrew Bennett, "Process Tracing and Causal Inference," in *Rethinking Social Inquiry: Diverse Tools, Shared Standards*, ed. Henry E. Brady and David Collier (Lanham, MD: Rowman and Littlefield, 2010), 208–209.

113. The book takes as its primary time frame the Bush and Obama administrations, in part due to data limitations. For the quantitative analysis, the information used to construct the key variables in the statistical models (an annual count of domestic terrorist attacks and partner states' counterterrorism operations) was only available for the 1996–2012 period at the time of writing. Therefore, as a complement to the quantitative analysis and its data restrictions, the case studies primarily focus on this same period to provide insights into the causal process taking place during the years that can be statistically tested. The focus on the Bush and Obama administrations also permitted greater access to declassified government documents and allowed me to conduct more open interviews with former officials from both administrations. Looking at the 1996–2012 period still allows me to compare pre- and post-9/11 counterterrorism policies and, during the war on terror, the resulting impact within partner states of counterterrorism efforts pursued by both administrations.

114. Author interview with Ambassador Aizaz Ahmad Chaudhry, former Pakistani foreign secretary and Pakistani ambassador to the United States, Islamabad, Pakistan, December 18, 2018.

115. Marcus Kreuzer, "The Structure of Description: Evaluating Descriptive Inferences and Conceptualizations," *Perspectives on Politics* 17, no. 1 (2019): 122–139.

## 2. WHAT'S IN A NAME?

1. "Letter from The President—War Powers Resolution," Office of the Press Secretary, the White House, June 13, 2016, https://obamawhitehouse.archives.gov/the-press-office/2016/06/13/letter-president-war-powers-resolution.

2. Matthew Weed, "Presidential References to the 2001 Authorization for Use of Military Force in Publicly Available Executive Actions and Reports to Congress," Congressional Research Service, May 11, 2016.

3. Vice Admiral Thomas R. Wilson, "Global Threats and Challenges: Statement for the Record," Testimony to the Senate Select Committee on Intelligence, February 6, 2002, https://irp.fas.org/congress/2002_hr/020602wilson.html.

4. George W. Bush, "Address to a Joint Session of Congress and the American People," the White House, September 20, 2001, https://georgewbush-whitehouse.archives.gov/news/releases/2001/09/20010920-8.html.

5. *National Intelligence Estimate: Trends in Global Terrorism*, Office of the Director of Central Intelligence, Central Intelligence Agency, 2006, https://www.dni.gov/files/documents/Special%20Report_Global%20Terrorism%20NIE%20Key%20Judgments.pdf.

6. Daniel L. Byman, *Al Qaeda, the Islamic State, and the Global Jihadist Movement* (New York: Oxford University Press, 2015); John L. Esposito, *Unholy War: Terror in the*

*Name of Islam* (New York: Oxford University Press, 2003); Fawaz A. Gerges, *The Far Enemy: Why Jihad Went Global* (Cambridge: Cambridge University Press, 2005); Mary Habeck, *Knowing the Enemy: Jihadist Ideology and the War on Terror* (New Haven, CT: Yale University Press, 2006); Barak Mendelsohn, *The Al-Qaeda Franchise: The Expansion of Al-Qaeda and Its Consequences* (New York: Oxford University Press, 2015); Bruce Riedel, *The Search for Al Qaeda: Its Leadership, Ideology, and Future* (Washington, DC: Brookings Institution Press, 2010); Michael W. S. Ryan, *Decoding Al-Qaeda's Strategy: The Deep Battle Against America* (New York: Columbia University Press, 2013); Michael Scheuer, *Osama Bin Laden* (New York: Oxford University Press, 2011); Lawrence Wright, *The Looming Tower: Al-Qaeda and the Road to 9/11* (New York: Vintage Books, 2006).

7. Steve Coll, *Ghost Wars: The Secret History of the CIA, Afghanistan, and Bin Ladin, from the Soviet Invasion to September 10, 2001* (London: Penguin, 2004).

8. Rob Johnson, *The Afghan Way of War: How and Why They Fight* (New York: Oxford University Press, 2012), 138–148.

9. Faridullah Bezhan, "The Pashtunistan Issue and Politics in Afghanistan, 1947–1952," *Middle East Journal* 68, no. 2 (2014): 197–209.

10. Mustafa Hamid and Leah Farrall, *The Arabs at War in Afghanistan* (London: Hurst and Company, 2015); Thomas Hegghammer, "The Rise of Muslim Foreign Fighters: Islam and the Globalization of Jihad," *International Security* 35, no. 3 (2010–2011): 53–94.

11. "International Terrorism—Usama Bin Laden/Al Qaeda," 9/11 Investigation Report, Federal Bureau of Investigation, July 25, 2002, FBI Vault.

12. Hamid and Farrall, *The Arabs at War in Afghanistan*, 291.

13. Alan Eastham, Memorandum for the Record: Interview, Team 3, 9/11 Commission, December 19, 2003, 9/11 Commission Papers, National Archives; Larry Goodson, Memorandum for the Record: Background briefing on Afghanistan and the Taliban, Team 3, 9/11 Commission, August 1, 2003, 9/11 Commission Papers, National Archives.

14. Eastham, Memorandum for the Record, 3; Peter Tomsen, Memorandum for the Record: Interview, Team 3, 9/11 Commission, October 8, 2003, 9/11 Commission Papers, National Archives.

15. Barnett R. Rubin, *Afghanistan from the Cold War Through the War on Terror* (New York: Oxford University Press, 2013), 86–90.

16. Hamid and Farrall, *The Arabs at War in Afghanistan*, 21.

17. Peter Bergen, *The Osama Bin Laden I Know: An Oral History of al Qaeda's Leader* (New York: Free Press, 2006), 50–57.

18. James Toth, *Sayyid Qutb: The Life and Legacy of a Radical Islamic Intellectual* (New York: Oxford University Press, 2013).

19. Coll, *Ghost Wars*, 319.

20. Tim Carney, Memorandum for the Record: Interview, Team 3, 9/11 Commission, December 4, 2003, 9/11 Commission Papers, National Archives.

21. Peter Bergen, *The Longest War: The Enduring Conflict Between America and Al-Qaeda* (New York: Free Press, 2011), 21.

22. Riedel, *The Search for Al Qaeda*, 59.

23. "Bin Ladin Determined to Strike in US," Presidential Daily Brief, the White House, August 6, 2001, National Security Archive.

24. "Interview with Donald A. Camp," Foreign Affairs Oral History Project, Association of Diplomatic Studies and Training, February 10, 2012, https://adst.org/OH%20TOCs /Camp-Donald.pdf.

25. "A New Bin Laden Strategy," Diplomatic Cable, U.S. Department of State, May 15, 1999, C186010175, State Department Reading Room.

26. "Interview with Donald A. Camp," 60.

27. Ahmed, *The Thistle and the Drone*, 98–104; Bruce Lawrence, ed., *Messages to the World: The Statements of Osama Bin Laden* (New York: Verso, 2005), 156.

28. Robert A. Pape, *Dying to Win: The Strategic Logic of Suicide Terrorism* (New York: Random House, 2005), 118.

29. Ayman al-Zawahiri, "The Seventh Interview: The Reality Between Pain and Hope," *As-Sabah*, May 2, 2014, https://jihadology.net/2014/05/02/as-sahab-media-presents-a-new-video-message-from-al-qaidahs-dr-ayman-al-ẓawahiri-the-seventh-interview-the-reality-between-pain-and-hope/.

30. Author interview with former senior ISI official, December 2018; Abbas, *The Taliban Revival*, 78. The number of al-Qaeda fighters present in Afghanistan has been difficult to pin down with any accuracy, in part of because of debates over who counts as an al-Qaeda member. Over the past decade, senior U.S. officials have consistently stated in public that there are between one and two hundred al-Qaeda members present in Afghanistan. See Richard Esposito, Matthew Cole, and Brian Ross, "President Obama's Secret: Only 100 al Qaeda Now in Afghanistan," ABC News, December 2, 2009, https:// abcnews.go.com/Blotter/president-obamas-secret-100-al-qaeda-now-afghanistan /story?id=9227861; Rob Taylor, "U.S. General Says al Qaeda Just Surviving in Afghanistan," Reuters, July 26, 2013, https://www.reuters.com/article/us-afghanistan-qaeda/u -s-general-says-al-qaeda-just-surviving-in-afghanistan-idUSBRE96P09M20130726; "Pompeo Says Fewer than 200 al Qaeda Left in Afghanistan Today," Reuters, September 15, 2020, https://www.reuters.com/article/us-usa-afghanistan-pompeo-al-qaeda/po mpeo-says-fewer-than-200-al-qaeda-left-in-afghanistan-today-idUSKBN26628E.

31. *National Intelligence Estimate*, 12.

32. *National Intelligence Estimate*, 17.

33. Ali Soufan, "Al-Qaeda Is Thriving, Despite Our Endless War. Can We Ever Defeat It?," BuzzFeed News, October 29, 2018, https://www.buzzfeednews.com/article/alisoufan /opinion-bin-laden-is-dead-so-why-is-al-qaeda-thriving.

34. Al-Zawahiri, "The Seventh Interview."

35. *Third Report of the Analytical Support and Sanctions Monitoring Team*, S/2005/572, 1267 Committee, UN Security Council, September 9, 2005: 8; John Brennan, "Securing the Homeland by Renewing American Strength, Resilience, and Values," Remarks by the Assistant to the President for Homeland Security and Counterterrorism, Center for Strategic and International, Washington, DC, May 26, 2010, https://obamawhitehouse

.archives.gov/the-press-office/remarks-assistant-president-homeland-security-and -counterterrorism-john-brennan-csi.

36. David Kilcullen, *Counterinsurgency* (New York: Oxford University Press, 2010), 165–227.

37. Kilcullen, 170–180.

38. Audrey Kurth Cronin, "The Evolution of Counter-Terrorism: Will Tactics Trump Strategy?," *International Affairs* 86, no. 4 (2010): 837–856.

39. *Eighth Report of the Analytical Support and Sanctions Monitoring Team*, S/2008/324, 1267 Committee, UN Security Council, May 14, 2008: 7.

40. Alexander Meleagrou-Hitchens, *Incitement: Anwar al-Awlaki's Western Jihad* (Cambridge, MA: Harvard University Press, 2020), 3.

41. Leah Farrall, "How al Qaeda Works: What the Organization's Subsidiaries Say About Its Strength," *Foreign Affairs* 90, no. 2 (2011): 128–138; Bruce Riedel, "The Return of the Knights: Al-Qaeda and the Fruits of Middle East Disorder," *Survival* 49, no. 3 (2007): 107–120.

42. Bergen, *The Longest War*, 197.

43. Marc Sageman, *Leaderless Jihad: Terror Networks in the Twenty-First Century* (Philadelphia: University of Pennsylvania Press, 2008), vii.

44. Elaine Sciolino and Eric Schmitt, "A Not Very Private Feud Over Terrorism," *New York Times*, June 8, 2008.

45. Bruce Hoffman, "The Myth of Grass-Roots Terrorism: Why Osama Bin Laden Still Matters," *Foreign Affairs* 87, no. 3 (2008): 133–138.

46. Anthony N. Ceslo, "Al Qaeda's Post-bin Laden Resurgence: The Paradox of Resilience and Failure," *Mediterranean Quarterly* 25, no. 2 (2014): 33–47; Barak Mendelsohn, "Al-Qaeda's Franchising Strategy," *Survival* 53, no. 3 (2011): 29–50; Mendelsohn, *The Al-Qaeda Franchise*; Shawn L. Ramirez and Arianna J. Robbins, "Targets and Tactics: Testing for a Duality within Al Qaeda's Network," *International Interactions* 44, no. 3 (2018): 559–581.

47. Barak Mendelsohn, *Jihadism Constrained: The Limits of Transnational Jihadism and What It Means for Counterterrorism* (Lanham, MD: Rowman and Littlefield, 2019).

48. Jacob N. Shapiro, *The Terrorist's Dilemma: Managing Violent Covert Operations* (Princeton, NJ: Princeton University Press, 2013), 232.

49. *Fourteenth Report of the Analytical Support and Sanctions Monitoring Team*, S/2013/467, 1267 Committee, UN Security Council, August 2, 2013: 6; Ramirez and Robbins, "Targets and Tactics."

50. *Eighth Report of the Analytical Support and Sanctions Monitoring Team*, 7.

51. *Second Report of the Analytical Support and Sanctions Monitoring Team*, S/2005/83, 1267 Committee, UN Security Council, February 15, 2005: 6.

52. John Turner, "From Cottage Industry to International Organisation: The Evolution of Salafi-Jihadism and the Emergence of the Al Qaeda Ideology," *Terrorism and Political Violence* 22, no. 4 (2010): 541–558.

53. National Consortium for the Study of Terrorism and Responses to Terrorism, Global Terrorism Database [data file], 2018, http://www.start.umd.edu/gtd.

54. *Sixteenth Report of the Analytical Support and Sanctions Monitoring Team*, S/2014/770, 1267 Committee, UN Security Council, October 29, 2014: 4.

55. Author interview with senior Yemeni diplomat, Washington, DC, October 2018.

56. Joe Bavier, "Who Are Boko Haram and Why Are They Terrorizing Nigerian Christians?," *The Atlantic*, January 24, 2012.

57. Author interview with Ambassador Akbar Ahmed, Ibn Khaldun Chair of Islamic Studies at American University and former political agent of South Waziristan and Orakzai Agencies in Pakistan's FATA, Washington, DC, December 7, 2018.

58. Interview with General Abdullah Dogar.

59. Bahadar Nawab Shakirullah, Ingrid Nyborg, and Noor Elahi, "The Underlying Causes of Violent Conflict in the North Waziristan Tribal Areas of Pakistan," *Civil Wars* 22, no. 1 (2020): 114–136.

60. Al-Qaeda, "Three Stages Letter," January 19, 2017 (Date of Declassification), Bin Laden's Bookshelf, Office of the Director of National Intelligence.

61. Osama bin Laden, "Letter from UBL to Atiyatullah Al Libi," SOCOM-2012-0000019-HT, Harmony Program, Combating Terrorism Center at West Point.

62. Al-Qaeda, "Letter to Abu Basir."

63. Bergen, *The Longest War*, 24; Ayman al-Zawahiri, "Letter to Zarqawi," July 9, 2005, Harmony Program, Combating Terrorism Center at West Point.

64. Al-Qaeda, "Letter to Abu Basir."

65. Al-Qaeda, "Letter to Abu Basir."

66. Al-Qaeda, "Letter to Nasir al-Wuhayshi."

67. Al-Qaeda, "Three Stages Letter."

68. Al-Qaeda, "Letter to Abu Basir."

69. Al-Qaeda, "Letter to Nasir al-Wuhayshi"; Al-Qaeda, "Letter Dated 18 July 2010," July 18, 2010, Bin Laden's Bookshelf, Office of the Director of National Intelligence; Al-Qaeda, "Letter to Shaykh Abu Abdallah dated 17 July 2010," July 17, 2010, Bin Laden's Bookshelf, Office of the Director of National Intelligence.

70. Bin Laden, "Letter from UBL to Atiyatullah Al Libi."

71. Vidar B. Skretting, "Al-Qaida in the Islamic Maghrib's Expansion in the Sahara: New Insights from Primary Sources," *Studies in Conflict & Terrorism*, September 24, 2020, 17, https://doi.org/10.1080/1057610X.2020.1822593.

72. Daniel L. Byman, "Comparing Al Qaeda and ISIS: Different Goals, Different Targets," Brookings Institution, April 29, 2015, https://www.brookings.edu/testimonies/comparing-al-qaeda-and-isis-different-goals-different-targets/.

73. Hassan Hassan, "The True Origins of ISIS," *The Atlantic*, November 30, 2018.

74. Fawaz A. Gerges, *ISIS: A History* (Princeton, NJ: Princeton University Press, 2016); David Kilcullen, *Blood Year: The Unraveling of Western Counterterrorism* (New York: Oxford University Press, 2016), 31–32, 41.

75. *Takfir*, derived from the Arabic term *kafir* (infidel or unbeliever), is the practice of a Muslim declaring other Muslims to be apostates, often over theological disputes, who are then, as apostates, liable to be victims of violence. Such a declaration has been used as justification for attacks against differing Islamic sects, including Sunni groups

targeting Shia or Ahmadi Muslims. See V. G. Julie Rajan, *Al Qaeda's Global Crisis: The Islamic State, Takfir, and the Genocide of Muslims* (Abingdon, UK: Routledge, 2015).

76. Al-Zawahiri, "Letter to Zarqawi."

77. Atiyah Abd al-Rahman, "Atiyah's Letter to Zarqawi," December 10, 2005, Harmony Program, Combating Terrorism Center at West Point.

78. Oren Dorell, "New Documents Show bin Laden was Warned of ISIL's Brutality Against Muslims," *USA Today*, March 1, 2016.

79. Ali Soufan and Daniel Freedman, *The Black Banners Declassified: How Torture Derailed the War on Terror after 9/11* (New York: W. W. Norton and Company, 2020), 324.

80. Daniel L. Byman and Jennifer R. Williams, "ISIS vs. Al Qaeda: Jihadism's Global Civil War," Brookings Institution, February 24, 2015, https://www.brookings.edu /articles/isis-vs-al-qaeda-jihadisms-global-civil-war/.

81. Liz Sly, "Al-Qaeda Disavows Any Ties with Radical Islamist ISIS Group in Syria, Iraq," *Washington Post*, February 3, 2014.

82. Nelly Lahoud et al., *Letters from Abbottabad: Bin Ladin Sidelined?* (West Point, NY: Combating Terrorism Center, 2012), https://apps.dtic.mil/sti/pdfs/ADA560875.pdf.

83. Al-Qaeda, "Letter Dated 07 August 2010," August 7, 2010, Bin Laden's Bookshelf, Office of the Director of National Intelligence.

84. Al-Qaeda, "Letter Dated 07 August 2010"; Aisha Ahmad, *Jihad & Co.: Black Markets and Islamist Power* (New York: Oxford University Press, 2017); Richard Philippe Chelin, "From the Islamic State of Algeria to the Economic Caliphate of the Sahel: The Transformation of Al Qaeda in the Islamic Maghreb," *Terrorism and Political Violence* 32, no. 6 (2020): 1186–1205; Katharine Petrich, "Cows, Charcoal, and Cocaine: Al-Shabaab's Criminal Activities in the Horn of Africa," *Studies in Conflict & Terrorism* 45, nos. 5–6 (2022): 479–500; James A. Piazza, "The Opium Trade and Patterns of Terrorism in the Provinces of Afghanistan: An Empirical Analysis," *Terrorism and Political Violence* 24, no. 2 (2012): 213–234.

85. David Rohde, "Biden's Chaotic Withdrawal from Afghanistan Is Complete," *New Yorker*, August 30, 2021.

86. Al-Qaeda, "Dear Muslim brothers and sisters," March 1, 2016 (Date of Declassification), Bin Laden's Bookshelf, Office of the Director of National Intelligence.

87. Osama Bin Laden, "To Our Honorable Emir the Emir of All Believers," December 3, 2010, Bin Laden's Bookshelf, Office of the Director of National Intelligence.

88. Al-Qaeda, "Letter to Hakimullah Mahsud," December 3, 2010, SOCOM-2012-0000007, Harmony Program, Combating Terrorism Center at West Point.

89. Al-Qaeda, "Letter Dated 07 August 2010."

90. Al-Qaeda, "Dear Brother Shaykh Mahmud," December 27, 2009, Bin Laden's Bookshelf, Office of the Director of National Intelligence.

91. *Indonesia Backgrounder: How the Jemaah Islamiyah Terrorist Network Operates* (Jakarta: International Crisis Group, 2002), 30.

92. Don Rassler and Vahid Brown, *The Haqqani Nexus and the Evolution of al-Qa'ida* (West Point, NY: Combating Terrorism Center, 2011), 10.

93.  "Sunni Terrorist Threat Growing," Senior Executive Intelligence Brief, Central Intelligence Agency, February 6, 2001, National Security Archive.

94.  Steve Coll, *Directorate S: The C.I.A. and America's Secret Wars in Afghanistan and Pakistan* (New York: Penguin Press, 2018), 551–556.

95.  Bergen, *The Longest War*, 254.

96.  AQIM Shura Council, "Letter from the Organization of al-Qaida in the Islamic Maghreb's Shura Council to Our Good Brothers in the Shura Council of the Masked Brigade," Al-Qaida Papers, Associated Press, October 3, 2012, http://hosted.ap.org /specials/interactives/_international/_pdfs/al-qaida-belmoktar-letter-english.pdf. The Associated Press's Al-Qaida Papers project is based on documents its reporters discovered in 2013 in a building formerly occupied by AQIM fighters in Timbuktu, Mali. See "Excerpts from al-Qaida Manifesto Left in Timbuktu," Associated Press, February 14, 2013, https://apnews.com/article/africa-mali-al-qaida-52f9b3f06e004a 0684181e7b27eb6c30.

97.  *Thirteenth Report of the Analytical Support and Sanctions Monitoring Team*, S/2012/968, 1267 Committee, UN Security Council, December 31, 2012: 5.

98.  White House Office of the Press Secretary, Background Briefing by Senior Administration Officials on the President's Speech on Counterterrorism, May 23, 2013, C06594688, State Department Reading Room.

99.  Brian Fishman, "Using the Mistakes of Al Qaeda's Franchises to Undermine Its Strategies," *Annals of the American Academy of Political and Social Science* 618 (2008): 46–54; Barbara F. Walter, "The Extremist's Advantage in Civil Wars," *International Security* 42, no. 2 (2017): 7–39.

100.  Harun Maruf and Dan Joseph, *Inside Al-Shabaab: The Secret History of Al-Qaeda's Most Powerful Ally* (Bloomington: Indiana University Press, 2018), 260.

101.  *Al Qaeda in Yemen and Somalia: A Ticking Time Bomb*, Report to the Committee on Foreign Relations, U.S. Senate, 111th Congress, S. Prt. 111–40, January 21, 2010; Bruce Hoffman, "Al Qaeda's Uncertain Future," *Studies in Conflict & Terrorism*, 36, no. 8 (2003): 635–653; Barack Obama, "Full Transcript of President Obama's Commencement Address at West Point," *Washington Post*, May 28, 2014.

102.  Phil Stewart, "Leon Panetta Says al Qaeda's Defeat 'Within Reach,'" Reuters, July 9, 2011, https://www.reuters.com/article/us-afghanistan-usa-panetta/leon-panetta-says -al-qaedas-defeat-within-reach-idUKTRE76818V20110709.

103.  "A Conversation with the Honorable Leon Panetta," Center for a New American Security, November 20, 2012, https://www.cnas.org/events/a-conversation-with-the -honorable-leon-panetta.

104.  Byman, "Friends Like These"; Caitriona Dowd and Clionadh Raleigh, "The Myth of Global Islamic Terrorism and Local Conflict in Mali and the Sahel," *African Affairs* 112, no. 448 (2013): 498–509; Elena Pokalova, "The Al Qaeda Brand: The Strategic Use of the 'Terrorist' Label," *Terrorism and Political Violence* 30, no. 3 (2018): 408–427; Eric Rosand, "The Security Council's Efforts to Monitor the Implementation of al Qaeda/ Taliban Sanctions," *American Journal of International Law* 98, no. 4 (2004): 745–763.

105.   Vladimir Putin, "Remarks by President Vladimir Putin to US Mass Media," Official Kremlin International News Broadcast, November 13, 2001; Sharon LaFraniere, "How Jihad Made Its Way to Chechnya," *Washington Post*, April 26, 2003.

106.   Michael Clarke, "China's 'War on Terrorism,' " in *Terrorism and Counter-Terrorism in China: Domestic and Foreign Policy Dimensions*, ed. Michael Clarke (New York: Oxford University Press, 2018), 17–38; Elena Pokalova, "Authoritarian Regimes Against Terrorism: Lessons from China," *Critical Studies on Terrorism* 6, no. 2 (2013): 279–298; Sean R. Roberts, *The War on the Uyghurs: China's Internal Campaign Against a Muslim Minority* (Princeton, NJ: Princeton University Press, 2020).

107.   Joseph Allchin, "Myanmar: The Invention of Rohingya Extremists," *New York Review of Books*, October 2, 2017.

108.   Allchin; "Secretary Antony J. Blinken on the Genocide and Crimes Against Humanity in Burma," U.S. State Department, March 21, 2022, https://www.state.gov/secretary -antony-j-blinken-at-the-united-states-holocaust-memorial-museum/.

109.   Author interview with Lawrence Wilkerson, former chief of staff to Secretary of State Colin Powell, Falls Church, VA, November 22, 2018.

110.   Author interview with Lawrence Wilkerson.

111.   Eric Schmitt and Thom Shanker, *Counterstrike: The Untold Story of America's Secret Campaign Against Al Qaeda* (New York: St. Martin's Press, 2011), 229–230.

112.   Robert Gates Oral History, Transcript, Presidential Oral Histories, Miller Center, University of Virginia, July 8, 2013.

113.   NSA Official [name redacted], Memorandum for the Record: Interview, Team 4, 9/11 Commission, March 3, 2004, 9/11 Commission Papers, National Archives.

114.   Eastham, Memorandum for the Record, 15.

115.   Steve Kashkett, Memorandum for the Record: Interview, Team 4, 9/11 Commission, November 4, 2003, 9/11 Commission Papers, National Archives.

116.   Michael Scheuer, "Coalition Warfare, Part 11: How Zarqawi Fits Into Bin Laden's World Front," *Terrorism Focus* 2, no. 8 (2005), https://jamestown.org/program/coalition-warfare -part-ii-how-zarqawi-fits-into-bin-ladens-world-front/.

117.   Dowd and Raleigh, "The Myth of Global Islamic Terrorism," 505.

## 3. THE UNITED STATES AND ITS COUNTERTERRORISM PARTNERS

1.   James B. Steinberg, "Counterterrorism: A New Organizing Principle for American National Security?," Brookings Institution, June 1, 2002, https://www.brookings.edu /articles/counterterrorism-a-new-organizing-principle-for-american-national-security/; Stephen M. Walt, "Beyond bin Laden: Reshaping U.S. Foreign Policy," *International Security* 26, no. 3 (2002): 56–78.

2.   Joshua Bolten Oral History Part I with Joel Kaplan, Transcript, Presidential Oral Histories, Miller Center, University of Virginia, January 15, 2013.

3.  Michael V. Hayden, *Playing to the Edge: American Intelligence in the Age of Terror* (New York: Penguin Books, 2016), 290.

4.  Andrew Boutton and David B. Carter, "Fair-Weather Allies? Terrorism and the Allocation of US Foreign Aid," *Journal of Conflict Resolution* 58, no. 7 (2014): 1144–1173; Tobias Heinrich, Carla Martinez Machain, and Jared Oestman, "Does Counterterrorism Militarize Foreign Aid? Evidence from Sub-Saharan Africa," *Journal of Peace Research* 54, no. 4 (2017): 527–541; John L. Helgerson, "The Trauma of 9/11: 2001–2002," in *Truth to Power: A History of the U.S. National Intelligence Council*, ed. Robert Hutchings and Gregory F. Treverton (Oxford: Oxford University Press, 2019), 85–104; Jude Howell and Jeremy Lind, "Changing Donor Policy and Practice in Civil Society in the Post-9/11 Aid Context," *Third World Quarterly* 30, no. 7 (2009): 1279–1296.

5.  Condoleezza Rice, *No Higher Honor: A Memoir of My Years in Washington* (New York: Crown, 2011), 79.

6.  Maura Harty, Memorandum for the Record: Interview, Team 5, 9/11 Commission, September 20, 2003, 9/11 Commission Papers, National Archives; Helgerson, "The Trauma of 9/11," 189.

7.  Ben Rhodes, "The 9/11 Era Is Over," *The Atlantic*, April 6, 2020.

8.  Bush, "Address to a Joint Session of Congress and the American People."

9.  Tommy Franks Oral History, Transcript, Presidential Oral Histories, Miller Center, University of Virginia, October 22, 2014.

10.  Timothy Naftali, "US counterterrorism Before Bin Laden," *International Journal* 60, no. 1 (2004–2005): 25–34.

11.  Madeleine Albright, Memorandum for the Record: Interview, Team 3, 9/11 Commission, January 7, 2004, 9/11 Commission Papers, National Archives; William Boykin, Memorandum for the Record: Interview, Team 3, 9/11 Commission, November 7, 2003, 9/11 Commission Papers, National Archives; *Terrorism Counteraction Field Manual*, No. FM 100–37, U.S. Department of the Army, July 1987; *The Public Report of the Vice President's Task Force on Combatting Terrorism*, Office of the Vice President, the White House, February 1986; Steve Richter, Memorandum for the Record: Interview, Team 2, 9/11 Commission, September 15, 2003, 9/11 Commission Papers, National Archives; Peter Schoomaker, Memorandum for the Record: Interview, Team 3, 9/11 Commission, February 19, 2003, 9/11 Commission Papers, National Archives; Phillip Wilcox, Memorandum for the Record: Interview, Team 3, 9/11 Commission, November 17, 2003, 9/11 Commission Papers, National Archives.

12.  *Terrorism in the United States*, Counterterrorism Division, Federal Bureau of Investigation, 1999: i.

13.  Don Kerr, Memorandum for the Record: Interview, Team 2, 9/11 Commission, September 9, 2003, 9/11 Commission Papers, National Archives.

14.  "U.S. Policy on Counterterrorism," Presidential Decision Directive 39, the White House, June 21, 1995, William J. Clinton Presidential Library.

15.  "U.S. Policy on Counterterrorism."

16.  Antiterrorism and Effective Death Penalty Act, Public Law 104–132, 104th Congress, April 24, 1995.

17. *The Public Report of the Vice President's Task Force on Combatting Terrorism*, 13.

18. *A National Security Strategy for a Global Age*, Office of the President, the White House, December 2000, 29.

19. Thomas Pickering, Memorandum for the Record: Interview, Teams 3 and 4, 9/11 Commission, December 22, 2003, 9/11 Commission Papers, National Archives.

20. Wilcox, Memorandum for the Record.

21. Author interview with former U.S. military intelligence officer, Washington, DC, October 2018.

22. Bruce Berkowitz, Memorandum for the Record: Interview, Team 2, 9/11 Commission, September 2, 2003, 9/11 Commission Papers, National Archives; Dave Carey, Memorandum for the Record: Interview, Team 2, 9/11 Commission, October 31, 2003, 9/11 Commission Papers, National Archives; Britt Snider, Memorandum for the Record: Interview, Team 2, 9/11 Commission, September 4, 2003, 9/11 Commission Papers, National Archives.

23. Pat Hanback, Memorandum for the Record: Interview, Team 2, 9/11 Commission, September 12, 2003, 9/11 Commission Papers, National Archives.

24. Patrick Ducey, Memorandum for the Record: Interview, Team 2, 9/11 Commission, January 1, 2004, 9/11 Commission Papers, National Archives.

25. Joan Dempsey, Memorandum for the Record: Interview, Team 2, 9/11 Commission, November 12, 2003, 9/11 Commission Papers, National Archives.

26. George Tenet, "Usama Bin Ladin," Memorandum, Office of the Director, Central Intelligence Agency, December 4, 1998, 9/11 Commission Papers, National Archives.

27. Dempsey, Memorandum for the Record.

28. George Tenet, *At the Center of the Storm: My Years at the CIA* (New York: HarperCollins, 2007).

29. *The 9/11 Commission Report*, 121; Jim Bodner, Memorandum for the Record: Interview, Team 3, 9/11 Commission, March 1, 2004, 9/11 Commission Papers, National Archives.

30. *The 9/11 Commission Report*, 121.

31. Robert Newberry, Memorandum for the Record: Interview, Team 3, 9/11 Commission, June 21, 2004, 9/11 Commission Papers, National Archives.

32. Dempsey, Memorandum for the Record.

33. Author interview with former U.S. military intelligence officer.

34. Richard A. Clarke, *Against All Enemies: Inside America's War on Terror* (New York: Free Press, 2004).

35. Bob Woodward, *Bush at War* (New York: Simon and Schuster, 2002), 39.

36. *The 9/11 Commission Report*, 367.

37. *Quadrennial Defense Review Report*, U.S. Department of Defense, February 6, 2006, vi.

38. Bergen, *The Longest War*, 51.

39. Donald Rumsfeld, *Known and Unknown: A Memoir* (New York: Sentinel, 2012), 341–342.

40. Paul Wolfowitz, "What Was and What Might Have Been: The Threats and Wars in Afghanistan and Iraq," Hoover Institution, March 29, 2022, https://www.hoover.org/sites/default/files/research/docs/wolfowitz_webreadypdf.pdf.

41.  Eric V. Larson and Bogdan Savych, *American Public Support for U.S. Military Operations from Mogadishu to Baghdad* (Santa Monica, CA: RAND Corporation, 2005), 95–97.

42.  Authorization for Use of Military Force, Public Law 107–40, 107th Congress, September 14, 2001: Section 2.

43.  Harrison Akins, "The 2001 Authorization for the Use of Military Force and America's Endless War," *Oxford Middle East Review* 2, no. 1 (2018): 12–18; Weed, "Presidential References to the 2001 Authorization for Use of Military Force."

44.  Tara Copp, "The Forever War Is Over. Its 2001 Authorization Lives On," *Defense One*, September 30, 2021, https://www.defenseone.com/policy/2021/09/forever-war-over-its -2001-authorization-lives/185768/.

45.  Sean Naylor, *Relentless Strike: The Secret History of Joint Special Operations Command* (New York: St. Martin's Press, 2015), 165.

46.  Christopher McIntosh, "Counterterrorism as War: Identifying the Dangers, Risks, and Opportunity Costs of U.S. Strategy Toward Al Qaeda and Its Affiliates," *Studies in Conflict & Terrorism* 38, no. 1 (2015): 23–38; Richard H. Schultz and Andreas Vogt, "It's War! Fighting Post-11 September Global Terrorism Through a Doctrine of Preemption," *Terrorism and Political Violence* 15, no. 1 (2003): 1–30.

47.  Powell A. Moore, "Hearing Recommendations for the Armed Services Committees," Info Memo for Secretary of Defense, July 30, 2004, Rumsfeld Papers. Emphasis in the original.

48.  Hayden, *Playing to the Edge*, 219–220.

49.  Thomas L. Friedman, "Foreign Affairs; World War III," *New York Times*, September 13, 2001.

50.  "Interview with Thomas Friedman," *Charlie Rose*, May 30, 2003, https://charlierose .com/videos/26893.

51.  "Israeli Perspective on Conflict with Iraq," C-SPAN, September 12, 2002, https://www .c-span.org/video/?172612-1/israeli-perspective-conflict-iraq.

52.  Bob Woodward, *State of Denial: Bush at War, Part III* (New York: Simon and Schuster, 2006), 406–408.

53.  Peter Waldman, "A Historian's Take on Islam Steers U.S. in Terrorism Fight," *Wall Street Journal*, February 3, 2004.

54.  Jeffrey Goldberg, "Breaking Ranks," *New Yorker*, October 31, 2005.

55.  Bernard Lewis, *What Went Wrong?: The Clash Between Islam and Modernity in the Middle East* (New York: Perennial, 2002), 159.

56.  Bernard Lewis, "The Roots of Muslim Rage," *The Atlantic*, September 1990; Lewis, "The Lewis Doctrine," *Prospect*, February 20, 2005.

57.  John Richard Cookson, "The Legacy of Bernard Lewis," *National Interest*, May 21, 2018.

58.  Cookson.

59.  *Quadrennial Defense Review Report*, 22.

60.  Statement by Stephen Tankel, Middle East Institute, Washington, DC, October 12, 2018.

61. Author interview with Richard Armitage, former deputy secretary of state, Arlington, VA, November 27, 2018; Donald Rumsfeld, "Ambassadors," July 22, 2002, Rumsfeld Papers.
62. Author interview with General Stanley McChrystal, former JSOC and ISAF Commander, Washington, DC, January 8, 2019.
63. Author interview with Douglas Feith.
64. Author interview with Douglas Feith.
65. Douglas J. Feith, *War and Decision: Inside the Pentagon at the Dawn of the War on Terrorism* (New York: Harper, 2008), 50.
66. Author interview with Richard Armitage; Wolfowitz, "What Was and What Might Have Been."
67. "U.S. Strategy in Afghanistan," Briefing Memorandum, the White House, October 16, 2001, 13526, National Security Archive.
68. Donald Rumsfeld, "Thoughts on Kosovo," Letter to Governor George W. Bush, April 28, 1999, Rumsfeld Papers.
69. Author interview with Douglas Feith.
70. Wilson, "Global Threats and Challenges: Statement for the Record," 14.
71. Author interview with General Stanley McChrystal.
72. Soufan and Freedman, *The Black Banners Declassified*, 489–490.
73. 2006 *National Intelligence Estimate*, 6.
74. *National Intelligence Estimate*, 5, 12.
75. Peter Bergen and Alec Reynolds, "Blowback Revisited: Today's Insurgents in Iraq Are Tomorrow's Terrorists," *Foreign Affairs* 84, no. 6 (2005): 2–6; J. Michael McConnell, "Annual Threat Assessment of the Intelligence Community for the Senate Armed Services Committee," Office of the Director of National Intelligence, February 27, 2008, https://www.dni.gov/files/documents/Newsroom/Testimonies/20080227_testimony.pdf.
76. *National Intelligence Estimate*, 28.
77. Ahsan I. Butt, "Why Did the United States Invade Iraq in 2003?," *Security Studies* 28, no. 2 (2019): 250–285; James D. Fearon, "Signaling Foreign Policy Interests: Tying Hands Versus Sinking Costs," *Journal of Conflict Resolution* 41, no. 1 (1997): 68–90.
78. Donald Rumsfeld, "Strategic Thoughts," Memorandum for the President, September 30, 2001, 12598, National Security Archive.
79. "U.S. Strategy in Afghanistan."
80. "Presentation—the Case for Action," the White House, September 12, 2002, National Security Archive.
81. "Intelligence Community Assessment: [Redacted] Regional Consequences of Regime Change in Iraq," National Intelligence Council, January 2003, C05299385, National Security Archive.
82. Article 5 reads as follows: "The Parties agree that an armed attack against one or more of them in Europe or North America shall be considered an attack against them all and consequently they agree that, if such an armed attack occurs, each of them, in exercise of the right of individual or collective self-defence recognised by Article 51 of

the Charter of the United Nations, will assist the Party or Parties so attacked by taking forthwith, individually and in concert with the other Parties, such action as it deems necessary, including the use of armed force, to restore and maintain the security of the North Atlantic area." See The North Atlantic Treaty, NATO, April 4, 1949, https://www.nato.int/cps/en/natohq/official_texts_17120.htm.

83.   Mendelsohn, *Combating Jihadism.*

84.   "Fact Sheet: International Contributions to the War Against Terrorism," Office of Public Affairs, U.S. Department of Defense, June 28, 2002, https://2001-2009.state.gov /coalition/cr/fs/12753.htm.

85.   "Attacking Terrorist Networks at Home and Abroad," the White House, September 2003, https://georgewbush-whitehouse.archives.gov/homeland/progress/attacking.html.

86.   Kilcullen, *Blood Year.*

87.   Schmitt and Shanker, *Counterstrike,* 46–56, 198.

88.   Tony Blair, "The War Against Terrorism: The Second Phase," Top Secret Security Briefing for US/UK Eyes Only, Office of the Prime Minister, December 4, 2001, National Security Archive. This letter was declassified and publicly released by the British government in July 2016 as part of the Chilcot Report, an inquiry led by Sir John Chilcot into the British government's role in the 2003 invasion of Iraq. See Steven Erlanger and David E. Sanger, "Chilcot Report on Iraq War Offers Devastating Critique of Tony Blair," *New York Times,* July 6, 2016.

89.   Author interview with Lawrence Wilkerson.

90.   Steve Cambone, "Framing the War," Memorandum for the Secretary of Defense, May 25, 2004, Rumsfeld Papers.

91.   Scott Sigmund Gartner, "Ties to the Dead: Connections to the Iraq War and 9/11 Casualties and Disapproval of the President," *American Sociological Review* 73, no. 4 (2008): 690–695; Scott Sigmund Gartner and Gary M. Segura, "All Politics Are Still Local: The Iraq War and the 2006 Midterm Elections," *PS: Political Science and Politics* 41, no. 1 (2008): 95–100; Michael Grunwald, "Opposition to War Buoys Democrats," *Washington Post,* November 8, 2006; Andrew Payne, "Presidents, Politics, and Military Strategy: Electoral Constraints During the Iraq War," *International Security* 44, no. 3 (2019/20): 163–203.

92.   Joseph L. Votel and Eero R. Keravuori, "The By-With-Through Operational Approach," *Joint Force Quarterly* 89, no. 2 (2018): 40.

93.   *Quadrennial Defense Review Report,* 17.

94.   Subhayu Bandyopadhyay, Todd Sandler, and Javed Younas, "Foreign Aid as Counterterrorism Policy," *Oxford Economic Papers* 63 (2011): 423–447; Dafna H. Rand and Stephen Tankel, *Security Cooperation and Assistance: Rethinking the Return on Investment* (Washington, DC: Center for a New American Security, 2015).

95.   Author interview with former U.S. military intelligence officer.

96.   Dov S. Zakheim, "Acquisition and Cross-Servicing Agreement (ACSA) with Pakistan," Action Memo for Secretary of Defense, March 4, 2003, Rumsfeld Papers.

97.   Zakheim, 2.

98. *National Strategy for Combating Terrorism*, the White House, February 2003, 19.

99. *National Strategy for Combating Terrorism.*

100. National Defense Authorization Act, Public Law 108–375, 108th Congress, October 28, 2004.

101. 10 U.S. Code, Section 127e, 2016, https://www.govinfo.gov/app/details/USCODE-2016 -title10/USCODE-2016-title10-subtitleA-partI-chap3-sec127e/summary.

102. Kyle Rempfer, "Special Operations Launches 'Secret Surrogate' Missions in New Counter-Terrorism Strategy," *Military Times*, February 8, 2019, https://www.militarytimes.com /news/your-army/2019/02/08/fighting-terrorism-may-rely-on-secret-surrogate-forces -going-forward/.

103. Wesley Morgan, "Behind the Secret U.S. War in Africa," *Politico*, July 2, 2018.

104. Schmitt and Shanker, *Counterstrike*, 191.

105. Thom Shanker, "U.S. Military to Stay in Philippines," *New York Times*, August 20, 2009.

106. Schmitt and Shanker, *Counterstrike*, 192.

107. "Trans-Sahara Counterterrorism Partnership: Guiding Strategy," U.S. Department of State, January 2014, State Department Reading Room; "Programs and Initiatives," Bureau of Counterterrorism, U.S. Department of State, 2018, https://www.state.gov /bureau-of-counterterrorism-programs-and-initiatives/.

108. "USG Counterterrorism Priorities for Niger," Diplomatic Cable, U.S. Department of State, September 11, 2003, C18633679, State Department Reading Room.

109. "Programs and Initiatives," Bureau of Counterterrorism, U.S. Department of State, accessed September 16, 2022, https://www.state.gov/bureau-of-counterterrorism-pro grams-and-initiatives/.

110. Eric Schmitt and Thom Shanker, "U.S. Seeks $3 Billion for Pakistani Military," *New York Times*, April 2, 2009.

111. *The 9/11 Commission Report*, 366.

112. Bridget L. Coggins, "Does State Failure Cause Terrorism? An Empirical Analysis (1999–2008)," *Journal of Conflict Resolution* 59, no. 3 (2015): 455–483; James D. Fearon and David D. Laitin, "Ethnicity, Insurgency, and Civil War," *American Political Science Review* 97, no. 1 (2003): 75–90; Tiffany Howard, *Failed States and the Origins of Violence: A Comparative Analysis of State Failure as a Root Cause of Terrorism and Political Violence* (Surrey, UK: Ashgate, 2014); Seth G. Jones, "The Rise of Afghanistan's Insurgency: State Failure and Jihad," *International Security* 32, no. 4 (2008): 7–40; James A. Piazza, "Incubators of Terror: Do Failed and Failing States Promote Transnational Terrorism?," *International Studies Quarterly* 52, no. 3 (2008): 469–488; Chelli Plummer, "Failed States and Connections to Terrorist Activity," *International Criminal Justice Review* 22, no. 4 (2012): 416–449.

113. Elizabeth Grimm Arsenault and Tricia Bacon, "Disaggregating and Defeating Terrorist Safe Havens," *Studies in Conflict & Terrorism* 38, no. 2 (2015): 85–112.

114. Donald Rumsfeld, "Meeting w/George Shultz," Meeting Notes, May 21, 2001, Rumsfeld Papers.

115. "The Worldwide Threat in 2003: Evolving Dangers in a Complex World," Unclassified Threat Briefing to Congress, Office of Director of Central Intelligence, Central Intelligence Agency, February 11, 2003, National Security Archive.

116. *National Defense Strategy of the United States of America*, U.S. Department of Defense, 2004, 2–3.

117. Author interview with Richard Armitage.

118. Donald Rumsfeld, Memorandum, February 11, 2002, Rumsfeld Papers; Donald Rumsfeld, "Areas Not Being Governed," April 22, 2002, Rumsfeld Papers.

119. Author interview with Douglas Feith.

120. Tankel, *With Us and Against Us*, 239.

121. Alan Sipress and Peter Slevin, "Powell Wary of Iraq Move," *Washington Post*, December 21, 2001.

122. "Significant Indications of Al-Qaida Activity in North Africa, Names of Known Al-Qaida Operatives and Planners with Ties to the Region," Information Report, Defense Intelligence Agency, January 2003, Defense Intelligence Agency Reading Room.

123. "The Abu Sayyaf-Al Qaeda Connection," ABC News, December 20, 2001, https://abcnews.go.com/International/story?id=79205&page=1.

124. *National Military Strategy of the United States of America*, U.S. Joint Chiefs of Staff, 2004, 5.

125. *National Military Strategy of the United States of America*, 9–10.

126. Author interview with Douglas Feith.

127. Kilcullen, *Blood Year*, 9.

128. *The 9/11 Commission Report*, 366–367.

129. European cities have a different dynamic than the other safe havens outlined by the 9/11 Commission that fall under the center-versus-periphery framework. Therefore, European cities as safe havens are not part of this analysis. See Akbar Ahmed, *Journey into Europe: Islam, Immigration, and Identity* (Washington, DC: Brookings Institution Press, 2018), and Angel Rabasa and Cheryl Benard, *Eurojihad: Patterns of Islamist Radicalization and Terrorism in Europe* (Cambridge: Cambridge University Press, 2014).

130. The Intelligence Reform and Terrorism Prevention Act of 2004, Public Law 108–458, 108th Congress, December 17, 2004: Section 7102b.

131. The name of the annual State Department report on international terrorism was changed in 2004, when the department began incorporating data on global terrorism from the newly established National Counterterrorism Center to distinguish the more comprehensive reports from previous ones.

132. *Country Reports on Terrorism*, Office of the Coordinator for Counterterrorism, U.S. Department of State, 2005, https://www.state.gov/j/ct/rls/crt/index.htm.

133. *National Strategy for Combating Terrorism*, Office of the President, the White House, September 2006.

134. Donald Rumsfeld, "Being in Place for Any Future AQ Movement," Memo, January 10, 2006, National Security Archive; Donald Rumsfeld, "Thoughts on Being in Place for Any Possible Future AQ Movements," Memo to General Pete Pace, January 12, 2006, National Security Archive.

135. *Somalia: Expanding Crisis in the Horn of Africa*, Joint Hearing Before the Subcommittee on Africa, Global Human Rights and International Operations and the Subcommittee on International Terrorism and Nonproliferation of the House Committee on International Relations, 109th Congress, June 29, 2006.

136. Mazzetti, *The Way of the Knife*, 149.

137. Mary Harper, *Everything You Have Told Me Is True: The Many Faces of Al Shabaab* (London: Hurst and Company, 2019), 28.

138. Mohammed Ibrahim Shire, "Provocation and Attrition Strategies in Transnational Terrorism: The Case of Al-Shabaab," *Terrorism and Political Violence*, November 3, 2021, https://doi.org/10.1080/09546553.2021.1987896.

139. "Al-Shabab Statement on Deadly Campus Assault in Kenya," *Washington Post*, April 4, 2015.

140. Tricia Bacon and Daisy Muibu, "The Domestication of Al-Shabaab," *Journal of the Middle East and Africa* 10, no. 3 (2019): 239–305.

141. "McCain, Obama Spar Over Al Qaeda in Iraq," Associated Press, June 18, 2009, https://www.cbsnews.com/news/mccain-obama-spar-over-al-qaeda-in-iraq/.

142. Dan Pfeiffer, "The Same Old Washington Blame Game," *White House Blog*, December 30, 2009, https://obamawhitehouse.archives.gov/blog/2009/12/30/same-old-washington-blame-game.

143. Bob Woodward, *Obama's Wars* (New York: Simon and Schuster, 2010), 123.

144. Mike Allen, "CIA Chief Vows to Treat Congress Better," *Politico*, February 25, 2009, https://www.politico.com/story/2009/02/cia-chief-vows-to-treat-congress-better-019342.

145. *Hearing to Receive Testimony of Afghanistan*, Senate Committee on Armed Services, 111th Congress, December 2, 2009.

146. Jeremy Scahill, *Dirty Wars: The World Is a Battlefield* (New York: Nation Books, 2013), 263.

147. *National Security Strategy*, Office of the President, the White House, May 2010, 21.

148. "Al-Qaeda in Yemen," Event Transcript, Carnegie Endowment for International Peace, Washington, DC, July 7, 2009, http://carnegieendowment.org/files/0708carnegie-yemen.pdf.

149. Woodward, *Obama's War*, 227–228.

150. "Remarks of John O. Brennan, Assistant to the President for Homeland Security and Counterterrorism, on Ensuring al-Qa'ida's Demise," Office of the Press Secretary, the White House, June 29, 2011, https://obamawhitehouse.archives.gov/the-press-office/2011/06/29/remarks-john-o-brennan-assistant-president-homeland-security-and-counter.

151. "Remarks of John O. Brennan."

152. 2010 *National Security Strategy*, 18.

153. *National Security Strategy*, Office of the President, the White House, February 2015, 9.

154. 2010 *National Security Strategy*, 22.

155. "Remarks by President Bush at 2002 Graduation Exercise of the United States Military Academy," Office of the Press Secretary, the White House, June 1, 2002, https://georgewbush-whitehouse.archives.gov/news/releases/2002/06/20020601-3.html

156. "READ: President Obama's Speech on the Future of the War on Terror," *Washington Post*, May 23, 2013.

157. Barbara Starr and Ryan Browne, "U.S. Orders First Drone Strikes Under Trump," CNN, January 24, 2017, https://www.cnn.com/2017/01/23/politics/drone-strikes-president-trump.

158. "Remarks by President Biden on the End of the War in Afghanistan," Office of the Press Secretary, the White House, August 31, 2021, https://www.whitehouse.gov/briefing-room/speeches-remarks/2021/08/31/remarks-by-president-biden-on-the-end-of-the-war-in-afghanistan/.

159. Author interview with Ambassador Richard Boucher, former assistant secretary of state for South and Central Asian Affairs, Washington, DC, February 25, 2019.

## 4. OUR MAN IN ISLAMABAD

1. Imran Khan (@ImranKhanPTI), "Record needs to be put straight on Mr Trump's tirade against Pakistan: 1. No Pakistani was involved in 9/11 but Pak decided to participate in US War on Terror … ," Twitter, November 19, 2018, https://twitter.com/ImranKhanPTI/status/1064482777054220289; Salman Masood, "Pakistan Angered by Trump's Claim that It Does 'Nothing' for U.S.," *New York Times*, November 19, 2018.

2. C. Christine Fair and Sarah J. Watson, eds., *Pakistan's Enduring Challenges* (Philadelphia: University of Pennsylvania Press, 2015); Hussain Haqqani, *Magnificent Delusions: Pakistan, The United States, and an Epic History* (New York: PublicAffairs, 2013); Hathaway, *The Leverage Paradox*; Dennis Kux, *The United States and Pakistan, 1947–2000: Disenchanted Allies* (Baltimore: Johns Hopkins University Press, 2001); Daniel S. Markey, *No Exit from Pakistan: America's Tortured Relationship with Islamabad* (Cambridge: Cambridge University Press, 2013); Nawaz, *The Battle for Pakistan*; Bruce Riedel, *Deadly Embrace: Pakistan, America, and the Future of Global Jihad* (Washington, DC: Brookings Institution Press, 2011); Howard B. Schaffer and Teresita C. Schaffer, *How Pakistan Negotiates with the United States* (Washington, DC: United States Institute of Peace, 2011).

3. In May 2018, FATA was merged into the Khyber Pakhtunkhwa (KP) Province under the FATA Interim Governance Regulation. The seven tribal agencies constituting FATA are now designated as tribal districts under the KP provincial government. As the period under study here predates these administrative changes, I continue to refer to the region as FATA and its constituent administrative units as tribal agencies in this chapter.

4. Terence Hunt, "Rice: Pakistan Must Control Border Area," *Washington Post*, February 26, 2007.

5. "Remarks by the President on a New Strategy for Afghanistan and Pakistan," Office of the Press Secretary, the White House, March 27, 2009, https://obamawhitehouse.archives.gov/the-press-office/remarks-president-a-new-strategy-afghanistan-and-pakistan.

6.  George Curzon, *Lord Curzon in India: Being a Selection from His Speeches as Viceroy & Governor-General of India, 1898–1905* (London: Macmillan and Co., 1906), 37.

7.  As historian Sameetah Agha argues, the perspective that colonial officials had of the frontier at the time did not fully align with local economic conditions. There were some local resources that were exploited by the local community in small quantities, such as trading in salt. Agha points out that one of the grievances held by the Afridi tribe that contributed to the outbreak of the 1897 revolt against the British was the increase of the salt tax. See Sameetah Agha, "Trans-Indus Salt: Objects, Resistance, and Violence in the North-West Frontier of British India," in *Objects and Frontiers in Modern Asia: Between the Mekong and the Indus*, ed. Lipokmar Dzuvichu and Manjeet Baruah (Abingdon, UK: Routledge, 2019), 21–42.

8.  There often is not a clearly delineated line between tribal and non-tribal communities or the "ungoverned" periphery and areas under state control. With reference to the Pashtun of northern Pakistan, along with the Somalis, the Kurds, and the Yemenis, anthropologist Akbar Ahmed distinguished between the highly egalitarian *nang* (honor) and more hierarchical *qalang* (taxes) tribal societies. This distinction was based on the organizing principle of the different societies. *Nang* tribal societies of the rugged and isolated periphery live outside of government control and organize social interactions according to the prevailing code of honor, with a strong bond of kinship and social cohesion within their tribal identity known as *asabiyyah*, a concept described by Ibn Khaldun in his fourteenth-century study *Muqaddimah*. *Qalang* tribal societies, on the other hand, reside in more settled agricultural lands, which allowed for the emergence of largescale landowners and social hierarchies, often based in a feudal-like system to work the more fertile land. These communities live closer to government control and are therefore subject to the laws, taxes, and economic interests of the state, with social cohesion and the strength of the code of honor as ideals of behavior weakening over time. See Akbar S. Ahmed, *Millennium and Charisma Among Pathans: A Critical Essay in Social Anthropology* (Abingdon, UK: Routledge, 1976); Ahmed, *Pukhtun Economy and Society*; Ahmed, *The Thistle and the Drone*, 26–27.

9.  Hugh Beattie, "Negotiations with the Tribes of Waziristan 1849–1914—The British Experience," *Journal of Imperial and Commonwealth History* 39, no. 4 (2011): 575.

10. Howell, *Mizh*; Christian Tripodi, *Edge of Empire: The British Political Officer and Tribal Administration in the North-West Frontier, 1877–1947* (Abingdon, UK: Routledge, 2011).

11. Winston Churchill, *The Story of the Malakand Field Force: An Episode of Frontier War* (London: Longmans, Green, and Co., 1901), 4.

12. K. Sivaramakrishnan, *Statemaking and Environmental Change in Colonial Eastern India* (Stanford, CA: Stanford University Press, 1999), 38.

13. "Field Operations: Reports of progress of Events with the Waziristan Field Force," File No. 1895_447_644, Military Department, Government of India, 1895, National Archives of India; "Proposed Formation of a North-West Frontier Agency: Minute by His Excellency the Viceroy on the Administration of the North-West Frontier," File

No. 37, Foreign Department, Government of India, September 1900, National Archives of India; Sameetah Agha, "Sub-imperialism and the Loss of the Khyber: The Politics of Imperial Defence on British India's North-West Frontier," *Indian Historical Review* 40, no. 2 (2013): 307–330.

14.   Author interview with Shahid Ahmed Afridi, former counterinsurgency officer in the Pakistan Army, Islamabad, Pakistan, December 17, 2018.

15.   "Summary of the Administration of Lord Curzon of Kedleston, Viceroy and Governor General of India, January 1899–November 1905," Military Department, Government of India, 1906, Asian Reading Room, Library of Congress; Johnson, *The Afghan Way of War*, 149–173.

16.   Johnson, *The Afghan Way of War*, 171.

17.   "Proposed Formation of a North-West Frontier Agency."

18.   The FCR was used as a model for frontier administration in other parts of the British Empire, including in northern Kenya, Nigeria, Iraq, and the southern Negev area of the Palestine Mandate.

19.   "Proposed Formation of a North-West Frontier Agency."

20.   Curzon, *Lord Curzon in India*, 423.

21.   Frontier Regulations Enquiry Committee, *Report of the Frontier Regulations Enquiry Committee* (Simla: Government of India Press, 1931), 24–25.

22.   Benjamin D. Hopkins, *Ruling the Savage Periphery: Frontier Governance and the Making of the Modern State* (Cambridge, MA: Harvard University Press, 2020), 55.

23.   Nabi Sahak, "The Origins of Anglo-Afghan Relations Clarifying the Political Status of Durand Line 1893–2021," PhD diss., King's College London, 2021, 153–161.

24.   Christian Tripodi, *The Unknown Enemy: Counterinsurgency and the Illusion of Control* (Cambridge: Cambridge University Press, 2021), 87.

25.   Curzon, *Lord Curzon in India*, 422.

26.   Francis Leeson, *Frontier Legion: With the Khassadars of North Waziristan* (Ferring, UK: Selwood Printing, 2003); Philip Woodruff, *The Men Who Ruled India: The Guardians* (London: Jonathan Cape, 1954).

27.   "Control of Waziristan," File No. Defence_A_1924_MAR_391–400, Army Department, Government of India, March 1924, National Archives of India.

28.   "Control of Waziristan."

29.   John Masters, *Bugles and a Tiger: A Volume of Autobiography* (New York: Ballantine Books, 1956), 205.

30.   Author interview with Ambassador Akbar Ahmed.

31.   O. K. Afridi, *Mahsud Monograph*, Tribal Affairs Research Cell, Home and Tribal Affairs Department, Government of North-West Frontier Province, 1980, 49.

32.   *Speeches by Quaid-i-Azam Muhammad Ali Jinnah, Governor-General of Pakistan, 3rd June 1947 to 14th August 1948* (Karachi: Saifee Printers, 1948), 93.

33.   *Speeches by Quaid-i-Azam Muhammad Ali Jinnah*, 94.

34.   FATA's special administrative status was officially enshrined in Pakistan's 1973 constitution.

35.   Bezhan, "The Pashtunistan Issue and Politics in Afghanistan."

36. Ahmed, *Pukhtun Economy and Society*, 144; Harrison Akins, "Mashar Versus Kashar in Pakistan's FATA: Intra-tribal Conflict and the Obstacles to Reform," *Asian Survey* 58, no. 6 (2018): 1136–1159.

37. Lieut.-Colonel C. E. Bruce, *Waziristan, 1936-1937: The Problems of the North-West Frontiers of India and their Solutions* (London: Gale and Polden, 1938), 12.

38. Ahmed, *Resistance and Control in Pakistan*, 6.

39. Ahmed, 60.

40. Ahmed, 59.

41. Christian Tripodi, "Negotiating with the Enemy: 'Politicals' and Tribes 1901–47," *Journal of Imperial and Commonwealth History* 39, no. 4 (2011): 589–606; Alan Warren, *Waziristan, The Faqir of Ipi, and the Indian Army: The North West Frontier Revolt of 1936-37* (Oxford: Oxford University Press, 2000).

42. Ahmed Rashid, *Taliban: Militant Islam, Oil, and Fundamentalism in Central Asia* (New Haven, CT: Yale University Press, 2000).

43. Strobe Talbot, Memorandum for the Record: Interview, Team 3, 9/11 Commission, January 15, 2004, 9/11 Commission Papers, National Archives.

44. Kux, *The United States and Pakistan*, 315–316.

45. Walter Anderson, Memorandum for the Record: Interview, Team 3, 9/11 Commission, August 14, 2003, 9/11 Commission Papers, National Archives, 3; Camp, Memorandum for the Record.

46. Chamberlin, Memorandum for the Record.

47. Anderson, Memorandum for the Record; Richard Armitage, Memorandum for the Record: Interview, Team 3, 9/11 Commission, January 12, 2004, 9/11 Commission Papers, National Archives; "Pakistan: DepSec Talbott Presses PM Sharif on UBL," Diplomatic Cable, U.S. Department of State, February 5, 1999, C06770712, State Department Reading Room; "Pakistan: Leverage and Engagement," Diplomatic Cable, U.S. Department of State, January 12, 2000, C17640553, State Department Reading Room.

48. "Pakistan: Leverage and Engagement."

49. Author interview with Christina Rocca, former assistant secretary of state for South Asian affairs, Clarendon, VA, January 16, 2019.

50. Ahmed Rashid, *Descent Into Chaos: The United States and the Failure of Nation Building in Pakistan, Afghanistan, and Central Asia* (New York: Viking, 2008), 56–57.

51. "Memorandum of Conversation: Secretary's Fourth Restricted Session with Shevardnadze," U.S. Department of State, March 23, 1988, National Security Archive.

52. Ahmed, *The Thistle and the Drone*, 135; Chamberlin, Memorandum for the Record.

53. Author interview with Marvin Weinbaum, former analyst for Afghanistan and Pakistan in the State Department's Bureau of Intelligence and Research and director of Afghanistan and Pakistan studies at the Middle East Institute, Washington, DC, October 16, 2018.

54. Eastham, Memorandum for the Record, 12; Michelle Sison, Memorandum for the Record: Interview, Team 3, 9/11 Commission, December 11, 2003, 9/11 Commission Papers, National Archives.

55. Author interview with Richard Armitage.

56. "Deputy Secretary Armitage's Meeting with Pakistan Intel Chief Mahmud," Diplomatic Cable, U.S. Department of State, September 12, 2001, 200401239, National Security Archive.

57. Author interview with Richard Armitage.

58. Srinath Raghavan, *Fierce Enigmas: A History of the United States in South Asia* (New York: Basic Books, 2018), 387.

59. Rashid, *Descent Into Chaos*, 28.

60. "Musharraf," Diplomatic Cable, U.S. Department of State, September 13, 2001, 200701534, National Security Archive.

61. Coll, *Directorate S*, 53.

62. George W. Bush, *Decision Points* (New York: Random House, 2010), 188.

63. "Deputy Secretary Armitage's Meeting with General Mahmud: Actions and Support Expected of Pakistan in Fight Against Terrorism," Diplomatic Cable, U.S. Department of State, September 13, 2001, 200405012, National Security Archive.

64. Author interview with Richard Armitage.

65. "Deputy Secretary Armitage's Meeting with General Mahmud."

66. "Deputy Secretary Armitage's Meeting with General Mahmud."

67. "Secretary's 13 September 2001 Conversation with Pakistani President Musharraf," Diplomatic Cable, U.S. Department of State, September 18, 2001, 200604900, National Security Archive.

68. "Musharraf Accepts the Seven Points," Diplomatic Cable, U.S. Department of State, September 14, 2001, 200405012, National Security Archive.

69. "Scene-Setter for the Visit of Senators Levin and Warner," Diplomatic Cable, U.S. Department of State, November 16, 2001, 200402730, National Security Archive.

70. Colin L. Powell, "Your Meeting with Pakistan President Musharraf," Memorandum for the President, November 5, 2001, 200402730, National Security Archive.

71. "Interview with Donald A. Camp"; "Pakistan: Musharraf Is Key to Public Support of His Government's Counterterrorism Policies," Bureau of Intelligence and Research, U.S. Department of State, February 2, 2004, State Department Reading Room.

72. "Interview with Ambassador Alan Eastham," Foreign Affairs Oral History Project, Association for Diplomatic Studies and Training, July 28, 2010, https://adst.org/OH%20TOCs/Eastham-Alan1.pdf.

73. *Public Papers of the Presidents of the United States, George W. Bush: 2002*, book 1, *January 1 to June 30, 2002* (Washington, DC: United States Government Printing Office, 2002), 220, 224.

74. "Interview Richard Armitage," *Frontline*, PBS, July 20, 2006, https://www.pbs.org/wgbh/pages/frontline/taliban/interviews/armitage.html.

75. Bush, *Decision Points*; "President Musharraf's Support to Militants in Kashmir," Defense Executive Intelligence Note, Defense Intelligence Agency, July 30, 2003, Defense Intelligence Agency Reading Room; "Intelligence Community Assessment, Key Warning Concerns for 2003."

76. "Kashmiri Militants," Background Paper, Defense Intelligence Agency, January 13, 2002, Defense Intelligence Agency Reading Room.

77. CIA, "Terrorism: Extremists Planning Attacks Against US Interests in Pakistan," Analytic Report, November 29, 2001, National Security Archive.

78. "Ambassador's 11/15 Meeting with President Musharraf," Diplomatic Cable, U.S. Department of State, November 15, 2001, C17522049, State Department Reading Room.

79. *Progress Report on the Global War on Terrorism*, the White House, September 2003.

80. "2003 Terrorism Report for Pakistan," Diplomatic Cable, U.S. Department of State, December 1, 2003, C18599405, State Department Reading Room.

81. L. E. Jacoby, "Pakistan's Failure to Stem Islamic Extremism," Info Memo for the Secretary of Defense, Defense Intelligence Agency, December 3, 2003, Defense Intelligence Agency Reading Room.

82. Doug Stone, Memorandum for the Record: Interview, Team 3, 9/11 Commission, October 26, 2003, 9/11 Commission Papers, National Archives.

83. "Pakistan: Current Terrorist Threat in Pakistan Remains High Despite Government Crackdown," Defense Intelligence Agency, January 14, 2002, Defense Intelligence Agency Reading Room.

84. Author interview with General Stanley McChrystal.

85. Craig Whitlock, *The Afghanistan Papers: A Secret History of the War* (New York: Simon and Schuster, 2021), 83. Over the next two decades, Afghan leaders would continuously lay the blame for insecurity in Afghanistan on Pakistani support for the Taliban.

86. Author interview with Richard Armitage.

87. Mazzetti, *The Way of the Knife*, 39.

88. Donald Rumsfeld, "2002 Memo to Doug Feith About Pakistan and the 'War on Terror,'" June 25, 2002, National Security Archive.

89. Author interview with Richard Armitage.

90. Hayden, *Playing to the Edge*, 205–206.

91. Author interview with Richard Armitage.

92. Stone, Memorandum for the Record, 8.

93. Coll, *Directorate S*, 55.

94. Author interview with Imtiaz Gul, Pakistani journalist, Islamabad, Pakistan, December 18, 2018.

95. Coll, *Directorate S*, 202–203.

96. Coll, *Directorate S*, 199.

97. Ryan Crocker Oral History, Transcript, Presidential Oral Histories, Miller Center, University of Virginia, September 9–10, 2010.

98. David O. Smith, *The Quetta Experience: A Study of Attitudes and Values Within the Pakistan Army* (Washington, DC: Woodrow Wilson Center, 2018), 71.

99. Louis Dupree, *Afghanistan* (Oxford: Oxford University Press, 2002), 540.

100. Carey Schofield, *Inside the Pakistan Army* (London: Biteback Publishing, 2011), 134.

101. Author interview with Muhammad Amir Rana, member of the steering committee for Pakistan's National Counterterrorism Authority and director of the Pak Institute for Peace Studies, Islamabad, Pakistan, December 13, 2018.

102. "S/P Ambassador Haass' Call on [Redacted]," Diplomatic Cable, State Department, November 12, 2002, 200704080, National Security Archive.

103. Hasan Khan, "Policy Rethink Needed," *Dawn* (Pakistan), October 9, 2012.

104. Schofield, *Inside the Pakistan Army*, 170.

105. Author interview with Richard Armitage.

106. "Pakistan's Recent Actions in the GWOT: A Chronology and Scorecard," Diplomatic Cable, U.S. Department of State, February 27, 2004, C05772200, State Department Reading Room.

107. Imtiaz Gul, *The Most Dangerous Place: Pakistan's Lawless Frontier* (New York: Viking Press, 2009), 24.

108. Author interview with Imtiaz Gul.

109. Rashid, *Descent Into Chaos*, 230–231.

110. Coll, *Directorate S*, 209.

111. Schofield, *Inside the Pakistan Army*, 151.

112. Ahmed, *The Thistle and the Drone*, 70.

113. Abbas, *The Taliban Revival*, 106.

114. Bergen, *The Longest War*, 253.

115. Iqbal Khattak, "I Did Not Surrender to the Military," *Friday Times* (Pakistan), April 30–May 6, 2004.

116. K. Alan Kronstadt and Bruce Vaughn, *Terrorism in South Asia*, Report for Congress, Congressional Research Service, August 31, 2005, 23.

117. Whitlock, *The Afghanistan Papers*, 85.

118. "Musharraf Worried About Wana Operation Fallout," *Dawn* (Pakistan), June 21, 2004.

119. "Musharraf Worried About Wana Operation Fallout."

120. "Pakistan Kills Pro-al Qaeda tribal fighter," Reuters, June 19, 2004, https://timesofmalta .com/articles/view/pakistan-kills-pro-al-qaeda-tribal-fighter.119959; *Removing Terrorist Sanctuaries: The 9/11 Commission Recommendations and U.S. Policy*, Report for Congress, Congressional Research Service, August 10, 2004.

121. Author interview with Christina Rocca.

122. Mazzetti, *The Way of the Knife*, 171.

123. "Policy on Track, But Violence Will Rise," Diplomatic Cable, U.S. Department of State, February 21, 2006, 20070059, National Security Archive.

124. "Policy on Track, But Violence Will Rise," 220.

125. Pazeer Gul, "Militant Cleric's School Destroyed in Miramshah," *Dawn* (Pakistan), March 8, 2006.

126. Coll, *Directorate S*, 220–221.

127. Saeed Shah, "Pakistani Tribesmen Organize to Fight Taliban Insurgents," *McClatchy*, September 26, 2008, https://www.mcclatchydc.com/news/nation-world/world/article 24502456.html.

128. Donald Rumsfeld, "F-16s," Memo to Bill Luti, April 15, 2005, National Security Archive; Donald Rumsfeld, "F-16s for Pakistan," Memo to Peter Rodman, June 7, 2005, National Security Archive; "Defeating al-Qaeda's Air Force: Pakistan's F-16 Program

in the Fight Against Terrorism," Donald Camp, principal deputy assistant secretary for South and Central Asian affairs, Statement Before the U.S. House of Representatives Foreign Affairs Subcommittee on South Asia, U.S. Department of State, September 16, 2008, https://2001-2009.state.gov/p/sca/ci/af/2008/109757.htm; Franz-Stefan Gady, "US Will Sell 8 F-16 Fighter Jets to Pakistan," *The Diplomat*, October 23, 2015, https://thediplomat.com/2015/10/us-will-sell-8-f-16-fighter-jets-to-pakistan/.

129.    Transmittal No. 06–09, Pakistan—F-16C/D Block 50/52 Aircraft, Defense Security Cooperation Agency, June 28, 2006, https://nation.time.com/wp-content/uploads/sites/8/2011/09/pakistan_06-09.pdf.

130.    Gady, "US Will Sell 8 F-16 Fighter Jets to Pakistan"; "Defeating al-Qaeda's Air Force."

131.    Author interview with Ambassador Richard Boucher.

132.    Harrison Akins, "Tribal Militias and Political Legitimacy in British India and Pakistan," *Asian Security* 16, no. 3 (2020): 304–322; "Impressions of Waziristan," Diplomatic Cable, U.S. Department of State, January 20, 2005, 200704080, National Security Archive.

133.    "Tribal Elders Call for Raising Fata Force," *The News* (Pakistan), September 14, 2006.

134.    Bergen, *The Longest War*, 260.

135.    Donald Rumsfeld, "Conversation with Musharraf," Message to Stephen J. Hadley, October 13, 2006, Rumsfeld Papers.

136.    Mark Mazzetti, "Amid U.S. Policy Disputes, Qaeda Grows in Pakistan," *New York Times*, June 30, 2008.

137.    "Afghanistan: Where We Stand and What We Need," Diplomatic Cable, U.S. Department of State, August 26, 2006, 200805703, National Security Archive.

138.    Caren Bohan, "U.S. Boosts Pressure on Musharraf Over al Qaeda," Reuters, July 18, 2007, https://www.reuters.com/article/us-pakistan-usa/u-s-boosts-pressure-on-musharraf-over-al-qaeda-idUSN1832540420070718.

139.    Mazzetti, "Amid U.S. Policy Disputes, Qaeda Grows in Pakistan."

140.    "Meeting with Pakistani President Pervez Musharraf, 12 February 2007," Memorandum for the President, February 13, 2007, Defense Department Reading Room; Rashid, *Descent Into Chaos*, 384.

141.    Thom Shanker, "U.S. Defense Chief, in Pakistan, Offers Support on Policing Afghan Border," *New York Times*, February 12, 2007.

142.    Schmitt and Shanker, *Counterstrike*, 108.

143.    Abbas, *The Taliban Revival*, 8.

144.    Myra MacDonald, *Defeat Is an Orphan: How Pakistan Lost the Great South Asian War* (London: Hurst and Company, 2017), 218.

145.    Kilcullen, *The Accidental Guerilla*, 34.

146.    Author interview with Shahid Ahmed Afridi.

147.    Declan Walsh, *The Nine Lives of Pakistan: Dispatches from a Precarious State* (New York: W. W. Norton and Co., 2020), 77.

148.    Abbas, *The Taliban Revival*, 160.

149.    Zahid Hussain, *The Scorpion's Tail: The Relentless Rise of Islamic Militants in Pakistan—And How It Threatens America* (New York: Free Press, 2010), 77.

150. Adnan Naseemullah, "Police Capacity and Insurgency in Pakistan," in *Policing Insurgencies: Cops as Counterinsurgents*, ed. C. Christine Fair and Sumit Ganguly (New Delhi: Oxford University Press, 2014), 191.

151. Rashid, *Descent Into Chaos*, 275.

152. Amira Jadoon, "Conflict Aggravation or Alleviation? A Cross-National Examination of U.S. Military Aid's Effect on Conflict Dynamics with Insights from Pakistan," *Political Science Quarterly* 135, no. 4 (2020): 676.

153. Author interview with General Abdullah Dogar.

154. Abbas, *The Taliban Revival*, 120.

155. Interview with Ambassador Cameron Munter, former U.S. ambassador to Pakistan, Washington, DC, January 23, 2019.

156. Coll, *Directorate S*, 209.

157. Smith, *The Quetta Experience*, 79.

158. Jadoon, "Conflict Aggravation or Alleviation?," 674.

159. Author interview with former senior ISI official.

160. Owais Tohid and Scott Baldauf, "Pakistani Army Must Go Through the Pashtuns," *Christian Science Monitor*, June 25, 2004.

161. Karl Kaltenthaler and William Miller, "Ethnicity, Islam, and Pakistani Public Opinion Toward the Pakistani Taliban," *Studies in Conflict & Terrorism* 38, no. 11 (2015): 938–957; Qandeel Siddique, *Tehrik-e-Taliban Pakistan: An Attempt to Deconstruct the Umbrella Organization and the Reasons for Its Growth in Pakistan's North-West*, DIIS Report 2010, no. 12 (2010), Danish Institute for International Studies.

162. Ezra Schricker, "The Search for Rebel Interdependence: A Study of the Afghan and Pakistani Taliban," *Journal of Peace Research* 54, no. 1 (2017): 16–30; Mona Kanwal Sheikh, *Guardians of God: Inside the Religious Mind of the Pakistani Taliban* (New Delhi: Oxford University Press, 2016).

163. *Report on Waziristan and Its Tribes* (Lahore: Government of India Press, 1901), 21.

164. *Report on Waziristan and Its Tribes*, 29.

165. Ahmed, *Resistance and Control in Pakistan*, 30.

166. Caroe, *The Pathans*, 393.

167. *Jinnah Papers Volume V, Pakistan: Pangs of Birth, 15 August–30 September 1947* (Islamabad: Quaid-e-Azam Papers Project, Government of Pakistan, 2000), 307.

168. Abbas, *The Taliban Revival*; Ahmed, *The Thistle and the Drone*.

169. Schofield, *Inside the Pakistan Army*, 137.

170. Author interview with General Abdullah Dogar.

171. S. H. Tajik, "Insight Into a Suicide Bomber Training Camp in Waziristan," *CTC Sentinel* 3, no. 3 (2010): 10–13.

172. Hussain, *The Scorpion's Tail*, 78.

173. "FATA: Militants Capture Fort in South Waziristan," Diplomatic Cable, U.S. Department of State, January 18, 2008, C17576044, State Department Reading Room.

174. Syed Shoaib Hasan, "Profile: Islamabad's Red Mosque," BBC News, July 27, 2007, http://news.bbc.co.uk/1/hi/world/south_asia/6503477.stm; Hussain, *The Scorpion's Tail*, 113–116.

175. Syed Saleem Shahzad, "The Taliban's Brothers in Alms," *Asia Times* (Hong Kong), March 14, 2007.
176. Andrew Small, *The China-Pakistan Axis: Asia's New Geopolitics* (New York: Oxford University Press, 2015), ix–xvi.
177. Hussain, *The Scorpion's Tail*, 116.
178. "Pakistani Colonel Killed in Clash," BBC News, July 8, 2007, http://news.bbc.co.uk/2/hi/south_asia/6281404.stm.
179. "Lal Masjid Stand-Off Day 2: 1,200 Surrender, Desert," *Tribune* (India), July 4, 2007.
180. "103 People Killed in Lal Masjid Operation: Report," *Pakistan Today*, April 20, 2013.
181. Hussain, *The Scorpion's Tail*, 119–120.
182. Nicholas Schmidle, "My Buddy, the Jihadi," *Washington Post*, July 15, 2007.
183. Ahmed, *The Thistle and the Drone*, 72.
184. Syed Saleem Shahzad, *Inside Al-Qaeda and the Taliban: Beyond 9/11* (London: Pluto Press, 2011), 49.
185. Amir Mir, "Pakistan: The Suicide-Bomb Capital of the World," *Asia Times* (Hong Kong), September 16, 2011; Schofield, *Inside the Pakistan Army*, 179.
186. "Five Most Wanted Militants," *Dawn* (Pakistan), August 18, 2011.
187. Hakimullah Mehsud, "Hakimullah Mehsud Criticizes Qazi Hussain," 2012, Taliban Communications Archive, Danish Institute for International Studies.
188. The Provincially Administered Tribal Areas (PATA) was established by Articles 246 and 247 of the 1973 Pakistani Constitution and consisted of the former princely states of Swat, Dir, Chitral, and Amb (which were abolished and merged with Pakistan in 1969), along with various other tribal regions within northern Pakistan. Administrative and legal authority in PATA was vested directly with the NWFP provincial governor, similar to the president's authority in neighboring FATA, with PATA specific regulations replacing the FCR in the new administrative unit. In 2018, the Pakistani parliament repealed PATA's special status, and the region was merged into the now renamed Khyber Pakhtunkhwa Province, alongside FATA's tribal agencies.
189. Fredrik Barth, *The Last Wali of Swat: An Autobiography as told to Fredrik Barth* (New York: Columbia University Press, 1985).
190. Siddique, *Tehrik-e-Taliban Pakistan*, 40.
191. Sheikh, *Guardians of God*, 145.
192. Maulana Fazlullah, "Maulana Fazlullah Speech to Suicide Bombers," 2010, Taliban Communications Archive, Danish Institute for International Studies.
193. Hussain, *The Scorpion's Tail*, 120.
194. Malik Siraj Akbar, "Watch That Tail," *Friday Times* (Pakistan), February 11–17, 2011.
195. Coll, *Directorate S*, 262–263.
196. Hussain, *The Scorpion's Tail*, 132.
197. Tajik, "Insight Into a Suicide Bomber Training Camp in Waziristan."
198. Abbas, *The Taliban Revival*, 152.
199. Baitullah Mehsud, "New Law System," 2009, Taliban Communications Archive, Danish Institute for International Studies.

200.   Shuja Nawaz, *FATA—A Most Dangerous Place: Meeting the Challenge of Militancy and Terror in the Federally Administered Tribal Areas of Pakistan* (Washington, DC: Center for Strategic and International Studies, 2009), 22.

201.   Author interview with General Abdullah Dogar.

202.   Umar Farooq, "How War Altered Pakistan's Tribal Areas," *Foreign Affairs*, October 6, 2017, https://www.foreignaffairs.com/articles/pakistan/2017-10-06/how-war-altered-pakistans-tribal-areas.

203.   Ahmed, *The Thistle and the Drone*, 77.

204.   Iqbal Khattak, "Inside Militancy in Waziristan," in *Dispatches from Pakistan*, ed. Madiha R. Tahir, Qalander Bux Memon, and Vijay Prashad (Minneapolis: University of Minnesota Press, 2014), 211.

205.   Tehreek-e-Taliban Pakistan, "Bloodshed and Revenge," Umar Studio, July 2009, acceshttps://archive.org/details/Tehreek-e-talibanPakistan_umarStudiojuly2009.

206.   Siddique, *Tehrik-e-Taliban Pakistan*, 63.

207.   Tehreek-e-Taliban Pakistan, "Tehreek-e-Taliban Dara Adam Khel," 2011, Taliban Communications Archive, Danish Institute for International Studies.

208.   Muhammad Khurasani, "A Message to US President Elect Donald J Trump," 2016, https://jihadology.net/2016/11/11/new-statement-from-the-teḥrik-i-ṭaliban-pakistans-muḥammad-al-khurasani-a-message-to-us-president-elect-donald-j-trump/.

209.   Syed Manzar Abbas Zaidi, "The New Taliban Warlords and Organization," *Defense Against Terrorism Review* 1, no. 2 (2008): 85–86.

210.   Shakirullah, Nyborg, and Elahi, "The Underlying Causes of Violent Conflict in the North Waziristan Tribal Areas of Pakistan," 126.

211.   Pakistan Army, "Message from the Pak Army," 2009, Taliban Communications Archive, Danish Institute for International Studies.

212.   Shura Ittehad-ul Mujahideen, "Shura Ittehad-ul Mujahideen," 2009, Taliban Communications Archive, Danish Institute for International Studies.

213.   Mushtaq Yusufzai, "Taliban Warns of Attack on Capital," *The News* (Pakistan), June 10, 2008.

214.   "Points to Raise with European Union Partners in Advance of President Musharraf's Visit to Brussels," Briefing Memo, U.S. Department of State, January 17, 2008, C17571088, State Department Reading Room.

215.   "Undersecretary Burns Strategic Dialogue with Israel," Briefing Memo, U.S. Department of State, January 18, 2008, C17571089, State Department Reading Room.

216.   Stanley McChrystal, *My Share of the Task: A Memoir* (New York: Portfolio/Penguin, 2014), 358.

217.   Rohan Gunaratna and Anders Nielsen, "Al Qaeda in the Tribal Areas of Pakistan and Beyond," *Studies in Conflict & Terrorism* 31, no. 9 (2008): 800–801.

218.   Rashid, *Descent Into Chaos*, 407.

219.   Rashid, *Descent Into Chaos*, 409; Ismail Khan and Carlotta Gall, "Battle of Bajaur: A Critical Test for Pakistan's Military," *New York Times*, September 23, 2008.

220.   Anand Gopal, Mansur Khan Mahsud, and Brian Fishman, "The Taliban in North Waziristan," in *Talibanistan: Negotiating the Borders Between Terror, Politics, and*

*Religion*, ed. Peter Bergen and Katherine Tiedemann (Oxford: Oxford University Press, 2013), 132–146.

221.   "Location and Activities of the Training Centers Affiliated with the Haqqani Network, Taliban, and Al-Qaeda in Northern Waziristan and Future Plans and Activities of Sarajuddin (Haqqani)," Information Report, Defense Intelligence Agency, April 2008, Defense Intelligence Agency Reading Room.

222.   Karin Brulliard and Haq Nawaz Khan, "After Major South Waziristan Offensive, Pakistan Still Faces Serious Obstacles," *Washington Post*, November 19, 2010.

223.   "Late December 2009 Al Qaeda and Haqqani Network Senior Leadership Activities in Miram Shah, Pakistan and Khowst Province, Afghanistan," Information Report, Defense Intelligence Agency, January 11, 2010, Defense Intelligence Agency Reading Room.

224.   "Haqqanis: Growth of a Militant Network," BBC News, September 14, 2011, https://www.bbc.com/news/world-south-asia-14912957.

225.   Hayden, *Playing to the Edge*, 346.

226.   Bush, *Decision Points*, 217–218.

227.   Barack Obama, "Obama's Remarks on Iraq and Afghanistan," *New York Times*, July 15, 2008.

228.   Woodward, *Obama's War*, 3.

229.   "Interview with Donald A. Camp," 93.

230.   Author interview with Ambassador Richard Boucher.

231.   "Conclusions of Afghanistan-Pakistan Strategic Review," White Paper, U.S. Department of State, March 27, 2009, C05514443, State Department Reading Room.

232.   Woodward, *Obama's War*, 106.

233.   "Remarks by the President on a New Strategy for Afghanistan and Pakistan."

234.   Coll, *Directorate S*, 402.

235.   Coll, 536.

236.   Woodward, *Obama's War*, 187–188.

237.   Arshad Mohammed, "Clinton Says Pakistan Is Abdicating to the Taliban," Reuters, April 23, 2009, https://www.reuters.com/article/us-afghanistan-pakistan-usa/clinton-says-pakistan-is-abdicating-to-the-taliban-idUSTRE53L69J20090423.

238.   "Pakistan: Extrajudicial Executions by Army in Swat," Human Rights Watch, July 16, 2010, https://www.hrw.org/news/2010/07/16/pakistan-extrajudicial-executions-army-swat.

239.   Woodward, *Obama's War*, 116.

240.   Ahmed Rashid, *Pakistan on the Brink: The Future of America, Pakistan, and Afghanistan* (London: Penguin, 2012), 149.

241.   Woodward, *Obama's War*, 285.

242.   Woodward, 200–201.

243.   Schofield, *Inside the Pakistan Army*, 234.

244.   Woodward, *Obama's War*, 269.

245.   George Packer, *Our Man: Richard Holbrooke and the End of the American Century* (New York: Alfred A. Knopf, 2019), 509.

246. Ahmed, *The Thistle and the Drone*; Daniel L. Byman, "Why Drones Work: The Case for Washington's Weapon of Choice," *Foreign Affairs*, 92, no. 4 (July–August 2013): 32–43; C. Christine Fair, Karl Kaltenthaler, and William J. Miller, "Pakistani Opposition to American Drone Strikes," *Political Science Quarterly* 129, no. 1 (2014): 1–33; Patrick B. Johnston and Anoop K. Sarbahi, "The Impact of U.S. Drone Strikes on Terrorism in Pakistan," *International Studies Quarterly* 60, no. 2 (2016): 203–219; Asfandyar Mir, "What Explains Counterterrorism Effectiveness? Evidence from the U.S. Drone War in Pakistan," *International Security* 43, no. 2 (2018): 45–83; Anouk S. Rigterink, "The Wane of Command: Evidence on Drone Strikes and Control Within Terrorist Organizations," *American Political Science Review* 115, no. 1 (2021): 31–50; Aqil Shah, "Do U.S. Drone Strikes Cause Blowback? Evidence from Pakistan and Beyond," *International Security* 42, no. 4 (2018): 47–84.

247. Author interview with General Stanley McChrystal.

248. Author interview with Shahid Ahmed Afridi.

249. Woodward, *Obama's War*, 364, 367.

250. Author interview with Ambassador Aizaz Ahmad Chaudhry; Schmitt and Shanker, *Counterstrike*, 238–240.

251. Coll, *Directorate S*, 523; Packer, *Our Man*, 511.

252. Woodward, *Obama's War*, 369.

253. Hillary Rodham Clinton, "Remarks at the Launch of the Asia Society's Series of Richard C. Holbrooke Memorial Addresses," U.S. Department of State, February 18, 2011, https://2009-2017.state.gov/secretary/20092013clinton/rm/2011/02/156815.htm.

254. Barack Obama, *A Promised Land* (New York: Crown Publishing, 2020), 315, 686.

255. Schmitt and Shanker, *Counterstrike*, 198.

256. Coll, *Directorate S*, 440; "Casualty Status," U.S. Department of Defense, July 13, 2020, https://www.defense.gov/casualty.pdf.

257. Khattak, "Inside Militancy in Waziristan," 206.

258. "What Will Happen in Waziristan?," Diplomatic Cable, U.S. Department of State, July 19, 2009, C05158844, State Department Reading Room.

259. "Lack of Exact Data Raises Fear About Militants Escaping the Net," *Dawn* (Pakistan), June 3, 2009.

260. Aamir Latif, "Taliban Finds Fertile Recruiting Ground in Pakistan's Tribal Refugee Camps," *US News and World Report*, February 9, 2009.

261. Latif, "Taliban Finds Fertile Recruiting Ground in Pakistan's Tribal Refugee Camps."

262. Jane Perlez, "64 in Pakistan Die in Bombing at Arms Plant," *New York Times*, August 21, 2008.

263. Amir Muawiya, "Abdullah Azam Shaheed Brigade," 2009, Taliban Communications Archive, Danish Institute for International Studies.

264. Hussain, *The Scorpion's Tail*, 179.

265. Declan Walsh, "Pakistan Militants Launch Deadly Attack on Rawalpindi Mosque," *The Guardian* (UK), December 4, 2009.

266. Saud Mehsud, "Taliban Video Highlights Revenge on Pakistan Military," Reuters, January 21, 2012, https://www.reuters.com/article/us-pakistan-military-video/taliban-video-highlights-revenge-on-pakistan-military-idUSTRE80KoNT20120121.

267. Ahmed, *The Thistle and the Drone*, 74.

268. "Editorial: The Terrorism Threat and Response," *Daily Times* (Pakistan), August 15, 2013.

269. Sheikh, *Guardians of God*, 41.

270. Zahir Shah Sherazi, "Zarb-e-Azb Operation: 120 Suspected Militants Killed in N Waziristan," *Dawn* (Pakistan), June 15, 2014.

271. Jon Boone and Ewen MacAskill, "Pakistan Responds to Peshawar School Massacre with Strikes on Taliban," *The Guardian* (UK), December 16, 2014.

272. Fakhar Kakakhel and Umar Farooq, "Pakistan's War and Loss of Hope for Those Displaced," Al Jazeera English, June 15, 2015, https://www.aljazeera.com/features/2015/6/15/pakistans-war-and-loss-of-hope-for-those-displaced.

273. *Country Reports on Terrorism*, Bureau of Counterterrorism, U.S. Department of State, 2016, https://www.state.gov/wp-content/uploads/2019/04/crt_2016.pdf.

274. Paul Staniland, Asfandyar Mir, and Sameer Lalwani, "Politics and Threat Perception: Explaining Pakistani Military Strategy on the North West Frontier," *Security Studies* 27, no. 4 (2018): 535–574.

275. Ahmed, *The Thistle and the Drone*, 96–133.

276. Author interview with Abdul Basit Mujahid.

277. Author interview with former senior ISI official.

278. Author interview with Pakistani diplomat, Washington, DC, November 2018.

279. Author interview with former Pakistani Foreign Ministry official, Islamabad, Pakistan, December 2018.

280. Author interview with General Stanley McChrystal.

281. Author interview with Ambassador Cameron Munter.

282. Author interview with Ambassador Richard Boucher.

## 5. THE TERRORISM TRAP IN YEMEN, MALI, AND EGYPT

1. Benoit Challand and Joshua Rogers, "The Political Economy of Local Governance in Yemen: Past and Present," *Contemporary Arab Affairs* 13, no. 4 (2020): 56; Victoria Clark, *Yemen: Dancing on the Heads of Snakes* (New Haven, CT: Yale University Press, 2010), 118.

2. Shelagh Weir, *A Tribal Order: Politics and Law in the Mountains of Yemen* (Austin: University of Texas Press, 2007), 295, 304.

3. Steven C. Caton, *Yemen Chronicle: An Anthropology of War and Mediation* (New York: Hill and Wang, 2005), 279.

4. Robert F. Worth, "Ex-jihadist Defies Yemen's Leader, and Easy Labels," *New York Times*, February 26, 2010.

5.  Sarah Phillips, *Yemen's Democracy Experiment in Regional Perspective: Patronage and Pluralised Authoritarianism* (London: Palgrave Macmillan, 2008), 94; Sarah Phillips, *Yemen and the Politics of Permanent Crisis* (Abingdon, UK: Routledge, 2011).

6.  Challand and Rogers, "The Political Economy of Local Governance in Yemen"; Marie-Christine Heinze, "On 'Gun Culture' and 'Civil Statehood' in Yemen," *Journal of Arabian Studies* 4, no. 1 (2014): 70–95; Alexandra Lewis, *Security, Clans and Tribes: Unstable Governance in Somaliland, Yemen and the Gulf of Aden* (London: Palgrave Macmillan, 2015), 23.

7.  Clive Jones, "The Tribes that Bind: Yemen and the Paradox of Political Violence," *Studies in Conflict & Terrorism* 34, no. 12 (2011): 902–916.

8.  Paul Dresch, *Tribes, Government, and History in Yemen* (Oxford: Clarendon, 1989), 361.

9.  Scahill, *Dirty Wars*, 61.

10. "Interview with Ambassador Edmund Hull," *Yemen: Country Reader*, Association for Diplomatic Studies and Training, n.d., https://adst.org/Readers/Yemen.pdf.

11. Robert F. Worth, "The Man Who Danced on the Heads of Snakes," *New York Times*, December 7, 2017.

12. *Colonial Annual Reports: Aden, 1946* (London: His Majesty's Stationery Office, 1948), 70, 72; *Colonial Reports: Aden, 1949 & 1950* (London: His Majesty's Stationery Office, 1952), 52, 85.

13. Stephen Day, "Aden and the Gulf: The Reflections of a Political Officer," *Middle Eastern Studies* 53, no. 1 (2017): 136.

14. Simon C. Smith, "Rulers and Residents: British Relations with the Aden Protectorate, 1937–59," *Middle Eastern Studies* 31, no. 3 (1995): 516.

15. Harold Ingrams, *The Yemen: Imams, Rulers, and Revolution* (New York: Praeger, 1964), 80.

16. *Colonial Reports: Aden, 1949 & 1950*, 59; Day, "Aden and the Gulf," 137.

17. Author correspondence with Stephen Day, a British political officer in the Aden Protectorate, 1961–1967, May 8, 2013.

18. Clark, *Yemen*, 44.

19. Dresch, *Tribes, Government, and History in Yemen*, 262.

20. Ingrams, *The Yemen*, 144.

21. Donald Rumsfeld, "My Visits to Saudi Arabia, Oman, Egypt, Uzbekistan, and Turkey," Memorandum for the President, October 6, 2001, Rumsfeld Papers.

22. Edmund Hull, Memorandum for the Record: Interview, Teams 2 and 3, 9/11 Commission, October 18, 2003, 9/11 Commission Papers, National Archives.

23. Ahmed, *The Thistle and the Drone*, 106–122.

24. Marieke Brandt, "The Global and the Local: Al-Qaeda and Yemen's Tribes," in Collombier and Roy, eds., *Tribes and Global Jihadism*, 111.

25. Hamid and Farrall, *The Arabs at War in Afghanistan*, 25.

26. Walter Pincus, "Yemen Hears Benefits of Joining U.S. Fight; Officials Discuss up to $400 Million in Aid," *Washington Post*, November 28, 2001.

27. Barbara Bodine, Memorandum for the Record: Interview, Team 3, 9/11 Commission, October 21, 2003, 9/11 Commission Papers, National Archives.

28. Scahill, *Dirty Wars*, 132.

29. "Interview with Ambassador Edmund Hull."

30. Scahill, *Dirty Wars*, 64.

31. "Interview with Ambassador Edmund Hull."

32. "Interview with Ambassador Edmund Hull."

33. Gregory D. Johnsen, *The Last Refuge: Yemen, Al-Qaeda, and America's War in Arabia* (New York: W. W. Norton, 2013), 90, 111.

34. "Interview with Ambassador Edmund Hull."

35. Author interview with senior Yemeni diplomat.

36. "Yemen Advances in War on Terror: Iryani," *Yemen Times* (Sana'a), April 22, 2004.

37. "Yemen: Confronting al-Qaeda, Preventing State Failure," Hearing Before the Senate Foreign Relations Committee, 111th Congress, January 20, 2010, https://www.govinfo .gov/content/pkg/CHRG-111shrg62357/html/CHRG-111shrg62357.htm.

38. "While Security Forces Surround Kidnappers, German Hostages Reported in Good Condition," *Yemen Times* (Sana'a), December 17, 2008.

39. *2006 Country Reports on Human Rights Practices*, Bureau of Human Rights, Democracy, and Labor, U.S. Department of State, March 6, 2007.

40. *2008 Country Reports on Human Rights Practices*, Bureau of Human Rights, Democracy, and Labor, U.S. Department of State, February 25, 2009.

41. John O. Brennan, *Undaunted: My Fight Against America's Enemies, at Home and Abroad* (New York: Celadon Press, 2020), 341.

42. "Al-Qaeda and Yemen," *Washington Post*, December 31, 2009.

43. Gregory D. Johnsen, "The Expansion Strategy of Al-Qa'ida in the Arabian Peninsula," *CTC Sentinel* 2, no. 9 (January 2010): 4–7.

44. Johnsen, "The Expansion Strategy of Al-Qa'ida in the Arabian Peninsula."

45. James Gallagher, "Al Qaeda in the Arabian Peninsula in 2010: The Intensification of the Near War," *Critical Threats*, March 8, 2011, https://www.criticalthreats.org/ana lysis/al-qaeda-in-the-arabian-peninsula-in-2010-the-intensification-of-the-near -war.

46. Scahill, *Dirty Wars*, 305–306.

47. Nasir al-Wuhayshi, "Al-Qai'da in Arabian Peninsula Leader Urges Yemeni Tribes to Fight Government," February 20, 2009, Global Terrorism Research Project, Haverford College.

48. Al-Wuhayshi, "Al-Qai'da in Arabian Peninsula Leader Urges Yemeni Tribes to Fight Government."

49. Koehler-Derrick, *A False Foundation?*, 43–44.

50. Koehler-Derrick, 109.

51. Koehler-Derrick, 124.

52. Koehler-Derrick, 47.

53. Koehler-Derrick, 110.

54. Al-Qaeda in the Arabian Peninsula, "Letter from Basir to the Brother in Command," March 1, 2016 (Date of Declassification), Bin Laden's Bookshelf, Office of the Director of National Intelligence.

55. Nadwa Al-Dawsari, *Foe Not Friend: Yemeni Tribes and Al-Qaeda in the Arabian Peninsula*, Project on Middle East Democracy, February 2018, https://pomed.org/wp-content/uploads/2018/02/Dawsari_FINAL_180201.pdf.

56. Scahill, *Dirty Wars*, 465–466.

57. Stephen Day, "The Political Challenge of Yemen's Southern Movement," Carnegie Endowment for International Peace, March 2010, https://carnegieendowment.org/files/yemen_south_movement.pdf.

58. Al-Dawsari, *Foe Not Friend*, 21.

59. Worth, "Ex-jihadist Defies Yemen's Leader, and Easy Labels."

60. Oleh Siraaj, "Son of Last Sultan of Yemen Joins with His Children the Mujahideen of Al-Qaeda," Arrahmah.com, April 23, 2012, https://www.arrahmah.id/son-of-last-sultan-of-yemen-joins-with-his-children-the-mujahideen-of-al-qaeda/.

61. Oren Adaki, "Yemeni Tribal Leader Joins AQAP," *Long War Journal*, June 17, 2014, https://www.longwarjournal.org/archives/2014/06/yemeni_tribal_leader_joins_aqa.php.

62. "Terrorism Finance: Designation of U.S. Person and Al-Qa'ida in the Arabian Peninsula Leader Anwar Al-Aulaqi," Diplomatic Cable, U.S. Department of State, July 28, 2010, C06091897, State Department Reading Room.

63. White House Office of the Press Secretary, Background Briefing by Senior Administration Officials on the President's Speech on Counterterrorism, May 23, 2013, C06594688, State Department Reading Room.

64. *2010 Country Reports on Terrorism*, Office of the Coordinator for Counterterrorism, U.S. Department of State, https://www.state.gov/j/ct/rls/crt/index.htm.

65. START, Global Terrorism Database.

66. "Yemen Gunmen in Deadly Raid on Aden Security Service HQ," BBC News, June 19, 2010, https://www.bbc.com/news/10356975.

67. Gallagher, "Al Qaeda in the Arabian Peninsula in 2010."

68. Fawaz al Haidari, "Yemen Army 'Regains Control' of Southern Town," Agence France-Presse, August 25, 2010, https://eng-archive.aawsat.com/theaawsat/news-middle-east/yemen-army-regains-control-of-southern-town.

69. Scott Shane, Mark Mazzetti, and Robert F. Worth, "Secret Assault on Terrorism Widens on Two Continents," *New York Times*, August 14, 2010.

70. "Air Raid Kills Yemeni Mediator," Al Jazeera English, May 25, 2010, https://www.aljazeera.com/news/2010/5/25/air-raid-kills-yemeni-mediator.

71. Scahill, *Dirty Wars*, 460.

72. Koehler-Derrick, *A False Foundation?*, 42.

73. Scahill, *Dirty Wars*, 464.

74. Ali Almujahed and Sudarsan Raghavan, "Yemen Bombing Shows Reach of al-Qaeda Branch," *Washington Post*, May 21, 2012.

75. Laura Kasinof, "Yemeni Commander Killed in Suicide Bombing," *New York Times*, June 18, 2012.

76. Declan Walsh and Tyler Hicks, "The Tragedy of Saudi Arabia's War," *New York Times*, October 29, 2018.

77. Stephen Harmon, "From GSPC to AQIM: The Evolution of an Algerian Islamist Terrorist Group Into an Al-Qa'ida Affiliate and Its Implications for the Sahara-Sahel Region," in *US Militarization of the Sahara-Sahel Region*, vol. 85, ed. Jacob Mundy (East Lansing, MI: Association of Concerned African Scholars, 2010), 17, 20. As GSPC renamed itself AQIM in 2007, in the midst of the war on terror, I refer to the group as GSPC/AQIM in this chapter to avoid any potential confusion from switching between acronyms.

78. Elias Yousif and Nani Detti, "Factsheet: U.S. Security Assistance in the Sahel," Security Assistance Monitor, April 2021, https://securityassistance.org/publications/factsheet-u -s-security-assistance-in-the-sahel/.

79. Rene Caillie, *Travels Through Central Africa to Timbuctoo, Volume One* (London: Henry Colburn and Richard Bentley, 1830), 65.

80. Patrick Manning, *Francophone Sub-Saharan Africa, 1880–1995* (Cambridge: Cambridge University Press, 1988), 67–71.

81. Charles Grumont, "Villages and Crossroads: Changing Territorialities Among the Tuareg of Northern Mali," in *Saharan Frontiers: Space and Mobility in Northwest Africa*, ed. James McDougall and Judith Scheele (Bloomington: Indian University Press, 2012), 135–136.

82. Landor, *Across Widest Africa*, 319.

83. Lord Rennell of Rodd, *People of the Veil*, 361; Johannes Nicolaisen and Ida Nicolaisen, *The Pastoral Tuareg: Ecology, Culture and Society* (New York: Thames and Hudson, 1997), 289; Jeremy Keenan, *The Lesser Gods of the Sahara: Social Change and Indigenous Rights* (London: Frank Cass, 2004), 22–57.

84. Baz Lecocq and Georg Klute, "Tuareg Separatism in Mali," *International Journal* 68, no. 3 (2013): 425; Leela Jacinto, "Will Romanticising the Tuareg Threaten Peace in Mali?," *France 24*, May 2, 2013, https://www.france24.com/en/20130205-mali-france -tuareg-romanticising-mnla-islamist-war-peace.

85. Delphine Perrin, "Tuaregs and Citizenship: The Last Camp of Nomadism," *Middle East Law and Governance* 6 (2014): 303.

86. Thurston Clarke, *The Last Caravan* (New York: G. P. Putnam's Sons, 1978); Charles G. Thomas and Toyin Falola, *Secession and Separatist Conflicts in Postcolonial Africa* (Calgary, AB: University of Calgary Press, 2020), 231–262.

87. Tor A. Benjaminsen, "Does Supply-Induced Scarcity Drive Violent Conflicts in the African Sahel? The Case of the Tuareg Rebellion in Northern Mali," *Journal of Peace Research* 45, no. 6 (2008): 828.

88. *Disaster Relief*, Hearing Before the Committee on Foreign Relations, U.S. Senate, 93rd Congress, March 29, 1974 (Washington, DC: U.S. Government Printing Office, 1974), 72.

89. Perrin, "Tuaregs and Citizenship: The Last Camp of Nomadism," 299–300.

90. Baz Lecocq, *Disputed Desert: Decolonisation, Competing Nationalisms and Tuareg Rebellions in Northern Mali* (Leiden: Brill, 2010).

91. Jean Sebastian Lecocq, *That Desert Is Our Country: Tuareg Rebellions and Competing Nationalisms in Contemporary Mali (1946–1996)* (Amsterdam: Amsterdam University Press, 2002), 132–133.

92. Stephanie Pezard and Michael Shurkin, *Achieving Peace in Northern Mali: Past Agreements, Local Conflicts, and the Prospects for a Durable Settlement* (Santa Monica, CA: RAND Corporation, 2015), 19.

93. Tankel, *With Us and Against Us*, 248.

94. "Mali Still Reluctant to Sign Article 98 Agreement," Diplomatic Cable, U.S. Department of State, June 5, 2003, C18633636, State Department Reading Room.

95. "Pan Sahel Initiative," Press Statement, Office of Counterterrorism, U.S. Department of State, November 7, 2002, https://2001-2009.state.gov/s/ct/rls/other/14987.htm.

96. "Ambassador Perry and PSI Team Visit Malian State Security," Diplomatic Cable, U.S. Department of State, October 30, 2002, C18633583, State Department Reading Room.

97. "Mali Still Reluctant to Sign Article 98 Agreement."

98. "Mali Still Reluctant to Sign Article 98 Agreement."

99. "General Wald Meets Minister of Foreign Affairs Lassana Traore," Diplomatic Cable, U.S. Department of State, June 5, 2003, C18633637, State Department Reading Room.

100. "Ambassador Perry and PSI Team Visit Malian State Security."

101. "Ambassador Meets Minister of Defense on Article 98," Diplomatic Cable, U.S. Department of State, March 24, 2003, C18633622, State Department Reading Room.

102. "Meeting with President Toure and the Situation in Mali's North," Diplomatic Cable, U.S. Department of State, April 22, 2004, C18633767, State Department Reading Room; "Views on Security in Mali's North," Diplomatic Cable, U.S. Department of State, April 24, 2004, C18633766, State Department Reading Room.

103. *2005 Country Reports on Terrorism*.

104. Joshua Hammer, *The Bad-Ass Librarians of Timbuktu: And Their Race to Save the World's Most Precious Manuscripts* (New York: Simon and Schuster, 2016), 111.

105. Hammer, *The Bad-Ass Librarians of Timbuktu*, 107.

106. *Examining U.S. Counterterrorism Priorities and Strategy Across Africa's Sahel Region*, Hearing Before the Subcommittee on African Affairs, Committee on Foreign Relations, U.S. Senate, 111th Congress, November 17, 2009.

107. *2009 Country Reports on Terrorism*, Office of the Coordinator for Counterterrorism, U.S. Department of State, https://www.state.gov/j/ct/rls/crt/index.htm.

108. "Mali: More U.S. Military Aid," *New York Times*, October 20, 2009.

109. "U.S. Overseas Loans and Grants (Greenbook)," USAID, last updated May 20, 2022, https://data.usaid.gov/Administration-and-Oversight/U-S-Overseas-Loans-and-Grants-Greenbook-Data/7cnw-pw8v.

110. *Mali: Avoiding Escalation*, Africa Report No. 189, International Crisis Group, 2012, 7.

111. Alexis Arieff and Kelly Johnson, *Crisis in Mali*, Report for Congress, Congressional Research Service, August 16, 2012.

112. *Mali: Avoiding Escalation*, 26.
113. "Tuaregs Claim 'Independence from Mali,'" Al Jazeera English, April 6, 2012, https://www.aljazeera.com/news/2012/4/6/tuaregs-claim-independence-from-mali.
114. *The Tuareg Revolt and the Mali Coup*, Hearing Before the Subcommittee on Africa, Global Health, and Human Rights, Committee on Foreign Affairs, U.S. House of Representatives, 112th Congress, June 29, 2012.
115. *Mali: Avoiding Escalation*, 18.
116. "New Mali Leader Dioncounda Traore Warns Rebels of War," BBC News, April 12, 2012, https://www.bbc.com/news/world-africa-17686468.
117. Secretary of State Hillary Clinton, Remarks at a UN Secretary General Meeting on the Sahel, U.S. State Department, September 26, 2012, https://2009-2017.state.gov/secretary/20092013clinton/rm/2012/09/198233.htm.
118. "Al-Qaida-linked Islamists Seize North Mali Towns," Associated Press, June 29, 2012, http://archive.boston.com/news/world/africa/articles/2012/06/29/al_qaida_linked_islamists_seize_north_mali_towns/.
119. Skretting, "Al-Qaida in the Islamic Maghrib's Expansion in the Sahara," 12, 16–17.
120. Pascale Combelles Siegel, "AQIM's Playbook in Mali," *CTC Sentinel* 6, no. 3 (2013): 9–11.
121. Rukmini Callimachi, "Report: Al-Qaeda Manifesto Found in Mali," Associated Press, February 14, 2013, https://www.usatoday.com/story/news/nation/2013/02/14/in-timbuktu-al-qaida-left-behind-a-manifesto/1919831/; Mark Doyle, "Mali Islamists Warned About Sharia in al-Qaeda 'Manifesto,'" BBC News, February 26, 2013, https://www.bbc.com/news/world-africa-21587055; Siegel, "AQIM's Playbook in Mali."
122. Mathieu Guidere, "The Timbuktu Letters: New Insights About AQIM," *Res Militaris* 4, no. 1 (2014): 8.
123. Guidere, "The Timbuktu Letters," 11.
124. "Profile: Mokhtar Belmokhtar," BBC News, June 15, 2015, https://www.bbc.com/news/world-africa-21061480.
125. Hammer, *The Bad-Ass Librarians of Timbuktu*, 191.
126. Afua Hirsch, "Mali's Army Suspected of Abuses and Unlawful Killings as War Rages," *The Guardian* (UK), January 19, 2013.
127. Sudarsan Raghavan and Edward Cody, "French Troops Face Complicated Military Landscape in Mali," *Washington Post*, January 24, 2013.
128. Hirsch, "Mali's Army Suspected of Abuses and Unlawful Killings as War Rages."
129. Eric Schmitt, "American Commander Details Al Qaeda's Strength in Mali," *New York Times*, December 3, 2012.
130. Schmitt, "American Commander Details Al Qaeda's Strength in Mali."
131. Hammer, *The Bad-Ass Librarians of Timbuktu*, 188.
132. "France to Increase Troops in Mali Invasion," Al Jazeera English, January 15, 2013, https://www.aljazeera.com/news/2013/1/15/france-to-increase-troops-in-mali-invasion.
133. "French Special Forces 'to Protect' Niger Uranium Mines," *France 24*, January 25, 2013, https://www.france24.com/en/20130125-france-niger-uranium-areva-special-forces-mali-security-special-forces.

134. Alpha Mahamane Cisse, "Cohabitation entre les Fama et alliées dans le nord: Le malaise se confirme," Maliweb.net, April 14, 2014, https://www.maliweb.net/armee/cohabitation-les-fama-alliees-nord-malaise-se-confirme-250652.html.

135. William Nomikos, "How UN Peacebuilding Unintentionally Incentivizes Local-Level Violence," SSRN, last modified May 19, 2018, https://papers.ssrn.com/sol3/papers.cfm?abstract_id=3165775.

136. "Islamists 'Disqualified' from Talks, Mali's President Says," France 24, January 31, 2013, https://www.france24.com/en/20130131-mali-president-traore-rejects-talks-islamist-ansar-dine.

137. Kevin Sieff, "The World's Most Dangerous U.N. Mission," Washington Post, February 17, 2017.

138. Patterns of Global Terrorism, Office of the Coordinator for Counterterrorism, U.S. Department of State, 2002, https://2009-2017.state.gov/j/ct/rls/crt/2002/pdf/index.htm.

139. G. W. Murray, Sons of Ishmael: A Study of the Egyptian Bedouin (London: George Routledge and Sons, 1935), 200.

140. Clinton Bailey, Bedouin Law from Sinai and the Negev: Justice Without Government (New Haven, CT: Yale University Press, 2009), 17–18.

141. Bailey, Bedouin Law from Sinai and the Negev, 12.

142. Clinton Bailey, Bedouin Poetry from Sinai and Negev (Oxford: Clarendon Press, 1991), 344.

143. Martin Ira Glassner, "The Bedouin of Southern Sinai Under Israeli Administration," Geographical Review 64, no. 1 (1974): 37.

144. Hugh John Beadnell, The Wilderness of Sinai: A Record of Two Years' Recent Exploration (London: Edward Arnold and Co., 1927), 9.

145. Dan Rabinowitz, "Themes in the Economy of the Bedouin of South Sinai in the 19th and 20th Centuries," International Journal of Middle East Studies 17, no. 2 (1985): 211–228.

146. Mala Tabory, The Multinational Force and Observers in the Sinai: Organization, Structure, and Function (Boulder, CO: Westview Press, 1986).

147. John R. Bradley, Inside Egypt: The Land of the Pharaohs on the Brink of Revolution (New York: Palgrave Macmillan, 2008); "Egyptian Bedouins Claim Government Denying 75,000 Citizenship," Daily News Egypt (Giza), May 23, 2007.

148. Human Rights Watch, "Look for Another Homeland": Forced Evictions in Egypt's Rafah, September 22, 2015, https://www.hrw.org/report/2015/09/22/look-another-homeland/forced-evictions-egypts-rafah#.

149. Evrim Gormus, "Bedouins and In-Between Border Space in the Northern Sinai," Mediterranean Politics 25, no. 3 (2020): 289–309; Amr Yossef, "Securing the Sinai: More Troops Won't Keep the Peace or Save the Egyptian-Israeli Relationship," Foreign Affairs, September 28, 2011, https://www.foreignaffairs.com/articles/middle-east/2011-09-28/securing-sinai.

150. Adel Rady, Tourism and Sustainable Development in Egypt (Cairo: Tourism Development Authority, 2002), 15.

151. *South Sinai Environmental Action Plan*, SEAM Programme, Egyptian Environmental Affairs Agency, 2004, https://www.eeaa.gov.eg/portals/0/eeaaReports/seam/e1_5.pdf.

152. James Melik, "Sinai Bedouin 'Left Out of Region's Economic Development,'" BBC News, November 12, 2012, https://www.bbc.co.uk/news/business-19267223.

153. Heba Aziz, "Employment in a Bedouin Community: The Case of the Town of Dahab in South Sinai," *Nomadic Peoples* 4, no. 2 (2000): 28–47; Hilary Gilbert, "'This Is Not Our Life, It's Just a Copy of Other People's: Bedu and the Price of 'Development' in South Sinai," *Nomadic Peoples* 15, no. 2 (2011): 7–32; Ismail Alexandrani, "Sufi Jihad and Salafi Jihadism in Egypt's Sinai: Tribal Generational Conflict," in Collombier and Roy, eds., *Tribes and Global Jihadism*, 102–103.

154. Matt Bradley, "Egypt Plans to Build Villages for Sinai Bedouins," *The National* (UAE), November 5, 2010.

155. Joshua R. Goodman, *Contesting Identities in South Sinai: Development, Transformation, and the Articulation of a "Bedouin" Identity Under Egyptian Rule* (Tel Aviv: The Moshe Dayan Center for Middle Eastern and African Studies, 2013), 21.

156. *Egypt's Sinai Question*, Middle East/North Africa Report No. 61, International Crisis Group, January 30, 2007, 22.

157. "Relaunching the Propaganda War," *The Economist*, November 8, 2001.

158. *2006 Country Report on Terrorism*, U.S. Department of State.

159. "Death Toll Rises in Egypt Blasts," BBC News, October 9, 2004, http://news.bbc.co.uk/2/hi/middle_east/3728436.stm.

160. Human Rights Watch, *Egypt: Mass Arrests and Torture in Sinai*, February 2005, 10, https://www.hrw.org/sites/default/files/reports/egypt0205.pdf.

161. Amr Nabil, "Al-Qaeda Suspected in Attacks at Resorts in Egypt," Associated Press, October 9, 2004, https://products.kitsapsun.com/archive/2004/10-09/11996_al-qaida_suspected_in_suicide_at.html.

162. Human Rights Watch, *Egypt: Mass Arrests and Torture in Sinai*, 13.

163. Human Rights Watch, 10.

164. "Egyptian Forces Slay Suspect in Sinai Bombings During Mountain Shootout," *New York Times*, February 2, 2005; "Three Face Trial for Taba Blasts," Al Jazeera English, March 30, 2005, https://www.aljazeera.com/news/2005/3/30/three-face-trial-for-taba-blasts.

165. "Toll Climbs in Egyptian Attacks," BBC News, July 23, 2005, http://news.bbc.co.uk/2/hi/middle_east/4709491.stm.

166. *2005 Country Reports on Terrorism*, U.S. Department of State.

167. *2006 Country Reports on Terrorism*, U.S. Department of State.

168. *2006 Country Reports on Terrorism*, U.S. Department of State.

169. "Sinai Crisis: A Timeline of Key Events Since 2007," *Middle East Eye*, February 13, 2015, https://www.middleeasteye.net/news/sinai-crisis-timeline-key-events-2007.

170. Steven A. Cook, "The Eagle Has Landed . . . In Sinai?," Council on Foreign Relations, August 17, 2011, https://www.cfr.org/blog/eagle-has-landedin-sinai.

171. Alexandrani, "Sufi Jihad and Salafi Jihadism in Egypt's Sinai," 102–104; Asher Zeiger, "Single Terror Group Responsible for Most Attacks in Sinai, Intelligence Sources Say,"

*Times of Israel*, October 3, 2012, https://www.timesofisrael.com/one-terror-network
-responsible-for-most-attacks-in-south-intelligence-sources/.

172.   "Ansar Beit al-Maqdis Targets Egypt's Security," Al Jazeera English, January 27, 2014,
https://www.aljazeera.com/news/2014/1/28/ansar-beit-al-maqdis-targets-egypts
-security; Anup Kaphle, "Timeline: Attacks by Ansar Bayt al-Maqdis," *Washington
Post*, January 28, 2014.

173.   Mohamed Fadel Fahmy, "Officials: Egypt to Target al Qaeda Cells Said to Be Training
in Sinai," CNN, August 12, 2011, http://www.cnn.com/2011/WORLD/africa/08/12/egypt
.al.qaeda.operation/index.html.

174.   Joshua Goodman, "Egypt's Assault on Sinai," *Carnegie Endowment for International
Peace*, June 5, 2014.

175.   Ahmed Eleiba, "In Sinai Everything Is Possible: Egyptian Army's Operation Eagle Is
Open-Ended," *Ahram Online* (Egypt), August 26, 2011, https://english.ahram.org.eg
/News/19747.aspx.

176.   Harriet Sherwood, "Israel Launches Gaza Air Strikes in Retaliation for Eilat Attacks,"
*The Guardian* (UK), August 18, 2011.

177.   Maayan Lubell, "Israel to OK Thousands of Egyptian Troops in Sinai: Report," Reuters,
August 26, 2011, https://www.reuters.com/article/us-israel-egypt-barak/israel-to-ok
-thousands-of-egyptian-troops-in-sinai-report-idUSTRE77P1SI20110826.

178.   Fahmy, "Officials: Egypt to Target al Qaeda Cells Said to Be Training in Sinai."

179.   Mohamed Fadel Fahmy, "Egyptian Forces Kill 11 Militants in Sinai," CNN, August 29,
2011, https://www.cnn.com/2012/08/29/world/meast/egypt-sinai-operation/index.html.

180.   Mohannad Sabry, "Egyptian Government Crackdown Produces More Militants in
Sinai," *Al-Monitor* (Washington, DC), September 6, 2013, https://www.al-monitor
.com/originals/2013/09/sinai-salafists-persecution-increase-militants.html.

181.   Ahmed Eleiba, "Egypt's 'Operation Eagle' Sinai Campaign Draws Mixed Reviews," *Ahram
Online* (Egypt), September 4, 2012, https://english.ahram.org.eg/News/52021.aspx.

182.   Tankel, *With Us and Against Us*, 279.

183.   Tankel, 280.

184.   "Two Memos, Morsi's Moves," Confidential Memos for the Secretary of State, U.S.
Department of State, August 14, 2012, State Department Reading Room.

185.   "The Root of Egypt's Coup: Morsi Giving Free Hand to Sinai Islamists," Associated
Press, July 18, 2013, https://www.haaretz.com/2013-07-18/ty-article/root-of-egypt-coup
-morsi-favoring-sinai-islamists/0000017f-e199-d7b2-a77f-e39f56cf0000.

186.   *2013 Country Reports on Terrorism*, U.S. Department of State.

187.   Tankel, *With Us and Against Us*, 282.

188.   "Egypt Army Launches Offensive Against Sinai Militants," BBC News, September 7,
2013, https://www.bbc.com/news/world-middle-east-24001833.

189.   "Egypt Army Launches Large-Scale Sinai Operation," Ma'an News Agency (Palestinian Territories), September 7, 2013.

190.   David Barnett, "Ansar Jerusalem Claims Credit for Sinai Attacks, Challenges Army
Claims," *Long War Journal*, September 11, 2013, https://www.longwarjournal.org/arch
ives/2013/09/ansar_jerusalem_claims_credit.php.

191.  David Barnett, "Ansar Jerusalem Claims Tourist Bus Bombing in Egypt's Sinai," *Long War Journal*, February 17, 2014, https://www.longwarjournal.org/archives/2014/02/ansar_jerusalem_clai_8.php.

192.  David Barnett, "Jihadist media Unit Urges Fighters to Strike Egyptian Army," *Long War Journal*, September 23, 2013.

193.  Mokhtar Awad and Samuel Tadros, "Bay'a Remorse? Wilayat Sinai and the Nile Valley," *CTC Sentinel* 8, no. 8 (2015): 3.

194.  Nancy A. Youssef and Amina Ismail, "In Egypt's Sinai, Military's Harsh Campaign Earns Pledges of Retaliation," *McClatchy*, October 8, 2013, https://www.adn.com/nation-world/article/egypt-s-sinai-military-s-harsh-campaign-earns-pledges-retaliation/2013/10/08/.

195.  Youssef and Ismail, "In Egypt's Sinai, Military's Harsh Campaign Earns Pledges of Retaliation."

196.  Sabry, "Egyptian Government Crackdown Produces More Militants in Sinai."

197.  David Barnett, "Ansar Jerusalem Claims Responsibility for Car Bombing in Ismailia," *Long War Journal*, October 21, 2013, https://www.longwarjournal.org/archives/2013/10/ansar_jerusale_claim.php.

198.  *2013 Country Reports on Terrorism*, U.S. Department of State.

199.  "Terrorist Designation of Ansar Bayt al-Maqdis," Bureau of Counterterrorism, U.S. Department of State, April 9, 2014, https://2009-2017.state.gov/r/pa/prs/ps/2014/04/224566.htm.

200.  "U.S. Assistance to Egypt," Office of the Spokesperson, U.S. Department of State, October 9, 2013, https://2009-2017.state.gov/r/pa/prs/ps/2013/10/215258.htm.

201.  Agence France-Presse, "Egypt Declares State of Emergency in Sinai After Checkpoint Bombing," *The Guardian* (UK), October 24, 2014.

202.  "US Delivers 10 Apache Helicopters to Egypt," Agence France-Presse, December 21, 2014, https://www.defensenews.com/air/2014/12/21/us-delivers-10-apache-helicopters-to-egypt/.

203.  Tamer El-Ghobashy, "Egypt's Leader Reinvents Himself as Bulwark Against Terrorism," *Wall Street Journal*, May 18, 2015; "Commander of U.S. Air Forces Central Command Visits Egypt," Press Release, U.S. Embassy in Egypt, September 2, 2015, https://eg.usembassy.gov/commander-u-s-air-forces-central-command-visits-egypt/.

204.  Dong-Yoon Lee, "Politics of Anti-terrorism Policy in Southeast Asia: A Comparative Study of the Philippines and Indonesia," *Pacific Focus* 24, no. 2 (2009): 247–269.

205.  Larry Niksch, *Abu Sayyaf: Target of Philippine-U.S. Anti-Terrorism Cooperation*, Report for Congress, Congressional Research Service, January 24, 2007, 4.

206.  *U.S. Government Efforts to Counter Violent Extremism*, Hearing Before the Senate Committee on Armed Services, 111th Congress, March 10, 2010.

207.  Peter Pace, Memorandum for the Record: Interview, Team 3, 9/11 Commission, January 16, 2004, 9/11 Commission, National Archives.

208.  Rommel C. Banlaoi, "The Abu Sayyaf Group: Threat of Maritime Piracy and Terrorism," in *Violence at Sea: Piracy in the Age of Global Terrorism*, ed. Peter Lehr (Abingdon, UK: Routledge, 2007), 121.

209.  James D. Fearon, "Counterfactuals and Hypothesis Testing in Political Science," *World Politics* 43, no. 2 (1991): 169–195.

210.  Bob Jordan, Memorandum for the Record: Interview, Teams 4 and 1, 9/11 Commission, January 15, 2004, 9/11 Commission Papers, National Archives.

211.  Jordan, Memorandum for the Record.

212.  Scahill, *Dirty Wars*, 130.

213.  *Progress Report on the Global War on Terrorism*, 3.

214.  *2009 Country Reports on Terrorism*, U.S. Department of State.

215.  Albert A. Thibault, Memorandum for the Record: Interview, Team 5, 9/11 Commission, November 5, 2003, 9/11 Commission Papers, National Archives.

216.  Ali S. Awadh Asseri, *Combating Terrorism: Saudi Arabia's Role in the War on Terror* (New York: Oxford University Press, 2010); Tankel, *With Us and Against Us*, 189.

217.  Kevin Sullivan, "A Rare Look Inside a Saudi Prison that Showers Terrorists with Perks," *Washington Post*, March 1, 2015.

218.  Ahmed, *The Thistle and the Drone*, 109–122; Toby Craig Jones, "Rebellion on the Saudi Periphery: Modernity, Marginalization, and the Shia Uprising of 1979," *International Journal of Middle East Studies* 38, no. 2 (2006): 213–233.

219.  Thomas Hegghammer, *The Failure of Jihad in Saudi Arabia*, Occasional Paper Series, Combating Terrorism Center at West Point, February 25, 2010.

## CONCLUSION

1.  Lee Hamilton and Tom Kean, "9/11 Commission Leaders: Turning the Tide on Extremism in fragile states," *The Hill*, December 4, 2018.

2.  *Worldwide Threat Assessment of the US Intelligence Community*, Office of the Director of National Intelligence, January 29, 2019, https://www.odni.gov/files/ODNI/documents/2019-ATA-SFR---SSCI.pdf.

3.  Jeff Seldin, "US Warns Al-Qaida 'as Strong as It Has Ever Been,' " Voice of America, August 1, 2019, https://www.voanews.com/a/usa_us-warns-al-qaida-strong-it-has-ever-been/6173074.html.

4.  "Biden's Speech to Congress: Full Transcript," *New York Times*, April 29, 2021.

5.  Anne Gearan, "Biden, Pulling Combat Forces from Iraq, Seeks to End the Post-9/11 Era," *Washington Post*, July 26, 2021; *Hearing to Receive Testimony on the Conclusion of Military Operations in Afghanistan and Plans for Future Counterterrorism Operations*, Senate Armed Services Committee, September 28, 2021, https://www.armed-services.senate.gov/imo/media/doc/21-73_09-28-2021.pdf.

6.  Kilcullen, *Blood Year*, 12, 208–209.

7.  Kilcullen, 211.

8.  Stephen Tankel, "Universal Soldiers or Parochial Actors: Understanding Jihadists as Products of Their Environments," *Terrorism and Political Violence* 31, no. 2 (2019): 299–322.

9. Ahmed, *The Thistle and the Drone*; Max Abrahms, "Why Democracies Make Superior Counterterrorists," *Security Studies* 16, no. 2 (2007): 223–253; Deniz Aksoy, David B. Carter, and Joseph Wright, "Terrorism in Dictatorships," *Journal of Politics* 74, no. 3 (2012): 810–826; Jean-Paul Azam and Veronique Thelen, "Foreign Aid Versus Military Intervention in the War on Terror," *Journal of Conflict Resolution* 54, no. 2 (2010): 237–261; Sarah Brockhoff, Tim Krieger, and Daniel Meierrieks, "Great Expectations and Hard Times: The (Nontrivial) Impact of Education on Domestic Terrorism," *Journal of Conflict Resolution* 59, no. 7 (2015): 1186–1215; Brian Burgoon, "On Welfare and Terror: Social Welfare Policies and Political-Economic Roots of Terrorism," *Journal of Conflict Resolution* 50, no. 2 (2006): 176–203; Seung-Whan Choi, "Fighting Terrorism Through the Rule of Law?," *Journal of Conflict Resolution* 54, no. 6 (2010): 940–966; Orlandrew E. Danzell, Yao-Yuan Yeh, Melia Pfannenstiel, "Does Education Mitigate Terrorism? Examining the Effects of Educated Youth Cohorts on Domestic Terror in Africa," *Terrorism and Political Violence* 32, no. 8 (2020): 1731–1752; Findley and Young, "Terrorism, Democracy, and Credible Commitments"; Walsh and Piazza, "Why Respecting Physical Integrity Rights Reduces Terrorism."

10. *Al Qaeda in Yemen and Somalia: A Ticking Time Bomb*, Report to the Committee on Foreign Relations, U.S. Senate, 111th Congress, S. Prt. 111–40, January 21, 2010, 17.

11. "Factsheet: A Comprehensive U.S. Government Approach to Countering Violent Extremism," U.S. Department of Homeland Security, accessed October 4, 2022, https://www.dhs.gov/sites/default/files/publications/US%20Government%20Approach%20to%20CVE-Fact%20Sheet_0.pdf.

12. Admiral Michael Mullen, Chairman of the Joint Chiefs of Staff, Remarks at the Kansas State University Landon Lecture Series, Kansas State University, March 3, 2010, https://www.k-state.edu/landon/speakers/michael-mullen/transcript.html.

13. Author interview with General Stanley McChrystal.

14. Seth G. Jones and Martin G. Libicki, *How Terrorist Groups End: Lessons for Countering al Qa'ida* (Santa Monica, CA: RAND Corporation, 2008).

15. Author interview with Ambassador Akbar Ahmed.

16. Ahmed, *The Thistle and the Drone*, 349.

17. Liam Anderson, "Ethnofederalism: The Worst Form of Institutional Arrangement . . .?," *International Security* 39, no. 1 (2014): 165–204; Lars-Erik Cederman et al., "Territorial Autonomy in the Shadow of Conflict: Too Little, Too Late?," *American Political Science Review* 109, no. 2 (2015): 354–370; Horowitz, *Ethnic Groups in Conflict*, 601–628; Ian S. Lustick, Dan Miodownik, and Roy J. Eidelson, "Secessionism in Multicultural States: Does Sharing Power Prevent or Encourage It?," *American Political Science Review* 98, no. 2 (2004): 209–229; David S. Siroky and John Cuffe, "Lost Autonomy, Nationalism and Separatism," *Comparative Political Studies* 48, no. 1 (2014): 3–34. The effects of decentralization on conflict, however, are debated. Other scholars have noted that decentralization of political power, rather than resolving the sources of conflict, can indirectly foster ethnic conflict and separatism by strengthening local ethnic or regional identities, creating a mobilized power base for political

leaders to pursue secessionist policies or engage in ethnic conflict, while others highlight the conditional effects of a state's ethnic makeup or variations in the periphery's economic reliance on the state. See, for instance, Kristin M. Bakke and Erik Wibbels, "Diversity, Disparity, and Civil Conflict in Federal States," *World Politics* 59, no. 1 (2006): 1–50; Dawn Brancati, "Decentralization: Fueling the Fire or Dampening the Flames of Ethnic Conflict and Secessionism," *International Organization* 60 (2006): 651–685; Thomas Christin and Simon Hug, "Federalism, the Geographic Location of Groups, and Conflict," *Conflict Management and Peace Science* 29, no. 1 (2012): 93–122; David S. Siroky et al., "Containing Nationalism: Culture, Economics and Indirect Rule in Corsica," *Comparative Political Studies* 54, no. 6 (2021): 1023–1057.

18.  Jori Breslawski, "Keeping Armed Actors Out: The Protective Effect of Shuras in Afghanistan," *Journal of Global Security Studies* 6, no. 1 (2021): 1–8; Suzanne Levi-Sanchez, "Civil Society in an Uncivil State: Informal Organizations in Tajik/Afghan Badakhshan," *Journal of International Affairs* 71, no. 2 (2018): 50–72.

19.  Jean-Paul Faguet, Ashley M. Fox, and Caroline Poschl, "Decentralizing for a Deeper, More Supple Democracy," *Journal of Democracy* 26, no. 4 (2015): 60–74; Roger Myerson, "Constitutional Structures for a Strong Democracy: Considerations on the Government of Pakistan," *World Development, Decentralization and Governance* 53 (2014): 46–54.

20.  For instance, see Eliot A. Cohen, *The Big Stick: The Limits of Soft Power and the Necessity of Military Force* (New York: Basic Books, 2016).

21.  Peter Bergen, *United States of Jihad: Investigating America's Homegrown Terrorists* (New York: Crown Publishers, 2016); Lehrke and Schomaker, "Kill, Capture, or Defend?," 761; Greg Miller, "Cheney Assertion of Lives Saved Hard to Support," *Los Angeles Times*, May 23, 2009.

22.  John Mueller and Mark G. Stewart, "Terrorism and Bathtubs: Comparing and Assessing the Risks," *Terrorism and Political Violence* 33, no. 1 (2021): 140.

23.  Audrey Kurth Cronin, "The 'War on Terrorism': What Does It Mean to Win?," *Journal of Strategic Studies* 37, no. 2 (2014): 174–197; Audrey Kurth Cronin, "U.S. Grand Strategy and Counterterrorism," *Orbis* 56, no. 2 (2012): 192–214; McIntosh, "Counterterrorism as War"; Donald Rumsfeld, "Global War on Terrorism," Memo to Gen. Dick Myers, Paul Wolfowitz, Gen. Pete Pace, and Doug Feith, October 16, 2003, National Security Archive.

24.  Schmitt and Shanker, *Counterstrike*, 160.

25.  Author interview with Douglas Feith.

26.  William Easterly, *The White Man's Burden: Why the West's Efforts to Aid the Rest Have Done So Much Ill and So Little Good* (New York: Penguin, 2006), 6, 383.

27.  Elinor Ostrom, "A Diagnostic Approach for Going Beyond Panaceas," *Proceedings of the National Academy of Sciences* 104, no. 39 (2007): 15181–15187.

28.  "Limit on the Expansion of the Authorization for Use of Military Force Act," H.R. 7500, 116th Congress, July 9, 2020, https://www.congress.gov/bill/116th-congress/house-bill/7500/all-actions?s=1&r=73&overview=closed.

29. Akins, "The 2001 Authorization for the Use of Military Force and America's Endless War," 18.

30. Stephen M. Walt, "Lessons of Two Wars: We Will Lose in Iraq and Afghanistan," *Foreign Policy*, August 16, 2011, https://foreignpolicy.com/2011/08/16/lessons-of-two-wars-we-will-lose-in-iraq-and-afghanistan/.

31. Aaron Y. Zelin, *Your Sons Are at Your Service: Tunisia's Missionaries of Jihad* (New York: Columbia University Press, 2020), 220.

32. Matthias Basedau, Birte Pfeiffer, and Johannes Vullers, "Bad Religion? Religion, Collective Action, and the Onset of Armed Conflict in Developing Countries," *Journal of Conflict Resolution* 60, no. 2 (2016): 226–255; Jori Breslawski and Brandon Ives, "Killing for God? Factional Violence on the Transnational Stage," *Journal of Conflict Resolution* 63, no. 3 (2019): 617–643; Matthew Isaacs, "Faith in Contention: Explaining the Salience of Religion in Ethnic Conflict," *Comparative Political Studies* 50, no. 2 (2017): 200–231; Nil S. Satana, Molly Inman, and Johanna Kristin Birnir, "Religion, Government Coalitions, and Terrorism," *Terrorism and Political Violence* 25, no. 1 (2012): 29–52; Davis S. Siroky et al., "Purifying the Religion: An Analysis of *Haram* Targeting Among Salafi Jihadi Groups," *Comparative Politics* 54, no. 3 (2022): 525–546; Monica D. Toft, "The Politics of Religious Outbidding," *Review of Faith and International Affairs* 11, no. 3 (2013): 10–19; Efe Tokdemir et al., "Rebel Rivalry and the Strategic Nature of Rebel Group Ideology and Demands," *Journal of Conflict Resolution* 65, no. 4 (2021): 729–758.

33. Charles Kurzman, *The Missing Martyrs: Why There Are So Few Muslim Terrorists* (New York: Oxford University Press, 2011).

34. Thomas Hegghammer, "The Last Jihadi Superstar," War on the Rocks, October 30, 2020, https://warontherocks.com/2020/10/the-last-jihadi-superstar/.

35. Scahill, *Dirty Wars*, 241.

36. Clark McCauley and Sophia Moskalenko, *Friction: How Conflict Radicalizes Them and Us* (New York: Oxford University Press, 2017), 280.

37. Jonathan Leader Maynard, "Ideology and Armed Conflict," *Journal of Peace Research* 56, no. 5 (2019): 636.

38. Sarah E. Parkinson, "Practical Ideology in Militant Organizations," *World Politics* 73, no. 1 (2021): 9.

39. Bruce Hoffman, "The Changing Face of Al Qaeda and the Global War on Terrorism," *Studies in Conflict & Terrorism* 27, no. 6 (2004): 549–560; Assaf Moghadam, "Motives for Martyrdom: Al-Qaida, Salafi Jihad, and the Spread of Suicide Attacks," *International Security* 33, no. 3 (2009): 46–78; Mara Redlich Revkin and Elisabeth Jean Wood, "The Islamic State's Pattern of Sexual Violence: Ideology and Institutions, Policies and Practices," *Journal of Global Security Studies* 6, no. 2 (2021): 1–20; Mehwish Sarwari, "Impact of Rebel Group Ideology on Wartime Sexual Violence," *Journal of Global Security Studies* 6, no. 2 (2021): 1–23.

40. Peter S. Henne, "The Ancient Fire: Religion and Suicide Terrorism," *Terrorism and Political Violence* 24, no. 1 (2012): 38–60; James A. Piazza, "Is Islamist Terrorism More Dangerous? An Empirical Study of Group Ideology, Organization, and Goal Structure," *Terrorism and Political Violence* 21, no. 1 (2009): 62–88.

41. Mora Deitch, "Is Religion a Barrier to Peace? Religious Influence on Violent Intrastate Conflict Termination," *Terrorism and Political Violence* 34, no. 7 (2022): 1454–1470; Isak Svensson, "Fighting with Faith: Religion and Conflict Resolution in Civil Wars," *Journal of Conflict Resolution* 51, no. 6 (2017): 930–949.

42. Tankel, "Universal Soldiers or Parochial Actors," 315. For an example of the influence of a terrorist group's operational environment on its ideological shifts, see Mark Youngman, "Broader, Vaguer, Weaker: The Evolving Ideology of the Caucasus Emirate Leadership," *Terrorism and Political Violence* 31, no. 2 (2019): 367–389. For an example of how changes in the political and conflict environment impact the ideology and behavior of other nonstate actors, such as warlords, see Romain Malejacq, *Warlord Survival: The Delusion of State Building in Afghanistan* (Ithaca, NY: Cornell University Press, 2019).

43. Shakirullah, Nyborg, and Elahi, "The Underlying Causes of Violent Conflict in the North Waziristan Tribal Areas of Pakistan," 126.

44. Victoria Williamson et al., "The Relationship Between of Moral Injury and Radicalisation: A Systematic Review," *Studies in Conflict & Terrorism* 45, no. 11 (2022): 977–1003.

45. Stefano Costalli and Andrea Ruggeri, "Emotions, Ideologies, and Violent Political Mobilization," *PS: Political Science and Politics* 50, no. 4 (2017): 923–927; Daniel W. Snook et al., "Crisis as Catalyst: Crisis in Conversion to Islam Related to Radicalism Intentions," *Terrorism and Political Violence*, July 26, 2021, https://doi.org/10.1080/09546553.2021.1938003; Speckhard and Ahkmedova, "The Making of a Martyr," 467.

46. Jeppe Fuglsang Larsen, "The Role of Religion in Islamist Radicalisation Process," *Critical Studies on Terrorism* 13, no. 3 (2020): 396–417; Anselm Rink and Kunaal Sharma, "The Determinants of Religious Radicalization: Evidence from Kenya," *Journal of Conflict Resolution* 62, no. 6 (2018): 1229–1261; Matteo Vergani et al., "The Three Ps of Radicalization: Push, Pull and Personal. A Systematic Scoping Review of the Scientific Evidence About Radicalization Into Violent Extremism," *Studies in Conflict & Terrorism* 43, no. 10 (2020): 854–885.

47. C. Christine Fair, Neil Malhotra, and Jacob Shapiro, "Islam, Militancy, and Politics in Pakistan: Insights from a National Sample," *Terrorism and Political Violence* 22, no. 4 (2010): 495–521.

48. Ahmed, *The Thistle and the Drone*, 76–79; Rubin, *Afghanistan from the Cold War Through the War on Terror*, 52–72; Michael Weddegjerde Skjelderup, "Jihadi Governance and Traditional Authority Structures: Al-Shabaab and Clan Elders in Southern Somalia, 2008–2012," *Small Wars & Insurgencies* 31, no. 6 (2020): 1174–1195.

49. Ahmad, *Jihad & Co.*; Aisha Ahmad, "The Security Bazaar: Business Interests and Islamist Power in Civil War Somalia," *International Security* 39, no. 3 (2014/15): 89–117.

50. Ahmed and Hart, *Islam in Tribal Societies*.

51. Konstantin Ash, "'The War Will Come to Your Street': Explaining Geographic Variation in Terrorism by Rebel Groups," *International Interactions* 44, no. 3 (2018): 411–436; Hansen, Nemeth, and Mauslein, "Ethnic Political Exclusion and Terrorism"; Ore

Koren and Anoop K. Sarbahi, "State Capacity, Insurgency, and Civil War: A Disaggregated Analysis," *International Studies Quarterly* 62, no. 2 (2018): 274–288; Josiah Marineau et al., "The Local Geography of Transnational Terrorism," *Conflict Management and Peace Science* 37, no. 3 (2020): 350–381; Carl Muller-Crepon, Philipp Hunziker, and Lars-Erik Cederman, "Roads to Rule, Roads to Rebel: Relational State Capacity and Conflict in Africa," *Journal of Conflict Resolution* 65, nos. 2–3 (2021): 563–590; Andreas Foro Tollefsen, "Experienced Poverty and Local Conflict Violence," *Conflict Management and Peace Science* 37, no. 3 (2020): 323–349.

52. Author interview with Lawrence Wilkerson.

53. Simon Staffell and Akil Awan, eds., *Jihadism Transformed: Al-Qaeda and Islamic State's Global Battle of Ideas* (New York: Oxford University Press, 2016).

54. Barack Obama, "Statement by the President on ISIL," the White House, September 10, 2014, https://obamawhitehouse.archives.gov/the-press-office/2014/09/10/statement-president-isil-1.

55. "2015–2016 Bureau of Counterterrorism 'Partnership Concept': Southeast Asia Region," U.S. Department of State, 2015, State Department Reading Room; "2015–2016 Bureau of Counterterrorism 'Partnership Concept': South and Central Asia," U.S. Department of State, 2015, State Department Reading Room; "2015–2016 Bureau of Counterterrorism 'Partnership Concept': Sahel region of Africa," U.S. Department of State, 2015, State Department Reading Room; "2015–2016 Bureau of Counterterrorism 'Partnership Concept': North Africa," U.S. Department of State, 2015, State Department Reading Room; "2015–2016 Bureau of Counterterrorism 'Partnership Concept': Horn of Africa," U.S. Department of State, 2015, State Department Reading Room; "2015–2016 Bureau of Counterterrorism 'Partnership Concept': Arabian Peninsula," U.S. Department of State, 2015, State Department Reading Room.

56. Tim Lister et al., "ISIS Goes Global: 143 Attacks in 29 Countries Have Killed 2,043," CNN, February 12, 2018, https://www.cnn.com/2015/12/17/world/mapping-isis-attacks-around-the-world/index.html.

57. 2019 *Worldwide Threat Assessment*, 11.

58. Kilcullen, *Blood Year*, 123–124.

59. Lizzie Dearden, "Isis Calls on Supporters to Wage 'All-Out War' on West During Ramadan with New Terror Attacks," *The Independent* (UK), May 26, 2017.

60. Asad Hashim, "Exclusive: Pakistani Taliban Down but Not Out, Says Ex-spokesman," Al Jazeera English, April 3, 2020, https://www.aljazeera.com/news/2020/4/3/exclusive-pakistani-taliban-down-but-not-out-says-ex-spokesman.

61. "Foreign Terrorist Organizations," Bureau of Counterterrorism, U.S. Department of State, accessed November 8, 2020, http://state.gov/foreign-terrorist-organizations.

62. "Transcript: Russ Travers Talks with Michael Morell on 'Intelligence Matters,'" CBS News, July 3, 2019, https://www.cbsnews.com/news/transcript-russ-travers-talks-with-michael-morell-on-intelligence-matters/.

63. Alexander Thurston, *Boko Haram: The History of an African Jihadist Movement* (Princeton, NJ: Princeton University Press, 2018), 272.

64. Maruf and Joseph, *Inside Al-Shabaab*, 256–264.

65. Mohamed Olad Hassan, "Somalia's Al-Shabab Declares War on Pro-Islamic State Group," Voice of America, December 21, 2018, https://www.voanews.com/a/somalia-al-shabab-declares-war-on-pro-islamic-state-group/4711075.html.

66. Carmela Fonbuena, "Terror in Mindanao: The Mautes of Marawi," Rappler, June 26, 2017, https://www.rappler.com/newsbreak/in-depth/173697-terrorism-mindanao-maute-family-marawi-city/.

67. Jon Boone, "Isis Ascent in Syria and Iraq Weakening Pakistani Taliban," *The Guardian* (UK), October 22, 2014.

68. Tahir Khan, "Senior TTP Commander Daud Khan Switches Loyalty to Daesh," *Daily Times* (Pakistan), July 31, 2017; Zia Ur Rehman, "Fazlullah Announces New TTP Karachi Chief," *The News* (Pakistan), November 28, 2016.

69. Priyanka Boghani, "ISIS Is in Afghanistan, But Who Are They Really," *PBS Frontline*, November 17, 2015, https://www.pbs.org/wgbh/frontline/article/isis-is-in-afghanistan-but-who-are-they-really/.

70. Borhan Osman, *Bourgeois Jihad: Why Young, Middle-Class Afghans Join the Islamic State*, Report No. 162 (Washington, DC: U.S. Institute of Peace, June 2020), 3.

71. "Islamic State Group Claims Deadly Attack on Afghanistan Prison," BBC News, August 3, 2020, https://www.bbc.com/news/world-asia-53633450.

72. Miriam Berger and Haq Nawaz Khan, "Islamic State in Afghanistan Claims Responsibility for Attacks Targeting the Taliban," *Washington Post*, September 19, 2021; "Afghanistan: Surge in Islamic State Attacks on Shia," Human Rights Watch, October 25, 2021, https://www.hrw.org/news/2021/10/25/afghanistan-surge-islamic-state-attacks-shia.

73. Kirsten E. Schulze and Joseph Chinyong Liow, "Making Jihadis, Waging Jihad: Transnational and Local Dimensions of the ISIS Phenomenon in Indonesia and Malaysia," *Asian Security* 15, no. 2 (2019): 122–139.

74. Ahmed, *Journey into Europe*, 460–472; Tamar Mitts, "From Isolation to Radicalization: Anti-Muslim Hostility and Support for ISIS in the West," *American Political Science Review* 113, no. 1 (2019): 173–194.

75. *2016 Country Reports on Terrorism*, U.S. Department of State.

76. "Duterte Declares Martial Law After Mindanao Attack," Al Jazeera English, May 24, 2017, https://www.aljazeera.com/news/2017/5/24/duterte-declares-martial-law-after-mindanao-attack.

77. Amnesty International, *Philippines: "Battle of Marawi": Death and Destruction in the Philippines* (London: Amnesty International, 2017), https://www.amnesty.org/en/documents/asa35/7427/2017/en/.

78. Caroe, *The Pathans*, 412.

# APPENDIX

1. The number of observations for the models varied between 1,357 and 1,970. As this analysis is focused on understanding the impact of U.S. counterterrorism within

America's partner states, rather than the impact of U.S. security policies on the levels of domestic terrorism in the United States, the models do not include the United States as one of the 173 states, and they only include data on U.S. foreign policy within the data set such as counterterrorism policy abroad and U.S. foreign assistance.

2.  I use a national-level measure of terrorist attacks as domestic terrorism is not localized to the periphery. As is evident from the case studies in chapters 4 and 5, terrorist groups commit attacks against domestic targets not only in their home regions but in other parts of the country as well in response to the indiscriminate violence associated with military operations targeting terrorist groups in the periphery. See Emil Aslan Souleimanov and David S. Siroky, "Random or Retributive? Indiscriminate Violence in the Chechen Wars," *World Politics* 68, no. 4 (2016): 677–712.

3.  Enders, Sandler, and Gaibulloev, "Domestic Versus Transnational Terrorism."

4.  Gaibulloev, Piazza, and Sandler, "Regime Types and Terrorism."

5.  START, Global Terrorism Database. This database, regularly used in quantitative studies of terrorism, is based on open-source information.

6.  Enders, Sandler, and Gaibulloev, "Domestic Versus Transnational Terrorism," 323.

7.  Poisson and negative binomial regressions are also used to estimate models with event counts as the dependent variable. A Poisson regression assumes that the variance is equal to the mean and is not appropriate for data with over-dispersion, which is often the case with data on terrorism as some states experience very high levels of terrorist attacks while others only experience a handful of attacks or even none at all. The likelihood ratio test statistic confirmed the presence of over-dispersion within the data. A negative binomial regression is appropriate for data with wide variance but not for data with excess zeros. There are a number of states that have never experienced an incident of either domestic or international terrorism, with many states only experiencing them intermittently. This leads to an excess number of zeros in the data. Further, many of these states have a very low likelihood of ever experiencing terrorism given particular conditions, such as a very small population, geographic isolation, a strongly homogenous society, or lack of a strategic position in international politics. This creates a subcategory within the data of states with zero terrorist attacks that are "certain zeros" and, regardless of variation in the independent variables, are not likely to experience a terrorist attack. A zero-inflated negative binomial regression accounts for this subcategory by relying on a two-step regression process using both a logistic regression to independently model the likelihood of a state being part of the "certain zero" subcategory and a negative binomial regression to estimate the relationship between the independent variables and the size of the event count. The result of a Vuong test confirmed that a zero-inflated negative binomial regression, rather than a negative binomial regression, is appropriate for the data.

8.  Luke Keele and Nathan J. Kelly, "Dynamic Models for Dynamics Theories: The Ins and Outs of Lagged Dependent Variables," *Political Analysis* 14, no. 2 (2006): 186–205; Quan Li, "Does Democracy Promote or Reduce Transnational Terrorist Incidents?," *Journal of Conflict Resolution* 49, no. 2 (2005): 278–297.

9. *Patterns of Global Terrorism*, Office of the Coordinator for Counterterrorism, U.S. Department of State, 1996–2003, https://1997-2001.state.gov/global/terrorism/annual _reports.html, https://2009-2017.state.gov/j/ct/rls/crt/index.htm.

10. *Country Reports on Terrorism*, Office of the Coordinator for Counterterrorism, U.S. Department of State, 2004–2012, https://2009-2017.state.gov/j/ct/rls/crt/index.htm.

11. *Country Reports on Terrorism.*

12. Enders, Sandler, and Gaibulloev, "Domestic Versus Transnational Terrorism."

13. Andreas Wimmer, Lars-Erik Cederman, and Brian Min, "Ethnic Politics and Armed Conflict. A Configurational Analysis of a New Global Dataset," *American Sociological Review* 74, no. 2 (2009): 316–337.

14. Minorities at Risk Project, "Minorities at Risk Dataset," College Park, MD: Center for International Development and Conflict Management, 2009, http://www.mar.umd .edu/mar_data.asp.

15. Monty Marshall and Keith Jaggers, *Polity IV Project: Political Regime Characteristics and Transitions, 1800–2010*, College Park, MD: Center for International Development and Conflict Management, University of Maryland, 2010, http://www.systemicpeace .org/inscrdata.html.

16. Aksoy, Carter, and Wright, "Terrorism in Dictatorships"; Walsh and Piazza, "Autocracies and Terrorism."

17. Erica Chenoweth, "Democratic Competition and Terrorist Activity," *Journal of Politics* 72, no. 1 (2010): 16–30; Erica Chenoweth, "Terrorism and Democracy," *Annual Review of Political Science* 16 (2013): 355–378; Michael G. Findley and Joseph K. Young. "Terrorism, Democracy, and Credible Commitments," *International Studies Quarterly* 55, no. 2 (2011): 357–378.

18. "Indicators," World Bank, accessed September 30, 2022, http://data.worldbank.org /indicator/.

19. "SIPRI Military Expenditure Database," Stockholm International Peace Research Institute, accessed September 30, 2022, www.sipri.org/databases/milex.

20. "U.S. Overseas Loans and Grants (Greenbook)," USAID, last updated May 20, 2022, https://data.usaid.gov/Administration-and-Oversight/U-S-Overseas-Loans-and -Grants-Greenbook-Data/7cnw-pw8v.

21. Cullen S. Hendrix and Joseph K. Young, "State Capacity and Terrorism: A Two-Dimensional Approach," *Security Studies* 23, no. 2 (2014): 329–363.

22. In addition to the robustness checks outlined in the appendix, I performed a wide range of other robustness checks, all of which supported the results of the presented statistical models. Regarding variables used, I ran models with varying combinations of the control variables, including using alternative measures when available and including control variables for the presence of civil conflict and government mass killings. To further test the robustness of the results, I relied on different model specifications, including rerunning the models using a negative binomial regression; running models with random effects and fixed effects; running a model using a generalized estimating equations, or GEE, estimator, a population-averaged estimator, with an AR(1) error structure; running a two-step Heckman probit model using U.S.-identified

safe havens as the dependent variable within the selection model; and running a bivariate probit model to account for any correlations between domestic terrorism and international terrorism (using a dummy variable for any terrorist attacks in a given year as the dependent variables).

23. Henne, *Islamic Politics, Muslim States, and Counterterrorism Tensions*; Henne, "Assessing the Impact of the Global War on Terrorism on Terrorism Threats in Muslim Countries."

24. The inclusion of the CTCS drops the number of observations in the model to 440.

25. Enders, Sandler, and Gaibulloev, "Domestic Versus Transnational Terrorism"; Gaibulloev, Piazza, and Sandler, "Regime Types and Terrorism."

# BIBLIOGRAPHY

## PRIMARY SOURCES AND ARCHIVES

9/11 Commission Papers, National Archives, Washington, DC

Asian Reading Room, Library of Congress, Washington, DC

Central Intelligence Agency Reading Room, McLean, VA

Defense Intelligence Agency Reading Room, Washington, DC

Department of Defense Reading Room, Arlington, VA

Department of Justice Reading Room, Washington, DC

Department of State Reading Room, Washington, DC

Director of National Intelligence Reading Room, McLean, VA

Donald Rumsfeld Papers, https://papers.rumsfeld.com

FBI Vault, Washington, DC

Foreign Affairs Oral History Program, Association for Diplomatic Studies and Training, https://adst.org

George W. Bush Presidential Library, Dallas, TX

Global Terrorism Research Project, Haverford College, Haverford, PA

Harmony Program, Combating Terrorism Center at West Point, West Point, NY

Jihadology.net

National Archives, London, UK

National Security Archive, George Washington University, Washington, DC

Presidential Oral History Project, Miller Center, University of Virginia, Charlottesville, VA

Taliban Communications Archive, Danish Institute for International Studies, Copenhagen, Denmark

William J. Clinton Presidential Library, Little Rock, AR

## MEDIA OUTLETS

ABC News, Agence France-Presse, *Ahram Online* (Egypt), Al Jazeera English, *Al-Monitor* (Washington, DC), Arrahmah.com (Indonesia), *Asia Times* (Hong Kong), Associated Press, *The Atlantic*, BBC News, BuzzFeed News, C-SPAN, CBS News, *Charlie Rose*, CNN, *Christian Science Monitor, Critical Threats, Daily News Egypt* (Egypt), *Daily Times* (Pakistan), *Dawn* (Pakistan), *Defense One, The Diplomat, The Economist*, Federal News Service, *Foreign Affairs, Foreign Policy, France 24, Friday Times* (Pakistan), *The Guardian* (UK), *The Hill, The Independent* (UK), *Long War Journal, Los Angeles Times*, Ma'an News Agency (Palestinian Territories), Maliweb.net (Mali), *McClatchy, Middle East Eye* (UK), *Military Times, The National* (UAE), *National Interest, The News* (Pakistan), *New Yorker, New York Times, New York Review of Books, Pakistan Today* (Pakistan), *PBS Frontline, Politico, Prospect Magazine* (UK), Rappler, Reuters, *The Tribune* (India), *USA Today, US News and World Report*, Voice of America, *Wall Street Journal*, War on the Rocks, *Washington Post, Yemen Times* (Sana'a)

## SECONDARY SOURCES

Abbas, Hassan. *The Taliban Revival: Violence and Extremism on the Pakistan-Afghanistan Frontier*. New Haven, CT: Yale University Press, 2014.

Abrahms, Max. "Why Democracies Make Superior Counterterrorists." *Security Studies* 16, no. 2 (2007): 223–253.

Addison, Tony, and S. Mansoob Murshed. "Transnational Terrorism as a Spillover of Domestic Disputes in Other Countries." *Defence and Peace Economics* 16, no. 2 (2005): 69–82.

Afridi, O. K. *Mahsud Monograph*. Peshawar: Tribal Affairs Research Cell, Home and Tribal Affairs Department, Government of North-West Frontier Province, 1980.

Agha, Sameetah. "Sub-imperialism and the Loss of the Khyber: The Politics of Imperial Defence on British India's North-West Frontier." *Indian Historical Review* 40, no. 2 (2013): 307–330.

Ahmad, Aisha. *Jihad & Co.: Black Markets and Islamist Power*. New York: Oxford University Press, 2017.

Ahmad, Aisha. "The Security Bazaar: Business Interests and Islamist Power in Civil War Somalia." *International Security* 39, no. 3 (2014–2015): 89–117.

Ahmed, Akbar. *Journey Into Europe: Islam, Immigration, and Identity*. Washington, DC: Brookings Institution Press, 2018.

Ahmed, Akbar. *The Thistle and the Drone: How America's War on Terror Became a Global War on Tribal Islam*. Washington, DC: Brookings Institution Press, 2013.

Ahmed, Akbar S. *Mataloona: Pukhto Proverbs*. Karachi: Oxford University Press, 1975.

Ahmed, Akbar S. *Millennium and Charisma Among Pathans: A Critical Essay in Social Anthropology*. Abingdon, UK: Routledge, 1976.

Ahmed, Akbar S. *Pukhtun Economy and Society: Traditional Structure and Economic Development in a Tribal Society.* Abingdon, UK: Routledge, 1980.

Ahmed, Akbar S. *Resistance and Control in Pakistan: Revised Edition.* Abingdon, UK: Routledge, 2004.

Ahmed, Akbar S. and David M. Hart, eds. *Islam in Tribal Societies: From the Atlas to the Indus.* Abingdon, UK: Routledge, 1984.

Akins, Harrison. "The Assam Rifles and India's North-East frontier policy." *Small Wars & Insurgencies* 31, no. 6 (2020): 1373–1394.

Akins, Harrison. "Mashar Versus Kashar in Pakistan's FATA: Intra-tribal Conflict and the Obstacles to Reform." *Asian Survey* 58, no. 6 (2018): 1136–1159.

Akins, Harrison. "Tribal Militias and Political Legitimacy in British India and Pakistan." *Asian Security* 16, no. 3 (2020): 304–322.

Akins, Harrison. "The 2001 Authorization for the Use of Military Force and America's Endless War." *Oxford Middle East Review* 2, no. 1 (2018): 12–18.

Akins, Harrison. "Violence on the Home Front: Interstate Rivalry and Pro-Government Militias." *Terrorism and Political Violence* 33, no. 3 (2021) 466–488.

Aksoy, Deniz, David B. Carter, and Joseph Wright. "Terrorism in Dictatorships." *Journal of Politics* 74, no. 3 (2012): 810–826.

Al-Dawsari, Nadwa, *Foe Not Friend: Yemeni Tribes and Al-Qaeda in the Arabian Peninsula.* Washington, DC: Project on Middle East Democracy, February 2018.

Anderson, Benedict. *Imagined Communities: Reflections on the Origin and Spread of Nationalism.* London: Verso, 1983.

Anderson, Liam. "Ethnofederalism: The Worst Form of Institutional Arrangement . . .?" *International Security* 39, no. 1 (2014): 165–204.

Arieff, Alexis, and Kelly Johnson. *Crisis in Mali.* Report for Congress, Congressional Research Service, August 16, 2012.

Arsenault, Elizabeth Grimm, and Tricia Bacon. "Disaggregating and Defeating Terrorist Safe Havens." *Studies in Conflict & Terrorism* 38, no. 2 (2015): 85–112.

Asal, Victor, Brian J. Phillips, R. Karl Rethemeyer, Corina Simonelli, and Joseph K. Young. "Carrots, Sticks, and Insurgent Targeting of Civilians." *Journal of Conflict Resolution* 63, no. 7 (2019): 1710–1735.

Ash, Konstantin. "Representative Democracy and Fighting Domestic Terrorism." *Terrorism and Political Violence* 28, no. 1 (2016): 114–134.

Ash, Konstantin. "'The War Will Come to Your Street': Explaining Geographic Variation in Terrorism by Rebel Groups." *International Interactions* 44, no. 3 (2018): 411–436.

Avdan, Nazli, and Gary Uzonyi. "V for Vendetta: Government Mass Killing and Domestic Terrorism." *Studies in Conflict & Terrorism* 40, no. 11 (2017): 934–965.

Awad, Mokhtar, and Samuel Tadros. "Bay'a Remorse? Wilayat Sinai and the Nile Valley." *CTC Sentinel* 8, no. 8 (2015): 1–7.

Awadh Asseri, Ali S. *Combating Terrorism: Saudi Arabia's Role in the War on Terror.* New York: Oxford University Press, 2010.

Azam, Jean-Paul, and Veronique Thelen. "Foreign Aid Versus Military Intervention in the War on Terror." *Journal of Conflict Resolution* 54, no. 2 (2010): 237–261.

Aziz, Heba. "Employment in a Bedouin Community: The Case of the Town of Dahab in South Sinai." *Nomadic Peoples* 4, no. 2 (2000): 28–47.

Bacon, Tricia, and Daisy Muibu. "The Domestication of Al-Shabaab." *Journal of the Middle East and Africa* 10, no. 3 (2019): 239–305.

Bailey, Clinton. *Bedouin Law from Sinai and the Negev: Justice Without Government.* New Haven, CT: Yale University Press, 2009.

Bailey, Clinton. *Bedouin Poetry from Sinai and Negev.* Oxford: Clarendon Press, 1991.

Bailey, Clinton. "Bedouin Religious Practices in Sinai and the Negev." *Anthropos* 77, nos. 1–2 (1982): 65–88.

Bakke, Kristin M., and Erik Wibbels. "Diversity, Disparity, and Civil Conflict in Federal States." *World Politics* 59, no. 1 (2006): 1–50.

Baldwin, Kate and Katharina Holzinger. "Traditional Political Institutions and Democracy: Reassessing Their Compatibility and Accountability." *Comparative Political Studies* 52, no. 12 (2019): 1747–1774.

Balthasar, Dominik. "State-Making at Gunpoint: The Role of Violent Conflict in Somaliland's March to Statehood." *Civil Wars* 19, no. 1 (2017): 65–86.

Bandyopadhyay, Subhayu, Todd Sandler, and Javed Younas. "Foreign Aid as Counterterrorism Policy." *Oxford Economic Papers* 63 (2011): 423–447.

Bapat, Navin. "The Internationalization of Terrorist Campaigns." *Conflict Management and Peace Science* 24, no. 4 (2007): 265–280.

Bapat, Navin. "Transnational Terrorism, US Military Aid, and the Incentive to Misrepresent." *Journal of Peace Research* 48, no. 3 (2011): 303–318.

Barth, Fredrik. *The Last Wali of Swat: An Autobiography as Told to Fredrik Barth.* New York: Columbia University Press, 1985.

Basedau, Matthias, Birte Pfeiffer, and Johannes Vullers. "Bad Religion? Religion, Collective Action, and the Onset of Armed Conflict in Developing Countries." *Journal of Conflict Resolution* 60, no. 2 (2016): 226–255.

Beadnell, Hugh John. *The Wilderness of Sinai: A Record of Two Years' Recent Exploration.* London: Edward Arnold and Co., 1927.

Beattie, Hugh. "Negotiations with the Tribes of Waziristan 1849–1914—The British Experience." *Journal of Imperial and Commonwealth History* 39, no. 4 (2011): 571–587.

Benjaminsen, Tor A. "Does Supply-Induced Scarcity Drive Violent Conflicts in the African Sahel? The Case of the Tuareg Rebellion in Northern Mali." *Journal of Peace Research* 45, no. 6 (2008): 819–836.

Bergen, Peter. *The Longest War: The Enduring Conflict Between America and Al-Qaeda.* New York: Free Press, 2011.

Bergen, Peter. *The Osama Bin Laden I Know: An Oral History of al Qaeda's Leader.* New York: Free Press, 2006.

Bergen, Peter. *United States of Jihad: Investigating America's Homegrown Terrorists.* New York: Crown Publishers, 2016.

Bergen, Peter, and Alec Reynolds. "Blowback Revisited: Today's Insurgents in Iraq Are Tomorrow's Terrorists." *Foreign Affairs* 84, no. 6 (2005): 2–6.

Bergen, Peter, and Katherine Tiedemann, eds. *Talibanistan: Negotiating the Borders Between Terror, Politics, and Religion*. Oxford: Oxford University Press, 2013.

Bezhan, Faridullah. "The Pashtunistan Issue and Politics in Afghanistan, 1947–1952." *Middle East Journal* 68, no. 2 (2014): 197–209.

Bloch, Marc. *The Historian's Craft*. Manchester, UK: Manchester University Press, 1954.

Boehm, Christopher. *Blood Revenge: The Enactment and Management of Conflict in Montenegro and Other Tribal Societies*. Philadelphia: University of Pennsylvania Press, 1986.

Boutton, Andrew. "US Foreign Aid, Interstate Rivalry, and Incentives for Counterterrorism Cooperation." *Journal of Peace Research* 51, no. 6 (2014): 741–754.

Boutton, Andrew, and David B. Carter. "Fair-Weather Allies? Terrorism and the Allocation of US Foreign Aid." *Journal of Conflict Resolution* 58, no. 7 (2014): 1144–1173.

Bradley, John R. *Inside Egypt: The Land of the Pharaohs on the Brink of Revolution*. New York: Palgrave Macmillan, 2008.

Brady, Henry E., and David Collier, eds. *Rethinking Social Inquiry: Diverse Tools, Shared Standards*. Lanham, MD: Rowman and Littlefield, 2010.

Braithwaite, Alex. "Transnational Terrorism as an Unintended Consequence of a Military Footprint." *Security Studies* 24, no. 2 (2015): 349–375.

Brancati, Dawn. "Decentralization: Fueling the Fire or Dampening the Flames of Ethnic Conflict and Secessionism." *International Organization* 60 (2006): 651–685.

Brennan, John O. *Undaunted: My Fight Against America's Enemies, at Home and Abroad*. New York: Celadon Press, 2020.

Breslawski, Jori. "Keeping Armed Actors Out: The Protective Effect of Shuras in Afghanistan." *Journal of Global Security Studies* 6, no. 1 (2021): 1–8.

Breslawski, Jori, and Brandon Ives. "Killing for God? Factional Violence on the Transnational Stage." *Journal of Conflict Resolution* 63, no. 3 (2019): 617–643.

Brinkerhoff, Derick W. "State Fragility and Governance: Conflict Mitigation and Subnational Perspectives." *Development Policy Review* 29, no. 2 (2011): 131–153.

Brockhoff, Sarah, Tim Krieger, and Daniel Meierrieks. "Great Expectations and Hard Times: The (Nontrivial) Impact of Education on Domestic Terrorism." *Journal of Conflict Resolution* 59, no. 7 (2015): 1186–1215.

Bromley, Daniel, and Glen Anderson. *Vulnerable People, Vulnerable States: Redefining the Development Challenge*. Abingdon, UK: Routledge, 2012.

Brower, Benjamin Claude. *A Desert Named Peace: The Violence of France's Empire in the Algerian Sahara, 1844–1902*. New York: Columbia University Press, 2009.

Bruce, Lieut.-Colonel C. E. *Waziristan, 1936–1937: The Problems of the North-West Frontiers of India and their Solutions*. London: Gale and Polden, 1938.

Bueno de Mesquita, Bruce, and Randolph M. Siverson. "War and the Survival of Political Leaders: A Comparative Study of Regime Types and Political Accountability." *American Political Science Review* 89, no. 4 (1995): 841–855.

Bueno de Mesquita, Ethan. "The Quality of Terror." *American Journal of Political Science* 49, no. 3 (2005): 515–530.

Bush, George W. *Decision Points*. New York: Random House, 2010.

Burgoon, Brian. "On Welfare and Terror: Social Welfare Policies and Political-Economic Roots of Terrorism." *Journal of Conflict Resolution* 50, no. 2 (2006): 176–203.

Butt, Ahsan I. "Why Did the United States Invade Iraq in 2003?" *Security Studies* 28, no. 2 (2019): 250–285.

Byman, Daniel L. *Al Qaeda, the Islamic State, and the Global Jihadist Movement.* New York: Oxford University Press, 2015.

Byman, Daniel L. "Comparing Al Qaeda and ISIS: Different Goals, Different Targets." Brookings Institution, April 29, 2015. https://www.brookings.edu/testimonies/comparing-al -qaeda-and-isis-different-goals-different-targets/.

Byman, Daniel L. "Friends Like These: Counterinsurgency and the War on Terrorism." *International Security* 31, no. 2 (2006): 79–115.

Byman, Daniel. "US Counterterrorism Intelligence Cooperation with the Developing World and Its Limits." *Intelligence and National Security* 32, no. 2 (2017): 145–160.

Byman Daniel L., and Jennifer R. Williams. "ISIS vs. Al Qaeda: Jihadism's Global Civil War." Brookings Institution, February 24, 2015. https://www.brookings.edu/articles/isis-vs-al -qaeda-jihadisms-global-civil-war/.

Caillie, Rene. *Travels Through Central Africa to Timbuctoo; and Across the Great Desert, to Morocco Performed in the Years 1824–1828 In Two Volumes, Volume One.* London: Henry Colburn and Richard Bentley, 1830.

Carey, Sabine C., Michael P. Colaresi, and Neil J. Mitchell. "Governments, Informal Links to Militias, and Accountability." *Journal of Conflict Resolution* 59, no. 5 (2015): 850–876.

Caroe, Olaf. *The Pathans: 550 B.C.—A.D. 1957.* New York: St. Martin's Press, 1958.

Caton, Steven C. *Yemen Chronicle: An Anthropology of War and Mediation.* New York: Hill and Wang, 2005.

Cederman, Lars-Erik, Simon Hug, Andreas Schadel, Julian Wucherpfennig. "Territorial Autonomy in the Shadow of Conflict: Too Little, Too Late?" *American Political Science Review* 109, no. 2 (2015): 354–370.

Ceslo, Anthony N. "Al Qaeda's Post–bin Laden Resurgence: The Paradox of Resilience and Failure." *Mediterranean Quarterly* 25, no. 2 (2014): 33–47.

Challand, Benoit, and Joshua Rogers. "The Political Economy of Local Governance in Yemen: Past and Present." *Contemporary Arab Affairs* 13, no. 4 (2020): 45–69.

Chelin, Richard Philippe. "From the Islamic State of Algeria to the Economic Caliphate of the Sahel: The Transformation of Al Qaeda in the Islamic Maghreb." *Terrorism and Political Violence* 32, no. 6 (2020): 1186–1205.

Chenoweth, Erica. "Democratic Competition and Terrorist Activity." *Journal of Politics* 72, no. 1 (2010): 16–30.

Chenoweth, Erica. "Terrorism and Democracy." *Annual Review of Political Science* 16 (2013): 355–378.

Choi, Seung-Whan. "Fighting Terrorism Through the Rule of Law?" *Journal of Conflict Resolution* 54, no. 6 (2010): 940–966.

Choi, Seung-Whan, and Patrick James. "Why Does the United States Intervene Abroad? Democracy, Human Rights Violations, and Terrorism." *Journal of Conflict Resolution* 60, no. 5 (2014): 899–926.

Choi, Seung-Whan, and James A. Piazza. "Ethnic Groups, Political Exclusion and Domestic Terrorism." *Defence and Peace Economics* 27, no. 1 (2016): 37–63.

Choi, Seung-Whan, and James A. Piazza. "Foreign Military Interventions and Suicide Attacks." *Journal of Conflict Resolution* 61, no. 2 (2017): 271–297.

Choi, Seung-Whan, and James A. Piazza. "Internally Displaced Populations and Suicide Terrorism." *Journal of Conflict Resolution* 60, no. 6 (2016): 1008–1040.

Christin, Thomas, and Simon Hug. "Federalism, the Geographic Location of Groups, and Conflict." *Conflict Management and Peace Science* 29, no. 1 (2012): 93–122.

Churchill, Winston. *The Story of the Malakand Field Force: An Episode of Frontier War.* London: Longmans, Green, and Co., 1901.

Clark, Victoria. *Yemen: Dancing on the Heads of Snakes.* New Haven, CT: Yale University Press, 2010.

Clarke, Michael, ed. *Terrorism and Counter-Terrorism in China: Domestic and Foreign Policy Dimensions.* New York: Oxford University Press, 2018.

Clarke, Richard A. *Against All Enemies: Inside America's War on Terror.* New York: Free Press, 2004.

Clarke, Thurston. *The Last Caravan.* New York: G. P. Putnam's Sons, 1978.

Clunan, Anne L., and Harold A. Trinkunas, eds. *Ungoverned Spaces: Alternatives to State Authority in an Era of Softened Sovereignty.* Palo Alto, CA: Stanford University Press, 2010.

Coggins, Bridget L. "Does State Failure Cause Terrorism? An Empirical Analysis (1999–2008)." *Journal of Conflict Resolution* 59, no. 3 (2015): 455–483.

Cohen, Eliot A. *The Big Stick: The Limits of Soft Power and the Necessity of Military Force.* New York: Basic Books, 2016.

Coll, Steve. *Directorate S: The C.I.A. and America's Secret Wars in Afghanistan and Pakistan.* New York: Penguin Press, 2018.

Coll, Steve. *Ghost Wars: The Secret History of the CIA, Afghanistan, and Bin Ladin, from the Soviet Invasion to September 10, 2001.* London: Penguin, 2004.

Collombier, Virginie, and Olivier Roy, eds. *Tribes and Global Jihadism.* London: C. Hurst and Company, 2017.

Connor, Walker. *Ethnonationalism: The Quest for Understanding.* Princeton, NJ: Princeton University Press, 1994.

Costalli, Stefano, and Andrea Ruggeri. "Emotions, Ideologies, and Violent Political Mobilization." *PS: Political Science and Politics* 50, no. 4 (2017): 923–927.

Crawford, Neta C. "The U.S. Budgetary Costs of the Post-9/11 Wars." Costs of War Project, Brown University, September 1, 2021. https://watson.brown.edu/costsofwar/files/cow/imce/papers/2021/Costs%20of%20War_U.S.%20Budgetary%20Costs%20of%20Post-9%2011%20Wars_9.1.21.pdf.

Crisman-Cox, Casey. "Enemies Within: Interactions Between Terrorists and Democracies." *Journal of Conflict Resolution* 62, no. 8 (2018): 1661–1685.

Cronin, Audrey Kurth. "The Evolution of Counter-Terrorism: Will Tactics Trump Strategy?" *International Affairs* 86, no. 4 (2010): 837–856.

Cronin, Audrey Kurth. "U.S. Grand Strategy and Counterterrorism." *Orbis* 56, no. 2 (2012): 192–214.

Cronin, Audrey Kurth. "The 'War on Terrorism:' What Does It Mean to Win?" *Journal of Strategic Studies* 37, no. 2 (2014): 174–197.

Curzon, George. *Lord Curzon in India: Being a Selection from His Speeches as Viceroy & Governor-General of India, 1898–1905*. London: Macmillan and Co., 1906.

Curzon, George. *The Romanes Lecture 1907: Frontiers*. Oxford: Clarendon Press, 1907.

Dafoe, Allan, Sophia Hatz, Baobao Zhang. "Coercion and Provocation." *Journal of Conflict Resolution* 65, nos. 2–3 (2021): 372–402.

Danzell, Orlandrew E., Yao-Yuan Yeh, and Melia Pfannenstiel. "Determinants of Domestic Terrorism: An Examination of Ethnic Polarization and Economic Development." *Terrorism and Political Violence* 31, no. 3 (2019): 536–558.

Danzell, Orlandrew E., Yao-Yuan Yeh, and Melia Pfannenstiel. "Does Education Mitigate Terrorism? Examining the Effects of Educated Youth Cohorts on Domestic Terror in Africa." *Terrorism and Political Violence* 32, no. 8 (2020): 1731–1752.

Day, Stephen. "Aden and the Gulf: The Reflections of a Political Officer." *Middle Eastern Studies* 53, no. 1 (2017): 136–151.

Deitch, Mora. "Is Religion a Barrier to Peace? Religious Influence on Violent Intrastate Conflict Termination." *Terrorism and Political Violence* 34, no. 7 (2022): 1454–1470.

Dowd, Caitriona, and Clionadh Raleigh. "The Myth of Global Islamic Terrorism and Local Conflict in Mali and the Sahel." *African Affairs* 112, no. 448 (2013): 498–509.

Dreher, Alex, and Justina A. V. Fischer. "Does Government Decentralization Reduce Domestic Terrorism? An Empirical Test." *Economics Letters* 111 (2011): 223–225.

Dupree, Louis. *Afghanistan*. Oxford: Oxford University Press, 2002.

Dzuvichu, Lipokmar, and Manjeet Baruah, eds. *Objects and Frontiers in Modern Asia: Between the Mekong and the Indus*. Abingdon, UK: Routledge, 2019.

Easterly, William. *The White Man's Burden: Why the West's Efforts to Aid the Rest Have Done So Much Ill and So Little Good*. New York: Penguin, 2006.

Enders, Walter, Gary A. Hoover, and Todd Sandler. "The Changing Nonlinear Relationship Between Income and Terrorism." *Journal of Conflict Resolution* 60, no. 2 (2016): 195–225.

Enders, Walter, Todd Sandler, and Khusrav Gaibulloev. "Domestic Versus Transnational Terrorism: Data, Decomposition, and Dynamics." *Journal of Peace Research* 48, no. 3 (2011): 319–337.

Esposito, John L. *Unholy War: Terror in the Name of Islam*. New York: Oxford University Press, 2003.

Evans-Pritchard, E. E. *The Nuer: A Description of the Modes of Livelihood and Political Institutions of a Nilotic People*. New York: Oxford University Press, 1940.

Evans-Pritchard, E. E. *The Sanusi of Cyrenaica*. Oxford: Clarendon Press, 1949.

Ezcurra, Roberto. "Group Concentration and Violence: Does Ethnic Segregation Affect Domestic Terrorism?" *Defence and Peace Economics* 30, no. 1 (2019): 46–71.

Faguet, Jean-Paul, Ashley M. Fox, and Caroline Poschl. "Decentralizing for a Deeper, More Supple Democracy." *Journal of Democracy* 26, no. 4 (2015): 60–74.

Fair, C. Christine, and Sumit Ganguly, eds. *Policing Insurgencies: Cops as Counterinsurgents*. New Delhi: Oxford University Press, 2014.

Fair, C. Christine, Karl Kaltenthaler, and William J. Miller. "Pakistani Opposition to American Drone Strikes." *Political Science Quarterly* 129, no. 1 (2014): 1–33.

Fair, C. Christine, Neil Malhotra, and Jacob Shapiro. "Islam, Militancy, and Politics in Pakistan: Insights from a National Sample." *Terrorism and Political Violence* 22, no. 4 (2010): 495–521.

Fair, C. Christine, and Sarah J. Watson, eds. *Pakistan's Enduring Challenges*. Philadelphia: University of Pennsylvania Press, 2015.

Faria, Joao Ricardo, and Daniel Arce. "Counterterrorism and Its Impact on Terror Support and Recruitment: Accounting for Backlash." *Defence and Peace Economics* 23, no. 5 (2012): 431–445.

Farrall, Leah. "How al Qaeda Works: What the Organization's Subsidiaries Say About Its Strength." *Foreign Affairs* 90, no. 2 (March–April 2011): 128–138.

Fearon, James D. "Counterfactuals and Hypothesis Testing in Political Science." *World Politics* 43, no. 2 (1991): 169–195.

Fearon, James D. "Domestic Political Audiences and the Escalation of International Disputes." *American Political Science Review* 88, no. 3 (1994): 577–592.

Fearon, James D. "Signaling Foreign Policy Interests: Tying Hands Versus Sinking Costs." *Journal of Conflict Resolution* 41, no. 1 (1997): 68–90.

Fearon, James D., and David D. Laitin. "Ethnicity, Insurgency, and Civil War." *American Political Science Review* 97, no. 1 (2003): 75–90.

Feith, Douglas J. *War and Decision: Inside the Pentagon at the Dawn of the War on Terrorism*. New York: Harper, 2008.

Findley, Michael G., and Joseph K. Young. "Fighting Fire with Fire? How (Not) to Neutralize an Insurgency." *Civil Wars* 9, no. 4 (2007): 378–401.

Findley, Michael G., and Joseph K. Young. "Terrorism, Democracy, and Credible Commitments." *International Studies Quarterly* 55, no. 2 (2011): 357–378.

Fishman, Brian. "Using the Mistakes of Al Qaeda's Franchises to Undermine Its Strategies." *Annals of the American Academy of Political and Social Science* 618 (2008): 46–54.

Gaibulloev, Khusrav, James A. Piazza, and Todd Sandler. "Regime Types and Terrorism." *International Organization* 71, no. 3 (2017): 491–522.

Gartner, Scott Sigmund. "Ties to the Dead: Connections to the Iraq War and 9/11 Casualties and Disapproval of the President." *American Sociological Review* 73, no. 4 (2008): 690–695.

Gartner, Scott Sigmund, and Gary M. Segura. "All Politics Are Still Local: The Iraq War and the 2006 Midterm Elections." *PS: Political Science and Politics* 41, no. 1 (2008): 95–100.

Geertz, Clifford. *The Interpretation of Cultures*. New York: Basic Books, 1973.

Gellner, Ernest. *Muslim Society*. Cambridge: Cambridge University Press, 1981.

Gerber, Theodore P., and Sarah E. Mendelson. "Security Through Sociology: The North Caucasus and the Global Counterinsurgency Paradigm." *Studies in Conflict & Terrorism* 32, no. 9 (2009): 831–851.

Gerges, Fawaz A. *The Far Enemy: Why Jihad Went Global*. Cambridge: Cambridge University Press, 2005.

Gerges, Fawaz A. *ISIS: A History*. Princeton, NJ: Princeton University Press, 2016.

Ghatak, Sambuddha. "The Role of Political Exclusion and State Capacity in Civil Conflict in South Asia." *Terrorism and Political Violence* 30, no. 1 (2018): 74–96.

Ghatak, Sambuddha, and Aaron Gold. "Development, Discrimination, and Domestic Terrorism: Looking Beyond a Linear Relationship." *Conflict Management and Peace Science* 34, no. 6 (2017): 618–639.

Ghatak, Sambuddha, Aaron Gold, and Brandon C. Prins. "Domestic Terrorism in Democratic States: Understanding and Addressing Minority Grievances." *Journal of Conflict Resolution* 63, no. 2 (2019): 439–467.

Gilbert, Hilary. "'This Is Not Our Life, It's Just a Copy of Other People's': Bedu and the Price of 'Development' in South Sinai." *Nomadic Peoples* 15, no. 2 (2011): 7–32.

Gill, Paul, James A. Piazza, and John Horgan. "Counterterrorism Killings and Provisional IRA Bombings, 1970–1998." *Terrorism and Political Violence* 28, no. 3 (2016): 473–496.

Goodman, Joshua R. *Contesting Identities in South Sinai: Development, Transformation, and the Articulation of a "Bedouin" Identity Under Egyptian Rule.* Tel Aviv: Moshe Dayan Center for Middle Eastern and African Studies, 2013.

Goodman, Joshua. "Egypt's Assault on Sinai." Carnegie Endowment for International Peace, June 5, 2014. https://carnegieendowment.org/sada/55810.

Grace, Emma. "Lex Talionis in the Twenty-First Century: Revenge Ideation and Terrorism." *Behavioral Sciences of Terrorism and Political Aggression* 10, no. 3 (2018): 249–263.

Gourevitch, Peter. "The Second Image Reversed: The International Sources of Domestic Politics." *International Organization* 32, no. 4 (1978): 881–912.

Guidere, Mathieu. "The Timbuktu Letters: New Insights About AQIM." *Res Militaris* 4, no. 1 (2014): 25–41.

Gul, Imtiaz. *The Most Dangerous Place: Pakistan's Lawless Frontier.* New York: Viking Press, 2009.

Gunaratna, Rohan, and Anders Nielsen. "Al Qaeda in the Tribal Areas of Pakistan and Beyond." *Studies in Conflict & Terrorism* 31, no. 9 (2008): 775–807.

Guyot-Rechard, Berenice. *Shadow States: India, China and the Himalayas, 1910–1962.* Cambridge: Cambridge University Press, 2017.

Habeck, Mary. *Knowing the Enemy: Jihadist Ideology and the War on Terror.* New Haven, CT: Yale University Press, 2006.

Hamid, Mustafa, and Leah Farrall. *The Arabs at War in Afghanistan.* London: C. Hurst and Company, 2015.

Hammer, Joshua. *The Bad-Ass Librarians of Timbuktu: And Their Race to Save the World's Most Precious Manuscripts.* New York: Simon and Schuster, 2016.

Hansen, Holly E., Stephen C. Nemeth, and Jacob A. Mauslein. "Ethnic Political Exclusion and Terrorism: Analyzing the Local Conditions for Violence." *Conflict Management and Peace Science* 37, no. 3 (2020): 280–300.

Haqqani, Hussain. *Magnificent Delusions: Pakistan, the United States, and an Epic History.* New York: PublicAffairs, 2013.

Harper, Mary. *Everything You Have Told Me Is True: The Many Faces of Al Shabaab.* London: C. Hurst and Company, 2019.

Hathaway, Robert M. *The Leverage Paradox: Pakistan and the United States.* Washington, DC: Woodrow Wilson International Center for Scholars, 2017.

Hayden, Michael V. *Playing to the Edge: American Intelligence in the Age of Terror.* New York: Penguin Books, 2016.

Hechter, Michael. *Internal Colonialism: The Celtic Fringe in British National Development.* Berkeley: University of California Press, 1975.

Hegghammer, Thomas. *The Failure of Jihad in Saudi Arabia.* Occasional Paper Series, Combating Terrorism Center at West Point, February 25, 2010.

Hegghammer, Thomas. "The Rise of Muslim Foreign Fighters: Islam and the Globalization of Jihad." *International Security* 35, no. 3 (2010/11): 53–94.

Heilbrunn, John R. "Paying the Price of Failure: Reconstructing Failed and Collapsed States in Africa and Central Asia." *Perspectives on Politics* 4, no. 1 (2006): 135–150.

Heinrich, Tobias, Carla Martinez Machain, and Jared Oestman. "Does Counterterrorism Militarize Foreign Aid? Evidence from sub-Saharan Africa." *Journal of Peace Research* 54, no. 4 (2017): 527–541.

Heinze, Marie-Christine. "On 'Gun Culture' and 'Civil Statehood' in Yemen." *Journal of Arabian Studies* 4, no. 1 (2014): 70–95.

Hendrix, Cullen S., and Joseph K. Young. "State Capacity and Terrorism: A Two-Dimensional Approach." *Security Studies* 23, no. 2 (2014): 329–363.

Henne, Peter S. "The Ancient Fire: Religion and Suicide Terrorism." *Terrorism and Political Violence* 24, no. 1 (2012): 38–60.

Henne, Peter S. "Assessing the Impact of the Global War on Terrorism on Terrorism Threats in Muslim Countries." *Terrorism and Political Violence* 33, no. 7 (2021): 1511–1529.

Henne, Peter S. "Government Interference in Religious Institutions and Terrorism." *Religion, State and Society* 47, no. 1 (2019): 67–86.

Henne, Peter S. *Islamic Politics, Muslim States, and Counterterrorism Tensions.* Cambridge: Cambridge University Press, 2016.

Henne, Peter S., Nilay Saiya, and Ashlyn W. Hand. "Weapon of the Strong? Government Support for Religion and Majoritarianism Terrorism." *Journal of Conflict Resolution* 64, no. 10 (2020): 1943–1967.

Hess, Robert L. "The 'Mad Mullah' and Northern Somalia." *Journal of African History* 5, no. 3 (1964): 415–433.

Hoffman, Bruce. "Al Qaeda's Uncertain Future." *Studies in Conflict & Terrorism* 36, no. 8 (2003): 635–653.

Hoffman, Bruce. "The Changing Face of Al Qaeda and the Global War on Terrorism." *Studies in Conflict & Terrorism* 27, no. 6 (2004): 549–560.

Hoffman, Bruce. "The Myth of Grass-Roots Terrorism: Why Osama Bin Laden Still Matters." *Foreign Affairs* 87, no. 3 (2008): 133–138.

Hopkins, Benjamin D. *Ruling the Savage Periphery: Frontier Governance and the Making of the Modern State.* Cambridge, MA: Harvard University Press, 2020.

Horowitz, Donald L. *Ethnic Groups in Conflict.* Berkeley: University of California Press, 1985.

Howard, Tiffany. *Failed States and the Origins of Violence: A Comparative Analysis of State Failure as a Root Cause of Terrorism and Political Violence.* Surrey, UK: Ashgate, 2014.

Howell, Evelyn. *Mizh: A Monograph on Government's Relations with the Mahsud Tribe.* Karachi: Oxford University Press, 1979.

Howell, Jude, and Jeremy Lind. "Changing Donor Policy and Practice in Civil Society in the Post-9/11 Aid Context." *Third World Quarterly* 30, no. 7 (2009): 1279–1296.

Hsu, Henda Y., and David McDowall. "Examining the State Repression-Terrorism Nexus: Dynamic Relationships Among Repressive Counterterrorism Actions, Terrorist Targets, and Deadly Terrorist Violence in Israel." *Criminology & Public Policy* 19 (2020): 483–514.

Hultman, Lisa. "Battle Losses and Rebel Violence: Raising the Costs for Fighting." *Terrorism and Political Violence* 19, no. 2 (2007): 205–222.

Hussain, Zahid. *The Scorpion's Tail: The Relentless Rise of Islamic Militants in Pakistan—and How It Threatens America.* New York: Free Press, 2010.

Hutchings, Robert, and Gregory F. Treverton, eds. *Truth to Power: A History of the U.S. National Intelligence Council.* Oxford: Oxford University Press, 2019.

Hwang, Julie Chernov, and Kirsten E. Schulze. "Why They Join: Pathways Into Indonesian Jihadist Organizations." *Terrorism and Political Violence* 30, no. 6 (2018): 911–932.

Isaacs, Matthew. "Faith in Contention: Explaining the Salience of Religion in Ethnic Conflict." *Comparative Political Studies* 50, no. 2 (2017): 200–231.

Jackson, Robert H. *Quasi-states: Sovereignty, International Relations and the Third World.* Cambridge: Cambridge University Press, 1990.

Jadoon, Amira. "Conflict Aggravation or Alleviation? A Cross-National Examination of U.S. Military Aid's Effect on Conflict Dynamics with Insights from Pakistan." *Political Science Quarterly* 135, no. 4 (2020): 665–695.

Janeczko, Matthew. "'Faced with Death, Even a Mouse Bites:' Social and Religious Motivations Behind Terrorism in Chechnya." *Small Wars & Insurgencies* 25, no. 2 (2013): 428–456.

Johnsen, Gregory D. "The Expansion Strategy of Al-Qa'ida in the Arabian Peninsula." *CTC Sentinel* 2, no. 9 (January 2010): 4–7.

Johnsen, Gregory D. *The Last Refuge: Yemen, Al-Qaeda, and America's War in Arabia.* New York: W. W. Norton, 2013.

Johnson, Rob. *The Afghan Way of War: How and Why They Fight.* New York: Oxford University Press, 2012.

Johnston, Patrick B., and Anoop K. Sarbahi. "The Impact of U.S. Drone Strikes on Terrorism in Pakistan." *International Studies Quarterly* 60, no. 2 (2016): 203–219.

Jones, Clive. "The Tribes that Bind: Yemen and the Paradox of Political Violence." *Studies in Conflict & Terrorism* 34, no. 12 (2011): 902–916.

Jones, Seth G. "The Rise of Afghanistan's Insurgency: State Failure and Jihad." *International Security* 32, no. 4 (2008): 7–40.

Jones, Seth G., and Martin G. Libicki. *How Terrorist Groups End: Lessons for Countering al Qa'ida.* Santa Monica, CA: RAND Corporation, 2008.

Jones, Sidney. "Radicalisation in the Philippines: The Cotabato Cell of the 'East Asia Wilayah.'" *Terrorism and Political Violence* 30, no. 6 (2018): 933–943.

Jones, Toby Craig. "Rebellion on the Saudi Periphery: Modernity, Marginalization, and the Shia Uprising of 1979." *International Journal of Middle East Studies* 38, no. 2 (2006): 213–233.

Kaltenthaler, Karl, and William Miller. "Ethnicity, Islam, and Pakistani Public Opinion Toward the Pakistani Taliban." *Studies in Conflict & Terrorism* 38, no. 11 (2015): 938–957.

Kattelman, Kyle T. "Assessing Success of the Global War on Terror: Terrorist Attack Frequency and the Backlash Effect." *Dynamics of Asymmetric Conflict* 13, no. 1 (2020): 67–86.

Keele, Luke, and Nathan J. Kelly. "Dynamic Models for Dynamics Theories: The Ins and Outs of Lagged Dependent Variables." *Political Analysis* 14, no. 2 (2006): 186–205.

Keenan, Jeremy. *The Lesser Gods of the Sahara: Social Change and Indigenous Rights.* London: Frank Cass, 2004.

Kilcullen, David. *The Accidental Guerilla: Fighting Small Wars in the Midst of a Big One.* New York: Oxford University Press, 2009.

Kilcullen, David. *Blood Year: The Unraveling of Western Counterterrorism.* New York: Oxford University Press, 2016.

Kilcullen, David. *Counterinsurgency.* New York: Oxford University Press, 2010.

Kirisci, Mustafa. "Militarized Law Enforcement Forces, State Capacity and Terrorism." *Terrorism and Political Violence* 34, no. 1 (2022): 93–112.

Kis-Katos, Krisztina, Helge Liebert, and Gunther G. Schulze. "On the Origin of Domestic and International Terrorism." *European Journal of Political Economy* 27 (2011): 517–536.

Koehler-Derrick, Gabriel. *A False Foundation? AQAP, Tribes, and Ungoverned Spaces.* West Point, NY: Combating Terrorism Center at West Point, September 2011. https://www.ctc .usma.edu/wp-content/uploads/2011/10/CTC_False_Foundation2.pdf.

Koren, Ore, and Anoop K. Sarbahi. "State Capacity, Insurgency, and Civil War: A Disaggregated Analysis." *International Studies Quarterly* 62, no. 2 (2018): 274–288.

Krause, Jonathan. "Islam and Anti-colonial Rebellions in North and West Africa, 1914–1918." *Historical Journal* 64, no. 3 (2021): 674–695.

Kreuzer, Marcus. "The Structure of Description: Evaluating Descriptive Inferences and Conceptualizations." *Perspectives on Politics* 17, no. 1 (2019): 122–139.

Kronstadt, K. Alan, and Bruce Vaughn. *Terrorism in South Asia.* Report for Congress, Congressional Research Service, August 31, 2005.

Kurzman, Charles. *The Missing Martyrs: Why There Are So Few Muslim Terrorists.* New York: Oxford University Press, 2011.

Kux, Dennis. *The United States and Pakistan, 1947–2000: Disenchanted Allies.* Baltimore: Johns Hopkins University Press, 2001.

Kymlicka, Will. *Multicultural Citizenship: A Liberal Theory of Minority Rights.* Oxford: Clarendon Press, 1995.

Ladwig, Walter C. *The Forgotten Front: Patron-Client Relationships in Counterinsurgency.* Cambridge: Cambridge University Press, 2017.

Lahoud, Nelly, Stuart Caudill, Liam Collins, Gabriel Koehler-Derrick, Don Rassler, and Muhammad al-Ubaydi. *Letters from Abbottabad: Bin Ladin Sidelined?* West Point, NY: Combating Terrorism Center, 2012. https://ctc.westpoint.edu/wp-content/uploads/2012 /05/CTC_LtrsFromAbottabad_WEB_v2.pdf.

Landor, Henry Savage. *Across Widest Africa: An Account of the Country and People of Eastern, Central and Western Africa as Seen During a Twelve Month Journey from Djibuti to Cape Verde*. London: Hurst and Blackett, 1907.

Larsen, Jeppe Fuglsang. "The Role of Religion in Islamist Radicalisation Process." *Critical Studies on Terrorism* 13, no. 3 (2020): 396–417.

Larson, Eric V., and Bogdan Savych. *American Public Support for U.S. Military Operations from Mogadishu to Baghdad*. Santa Monica, CA: RAND Corporation, 2005.

Larue, Patrick F., and Orlandrew E. Danzell. "Rethinking State Capacity: Conceptual Effects on the Incidence of Terrorism." *Terrorism and Political Violence* 34, no. 6 (2022): 1241–1258.

Lawrence, Bruce, ed. *Messages to the World: The Statements of Osama Bin Laden*. New York: Verso, 2005.

Lecocq, Baz. *Disputed Desert: Decolonisation, Competing Nationalisms and Tuareg Rebellions in Northern Mali*. Leiden: Brill, 2010.

Lecocq, Baz, and Georg Klute. "Tuareg Separatism in Mali." *International Journal* 68, no. 3 (2013): 424–434.

Lecocq, Jean Sebastian. *That Desert Is Our Country: Tuareg Rebellions and Competing Nationalisms in Contemporary Mali (1946–1996)*. Amsterdam: Amsterdam University Press, 2002.

Lee, Dong-Yoon. "Politics of Anti-terrorism Policy in Southeast Asia: A Comparative Study of the Philippines and Indonesia." *Pacific Focus* 24, no. 2 (2009): 247–269.

Leeson, Francis. *Frontier Legion: With the Khassadars of North Waziristan*. Ferring, UK: Selwood Printing, 2003.

Lehr, Peter, ed. *Violence at Sea: Piracy in the Age of Global Terrorism*. Abingdon, UK: Routledge, 2007.

Levi-Sanchez, Suzanne. "Civil Society in an Uncivil State: Informal Organizations in Tajik/Afghan Badakhshan." *Journal of International Affairs* 71, no. 2 (2018): 50–72.

Lewis, Alexandra. *Security, Clans and Tribes: Unstable Governance in Somaliland, Yemen and the Gulf of Aden*. London: Palgrave Macmillan, 2015.

Lewis, Bernard. *What Went Wrong? The Clash Between Islam and Modernity in the Middle East*. New York: Perennial, 2002.

Lehrke, Jesse Paul, and Rahel Schomaker. "Kill, Capture, or Defend? The Effectiveness of Specific and General Counterterrorism Tactics Against the Global Threats of the Post-9/11 Era." *Security Studies* 25, no. 4 (2016): 729–762.

LeoGrande, William M. "A Splendid Little War: Drawing the Line in El Salvador." *International Security* 6, no. 1 (1981): 27–52.

Lewis, I. M. *A Pastoral Democracy: A Study of Pastoralism and Politics Among the Northern Somali of the Horn of Africa*. London: Oxford University Press, 1961.

Li, Quan. "Does Democracy Promote or Reduce Transnational Terrorist Incidents?" *Journal of Conflict Resolution* 49, no. 2 (2005): 278–297.

Lustick, Ian S., Dan Miodownik, and Roy J. Eidelson. "Secessionism in Multicultural States: Does Sharing Power Prevent or Encourage It?" *American Political Science Review* 98, no. 2 (2004): 209–229.

Lyall, Alfred. "Frontiers and Protectorates." *Nineteenth Century: A Monthly Review* 30, no. 174 (1891): 312–328.

MacDonald, Myra. *Defeat Is an Orphan: How Pakistan Lost the Great South Asian War.* London: C. Hurst and Company, 2017.

Malejacq, Romain. *Warlord Survival: The Delusion of State Building in Afghanistan.* Ithaca, NY: Cornell University Press, 2019.

Manning, Patrick. *Francophone Sub-Saharan Africa, 1880–1995.* Cambridge: Cambridge University Press, 1988.

Marineau, Josiah, Henry Pascoe, Alex Braithwaite, Michael Findley, and Joseph Young. "The Local Geography of Transnational Terrorism." *Conflict Management and Peace Science* 37, no. 3 (2020): 350–381.

Markey, Daniel S. *No Exit from Pakistan: America's Tortured Relationship with Islamabad.* Cambridge: Cambridge University Press, 2013.

Maruf, Harun, and Dan Joseph. *Inside Al-Shabaab: The Secret History of Al-Qaeda's Most Powerful Ally.* Bloomington: Indiana University Press, 2018.

Masters, John. *Bugles and a Tiger: A Volume of Autobiography.* New York: Ballantine Books, 1956.

Matloff, Judith. *No Friends but the Mountains: Dispatches from the World's Violent Highlands.* New York: Basic Books, 2017.

Maynard, Jonathan Leader. "Ideology and Armed Conflict." *Journal of Peace Research* 56, no. 5 (2019): 635–649.

Mazzetti, Mark. *The Way of the Knife: The CIA, a Secret Army, and a War at the Ends of the Earth.* New York: Penguin Books, 2013.

McCauley, Clark, and Sophia Moskalenko. *Friction: How Conflict Radicalizes Them and Us.* New York: Oxford University Press, 2017.

McChrystal, Stanley. *My Share of the Task: A Memoir.* New York: Portfolio/Penguin, 2014.

McDougall, James, and Judith Scheele, eds. *Saharan Frontiers: Space and Mobility in Northwest Africa.* Bloomington: Indian University Press, 2012.

McDowall, David. *A Modern History of the Kurds.* London: I. B. Tauris, 2004.

McIntosh, Christopher. "Counterterrorism as War: Identifying the Dangers, Risks, and Opportunity Costs of U.S. Strategy Toward Al Qaeda and Its Affiliates." *Studies in Conflict & Terrorism* 38, no. 1 (2015): 23–38.

Meleagrou-Hitchens, Alexander. *Incitement: Anwar al-Awlaki's Western Jihad.* Cambridge, MA: Harvard University Press, 2020.

Mendelsohn, Barak. *The Al-Qaeda Franchise: The Expansion of Al-Qaeda and Its Consequences.* New York: Oxford University Press, 2015.

Mendelsohn, Barak. "Al-Qaeda's Franchising Strategy." *Survival* 53, no. 3 (2011): 29–50.

Mendelsohn, Barak. *Combating Jihadism: American Hegemony and Interstate Cooperation in the War on Terrorism.* Chicago: University of Chicago Press, 2009.

Mendelsohn, Barak. *Jihadism Constrained: The Limits of Transnational Jihadism and What It Means for Counterterrorism.* Lanham, MD: Rowman and Littlefield, 2019.

Miakhel, Shahmahmood. "Understanding Afghanistan: The Importance of Tribal Culture and Structure in Security and Governance." *Asian Survey* 35, no. 7 (1995): 1–22.

Mir, Asfandyar. "What Explains Counterterrorism Effectiveness? Evidence from the U.S. Drone War in Pakistan." *International Security* 43, no. 2 (2018): 45–83.

Mitts, Tamar. "From Isolation to Radicalization: Anti-Muslim Hostility and Support for ISIS in the West." *American Political Science Review* 113, no. 1 (2019): 173–194.

Moghadam, Assaf. "Motives for Martyrdom: Al-Qaida, Salafi Jihad, and the Spread of Suicide Attacks." *International Security* 33, no. 3 (2009): 46–78.

Mueller, John, and Mark G. Stewart. "Terrorism and Bathtubs: Comparing and Assessing the Risks." *Terrorism and Political Violence* 33, no. 1 (2021): 138–163.

Muller-Crepon, Carl, Philipp Hunziker, and Lars-Erik Cederman. "Roads to Rule, Roads to Rebel: Relational State Capacity and Conflict in Africa." *Journal of Conflict Resolution* 65, nos. 2–3 (2021): 563–590.

Mundy, Jacob, ed. *US Militarization of the Sahara-Sahel Region*, vol. 85. East Lansing, MI: Association of Concerned African Scholars, 2010.

Murphy, Paul J. *Allah's Angels: Chechen Women in War.* Annapolis, MD: Naval Institute Press, 2011.

Murray, G. W. *Sons of Ishmael: A Study of the Egyptian Bedouin.* London: George Routledge and Sons, 1935.

Murtazashvili, Jennifer. "A Tired Cliché: Why We Should Stop Worrying About Ungoverned Spaces and Embrace Self-Governance." *Journal of International Affairs* 71, no. 2 (2018): 11–29.

Murtazashvili, Jennifer Brick. *Informal Order and the State in Afghanistan.* Cambridge: Cambridge University Press, 2016.

Myerson, Roger. "Constitutional Structures for a Strong Democracy: Considerations on the Government of Pakistan." *World Development, Decentralization and Governance* 53 (2014): 46–54.

Naftali, Timothy. "US Counterterrorism Before Bin Laden." *International Journal* 60, no. 1 (2004–2005): 25–34.

Napps Cameron, and Walter Enders. "A Regional Investigation of the Interrelationships Between Domestic and Transnational Terrorism: A Time Series Analysis." *Defence and Peace Economics* 26, no. 2 (2015): 133–151.

National Commission on Terrorist Attacks Upon the United States. *The 9/11 Commission Report: Final Report of the National Commission on Terrorist Attacks Upon the United States.* New York: Norton, 2004.

Nawaz, Shuja. *The Battle for Pakistan: The Bitter US Friendship and a Tough Neighbourhood.* Delhi, IN: Penguin Random House, 2019.

Nawaz, Shuja. *FATA—A Most Dangerous Place: Meeting the Challenge of Militancy and Terror in the Federally Administered Tribal Areas of Pakistan.* Washington, DC: Center for Strategic and International Studies, 2009.

Naylor, Sean. *Relentless Strike: The Secret History of Joint Special Operations Command.* New York: St. Martin's Press, 2015.

Neumayer, Eric, and Thomas Plumper. "Foreign Terror on Americans." *Journal of Peace Research* 48, no. 1 (2011): 3–17.

Nicolaisen, Johannes, and Ida Nicolaisen. *The Pastoral Tuareg: Ecology, Culture and Society.* New York: Thames and Hudson, 1997.

Niksch, Larry. *Abu Sayyaf: Target of Philippine-U.S. Anti-terrorism Cooperation.* Report for Congress, Congressional Research Service, January 24, 2007.

Nomikos, William. "How UN Peacebuilding Unintentionally Incentivizes Local-Level Violence." *SSRN,* last modified May 19, 2018. https://papers.ssrn.com/sol3/papers.cfm?abstract _id=3165775.

Obama, Barack. *A Promised Land.* New York: Crown Publishing, 2020.

Osman, Borhan. *Bourgeois Jihad: Why Young, Middle-Class Afghans Join the Islamic State.* Report No. 162, U.S. Institute of Peace, June 2020.

Ostrom, Elinor. "A Diagnostic Approach for Going Beyond Panaceas." *Proceedings of the National Academy of Sciences* 104, no. 39 (2007): 15181–15187.

Packer, George. *Our Man: Richard Holbrooke and the End of the American Century.* New York: Alfred A. Knopf, 2019.

Pape, Robert A. *Dying to Win: The Strategic Logic of Suicide Terrorism.* New York: Random House, 2005.

Parkinson, Sarah E. "Practical Ideology in Militant Organizations." *World Politics* 73, no. 1 (2021): 52–81.

Payne, Andrew. "Presidents, Politics, and Military Strategy: Electoral Constraints During the Iraq War." *International Security* 44, no. 3 (2019/20): 163–203.

Perrin, Delphine. "Tuaregs and Citizenship: The Last Camp of Nomadism." *Middle East Law and Governance* 6 (2014): 296–326.

Petrich, Katharine. "Cows, Charcoal, and Cocaine: Al-Shabaab's Criminal Activities in the Horn of Africa." *Studies in Conflict & Terrorism* 45, nos. 5–6 (2022): 479–500.

Pezard, Stephanie, and Michael Shurkin. *Achieving Peace in Northern Mali: Past Agreements, Local Conflicts, and the Prospects for a Durable Settlement.* Santa Monica, CA: RAND Corporation, 2015.

Phillips, Sarah. *Yemen and the Politics of Permanent Crisis.* Abingdon, UK: Routledge, 2011.

Phillips, Sarah. *Yemen's Democracy Experiment in Regional Perspective: Patronage and Pluralised Authoritarianism.* London: Palgrave Macmillan, 2008.

Piazza, James A. "Incubators of Terror: Do Failed and Failing States Promote Transnational Terrorism?" *International Studies Quarterly* 52, no. 3 (2008): 469–488.

Piazza, James A. "Is Islamist Terrorism More Dangerous? An Empirical Study of Group Ideology, Organization, and Goal Structure." *Terrorism and Political Violence* 21, no. 1 (2009): 62–88.

Piazza, James A. "The Opium Trade and Patterns of Terrorism in the Provinces of Afghanistan: An Empirical Analysis," *Terrorism and Political Violence* 24, no. 2 (2012): 213–234.

Piazza, James A. "Politician Hate Speech and Domestic Terrorism." *International Interactions* 46, no. 3 (2020): 431–453.

Piazza, James A. "Poverty, Minority Economic Discrimination, and Domestic Terrorism." *Journal of Peace Research* 48, no. 3 (2011): 339–353.

Piazza, James A. "Repression and Terrorism: A Cross-National Empirical Analysis of Types of Repression and Domestic Terrorism." *Terrorism and Political Violence* 29, no. 1 (2017): 102–118.

Piazza, James A. "Terrorism and Party Systems in the States of India." *Security Studies* 19, no. 1 (2010): 99–123.

Piazza, James A. "Types of Minority Discrimination and Terrorism." *Conflict Management and Peace Science* 29, no. 5 (2012): 521–546.

Piazza, James A., and Seung-Whan Choi. "International Military Interventions and Transnational Terrorist Backlash." *International Studies Quarterly* 62, no. 3 (2018): 686–695.

Plummer, Chelli. "Failed States and Connections to Terrorist Activity." *International Criminal Justice Review* 22, no. 4 (2012): 416–449.

Pokalova, Elena. "The Al Qaeda Brand: The Strategic Use of the 'Terrorist' Label." *Terrorism and Political Violence* 30, no. 3 (2018): 408–427.

Pokalova, Elena. "Authoritarian Regimes Against Terrorism: Lessons from China." *Critical Studies on Terrorism* 6, no. 2 (2013): 279–298.

Polo, Sara M. T., and Kristian Skrede Gleditsch. "Twisting Arms and Sending Messages: Terrorist Tactics in Civil War." *Journal of Peace Research* 53, no. 6 (2016): 815–829.

Putnam, Robert D. "Diplomacy and Domestic Politics: The Logic of Two-Level Games." *International Organizations* 42, no. 3 (1988): 427–460.

Rabasa, Angel, and Cheryl Benard. *Eurojihad: Patterns of Islamist Radicalization and Terrorism in Europe.* Cambridge: Cambridge University Press, 2014.

Rabinowitz, Dan. "Themes in the Economy of the Bedouin of South Sinai in the 19th and 20th Centuries." *International Journal of Middle East Studies* 17, no. 2 (1985): 211–228.

Rady, Adel. *Tourism and Sustainable Development in Egypt.* Cairo: Tourism Development Authority, 2002.

Raghavan, Srinath. *Fierce Enigmas: A History of the United States in South Asia.* New York: Basic Books, 2018.

Rajan, V. G. Julie. *Al Qaeda's Global Crisis: The Islamic State, Takfir, and the Genocide of Muslims.* Abingdon, UK: Routledge, 2015.

Ramirez, Shawn L., and Arianna J. Robbins. "Targets and Tactics: Testing for a Duality Within Al Qaeda's Network." *International Interactions* 44, no. 3 (2018): 559–581.

Rand, Dafna H., and Stephen Tankel. *Security Cooperation and Assistance: Rethinking the Return on Investment.* Washington, DC: Center for a New American Security, 2015.

Rashid, Ahmed. *Descent Into Chaos: The United States and the Failure of Nation Building in Pakistan, Afghanistan, and Central Asia.* New York: Viking, 2008.

Rashid, Ahmed. *Pakistan on the Brink: The Future of America, Pakistan, and Afghanistan.* London: Penguin, 2012.

Rashid, Ahmed. *Taliban: Militant Islam, Oil, and Fundamentalism in Central Asia.* New Haven, CT: Yale University Press, 2000.

Rassler, Don, and Vahid Brown. *The Haqqani Nexus and the Evolution of al-Qa'ida.* West Point, NY: Combating Terrorism Center, 2011.

Ratelle, Jean-Francois, and Emil Aslan Souleimanov. "Retaliation in Rebellion: The Missing Link to Explaining Insurgent Violence in Dagestan." *Terrorism and Political Violence* 29, no. 4 (2017): 573–592.

*Removing Terrorist Sanctuaries: The 9/11 Commission Recommendations and U.S. Policy*. Report for Congress, Congressional Research Service, August 10, 2004.

Revkin, Mara Redlich, and Elisabeth Jean Wood. "The Islamic State's Pattern of Sexual Violence: Ideology and Institutions, Policies and Practices." *Journal of Global Security Studies* 6, no. 2 (2021): 1–20.

Rice, Condoleezza. *No Higher Honor: A Memoir of My Years in Washington*. New York: Crown, 2011.

Riedel, Bruce. *Deadly Embrace: Pakistan, America, and the Future of Global Jihad*. Washington, DC: Brookings Institution Press, 2011.

Riedel, Bruce. "The Return of the Knights: Al-Qaeda and the Fruits of Middle East Disorder." *Survival* 49, no. 3 (2007): 107–120.

Riedel, Bruce. *The Search for Al Qaeda: Its Leadership, Ideology, and Future*. Washington, DC: Brookings Institution Press, 2010.

Rigterink, Anouk S. "The Wane of Command: Evidence on Drone Strikes and Control Within Terrorist Organizations." *American Political Science Review* 115, no. 1 (2021): 31–50.

Rink, Anselm, and Kunaal Sharma. "The Determinants of Religious Radicalization: Evidence from Kenya." *Journal of Conflict Resolution* 62, no. 6 (2018): 1229–1261.

Roberts, Sean R. *The War on the Uyghurs: China's Internal Campaign Against a Muslim Minority*. Princeton, NJ: Princeton University Press, 2020.

Rodd, Francis Rennell. *People of the Veil: Being an Account of the Habits, Organisation and History of the Wandering Tuareg Tribes Which Inhabit the Mountains of Air or Asben in the Central Sahara*. Oosterhout, NL: Anthropological Publications, 1966.

Rosand, Eric. "The Security Council's Efforts to Monitor the Implementation of al Qaeda/Taliban Sanctions." *American Journal of International Law* 98, no. 4 (2004): 745–763.

Rosen, Lawrence. *Bargaining for Reality: The Construction of Social Relations in a Muslim Community*. Chicago: University of Chicago Press, 1984.

Rosendorff, B. Peter, and Todd Sandler. "Too Much of a Good Thing? The Proactive Response Dilemma." *Journal of Conflict Resolution* 48, no. 5 (2004): 657–671.

Rubin, Barnett R. *Afghanistan from the Cold War Through the War on Terror*. New York: Oxford University Press, 2013.

Rumsfeld, Donald. *Known and Unknown: A Memoir*. New York: Sentinel, 2012.

Ryan, Michael W. S. *Decoding Al-Qaeda's Strategy: The Deep Battle Against America*. New York: Columbia University Press, 2013.

Sageman, Marc. *Leaderless Jihad: Terror Networks in the Twenty-First Century*. Philadelphia: University of Pennsylvania Press, 2008.

Sahak, Nabi. "The Origins of Anglo-Afghan Relations Clarifying the Political Status of Durand Line 1893–2021." PhD dissertation, King's College London, 2021.

Sanchez-Cuenca, Ignacio, and Luis de la Calle. "Domestic Terrorism: The Hidden Side of Political Violence." *Annual Review of Political Science* 12 (2009): 31–49.

Sarwari, Mehwish. "Impact of Rebel Group Ideology on Wartime Sexual Violence." *Journal of Global Security Studies* 6, no. 2 (2021): 1–23.

Satana, Nil S., Molly Inman, and Johanna Kristin Birnir. "Religion, Government Coalitions, and Terrorism." *Terrorism and Political Violence* 25, no. 1 (2012): 29–52.

Savun, Burcu, and Brian J. Phillips. "Democracy, Foreign Policy, and Terrorism." *Journal of Conflict Resolution* 53, no. 6 (2009): 878–904.

Scahill, Jeremy. *Dirty Wars: The World Is a Battlefield.* New York: Nation Books, 2013.

Schaffer, Howard B., and Teresita C. Schaffer. *How Pakistan Negotiates with the United States.* Washington, DC: United States Institute of Peace, 2011.

Scheuer, Michael. "Coalition Warfare, Part 11: How Zarqawi Fits Into Bin Laden's World Front." *Terrorism Focus* 2, no. 8 (2005). https://jamestown.org/program/coalition-warfare -part-ii-how-zarqawi-fits-into-bin-ladens-world-front/.

Scheuer, Michael. *Osama Bin Laden.* New York: Oxford University Press, 2011.

Schmitt, Eric, and Thom Shanker. *Counterstrike: The Untold Story of America's Secret Campaign Against Al Qaeda.* New York: St. Martin's Press, 2011.

Schofield, Carey. *Inside the Pakistan Army.* London: Biteback Publishing, 2011.

Schricker, Ezra. "The Search for Rebel Interdependence: A Study of the Afghan and Pakistani Taliban." *Journal of Peace Research* 54, no. 1 (2017): 16–30.

Schultz, Richard H., and Andreas Vogt. "It's War! Fighting Post-11 September Global Terrorism Through a Doctrine of Preemption." *Terrorism and Political Violence* 15, no. 1 (2003): 1–30.

Schulze, Kirsten E., and Joseph Chinyong Liow. "Making Jihadis, Waging Jihad: Transnational and Local Dimensions of the ISIS Phenomenon in Indonesia and Malaysia." *Asian Security* 15, no. 2 (2019): 122–139.

Scott, James C. *Against the Grain: A Deep History of the Earliest States.* New Haven, CT: Yale University Press, 2017.

Scott, James C. *The Art of Not Being Governed: An Anarchist History of Southeast Asia.* New Haven, CT: Yale University Press, 2009.

Shah, Aqil. "Do U.S. Drone Strikes Cause Blowback?: Evidence from Pakistan and Beyond." *International Security* 42, no. 4 (2018): 47–84.

Shakirullah, Bahadar Nawab, Ingrid Nyborg, and Noor Elahi. "The Underlying Causes of Violent Conflict in the North Waziristan Tribal Areas of Pakistan." *Civil Wars* 22, no. 1 (2020): 114–136.

Shapiro, Jacob N. *The Terrorist's Dilemma: Managing Violent Covert Operations.* Princeton, NJ: Princeton University Press, 2013.

Shahzad, Syed Saleem. *Inside Al-Qaeda and the Taliban: Beyond 9/11.* London: Pluto Press, 2011.

Sheikh, Mona Kanwal. *Guardians of God: Inside the Religious Mind of the Pakistani Taliban.* New Delhi: Oxford University Press, 2016.

Shire, Mohammed Ibrahim. "Provocation and Attrition Strategies in Transnational Terrorism: The Case of Al-Shabaab." *Terrorism and Political Violence*, November 3, 2021. https:// doi.org/10.1080/09546553.2021.1987896.

Siddique, Qandeel. *Tehrik-e-Taliban Pakistan: An Attempt to Deconstruct the Umbrella Organization and the Reasons for Its Growth in Pakistan's North-West*. DIIS Report 2010, no. 12 (2010), Danish Institute for International Studies. https://pure.diis.dk/ws/files/104682/RP2010_12_Tehrik_e_Taliban_web.pdf.

Siegel, Pascale Combelles. "AQIM's Playbook in Mali." *CTC Sentinel* 6, no. 3 (2013): 9–11.

Siroky, David S., and John Cuffe. "Lost Autonomy, Nationalism and Separatism." *Comparative Political Studies* 48, no. 1 (2014): 3–34.

Siroky, David S., Sean Mueller, Andre Fazi, and Michael Hechter. "Containing Nationalism: Culture, Economics and Indirect Rule in Corsica." *Comparative Political Studies* 54, no. 6 (2021): 1023–1057.

Siroky, Davis S., Emil Aslan Souleimanov, Jean-Francois Ratelle, and Milos Popovic. "Purifying the Religion: An Analysis of *Haram* Targeting Among Salafi Jihadi Groups." *Comparative Politics* 54, no. 3 (2022): 525–546.

Sivaramakrishnan, K. *Statemaking and Environmental Change in Colonial Eastern India*. Stanford, CA: Stanford University Press, 1999.

Skjelderup, Michael Weddegjerde. "Jihadi Governance and Traditional Authority Structures: Al-Shabaab and Clan Elders in Southern Somalia, 2008–2012." *Small Wars & Insurgencies* 31, no. 6 (2020): 1174–1195.

Skretting, Vidar B. "Al-Qaida in the Islamic Maghrib's Expansion in the Sahara: New Insights from Primary Sources." *Studies in Conflict & Terrorism*, September 24, 2020. https://doi.org/10.1080/1057610X.2020.1822593.

Smith, David O. *The Quetta Experience: A Study of Attitudes and Values Within the Pakistan Army*. Washington, DC: Woodrow Wilson Center, 2018.

Smith, Simon C. "Rulers and Residents: British Relations with the Aden Protectorate, 1937–59." *Middle Eastern Studies* 31, no. 3 (1995): 509–523.

Soufan, Ali, and Daniel Freedman. *The Black Banners Declassified: How Torture Derailed the War on Terror After 9/11*. New York: W. W. Norton and Co., 2020.

Souleimanov, Emil Aslan, and Huseyn Aliyev. "Blood Revenge and Violent Mobilization: Evidence from the Chechen Wars." *International Security* 40, no. 2 (2015): 158–180.

Souleimanov, Emil Aslan, and Huseyn Aliyev. *How Socio-cultural Codes Shaped Violent Mobilization and Pro-Insurgent Support in the Chechen Wars*. Basingstoke, UK: Palgrave Macmillan, 2017.

Small, Andrew. *The China-Pakistan Axis: Asia's New Geopolitics*. New York: Oxford University Press, 2015.

Snook, Daniel W., Ari D. Fodeman, Scott M. Kleinmann, and John G. Horgan. "Crisis as Catalyst: Crisis in Conversion to Islam Related to Radicalism Intentions." *Terrorism and Political Violence*, July 26, 2021. https://doi.org/10.1080/09546553.2021.1938003.

Speckhard, Anne and Khapta Ahkmedova. "The Making of a Martyr: Chechen Suicide Terrorism." *Studies in Conflict & Terrorism* 29, no. 5 (2006): 429–492.

*Speeches by Quaid-i-Azam Muhammad Ali Jinnah, Governor-General of Pakistan, 3rd June 1947 to 14th August 1948*. Karachi: Saifee Printers, 1948.

Staffell, Simon, and Akil Awan, eds. *Jihadism Transformed: Al-Qaeda and Islamic State's Global Battle of Ideas*. New York: Oxford University Press, 2016.

Staniland, Paul, Asfandyar Mir, and Sameer Lalwani. "Politics and Threat Perception: Explaining Pakistani Military Strategy on the North West Frontier." *Security Studies* 27, no. 4 (2018): 535–574.

Stanton, Jessica A. "Terrorism in the Context of Civil War." *Journal of Politics* 75, no. 4 (2013): 1009–1022.

Steinberg, James B. "Counterterrorism: A New Organizing Principle for American National Security?" Brookings Institution, June 1, 2002. https://www.brookings.edu/articles/counter terrorism-a-new-organizing-principle-for-american-national-security/.

Stone, John. "Escalation and the War on Terror." *Journal of Strategic Studies* 35, no. 5 (2012): 639–661.

Stremlau, Nicole. "Governance Without Government in the Somali Territories." *Journal of International Affairs* 71, no. 2 (2018): 73–89.

Svensson, Isak. "Fighting with Faith: Religion and Conflict Resolution in Civil Wars." *Journal of Conflict Resolution* 51, no. 6 (2017): 930–949.

Tabory, Mala. *The Multinational Force and Observers in the Sinai: Organization, Structure, and Function.* Boulder, CO: Westview Press, 1986.

Tahir, Madiha R., Qalander Bux Memon, and Vijay Prashad, eds. *Dispatches from Pakistan.* Minneapolis: University of Minnesota Press, 2014.

Tajik, S. H. "Insight Into a Suicide Bomber Training Camp in Waziristan." *CTC Sentinel* 3, no. 3 (2010): 10–13.

Tankel, Stephen. "Universal Soldiers or Parochial Actors: Understanding Jihadists as Products of Their Environments." *Terrorism and Political Violence* 31, no. 2 (2019): 299–322.

Tankel, Stephen. *With Us and Against Us: How America's Partners Help and Hinder the War on Terror.* New York: Columbia University Press, 2018.

Taylor, Andrew J. "Thoughts on the Nature and Consequence of Ungoverned Spaces." *SAIS Review of International Affairs* 36, no. 1 (2016): 5–15.

Tenet, George. *At the Center of the Storm: My Years at the CIA.* New York: HarperCollins, 2007.

Teo, Shu De. "Evaluating the Concept of Ungoverned Spaces: The Limitations of a Two Dimensional Worldview." *Journal of International Affairs* 71, no. 2 (2018): 125–133.

Thomas, Charles G., and Toyin Falola. *Secession and Separatist Conflicts in Postcolonial Africa.* Calgary, AB: University of Calgary Press, 2020.

Thurston, Alexander. *Boko Haram: The History of an African Jihadist Movement.* Princeton, NJ: Princeton University Press, 2018.

Toft, Monica D. "The Politics of Religious Outbidding." *Review of Faith and International Affairs* 11, no. 3 (2013): 10–19.

Toft, Monica Duffy, and Yuri M. Zhukov. "Denial and Punishment in the North Caucasus: Evaluating the Effectiveness of Coercive Counter-Insurgency." *Journal of Peace Research* 49, no. 6 (2012): 785–800.

Tokdemir, Efe, Evgeny Sedashov, Sema Hande Ogutcu-Fu, Carlos E. Moreno Leon, Jeremy Berkowitz, and Seden Akcinaroglu. "Rebel Rivalry and the Strategic Nature of Rebel Group Ideology and Demands." *Journal of Conflict Resolution* 65, no. 4 (2021): 729–758.

Tollefsen, Andreas Foro. "Experienced Poverty and Local Conflict Violence." *Conflict Management and Peace Science* 37, no. 3 (2020): 323–349.

Toth, James. *Sayyid Qutb: The Life and Legacy of a Radical Islamic Intellectual*. New York: Oxford University Press, 2013.

Toukan, Mark. "International Politics by Other Means: External Sources of Civil War." *Journal of Peace Research* 56, no. 6 (2019): 812–826.

Tripodi, Christian. *Edge of Empire: The British Political Officer and Tribal Administration in the North-West Frontier, 1877–1947*. Abingdon, UK: Routledge, 2011.

Tripodi, Christian. "Negotiating with the Enemy: 'Politicals' and Tribes 1901–47." *Journal of Imperial and Commonwealth History* 39, no. 4 (2011): 589–606.

Tripodi, Christian. *The Unknown Enemy: Counterinsurgency and the Illusion of Control*. Cambridge: Cambridge University Press, 2021.

Tschantret, Joshua. "Democratic Breakdown and Terrorism." *Conflict Management and Peace Science* 38, no. 4 (2021): 369–390.

Turner, John. "From Cottage Industry to International Organisation: The Evolution of Salafi-Jihadism and the Emergence of the Al Qaeda Ideology." *Terrorism and Political Violence* 22, no. 4 (2010): 541–558.

Ugarte, Eduardo F. "The Alliance System of the Abu Sayyaf, 1993–2000." *Studies in Conflict & Terrorism* 31, no. 2 (2008): 125–144.

Unal, Mustafa Cosar, and Petra Cafnik Uludag. "Eradicating Terrorism in Asymmetric Conflict: The Role and Essence of Military Deterrence." *Terrorism and Political Violence* 34, no. 4 (2022): 772–816.

Uzonyi, Gary. "Interstate Rivalry, Genocide, and Politicide." *Journal of Peace Research* 55, no. 4 (2018): 476–490.

Vergani, Matteo, Muhammad Iqbal, Ekin Ilbahar, and Greg Barton. "The Three Ps of Radicalization: Push, Pull and Personal. A Systematic Scoping Review of the Scientific Evidence About Radicalization Into Violent Extremism." *Studies in Conflict & Terrorism* 43, no. 10 (2020): 854–885.

Votel, Joseph L., and Eero R. Keravuori. "The By-With-Through Operational Approach." *Joint Force Quarterly* 89, no. 2 (2018): 40–47.

Van de Walle, Nicolas. *African Economies and the Politics of Permanent Crisis, 1979–1999*. Cambridge: Cambridge University Press, 2001.

Walsh, Declan. *The Nine Lives of Pakistan: Dispatches from a Precarious State*. New York: W.W. Norton and Co., 2020.

Walsh, James I., and James A. Piazza. "Autocracies and Terrorism: Conditioning Effects of Authoritarian Regime Types on Terrorist Attacks." *American Journal of Political Science* 57, no. 4 (2013): 941–955.

Walsh, James I., and James A. Piazza. "Why Respecting Physical Integrity Rights Reduces Terrorism." *Comparative Political Studies* 43, no. 5 (2010): 551–577.

Walt, Stephen M. "Beyond bin Laden: Reshaping U.S. Foreign Policy." *International Security* 26, no. 3 (2002): 56–78.

Walter, Barbara F. "The Extremist's Advantage in Civil Wars." *International Security* 42, no. 2 (2017): 7–39.

Waltz, Kenneth N. *Man, State, and War: A Theoretical Analysis*. New York: Columbia University Press, 1954.

Warren, Alan. *Waziristan, The Faqir of Ipi, and the Indian Army: The North West Frontier Revolt of 1936–37*. Oxford: Oxford University Press, 2000.

Weed, Matthew. "Presidential References to the 2001 Authorization for Use of Military Force in Publicly Available Executive Actions and Reports to Congress." Congressional Research Service, May 11, 2016.

Weir, Shelagh. *A Tribal Order: Politics and Law in the Mountains of Yemen*. Austin: University of Texas Press, 2007.

Whitlock, Craig. *The Afghanistan Papers: A Secret History of the War*. New York: Simon and Schuster, 2021.

Williamson, Victoria, Dominic Murphy, Sharon A. M. Stevelink, Edgar Jones, Shannon Allen, and Neil Greenberg. "The Relationship Between of Moral Injury and Radicalisation: A Systematic Review." *Studies in Conflict & Terrorism* 45, no. 11 (2022): 977–1003.

Wimmer, Andreas, Lars-Erik Cederman, and Brian Min. "Ethnic Politics and Armed Conflict. A Configurational Analysis of a New Global Dataset." *American Sociological Review* 74, no. 2 (2009): 316–337.

Wolfowitz, Paul. "What Was and What Might Have Been: The Threats and Wars in Afghanistan and Iraq." Hoover Institution, March 29, 2022. https://www.hoover.org/sites/default /files/research/docs/wolfowitz_webreadypdf.pdf.

Woodruff, Philip. *The Men Who Ruled India: The Guardians*. London: Jonathan Cape, 1954.

Woodward, Bob. *Bush at War*. New York: Simon and Schuster, 2002.

Woodward, Bob. *Obama's Wars*. New York: Simon and Schuster, 2010.

Woodward, Bob. *State of Denial: Bush at War, Part III*. New York: Simon and Schuster, 2006.

Wright, Lawrence. *The Looming Tower: Al-Qaeda and the Road to 9/11*. New York: Vintage Books, 2006.

Wucherpfennig, Julian, Philipp Hunziker, and Lars-Erik Cederman. "Who Inherits the State? Colonial Rule and Postcolonial Conflict." *American Journal of Political Science* 60, no. 4 (2016): 882–898.

Younas, Javed, and Todd Sandler. "Gender Imbalance and Terrorism in Developing Countries." *Journal of Conflict Resolution* 61, no. 3 (2017): 483–510.

Youngman, Mark. "Broader, Vaguer, Weaker: The Evolving Ideology of the Caucasus Emirate Leadership." *Terrorism and Political Violence* 31, no. 2 (2019): 367–389.

Zaidi, Z. H., ed. *Jinnah Papers Volume V, Pakistan: Pangs of Birth, 15 August—30 September 1947*. Islamabad: Quaid-e-Azam Papers Project, Government of Pakistan, 2000.

Zelin, Aaron Y. *Your Sons Are at Your Service: Tunisia's Missionaries of Jihad*. New York: Columbia University Press, 2020.

Zeman, Phillip M. "Tribalism and Terror: Report from the field." *Small Wars & Insurgencies* 20, nos. 3–4 (2009): 681–709.

# INDEX

Bin Laden, Mohammed, 34
Bin Laden, Omar, 36
Bin Laden, Osama, 41, 64, 75, 130, 159, 163,
    191; 9/11 attacks, 37; and affiliates, 24, 39,
    47–51, 53–55, 58, 108; in Afghanistan,
    34–35, 36–37, 155; focus of U.S.
    counterterrorism, 58, 64, 107, founding
    al-Qaeda, 35–36; in Pakistan, 54, 111, 139;
    in Sudan, 36; and Taliban, 37; war
    declaration, 36; Yemeni background,
    34–35, 155
Blair, Dennis, 199
Blair, Tony, 75–76, 125
Blee, Rich, 114
Bloch, Marc, 7
Bodine, Barbara, 156
Boko Haram, 8, 46, 199, 221–222
Boucher, Richard, 90, 146
Brennan, John, 87–88, 137, 159, 165
British India, 93–95. See also India
Brookings Institution, 135
Bugti, Akbar Khan, 14
Burkina Faso, 171
Bush, George W., 28, 76, 92; and 9/11 attacks,
    65–66; and bin Laden, 64–65; and Blair,
    75–76; counterterrorism policy, 4, 20,
    32–33, 66, 71–73, 75, 86, 88–89; drone
    program, 138; influences, 68; and
    Musharraf, 104, 106–108, 119; and partner
    states, 60, 133; and Saleh, 156

Caillie, Rene, 169
Cambone, Steve, 76
Camp David Accords, 184–185, 187
Camus, Albert: *The Plague*, 41
Carnegie Endowment for International
    Peace, 87
Caroe, Olaf, 9, 123–124
Caucasus, 10, 84
Center for a New American Security, 55
center versus periphery, 5, 9–19, 21, 90, 147,
    205–206, 209–210; conflict resolution,

211, 301–302n17; and terrorist groups,
    253n25
Central Intelligence Agency (CIA), 34, 39,
    54, 57, 59, 63–64, 73, 102, 108, 110, 136;
    Alec Station, 36; intelligence sharing,
    113
Chad, 174
Chamberlin, Wendy, 106, 107, 111
*Charlie Rose Show*, 67
Chechnya: al-Qaeda connections, 56; and
    Islam, 15–16; Russian military operations,
    15–16, 18, 25
Cheney, Dick, 57, 69, 72, 120
Chilcot Report, 272n88
China: and India, 12; and Pakistan, 125–126;
    and Uighurs, 56
Christmas Day attempted bombing, 149
Churchill, Winston, 94
Clarke, Richard, 64, 71
clash of civilizations, 69
Clinton, Bill, 62
Clinton, Hillary, 87, 164, 180
Coalition Support Funds, 77–78
Cold War, 3, 12, 63, 102, 103
Coll, Steve, 122
colonialism: British India, 93–95; British in
    Yemen, 150–151; and Egypt, 186–187; Italy
    in Africa, 11; and Middle East, 68–69;
    Mali, 169–171; Spanish Morocco, 10–11;
    use of military force, 9–11
Combined Joint Task Force—Horn of
    Africa, 78
Common Organization of the Saharan
    Regions, 171
Connor, Walker, 11
Coulibaly, Malick, 182
Council on Foreign Relations, 67
*Country Reports on Terrorism* (U.S. State
    Department), 83–84, 232–233, 244
Coultrup, Bill, 79
countering violent extremism,
    208–209

## COLUMBIA STUDIES IN TERRORISM AND IRREGULAR WARFARE

*Bruce Hoffman, Series Editor*

Ami Pedahzur, *The Israeli Secret Services and the Struggle Against Terrorism*

Ami Pedahzur and Arie Perliger, *Jewish Terrorism in Israel*

Lorenzo Vidino, *The New Muslim Brotherhood in the West*

Erica Chenoweth and Maria J. Stephan, *Why Civil Resistance Works: The Strategic Logic of Nonviolent Conflict*

William C. Banks, editor, *New Battlefields/Old Laws: Critical Debates on Asymmetric Warfare*

Blake W. Mobley, *Terrorism and Counterintelligence: How Terrorist Groups Elude Detection*

Jennifer Morrison Taw, *Mission Revolution: The U.S. Military and Stability Operations*

Guido W. Steinberg, *German Jihad: On the Internationalization of Islamist Terrorism*

Michael W. S. Ryan, *Decoding Al-Qaeda's Strategy: The Deep Battle Against America*

David H. Ucko and Robert Egnell, *Counterinsurgency in Crisis: Britain and the Challenges of Modern Warfare*

Bruce Hoffman and Fernando Reinares, editors, *The Evolution of the Global Terrorist Threat: From 9/11 to Osama bin Laden's Death*

Boaz Ganor, *Global Alert: The Rationality of Modern Islamist Terrorism and the Challenge to the Liberal Democratic World*

M. L. R. Smith and David Martin Jones, *The Political Impossibility of Modern Counterinsurgency: Strategic Problems, Puzzles, and Paradoxes*

Elizabeth Grimm Arsenault, *How the Gloves Came Off: Lawyers, Policy Makers, and Norms in the Debate on Torture*

Assaf Moghadam, *Nexus of Global Jihad: Understanding Cooperation Among Terrorist Actors*

Bruce Hoffman, *Inside Terrorism*, 3rd edition

Stephen Tankel, *With Us and Against Us: How America's Partners Help and Hinder the War on Terror*

Wendy Pearlman and Boaz Atzili, *Triadic Coercion: Israel's Targeting of States That Host Nonstate Actors*

Bryan C. Price, *Targeting Top Terrorists: Understanding Leadership Removal in Counterterrorism Strategy*

Mariya Y. Omelicheva and Lawrence P. Markowitz, *Webs of Corruption: Trafficking and Terrorism in Central Asia*

Aaron Y. Zelin, *Your Sons Are at Your Service: Tunisia's Missionaries of Jihad*

Printed in the USA
CPSIA information can be obtained
at www.ICGtesting.com
LVHW092102241124
797511LV00001B/23